Introduction to

Google™
Apps

Personal Apps

Introduction to

Google
Apps

Personal Apps

Michael Miller

Boston   Columbus   Indianapolis   New York   San Francisco   Upper Saddle River
Amsterdam   Cape Town   Dubai   London   Madrid   Milan   Munich   Paris   Montreal   Toronto
Delhi   Mexico City   São Paulo   Sydney   Hong Kong   Seoul   Singapore   Taipei   Tokyo

Editor in Chief: Michael Payne
Product Development Manager: Laura Burgess
Editorial Project Manager: Meghan Bisi
Development Editor: Karen Misler
Editorial Assistant: Carly Prakapas
Director of Digital Development: Zara Wanlass
Executive Editor, Digital Learning & Assessment: Paul Gentile
Director, Media Development: Cathi Profitko
Senior Editorial Media Project Manager: Alana Coles
Production Media Project Manager: John Cassar
Director of Marketing for Business & Technology: Patrice Jones
Marketing Coordinator: Susan Osterlitz
Marketing Assistant: Darshika Vyas
Senior Managing Editor: Cynthia Zonneveld
Associate Managing Editor: Camille Trentacoste
Manager of Rights & Permissions: Hessa Albader
Operations Specialist: Renata Butera
Production Manager: Renata Butera
Creative Art Director: Jayne Conte
Interior Design: Anthony Gemmellaro
Cover Design: Anthony Gemmellaro
Manager, Cover Visual Research & Permissions: Karen Sanatar
Full-Service Project Management: Saraswathi Muralidhar
Composition: PreMediaGlobal
Printer/Binder: Banta Menasha
Cover Printer: Banta Menasha
Text Font: 10.5/12 Garamond3

All screenshots are reused by Permission of Google, Inc.

Library of Congress Cataloging-in-Publication Data

Miller, Michael
    Introduction to Google Apps—personal apps / Michael Miller.
        p. cm.
    Includes index.
    ISBN-13: 978-0-13-255212-7
    ISBN-10: 0-13-255212-4
1. Google. 2. Web search engines. 3. Application software. 4. Cloud computing.
5. Personal information management. I. Title.
    TK5105.885.G66M574 2012
    025.04—dc23

                                                                    2011027585

10 9 8 7 6 5 4 3 2 1

ISBN 13: 978-0-13-255212-7
ISBN 10:   0-13-255212-4

About the Author

Michael Miller has written more than 100 nonfiction how-to books over the last two decades, including *Absolute Beginner's Guide to Computer Basics, Windows 7 Your Way, YouTube for Business, The Complete Idiot's Guide to Music Theory, Facebook for Grown-Ups,* and *Introduction to Social Networking* textbook. His books have collectively sold more than 1 million copies worldwide. Miller has established a reputation for his conversational writing style and for clearly explaining complex topics to casual readers. More information can be found at the author's website, located at **www.molehillgroup.com.**

Dedication: To Sherry, of course

Contents

Chapter One | Creating and Managing a Google Account   1

Objective 1
Sign Up for a Google Account   2

  Hands-On Exercises 1
  Signing Up for a Google Account   4

Objective 2
Change Your Google Account Settings   6

  Hands-On Exercises 2
  Changing Google Account Settings   7

Chapter Two | Using Google Search   11

Objective 1
Conduct a Basic Search   12

  Hands-On Exercises 1
  Conducting a Basic Search   18

Objective 2
Refine Your Search   21

  Hands-On Exercises 2
  Refining Your Search   23

Objective 3
Conduct an Advanced Search   34

  Hands-On Exercises 3
  Conducting an Advanced Search   35

Objective 4
Search for Images   41

  Hands-On Exercises 4
  Searching for Images   41

Chapter Three | Using Other Google Search Tools   51

Objective 1
Search for Scholarly and Legal Information   52

  Hands-On Exercises 1
  Searching for Scholarly and Legal Information   53

Objective 2
Search for News Articles   57

  Hands-On Exercises 2
  Searching for News Articles   58

Objective 3
Search for Bargains   62

  Hands-On Exercises 3
  Searching for Bargains   65

Chapter Four | Using Google's Nonsearch Features   71

Objective 1
Customize Your iGoogle Page   72

  Hands-On Exercises 1
  Customizing Your iGoogle Page   73

Objective 2
Use Google Translate   79

  Hands-On Exercises 2
  Using Google Translate   79

Objective 3
Use Google for Definitions, Calculations, and Conversions   82

  Hands-On Exercises 3
  Using Google for Definitions, Calculations, and Conversions   85

Chapter Five | Using Google Books   93

Objective 1
Search for Books and View Book Content   94

  Hands-On Exercises 1
  Searching for Books and Viewing Book Content   97

Objective 2
Review Books   100

  Hands-On Exercises 2
  Reviewing Books   101

Objective 3
Purchase and Download Books   102

  Hands-On Exercises 3
  Purchasing and Downloading Books   103

Objective 4
Manage Your Library   105

  Hands-On Exercises 4
  Managing Your Library   105

Chapter Six | Using Google Groups and Google Reader   111

Objective 1
Search Google Groups   112

  Hands-On Exercises 1
  Searching Google Groups   112

Objective 2
Visit and Participate in Groups   115

  Hands-On Exercises 2
  Visiting and Participating in Groups   116

Objective 3
Create a New Group   119

  Hands-On Exercises 3
  Creating a New Group   120

Objective 4
Use Google Reader   123

  Hands-On Exercises 4
  Using Google Reader   123

Chapter Seven | Using Google Maps and Google Earth   129

Objective 1
Map a Location   130

  Hands-On Exercises 1
  Mapping a Location   131

Objective 2
Search for a Nearby Business   141

  Hands-On Exercises 2
  Searching for a Nearby Business   142

Objective 3
Create a Custom Map   145

  Hands-On Exercises 3
  Creating a Custom Map   145

Objective 4
Generate Turn-by-Turn Directions   150

  Hands-On Exercises 4
  Generating Turn-by-Turn Directions   151

Objective 5
Navigate Google Earth   154

  Hands-On Exercises 5
  Navigating Google Earth   154

Objective 6
Use Layers   156

  Hands-On Exercises 6
  Using Layers   157

Objective 7
Generate Google Earth Driving Directions   159

  Hands-On Exercises 7
  Generating Google Earth Driving Directions   159

Chapter Eight | Using Gmail   165

Objective 1
Sign Up for a Gmail Account   166

  Hands-On Exercises 1
  Signing Up for a Gmail Account   166

Objective 2
Manage Your Inbox   169

  Hands-On Exercises 2
  Managing Your Inbox   172

Objective 3
Send and Receive Email Messages   179

  Hands-On Exercises 3
  Sending and Receiving Email Messages   180

Objective 4
Protect against Spam and Viruses   187

  Hands-On Exercises 4
  Protecting against Spam   188

Objective 5
Manage Your Contacts   190

  Hands-On Exercises 5
  Managing Your Contacts   190

Objective 6
Customize Gmail   196

  Hands-On Exercises 6
  Customizing Gmail   198

Chapter Nine | Using Google Calendar   207

Objective 1
Create a New Calendar   208

  Hands-On Exercises 1
  Creating a New Calendar   208

Objective 2
View Your Calendars   211

   Hands-On Exercises 2
   Viewing Your Calendars   212

Objective 3
Add New Events   217

   Hands-On Exercises 3
   Adding New Events   218

Objective 4
Share a Public Calendar   224

   Hands-On Exercises 4
   Sharing a Public Calendar   224

Objective 5
Create and Manage a To-Do List   228

   Hands-On Exercises 5
   Creating and Managing
   a To-Do List   228

Chapter Ten | Using the Google
Chrome Browser   237

Objective 1
Navigate the Web with
Google Chrome   238

   Hands-On Exercises 1
   Navigating the Web with
   Google Chrome   242

Objective 2
Manage Tabs and Homepages   245

   Hands-On Exercises 2
   Managing Tabs and Homepages   246

Objective 3
Add and Manage Bookmarks
and History   248

   Hands-On Exercises 3
   Adding and Managing Bookmarks
   and History   249

Objective 4
Use Google Chrome with
Google Apps   257

   Hands-On Exercises 4
   Using Google Chrome with
   Google Apps   257

Chapter Eleven | Using Google Buzz   263

Objective 1
Configure Google Buzz   264

   Hands-On Exercises 1
   Configuring Google Buzz   265

Objective 2
Follow and Post to Google Buzz   268

   Hands-On Exercises 2
   Following and Posting to Google Buzz   269

Chapter Twelve | Using Blogger   277

Objective 1
Create a New Blog   278

   Hands-On Exercises 1
   Creating a New Blog   279

Objective 2
Create New Blog Posts   282

   Hands-On Exercises 2
   Creating New Blog Posts   283

Objective 3
Customize Your Blog   291

   Hands-On Exercises 3
   Customizing Your Blog   293

Objective 4
Manage Blog Comments   300

   Hands-On Exercises 4
   Managing Blog Comments   301

Chapter Thirteen | Using Picasa   309

Objective 1
Organize Your Photographs   310

   Hands-On Exercises 1
   Organizing Your Photographs   312

Objective 2
Edit Your Photographs   315

   Hands-On Exercises 2
   Editing Your Photographs   316

Objective 3
Print and Share Your Photographs   323

   Hands-On Exercises 3
   Printing and Sharing Your Photographs   323

Objective 4
Share Your Photographs with Picasa
Web Albums   327

Hands-On Exercises 4
Sharing Your Photographs with Picasa
Web Albums   327

Chapter Fourteen | Using YouTube   335

Objective 1
Search for and Watch Videos   336

Hands-On Exercises 1
Searching for and Watching Videos   337

Objective 2
Share Your Favorite Videos   339

Hands-On Exercises 2
Sharing Your Favorite Videos   340

Objective 3
Upload Videos   343

Hands-On Exercises 3
Uploading Videos   344

Glossary   **353**
Index   **357**

Visual Walk-Through

Many of today's introductory computing courses are moving beyond coverage of just the traditional Microsoft® Office applications. Instructors are looking to incorporate newer technologies and software applications into their courses, and on some college campuses new alternative courses based on emerging technologies are being offered.

The NEXT Series was developed to provide innovative instructors with a high-quality, academic teaching solution that focuses on the next great technologies. There is more to computing than Microsoft® Office, and the books in *The NEXT Series* enable students to learn about some of the newer technologies that are available and becoming part of our everyday lives.

The NEXT Series…making it easy to teach what's *NEXT!*

▶ Whether you are interested in creating a new course or you want to enhance an existing class by incorporating new technology, *The NEXT Series* is your solution.

Included in this series are books on alternative productivity software application products, Google Apps—Productivity Apps, Google Apps—Personal Apps, and OpenOffice.org, as well as new technologies encompassed in Web 2.0, and Social Networking.

► *Introduction to Google Apps—Personal Apps* is a teaching and learning tool that was designed for use in a classroom setting, encouraging students to learn by using these new technologies hands-on.

The text includes in-chapter Hands-On Exercises, end-of-chapter exercises, and instructor supplements.

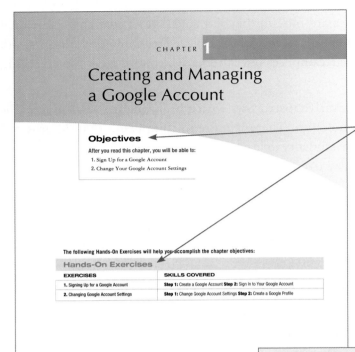

Each chapter opens with a list of numbered **Objectives**, clearly outlining what students will be able to accomplish after completing the chapter. The **Hands-On Exercises** are also outlined at the beginning of the chapter, letting students know what they will be doing in each chapter.

Learn-by-doing approach

Students learn how to use Google Apps by completing a series of **Hands-On Exercises**. These exercises are clearly distinguished from the explanatory text because the pages are shaded in green.

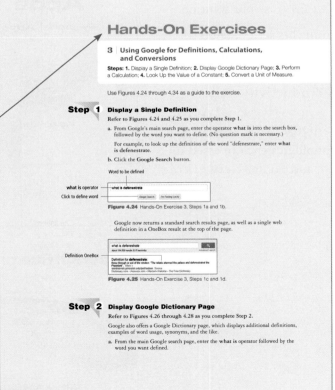

Question & Answer Format

Each section begins with a question, engaging students in a dialog with the authors and drawing them into the content.

Key terms are defined in the margins.

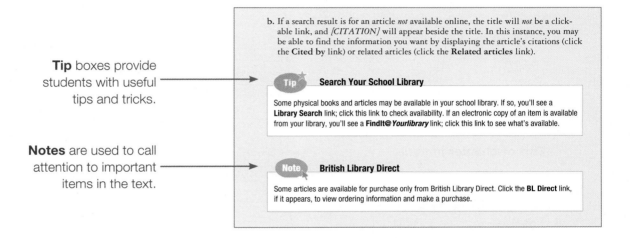

Objective 2

Search for News Articles

What is Google News?

Google News is a news-gathering service that identifies, assembles, and displays the latest news headlines from more than 4,500 different news organizations. It also offers a comprehensive news archive search.

Is Google News just for current news?

By default, Google News uses the last 30 days' worth of articles in its search results. If you want to find older news—up to 200 years old, in some cases—you can use Google's *News Archive Search*. In addition to finding recent, but not too recent, news headlines, it's also a great tool for learning about historical events.

Where does Google News get its news?

Google News sources its articles from a variety of different newspapers, magazines, and other news-gathering organizations. Sources include the *New York Times*, *Washington Post*, *Los Angeles Times*, *International Herald Tribune*, *Wall Street Journal*, *USA Today*, *Forbes*, Bloomberg, Reuters, CBS News, ABC News, Fox News, MSNBC, BBC, CNN, and ESPN.

Google News Google's news aggregation service.

News Archive Search Google's database of older news articles—up to 200 years old.

Tip boxes provide students with useful tips and tricks.

Notes are used to call attention to important items in the text.

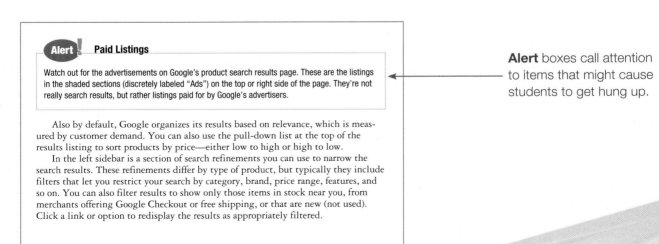

b. If a search result is for an article *not* available online, the title will *not* be a clickable link, and *[CITATION]* will appear beside the title. In this instance, you may be able to find the information you want by displaying the article's citations (click the **Cited by** link) or related articles (click the **Related articles** link).

Tip **Search Your School Library**

Some physical books and articles may be available in your school library. If so, you'll see a **Library Search** link; click this link to check availability. If an electronic copy of an item is available from your library, you'll see a **FindIt@Yourlibrary** link; click this link to see what's available.

Note **British Library Direct**

Some articles are available for purchase only from British Library Direct. Click the **BL Direct** link, if it appears, to view ordering information and make a purchase.

Alert **Paid Listings**

Watch out for the advertisements on Google's product search results page. These are the listings in the shaded sections (discretely labeled "Ads") on the top or right side of the page. They're not really search results, but rather listings paid for by Google's advertisers.

Alert boxes call attention to items that might cause students to get hung up.

Also by default, Google organizes its results based on relevance, which is measured by customer demand. You can also use the pull-down list at the top of the results listing to sort products by price—either low to high or high to low.

In the left sidebar is a section of search refinements you can use to narrow the search results. These refinements differ by type of product, but typically they include filters that let you restrict your search by category, brand, price range, features, and so on. You can also filter results to show only those items in stock near you, from merchants offering Google Checkout or free shipping, or that are new (not used). Click a link or option to redisplay the results as appropriately filtered.

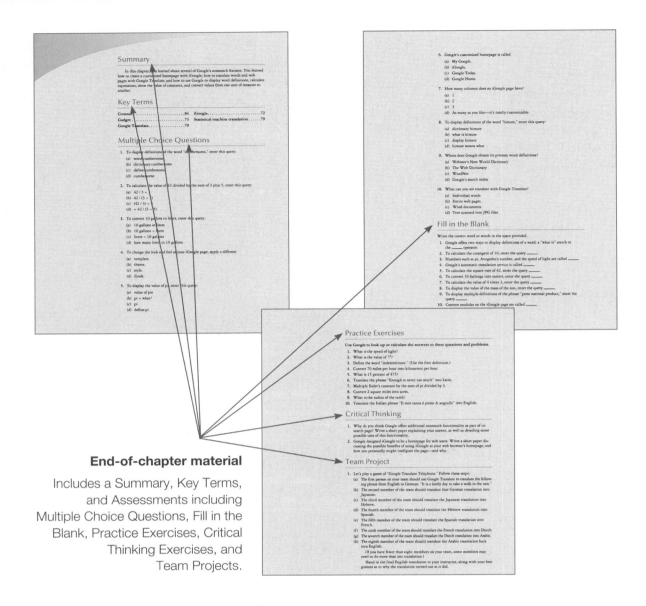

End-of-chapter material

Includes a Summary, Key Terms, and Assessments including Multiple Choice Questions, Fill in the Blank, Practice Exercises, Critical Thinking Exercises, and Team Projects.

Supplements for Instructors

Online Instructor Resource Center with:

- Instructor's Manual
- Solution Files

www.pearsonhighered.com/nextseries

Supplements for Students

Companion Website with:

- Objectives
- Glossary
- Chapter Summaries
- Appendix A
- Student Data Files

www.pearsonhighered.com/nextseries

CHAPTER 1

Creating and Managing a Google Account

Objectives

After you read this chapter, you will be able to:

1. Sign Up for a Google Account
2. Change Your Google Account Settings

The following Hands-On Exercises will help you accomplish the chapter objectives:

Hands-On Exercises

EXERCISES	SKILLS COVERED
1. Signing Up for a Google Account	**Step 1:** Create a Google Account **Step 2:** Sign In to Your Google Account
2. Changing Google Account Settings	**Step 1:** Change Google Account Settings **Step 2:** Create a Google Profile

Objective 1

Sign Up for a Google Account

What is a Google account?

Google account An individual user account for all Google services.

A *Google account* is a personal user account that provides access to services provided by Google. A Google account functions as a single log-on across Google; you need to create only a single Google account to access all Google services.

Why do you need a Google account?

While you can use many Google services, including its main search page, without a Google account, other services require the user to establish an account and to be signed in to the account in order to use that service. For example, to access your individual Google Docs documents, you need to be signed in to your Google account; all your documents are stored under your account name. Similarly, you need a Google account to access your email messages in Gmail.

In addition, many Google services provide further functionality when a user is signed in to his or her Google account. For example, when signed in to your Google account, you can customize the functionality and results display for Google search.

Which Google services require a Google account?

Those services (what Google calls "products") that store personal information are more likely to require the establishment of a Google account. They include Google Docs, Google Calendar, Gmail, Blogger, YouTube, and iGoogle.

How much does it cost to create a Google account?

Google accounts are free and anyone can sign up for one of them.

What services and applications does Google offer?

You probably know Google as the web's premiere search engine. While search is at the heart of most of Google's activities, it's only a part of what the company does. Google also offers a variety of web-based applications and services, as well as some freestanding software programs, covering everything from online calendars to word processing to photo editing. Table 1.1 details Google's current offerings.

Table 1.1—Google Applications and Services		
Google Service/Application	**Description**	**Web Address**
Blogger	Blog hosting	www.blogger.com
Gmail	Web-based email	mail.google.com
Google Blog Search	Blog search	www.google.com/blogsearch
Google Books	Book search	books.google.com
Google Calendar	Online calendar and task lists	calendar.google.com
Google Checkout	Online checkout service (for online retailers)	checkout.google.com
Google Chrome	Web browser	www.google.com/chrome
Google Code	Developer tools	code.google.com
Google Desktop	Computer file search and personalization	desktop.google.com
Google Directory	Web directory	directory.google.com

Google Service/Application	Description	Web Address
Google Docs	Web-based word processor, spreadsheet, and presentation applications	docs.google.com
Google Earth	Mapping and exploration software	earth.google.com
Google Finance	Business and financial information	www.google.com/finance
Google Groups	Online discussion groups and USENET search	groups.google.com
Google Health	Electronic health records	www.google.com/health
Google Images	Image search	images.google.com
Google Knol	Wiki-like information sharing	knol.google.com
Google Labs	Experimental features	labs.google.com
Google Maps	Mapping and directions	maps.google.com
Google Mobile	Services for mobile phones	www.google.com/mobile
Google News	Current and archived news stories	news.google.com
Google Patent Search	Patent search	www.google.com/patents
Google Product Search	Online shopping directory	www.google.com/products
Google Reader	News reader	www.google.com/reader
Google Realtime Search	Real-time search of social networks, news articles, and blog posts	www.google.com/realtime
Google Scholar	Search of scholarly papers	scholar.google.com
Google Sites	Website creation and hosting	sites.google.com
Google Talk	Instant messaging	www.google.com/talk
Google Toolbar	Search toolbar for web browsers	toolbar.google.com
Google Translate	Web page translation	translate.google.com
Google Trends	Current and past search trends	www.google.com/trends
Google Videos	Video search	video.google.com
Google Voice	Telephone and voicemail management	voice.google.com
Google Web Search	Web search	www.google.com
iGoogle	Personalized homepage	www.google.com/ig
Orkut	Social networking	www.orkut.com
Panoramio	Photo sharing	www.panoramio.com
Picasa	Photo editing software	www.picasa.com
Picasa Web Albums	Photo sharing	picasaweb.google.com
Picnik	Online photo editing	www.picnik.com
SketchUp	3D modeling software	sketchup.google.com
YouTube	Video sharing	www.youtube.com

Hands-On Exercises

1 | Signing Up for a Google Account

Steps: 1. Create a Google Account; **2.** Sign In to Your Google Account.

Use Figures 1.1 through 1.4 as a guide in the exercise.

 Step 1 **Create a Google Account**

Refer to Figures 1.1 and 1.2 as you complete Step 1.

a. Go to the main Google search page at **www.google.com**.

b. Click the **Sign in** link.

c. When the *Google accounts* page appears, click the **Create an account now** link.

d. When the *Create an Account* page appears, enter your email address into the *Your current email address* box.

e. Enter your desired password into the *Choose a password* box and then re-enter it into the *Re-enter password* box.

 Note **Password Length**

> Your Google account password must be at least eight characters long. For improved security, use a longer password that contains a combination of letters, numbers, and other characters.

f. If you want to stay signed in across multiple Google services after you sign in to the first service, check the **Stay signed in** option.

g. To let Google track your usage across its services, check the **Enable Web History** option.

h. If you want Google as your browser's homepage, check the **Set Google as my default homepage** option.

i. Click the **Location** drop-down menu and select your current country.

j. Enter your date of birth, in the form of MM/DD/YYYY, into the *Birthday* box.

Enter current email address

Enter desired password

Check to stay signed in

Check to enable web history tracking

Check to set Google as your homepage

Enter birthday

Select location

Figure 1.1 Hands-On Exercise 1, Steps 1d through 1j.

k. Enter the generated characters into the *Word Verification* box.

l. Read the **Terms of Service**, if you wish.

m. Click the **I accept. Create my account.** button.

Enter word verification characters

Click to create new account

Figure 1.2 Hands-On Exercise 1, Steps 1k through 1m.

Step 2   Sign In to Your Google Account

Refer to Figures 1.3 and 1.4 as you complete Step 2.

Once you've created your Google account, you can sign in to that account from most Google services, such as the main Google search page.

a. Go to the main Google search page at **www.google.com**.

b. Click the **Sign in** link.

Click to sign in

Figure 1.3 Hands-On Exercise 1, Steps 2a and 2b.

c. When the *Google accounts* page appears, enter your email address into the *Email* box.

d. Enter your password into the *Password* box.

e. If you wish to stay signed in across multiple Google services, check the **Stay signed in** option.

f. Click the **Sign in** button.

Enter password

Enter email address

Check to stay signed in across other services

Click to sign in

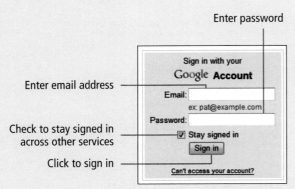

Figure 1.4 Hands-On Exercise 1, Steps 2c through 2f.

Objective 2

Change Your Google Account Settings

What information can you store in your Google account?

When you first create your Google account, the only information Google has is your email address, location, and birthday. However, you can add other information to your account if you choose. For example, you can create a complete user profile, including first and last name, gender, occupation, employer, schools attended, and a short bio. You can even add a personal photo to your profile. (Note that all profile information is optional.) In addition, many individual Google services include their own settings that are part of your Google account.

How do you change or add to your Google account settings?

You can access your Google account settings from the Settings option found on many Google services pages, including the main Google search page.

Hands-On Exercises

2 | Changing Google Account Settings

Steps: 1. Change Google Account Settings; **2.** Create a Google Profile.

Use Figures 1.5 through 1.7 as a guide in the exercise.

Step 1 Change Google Account Settings

Refer to Figures 1.5 and 1.6 as you complete Step 1.

a. Go to the main Google search page at **www.google.com** and sign in to your Google account.

b. Click the **Settings** link at the top of the page and then select **Google Account settings**. (If you're using Internet Explorer, click your name or email address at the top of the page and select **Account settings**.)

Click to edit account settings ————

Figure 1.5 Hands-On Exercise 2, Steps 1a and 1b.

c. To change your password, click the **Changing your password** link. When the *Change password* page appears, enter your current password and new password, confirm the new password, and click the **Save** button.

d. To associate another email address with this account, click the **Edit** link in the *Email addresses* section. When the next page appears, enter a new address into the *Add an additional email address* box and click the **Save** button.

e. To view data for Google services stored with your Google account, click the **View data stored with this account** link.

Click to change password ————
Click to create or edit account profile ————
Click to edit email address ————

Figure 1.6 Hands-On Exercise 2, Steps 1c through 1e.

Step 2 Create a Google Profile

Refer to Figure 1.7 as you complete Step 2.

a. Go to the main Google search page at **www.google.com** and sign in to your Google account.

b. Click the **Settings** link at the top of the page, and then select **Google Account settings**. (If you're using Internet Explorer, click your name or email address at the top of the page and select **Account settings**.)

c. When the *Google accounts* page appears, click the **Create a profile** link in the *Profile* section.

d. When the *Create a public profile* page appears, enter your first and last names; then click the **Create profile & continue** button.

e. When the *Create your profile* page appears, make sure the **About me** tab is selected.

f. Enter information into the various sections as desired. All information is optional.

g. To add a personal photo, click the **change photo** link. When the *Select profile photo* page appears, click **Upload from my computer**, click the **Browse** or **Choose File** button, and then navigate to and select the file to upload. When the *Crop this picture of yourself* box appears, drag the corner handles to crop the photo and then click the **Apply Changes** button.

h. When you're done creating your profile, click the **Done editing** button.

Figure 1.7 Hands-On Exercise 2, Steps 2d through 2h.

Summary

In this chapter, you learned how to create a new Google account, as well as how to change your account settings and create a personal profile.

Key Term

Google account .2

Multiple Choice Questions

1. Which of the following is true?

   (a) A Google account is necessary to use all Google services.

   (b) A Google account is necessary to use some Google services.

   (c) A Google account is not necessary to use any Google services.

   (d) None of the above.

2. What is the cost to create and maintain a single Google account?

   (a) Free

   (b) $9.95 one-time charge

   (c) $9.95/year

   (d) $9.95 one-time charge plus $9.95/year

3. Which of the following information is required to create a basic Google account?

   (a) First and last names

   (b) Current email address

   (c) Phone number

   (d) Street address

4. Which of the following is *not* a current Google service or application?

   (a) Google Books

   (b) Google Docs

   (c) Google Law

   (d) Google News

5. Which of the following information is *not* part of a Google profile?

   (a) Places you've lived

   (b) Places you've worked

   (c) Schools you've attended

   (d) Pets you've owned

Critical Thinking

1. Google wants users to link usage of all its applications and services via a single Google account. Write a short paper discussing the pros and cons of linking various applications and services in this manner; discuss the privacy implications as well as the convenience factor.

Credits

Google, Blogger, and Picasa screenshots reprinted by permission.

CHAPTER 2

Using Google Search

Objectives

After you read this chapter, you will be able to:

1. Conduct a Basic Search

2. Refine Your Search

3. Conduct an Advanced Search

4. Search for Images

The following Hands-On Exercises will help you accomplish the chapter objectives:

Hands-On Exercises

EXERCISES	SKILLS COVERED
1. Conducting a Basic Search	**Step 1:** Enter a Search Query **Step 2:** Extend Your Search Results **Step 3:** Refine Your Search Results with Google's Search Tools
2. Refining Your Search	**Step 1:** Conduct an AND/OR Search **Step 2:** Work with Stop Words **Step 3:** Exclude Words from Your Results **Step 4:** Search for Similar Words **Step 5:** Search for an Exact Phrase **Step 6:** Restrict Your Search to Specific File Types **Step 7:** Restrict Your Search to a Specific Domain or Website **Step 8:** Restrict Your Search to the Page's Title **Step 9:** Restrict Your Search to the Page's URL **Step 10:** Restrict Your Search to the Page's Body Text **Step 11:** Restrict Your Search to the Page's Anchor Text **Step 12:** Search for Similar Pages
3. Conducting an Advanced Search	**Step 1:** Access Google's Advanced Search Page **Step 2:** Conduct an OR Search **Step 3:** Search for an Exact Phrase **Step 4:** Search for Pages in a Specific Language **Step 5:** Search for Recent Web Pages **Step 6:** Search within a Numeric Range **Step 7:** Activate SafeSearch Filtering
4. Searching for Images	**Step 1:** Enter a Basic Query **Step 2:** View Image Search Results **Step 3:** Search by Image Size **Step 4:** Search by Type of Image **Step 5:** Search for Black and White Images

Objective 1

Conduct a Basic Search

What is Google?

Google **The Internet's most popular search engine.**

Search engine **A website that enables users to search the web for specific information.**

Search index **A database that stores information about web pages, in order to provide fast and accurate searching.**

Database **An organized collection of related information.**

Google is the Internet's most popular *search engine*. It has the largest *search index*, which is the *database* Google uses to store the pages it catalogs on the web. Google also has the most users of any search site, and for good reason: Google is both easy to use and returns highly relevant results. From the spartan nature of the main Google search page to the ease-of-use of the search feature, a Google search is so effortless that just about anyone can do it, without a lot of effort or instruction.

> **Note Google, Inc.**
>
> The Google search engine is just one offering from Google, Inc., the company behind the technology. While Google's stated mission is search related ("to organize the world's information and make it universally accessible and useful"), in reality the company generates very little money from its search technologies. Instead, Google generates most of its revenues from selling advertising based on its search results—and has become the largest advertising-related firm on the web.

> **Note To Google**
>
> Because of its dominance in the search engine market, Google has become synonymous with using the web to search for information. In June 2006, the verb "to google" was added to the *Oxford English Dictionary*.

How does a Google search work?

Web server **A specialized computer, connected to the Internet, that hosts web content.**

The typical Google search takes less than half a second to complete. That's because all the searching takes place on Google's own *web servers*. You may think that you're searching the web when you enter a Google query, but in effect you're searching a huge index of websites stored on Google's servers. That index was created previously, over a period of time; because you're only searching a server, not the entire web, your searches can be completed in the blink of an eye.

> **Note Servers**
>
> Google uses more than a half-million servers, located in clusters in its technology centers around the world. All of these servers run the Linux operating system. Google uses three types of servers: web servers (which host Google's public website), index servers (which hold the searchable index to the bigger document database), and document servers (which house copies of all the individual web pages in Google's database).

Of course, you're unaware of all this behind-the-scenes activity. You simply type your query into the search box on Google's main web page, click the **Google Search** button, and then view the search results page when it appears. All the shuffling of data from server to server is invisible to you.

How does Google build its search index?

At the heart of Google's search system is the database of web pages stored on Google's document servers. These servers hold billions of individual web pages—not the entire web, but a good portion of it.

Crawler A software program that automatically and regularly visits websites to read and index them for search engine use. It is also known as a *spider*.

GoogleBot Google's web crawler software.

How does Google determine which web pages to index and store on its servers? Most of the pages in the Google database are found by Google's special *crawler* or spider software, which automatically crawls the web, looking for new and updated web pages. Google's crawler, known as *GoogleBot*, not only searches for new web pages (by exploring links to other pages on the pages it already knows about), but also re-crawls pages already in the database, checking for changes and updates. A complete re-crawling of the web pages in the Google database takes place every few weeks, so no individual page is more than a few weeks out of date.

> **Note** **Smart Crawling**
>
> GoogleBot is smart about how it updates the Google database. Web pages that are known to be frequently updated are crawled more frequently than other pages. For example, pages on a news site might be crawled hourly.

The GoogleBot crawler reads each page it encounters, much like a web browser does. It follows every link on every page until all the links have been followed. New pages are added to the Google database by following those links GoogleBot hasn't seen before.

How does Google rank its search results?

Searching the Google index for all occurrences of a given word isn't all that difficult, especially with the computing power of a half-million servers driving things. What is difficult is returning the results in a format that is usable by and relevant to the person doing the searching. You can't just list the matching web pages in random order, nor is alphabetical or chronological order all that useful. No, Google has to return its search results with the most important or relevant pages listed first; it has to rank the results for its users.

How does Google determine which web pages are the best match to a given query? The exact methodology is top secret, but Google does provide some hints as to how its ranking system works. There are three components to the ranking:

- **Text analysis.** Google looks not only for matching words on a web page but also for how those words are used. That means examining font size, usage, proximity, and more than a hundred other factors to help determine relevance. Google also analyzes the content of neighboring pages on the same website to ensure that the selected page is the best match.

- **Links and link text.** Google then looks at the links (and the text for those links) on the web page, making sure that they link to pages that are relevant to the searcher's query.

PageRank Google's algorithm for ranking web pages in its search results.

- **PageRank.** Finally, Google relies on its own proprietary *PageRank* technology to give an objective measurement of web page importance and popularity. PageRank determines a page's importance by counting the number of other pages that link to that page. The more pages that link to a page, the higher that page's PageRank—and the higher it will appear in the search results. The PageRank is a numerical ranking from 0 to 10, expressed as PR0, PR1, PR2, and so forth—the higher the better.

> **Note** **Page Specific**
>
> PageRank is page specific, not site specific. This means that the PageRank of the individual pages on a website can (and probably will) vary from page to page.

How is the Google search page organized?

Google's homepage is stunning in its simplicity. All you see is the Google logo, the search box, some links to additional search services, and two search buttons. The two search buttons are **Google Search**, which returns a long list of results to choose from, and **I'm Feeling Lucky**, which takes you directly to the most relevant result page (Figure 2.1).

Additional search links

Click to configure search settings

Search box

Click to search

Click to return the one best search result

Figure 2.1 The Google search page.

 Note   **Comparing Your Screen with the Figures in This Book**

Since Google is constantly updating its feature set, the pages you see on your own computer might not always match those displayed in this book. In addition, since Google's search results are updated daily (if not hourly!), the search results displayed here may be different from the search results you obtain when you work through these exercises.

How do you conduct a Google search?

Query A search for information.

Keyword A term used in a search query.

You start a Google search, also called a *query*, from Google's homepage, located at **www.google.com**. Your query can include one or more *keywords*, which are the terms used in your search.

 Note   **Not Case Sensitive**

Google searches are not case sensitive, which means there's no need to capitalize words in your queries.

What does a search results page look like?

All Google search results pages are different, because each search is different. The results that Google displays are fine-tuned to the query you entered (Figure 2.2).

Advertisements

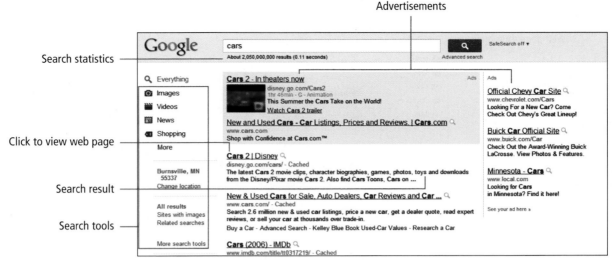

Search statistics

Click to view web page

Search result

Search tools

Figure 2.2 A typical search results page.

Let's start at the top of the page, where Google displays a search box and Search button, in case you want to conduct another search from this search results page. Directly underneath the search box are statistics related to your query. You'll see how many results were returned for your query, and how long it took to display those results.

On the left side of the search results page is a sidebar that contains various *search tools* for fine-tuning your search results. Click any link to display only that type of result.

In most instances, the first freestanding search result on the page is the page that Google ranks number one for the query you entered. This page is most likely to provide the information you were looking for. The result includes the page's title, along with a short description of the page. To view the page, click the blue underlined title link.

In some instances, there may be other relevant pages from the same site. If this is the case, Google displays a **Show more results from site** link beneath the initial search result; click this link to display more pages from this site.

If, for some reason, a given page is no longer available when you click its link in Google's search results, you can click the **Cached** link. A *cached page* is an older version of the current web page stored on Google's document servers.

Search tools A means of filtering Google search results.

Cached page A page that is stored on Google's document servers, and that may be slightly older than the current version of the page, or outdated.

Organic Nonpaid search results; results generated directly from a Google search.

Alert!   **Paid Results**

Not all the pages listed on a search results page are *organic*; some are paid for by Google's advertisers. These ads are typically above and sometimes to the right of the legitimate search results. You should not confuse these links with the main search results; they may have only indirect relevance to your query.

You can view a small representation (thumbnail) of any results page while remaining on the search results page by clicking the magnifying glass icon next to the result. Click the icon again to hide the thumbnail (Figure 2.3).

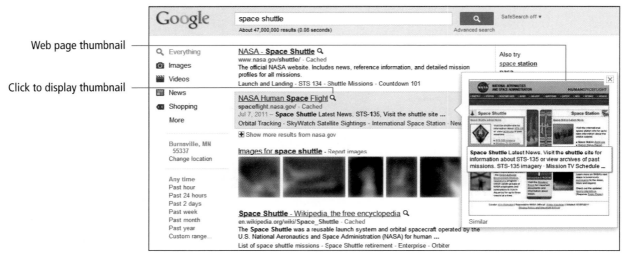

Web page thumbnail ———

Click to display thumbnail ———

Figure 2.3 Viewing search results.

OneBox Specialized search results.

Google sometimes displays specialized search results, called *OneBox* results, located near the top of the page. For example, Google might display matching news results for a query about a current event, or images for a query about a celebrity; sometimes more than one OneBox is displayed. If this is the type of information you're looking for, click the **OneBox** link (typically with its own content-specific label, such as *News* or *Images*) to see more pages like the one listed (Figure 2.4).

OneBox results ———

Figure 2.4 OneBox search results.

At the bottom of each search results page is a list of related searches. You may find that one of these searches is more targeted than the original query you entered; click a related search to see those results (Figure 2.5).

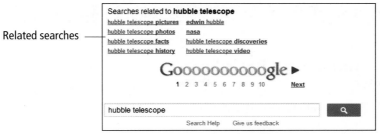

Related searches ———

Figure 2.5 The bottom of a search results page.

Universal Search The display of different types of search results on a single results page.

How can you fine-tune Google's search results?

There are many ways to fine-tune Google's search results to better answer your queries. Perhaps the most useful method is to use Google's search tools, located in the left-hand sidebar of the search results page. These search tools let you filter your results in several different ways. For example, you can opt to display only certain types of results (images, videos, news, shopping, etc.), or pages created or updated within a given time period. You employ these search tools *after* you've entered your query, thus redisplaying the (newly filtered) results (Figure 2.6).

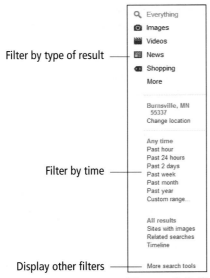

Filter by type of result ———

Filter by time ———

Display other filters ———

Figure 2.6 Google's search tools.

What is Google Instant?

Google Instant Technology on the Google site that displays search results as a query is entered.

One of Google's newest features is *Google Instant*. When activated, Google Instant displays predicted search results as you type, instead of waiting for you to click the **Google Search** button. These instant search results can save time and help you fine-tune your query as you're typing it.

If Google Instant is not activated by default, click the **Settings** or **Options** (gear) button at the top of any Google page and select **Search settings.** When the *Preferences* page appears, scroll to the Google Instant section and select the **Use Google Instant** option and then click the **Save Preferences** button.

Hands-On Exercises

1 | Conducting a Basic Search

Steps: 1. Enter a Search Query; **2.** Extend Your Search Results; **3.** Refine Your Search Results with Google's Search Tools.

Use Figures 2.7 through 2.10 as a guide to the exercise.

Step 1 | Enter a Search Query

Refer to Figure 2.7 as you complete Step 1.

a. From your web browser, go to Google's main page, located at **www.google.com**.

b. Enter your query, consisting of one or more keywords, into the search box.

c. Click the **Google Search** button.

> **Tip ★ Suggested Queries**
>
> Google will display possible queries in a drop-down box as you type. If you wish, you can select one of these queries to begin your search without clicking the **Google Search** button.

> **Tip ★ Google Instant**
>
> If Google Instant is activated, search results will appear as you type your query. You can accept these preliminary search results, or continue to enter your full query and then click the **Google Search** button.

After you click the **Google Search** button, Google searches its index for all the web pages that match your query and then displays the results on a separate search results page.

Enter query —
Click to search —

Figure 2.7 Hands-On Exercise 1, Step 1.

Step 2 | Extend Your Search Results

Refer to Figure 2.8 as you complete Step 2.

For many searches, you can find what you want simply by clicking a few page links on the first search results page. Don't assume, however, that the only relevant results will appear on the first page. Some queries return literally thousands (if not *millions*) of matching pages. Even though the most relevant results are supposed to be listed first, it's possible to find much useful information buried deeper in the results.

a. Enter your query the usual way to display the first page of search results.

b. To display the next page of search results, scroll to the bottom of the first page and click the **Next** link or blue right arrow.

c. To go directly to a specific page in the search results, scroll to the bottom of any search results page and click a page number.

d. To view a page beyond the first ten listed, click on the **10** link. (This may be a different number, depending on your specific search results.)

This displays page 10 of the search results, along with links to pages 1–19 at the bottom; keep clicking to the right to view more and more pages of results.

Click to view next page of results

Click to go to a specific results page

Figure 2.8 Hands-On Exercise 1, Step 2.

Step ③ Refine Your Search Results with Google's Search Tools

Refer to Figures 2.9 and 2.10 as you complete Step 3.

You can use Google's search tools to refine the results of any query.

a. Enter your query the usual way to display the first page of search results.

By default, Google displays all types of results, as evidenced by the selection of **Everything** in the search tools.

b. To display only certain types of results, click that link in the search tools sidebar:

- Images
- Videos
- News
- Shopping

Click the **More** link to display even more types of results, including Books, Places, Blogs, Discussions, and Recipes.

c. To narrow the results by date, click a date range in the search tools sidebar:

- Latest
- Past 24 Hours
- Past week
- Past month
- Past year

 Options Vary by Search

The options available in the sidebar vary by what you're searching for. You may not always see all the search options described here.

To select a custom date range, click **Custom range** and then enter a beginning and end date.

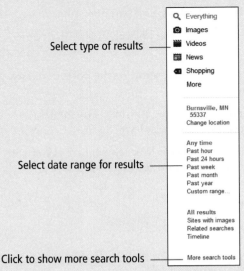

Select type of results

Select date range for results

Click to show more search tools

Figure 2.9 Hands-On Exercise 1, Steps 3a through 3c.

d. To filter by additional search tools, click the **More search tools** link in the sidebar and then select from the additional tools:

- Sites with images (displays sites that include images)
- Related searches (displays a list of searches related to the current query)
- Timeline (displays results by date, including a visual timeline)
- Visited pages (displays only those pages recently visited)
- Not yet visited (displays only pages not yet viewed)
- Dictionary (displays a Dictionary page with the word or phrase's definition, usage, and the like)
- Reading level (filters results by reading level)
- Social (displays results from blogs, tweets, and other social media)
- Nearby (displays only results from nearby businesses)
- Translated foreign pages (displays only non-English pages, translated into English)

The filtered results are displayed when you click a search tools link; you don't have to click the **Search** button to initiate a new search.

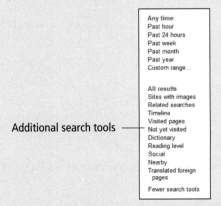

Additional search tools

Figure 2.10 Hands-On Exercise 1, Step 3d.

Objective 2

Refine Your Search

Search operator A symbol or word that causes a search engine to do something special with the word directly following the symbol.

Boolean operators Words that are used to refine a search and that come from Boolean logic and mathematics, such as AND, OR, and NOT. Google supports only the Boolean OR operator.

Stop word A small, common word, such as "and," "the," "where," "how," and "what," that Google ignores when performing a query.

How can you produce better search results?

Most users enter a keyword or two into Google's search box, click the Google Search button, and are satisfied with the results. This is a rather brute force method of searching, however, and typically generates a multitude of (mostly unwanted) results.

To generate a smaller, more targeted list of results, you have to refine your query using a defined series of *search operators*. These words and symbols instruct Google to fine-tune your query accordingly.

> **Note** **Boolean Operators**
>
> **Boolean operators** come from Boolean logic and mathematics, and are words used to refine a search. The OR operator is the only Boolean operator accepted by the Google search engine. The Boolean AND operator is assumed in all Google searches; the Boolean NOT operator is replaced by the Google – (minus sign) operator.

How do you construct an AND/OR query?

When constructing a query from multiple keywords, Google automatically assumes the word "and" between all the words in your query. That is, if you enter two words, it assumes you're looking for pages that include *both* those words—word one *and* word two. It doesn't return pages that include only one or the other.

This is different from assuming the **OR** operator between the words in your query. With an "and" query, the results include pages that include both words. With an "or" query, the results include pages that include either word—potentially a much larger set of results.

So, for example, if you entered the query "chevrolet camaro," Google reads this as "chevrolet AND camaro," and searches for pages that include both words. If you want to search for pages that include either of the two words, you'd instead enter "chevrolet OR camaro."

What are stop words?

Google automatically ignores small, common words, called *stop words*, in a query. Stop words include "and," "the," "where," "how," "what," "or" (unless uppercase), and other similar words, along with certain single digits and single letters (such as "a").

Including a stop word in a search normally does nothing but slow the search down, which is why Google excises them. As an example, Google takes the query "how a toaster works," removes the words "how" and "a," and creates the new, shorter query "toaster works."

You can override the stop word exclusion by telling Google that it *must* include specific words in the query. You do this by putting the + (plus sign) operator in front of the otherwise excluded word.

How can you exclude specific words from your results?

Sometimes you want to refine your results by excluding pages that include a specific word. You can exclude words from your search by using the – (minus sign) operator; any word in your query preceded by the – sign is automatically excluded from the search results. (Remember to always include a space before the – sign, and none after.)

For example, if you want to search for pages about apples, but not about Apple iPods, you would enter the query "apple –ipod." This search returns all pages that include the word apple but *not* the word iPod.

How can you search if you're not sure of what you're searching for?

If you're not sure you're thinking of the right word for a query, you can tell Google to search for words similar to a given word. You do this by adding the ~ (tilde) operator. Just include the ~ character (located to the left of the 1 key on your keyboard) immediately before the word in question, no spaces, and Google will search for all pages that include that word and all appropriate synonyms. For example, to search for words similar to the word "warming," enter the query "~warming." This will return pages about warming, heating, climate change, and the like.

Can you use wildcards in a query?

Wildcard A character that enables you to search for all words that include the first part of a keyword. Google does not support wildcard searches.

Unlike some other search engines, Google doesn't let you use *wildcards* to indicate the variable ends of words. Wildcards let you search for all words that include the first part of a keyword; for example, a search for book* (with the * wildcard) would typically return results for "books," "bookstore," "bookkeeper," and so on.

Automatic word stemming A feature that enables Google to automatically search for all possible word variations.

Instead, Google incorporates *automatic word stemming*, which enables Google to automatically search for all possible word variations. This is a great way to search for both singular and plural forms of a word, as well as different tenses and forms. Using our "book" example, entering the query book in a Google search should return pages that include all forms of the word book—"books," "booked," and so forth.

 Tip   **Reverse Stemming**

Automatic word stemming also works in the opposite direction. For example, a search for rains will return both the words "rains" and "rain."

Can Google search for files on the web?

Google can search for information contained in all sorts of documents, not just HTML web pages. Each document format is called a *file type*, and Google can search by file type using the file's three- or four-character *file extension*, which indicates the program a file was created in.

File type A particular way of encoding data in a computer file. Most programs store their data in their own file types; file types are indicated by specific file extensions.

Google can recognize and search for the following file types:

File extension A three- or four-character suffix that usually indicates the program in which a file was created.

- Adobe Acrobat (*.pdf*)
- Adobe PostScript (*.ps*)
- Autodesk (*.dwf*)
- Google Earth (*.kml, .kmz*)
- Lotus 1-2-3 (*.wk1, .wk2, .wk3, .wk4, .wk5, .wki, .wks, .wku*)
- MacWrite (*.mw*)
- Microsoft Excel (*.xls, .xlsx*)
- Microsoft PowerPoint (*.ppt, .pptx*)
- Microsoft Word (*.doc, .docx*)
- Microsoft Works (*.wdb, .wks, .wps*)
- Microsoft Write (*.wri*)
- Rich Text Format (*.rtf*)
- Shockwave Flash (*.swf*)
- Text (*.ans, .txt*)

If you want to restrict your results to a specific file type, use the **filetype:** operator followed by the file extension, in this format: filetype:*filetype*. To eliminate a particular file type from your search results, use the filetype: operator preceded by the – operator and followed by the file extension, like this: –filetype:*filetype*.

For example, to search only for PowerPoint *.ppt* files, use this query: filetype:ppt. To exclude *.ppt* files from your search, enter this query: –filetype:ppt.

Domain A specific type of site on the web, indicated by the domain name after the final "dot" separator. For example, the *.edu* domain is used to indicate education sites.

URL Short for uniform resource locator; a web address.

Can you use Google to search within a given website?

Websites are organized by top-level *domain*, which is the two- or three-character name that defines a type of Internet site. Google lets you search for sites within a specific top-level web domain, such as *.com* or *.org* or *.edu*—or, perhaps, within a specific country's domain, such as *.uk* (United Kingdom) or *.ca* (Canada). You do this by using the **site:** operator. Just enter the operator followed by the domain name, like this: **site:***domain*.

The site: operator can also be used to restrict your search to a specific website. In this instance, you enter the site's top-level *URL*, or web address, like this: site: www.*website.domain*.

Hands-On Exercises

2 | Refining Your Search

Steps: 1. Conduct an AND/OR Search; **2.** Work with Stop Words; **3.** Exclude Words from Your Results; **4.** Search for Similar Words; **5.** Search for an Exact Phrase; **6.** Restrict Your Search to Specific File Types; **7.** Restrict Your Search to a Specific Domain or Website; **8.** Restrict Your Search to the Page's Title; **9.** Restrict Your Search to the Page's URL; **10.** Restrict Your Search to the Page's Body Text; **11.** Restrict Your Search to the Page's Anchor Text; **12.** Search for Similar Pages.

Use Figures 2.11 through 2.34 as a guide to the exercise.

Step 1 Conduct an AND/OR Search

Refer to Figures 2.11 and 2.12 as you complete Step 1.

a. As previously noted, Google assumes the AND operator between any two keywords—which means you don't have to enter it in your query. For this example, enter the query **birds fish** into the search box and then click the **Google Search** button.

The results for this query return pages that include *both* keywords.

No AND operator —
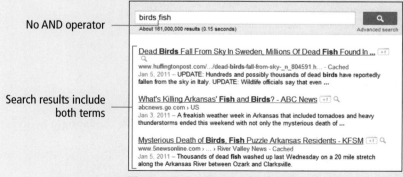
Search results include
both terms —

Figure 2.11 Hands-On Exercise 2, Step 1a.

b. To conduct an "or" query, to search for pages that include either of two keywords, enter the **OR** operator between the two keywords. For example, enter the query **birds OR fish** into the search box and then click the **Google Search** button.

The results for this query include pages that include either word, not necessarily both.

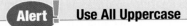
OR operator

Search results include at least one of the terms

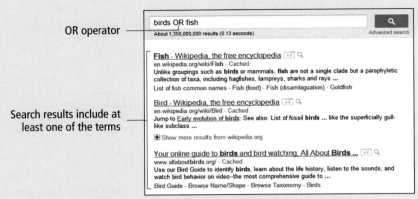

Figure 2.12 Hands-On Exercise 2, Step 1b.

Step 2 Work with Stop Words

Refer to Figures 2.13 and 2.14 as you complete Step 2.

a. In the Google search box, enter the query **where is mars** and then click the **Google Search** button.

The results ignore the stop words "where" and "is."

Stop words

Search results ignore stop words

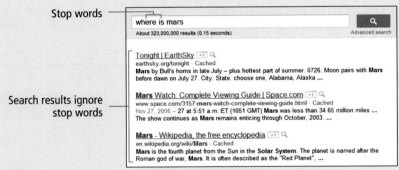

Figure 2.13 Hands-On Exercise 2, Step 2a.

b. Now enter the query **+where +is mars** and then click the **Google Search** button.

These results include the words "where" and "is."

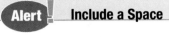

+ sign

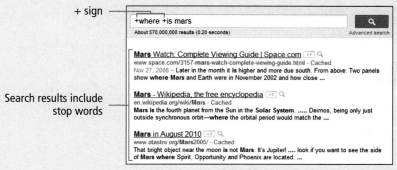

Search results include
stop words

Figure 2.14 Hands-On Exercise 2, Step 2b.

Step 3 Exclude Words from Your Results

Refer to Figures 2.15 and 2.16 as you complete Step 3.

In this activity, we examine word exclusion by looking at a word that has several meanings—"bass," which can be a fish, a brand of shoe, a male singer, a type of guitar, a type of drum, or a brand of beer.

a. In the Google search box, enter **bass** and then click the **Google Search** button.

The results include pages about fish, shoes, singers, and the like.

Query

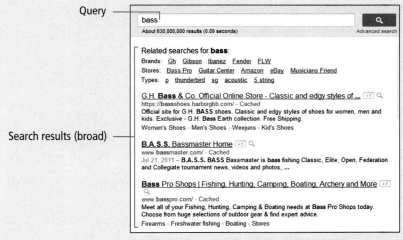

Search results (broad)

Figure 2.15 Hands-On Exercise 2, Step 3a.

b. To focus your results more closely on the bass that's a male vocalist, you want to exclude pages that include the word "fish," "shoe," "guitar," "drum," and "beer." Enter the query **bass –fish –shoe –guitar –drum –beer** and click the **Google Search** button.

The results no longer include pages that talk about fish, guitars, drums, beer, and shoes.

Excluded words

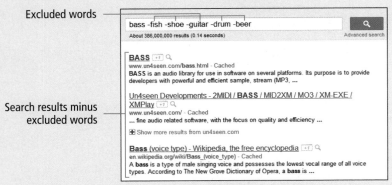

Search results minus
excluded words

Figure 2.16 Hands-On Exercise 2, Step 3b.

Step 4 **Search for Similar Words**

Refer to Figures 2.17 and 2.18 as you complete Step 4.

a. In the Google search box, enter the query **elderly** and then click the **Google Search** button.

The results include only pages with the word "elderly."

Query (standard)

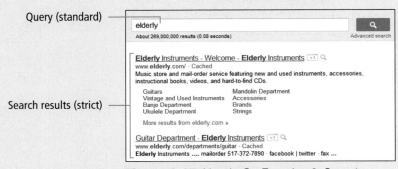

Search results (strict)

Figure 2.17 Hands-On Exercise 2, Step 4a.

b. To expand your search, enter the query **~elderly** and then click the **Google Search** button.

The results now include pages that include not just the word "elderly," but also the words "senior," "old," "aged," and so on.

~ operator

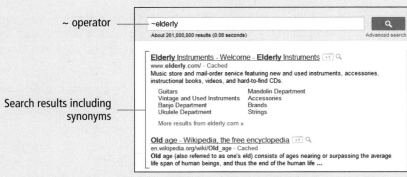

Search results including
synonyms

Figure 2.18 Hands-On Exercise 2, Step 4b.

Tip ★ **Listing Synonyms Only**

To list *only* synonyms without returning matches for the original word, combine the ~ operator with the – operator, like this: ~keyword –keyword. This excludes the original word from the synonymous results. Using the previous example, to list only synonyms for the word "elderly," enter ~elderly –elderly.

Step 5   Search for an Exact Phrase

Refer to Figures 2.19 and 2.20 as you complete Step 5.

When you want to search for an exact phrase, you should enclose the entire phrase in quotation marks. This tells Google to search for the precise keywords in the prescribed order.

a. In the Google search box, enter the query **summer vacation package** (no quotation marks) and then click the **Google Search** button.

The results include pages that include all the words "summer," "vacation," and "package"—but not necessarily in that order, or even used consecutively.

Query (string of words) ——

Search results include all words in any order ——

Figure 2.19 Hands-On Exercise 2, Step 5a.

b. To limit the results just to pages about summer vacation packages, you have to search for pages that include the three words in that precise order as a phrase. To do this, enter the query **"summer vacation package,"** making sure to surround the phrase with the quotation marks; then click the **Google Search** button.

The results include only those pages that include the exact phrase "summer vacation package"—and no pages where the word "summer" appears at the top of a page and "vacation" appears at the bottom.

Quotation marks ——

Search results for exact phrase only ——

Figure 2.20 Hands-On Exercise 2, Step 5b.

Step 6 Restrict Your Search to Specific File Types

Refer to Figures 2.21 and 2.22 as you complete Step 6.

In this exercise, we'll search for PDF files—and then exclude PDF files from our search.

a. To limit your search to only Adobe PDF documents about NASA, enter **nasa filetype:pdf** into the search box and then click the **Google Search** button.

The results include only PDF files.

Search for a specific file type

Search results—PDF files only

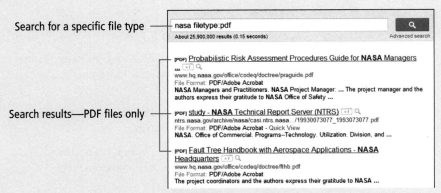

Figure 2.21 Hands-On Exercise 2, Step 6a.

b. To exclude PDF files from your search results, enter **nasa –filetype:pdf** and click the **Google Search** button.

Google now returns only web pages and no PDF files.

Excluding PDF files

Search results do not include PDF files

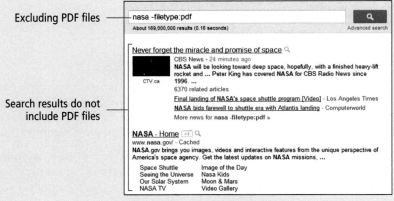

Figure 2.22 Hands-On Exercise 2, Step 6b.

Step 7 Restrict Your Search to a Specific Domain or Website

Refer to Figures 2.23 and 2.24 as you complete Step 7.

In this exercise, you will search for information about NASA at both a specified domain and a specified website.

a. To limit your search to sites in the *.edu* domain, enter the query **nasa site:.edu**, and then click the **Google Search** button.

Google returns only matching pages from the *.edu* domain.

Search the .edu domain

Search results for pages
in the .edu domain

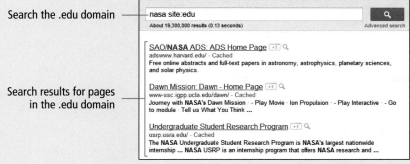

Figure 2.23 Hands-On Exercise 2, Step 7a.

b. To limit your search to pages within the White House website (**www.whitehouse.gov**), enter the query **nasa site:www.whitehouse.gov,** and then click the **Google Search** button.

Google returns only matching pages from the White House website.

Search the whitehouse.gov
website

Search results for pages on the
whitehouse.gov site

Figure 2.24 Hands-On Exercise 2, Step 7b.

Step 8 Restrict Your Search to the Page's Title

Refer to Figures 2.25 and 2.26 as you complete Step 8.

The title of a web page appears in the browser Title bar. Sometimes you want to search only the titles of web pages, while ignoring the pages' body text; this helps focus your search on those pages that are primarily, rather than peripherally, focused on the topic at hand. Google offers two ways to do this, depending on how many words you have in your query.

If your query contains a single word, use the **intitle:** operator at the beginning of your query. If your query contains multiple words, use the **allintitle:** operator.

a. To look for pages with the word "football" in the title, enter the query **intitle:football** and click the **Google Search** button. (Make sure not to leave a space between the intitle: operator and the keyword.)

Only those pages with the word "football" in the title are returned.

Limit search to page titles ——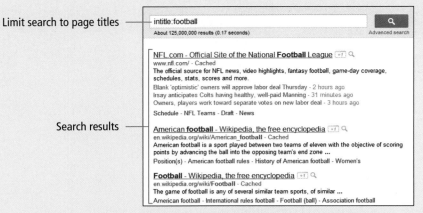

Search results ——

Figure 2.25 Hands-On Exercise 2, Step 8a.

b. To look for pages with the words "football arena" in the title, perform the query **allintitle:football arena.**

Google returns pages with both words in the title.

Limit search to page titles ——

Search results ——

Figure 2.26 Hands-On Exercise 2, Step 8b.

 Multiple Keywords with the intitle: Operator

When you use the allintitle: operator, Google searches for all the keywords after the operator. If you use the intitle: operator, Google searches only for the first word after the operator; all subsequent words are subject to a normal full-page search.

Step 9 **Restrict Your Search to the Page's URL**

Refer to Figures 2.27 and 2.28 as you complete Step 9.

The **inurl:** and **allinurl:** operators are similar to the **intitle:** and **allintitle:** operators, but restrict your search to words that appear in web page addresses (URLs). You use these operators in the same fashion—**inurl:** to search for single words and **allinurl:** to search for multiple words.

a. To search for sites that have the word "molehill" in their URLs, enter the query **inurl:molehill** and click the **Google Search** button. (Make sure not to leave a space between the inurl: operator and the keyword.)

Google returns sites with molehill in the URL.

Limit search to URLs ——

Search results ——

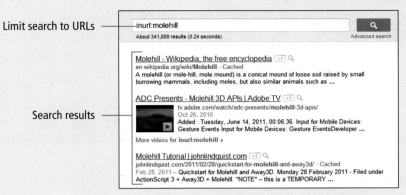

Figure 2.27 Hands-On Exercise 2, Step 9a.

b. To search for sites that have both the words "molehill" and "group" in their URLs, perform the query **allinurl:molehill group**.

As with the allintitle: operator, all the keywords you enter after the allinurl: operator are included in the search.

Limit search to URLs ——

Search results ——

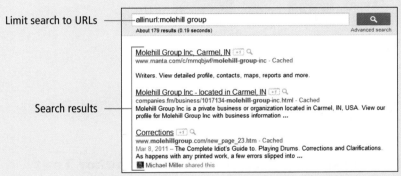

Figure 2.28 Hands-On Exercise 2, Step 9b.

Step 10   Restrict Your Search to the Page's Body Text

Refer to Figure 2.29 and 2.30 as you complete Step 10.

While you can limit your searches to page titles and URLs, it's more likely that you'll want to search the body text of web pages. To restrict your search to body text only (regardless of whether the search item appears in the page title, URL, or link text), use the **intext:** and **allintext:** operators. The syntax is the same as the previous operators; use **intext:** to search for single words and **allintext:** to search for multiple words.

a. To search for pages that include the word "bird" in their body text, perform the query **intext:bird**. (Make sure not to leave a space between the intext: operator and the keyword.)

Pages that include the word "bird" in their main content are now returned.

Limit search to page text —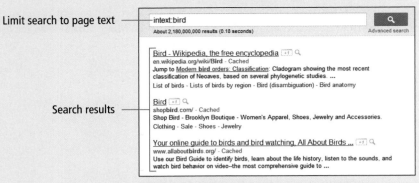

Search results —

Figure 2.29 Hands-On Exercise 2, Step 10a.

b. To search for pages that include both the words "bird" and "feathers" in the body text, perform the query **allintext:bird feathers**.

Google now returns pages that include both these words in the main body.

Limit search to page text —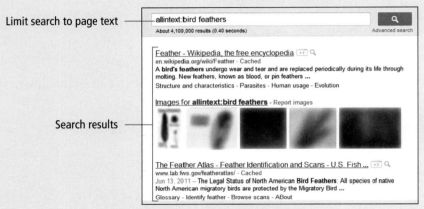

Search results —

Figure 2.30 Hands-On Exercise 2, Step 10b.

Step 11 Restrict Your Search to the Page's Anchor Text

Refer to Figures 2.31 and 2.32 as you complete Step 11.

The web is built around hyperlinking—the ability to click on an underlined piece of text to jump to a related web page. The underlined text that links to another web page is called the *anchor text*, and Google lets you search only the anchor text on a web page. You use the **inanchor:** operator to restrict your search to a single word in the anchor text; the **allinanchor:** variation lets you search for multiple words in the anchor text.

Anchor text The text that links to another web page.

a. To search for links that reference the word "goose," enter the query **inanchor:goose** and click the **Google Search** button. (Make sure not to leave a space between the **inanchor:** operator and the keyword.)

Google returns pages that include links with the word "goose."

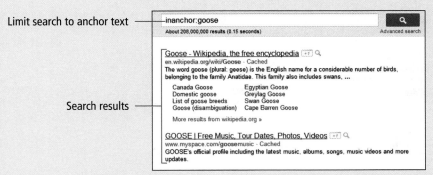

Limit search to anchor text ——

Search results ——

Figure 2.31 Hands-On Exercise 2, Step 11a.

b. To search for links that reference the words "goose" and "duck," perform the query **allinanchor:goose duck**.

Google now returns pages that include links with both the words "goose" and "duck."

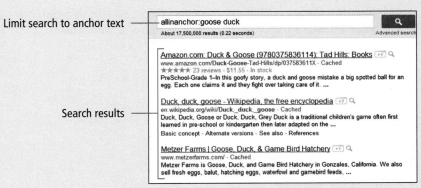

Limit search to anchor text ——

Search results ——

Figure 2.32 Hands-On Exercise 2, Step 11b.

Step 12 Search for Similar Pages

Refer to Figures 2.33 and 2.34 as you complete Step 12.

Have you ever found a web page you liked or found helpful and then wondered if there were any more like it? Fortunately, you can use Google's **related:** operator to display pages that are in some way similar to the specified page.

a. If you enter only a page's URL as your query, Google returns various pages on that website. For example, enter **www.pearsoned.com** into the search box and click the **Google Search** button.

The results are all pages on the Pearson Education website.

Website search ———

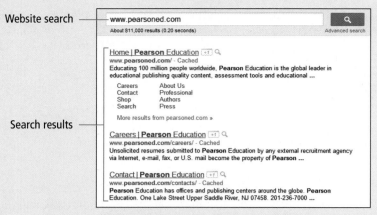

Search results ———

Figure 2.33 Hands-On Exercise 2, Step 12a.

b. To find websites that are like the Pearson Education site, enter **related:www. pearsoned.com** as your query.

The results now include sites similar to Pearson Education—in this instance, pages from other Pearson companies and other educational publishers.

Search related sites ———

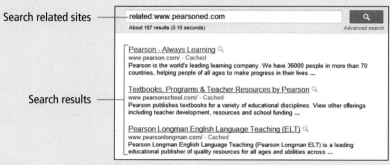

Search results ———

Figure 2.34 Hands-On Exercise 2, Step 12b.

Objective 3

Conduct an Advanced Search

Is there a way to enter an advanced query without using search operators?

If you don't want to spend the time to learn all of Google's complicated search operators, but still want to fine-tune your search beyond the basic keyword query, you can use Google's Advanced Search page. This page performs most of these same advanced search functions using a series of simple pull-down menus and checkboxes. You open the Advanced Search page by clicking the **Options** (gear) button on the main Google search page and then selecting **Advanced search**, or by clicking the **Advanced search** link by the Search button on any search results page.

What can you filter from the Advanced Search page?

The top of the Advanced Search page is where you enter your query. This section functions much like Google's various search operators; you can choose to search for *all these words* (the default "and" search), *this exact wording or phrase* (the quotation marks operator), or *one or more of these words* (the OR operator). You can also choose to not show pages that include selected words, by using the *But don't show pages that have any of these unwanted words* option.

Usage rights The permissions that specify in what context web page content can be reused.

Additional filters are also available. You can filter results based on reading level, language, or file type, or choose to search within a specific site or domain. You can also search by date, *usage rights*, where on the page keywords appear, region, or numeric range. The Advanced Search page also lets you search for similar pages, or for pages that link to a specific page.

How can you filter offensive pages from your search results?

SafeSearch Google's content filter for search results.

Another important option on Google's Advanced Search page is *SafeSearch* content filtering. You use SafeSearch to filter adult websites and images from your Google search results—an effective way to ensure that younger computer users aren't exposed to unwanted content.

Google provides two levels of SafeSearch filtering. Moderate filtering affects only the images returned on Google's search results pages, and is activated from Google's Image Search page; it blocks the display of potentially offensive images. (Moderate SafeSearch filtering is activated by default for all Google Image Search.) Strict filtering, activated from the Advanced Search page, applies the same standards to all your search results, whether image or text-based.

Hands-On Exercises

3 | Conducting an Advanced Search

Steps: 1. Access Google's Advanced Search Page; **2.** Conduct an OR Search; **3.** Search for an Exact Phrase; **4.** Search for Pages in a Specific Language; **5.** Search for Recent Web Pages; **6.** Search within a Numeric Range; **7.** Activate SafeSearch Filtering.

Use Figures 2.35 through 2.45 as a guide to the exercise.

Step 1 Access Google's Advanced Search Page

Refer to Figures 2.35 and 2.36 as you complete Step 1.

a. Go to Google's main search page, located at **www.google.com**.

b. Click the **Options** (gear) button and select **Advanced search**.

Click to display Advanced Search page

Figure 2.35 Hands-On Exercise 3, Steps 1a and 1b.

This displays the *Advanced Search* page.

c. Make your selections and then click the **Advanced Search** button.

Select number of
results/page   Click to execute search

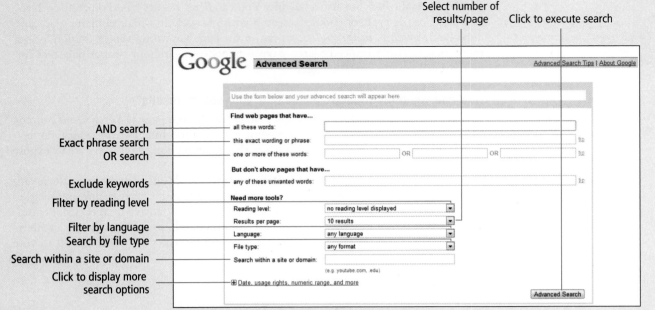

AND search
Exact phrase search
OR search

Exclude keywords
Filter by reading level

Filter by language
Search by file type
Search within a site or domain
Click to display more
search options

Figure 2.36 Hands-On Exercise 3, Step 1c.

Step 2 Conduct an OR Search

Refer to Figure 2.37 as you complete Step 2.

a. From the main Google search page, click the **Advanced search** link.

b. Go to the *Find web pages that have . . . one or more of these words* section.

c. Enter the first keyword into the first box.

d. Enter the second keyword into the second box, after the "OR."

e. Enter the third (optional) keyword into the third box, after the "OR."

f. Click the **Advanced Search** button.

Enter keywords

Final query

Click to execute search

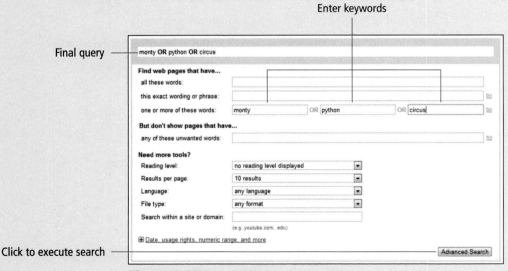

Figure 2.37 Hands-On Exercise 3, Step 2.

Step 3   Search for an Exact Phrase

Refer to **Figure 2.38** as you complete Step 3.

a. From the main Google search page, click the **Options** (gear) button and select **Advanced search**.

b. Go to the *Find web pages that have . . . this exact wording or phrase* section.

c. Enter the phrase into the box.

d. Click the **Advanced Search** button.

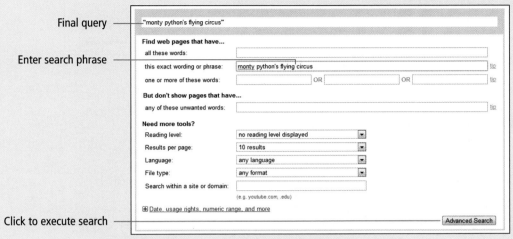

Final query —

Enter search phrase —

Click to execute search —

Figure 2.38 Hands-On Exercise 3, Step 3.

Step 4   Search for Pages in a Specific Language

Refer to **Figure 2.39** as you complete Step 4.

a. From the main Google search page, click the **Options** (gear) button and select **Advanced search**.

b. Enter your query into one of the three boxes in the *Find web pages that have . . .* section of the page.

c. In the *Need more tools?* section, click the **Language** list arrow, and select the language you want to search for.

d. Click the **Advanced Search** button.

Enter query

Select language

Click to execute search

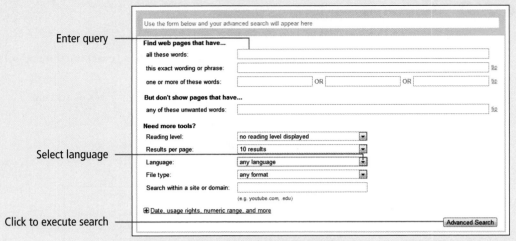

Figure 2.39 Hands-On Exercise 3, Step 4.

Step 5 Search for Recent Web Pages

Refer to Figures 2.40 and 2.41 as you complete Step 5.

a. From the main Google search page, click the **Options** (gear) button and select **Advanced search**.

b. Enter your query into one of the three boxes in the *Find web pages that have . . .* section of the page.

c. In the *Need more tools?* section, click the **Date, usage rights, numeric range, and more** link.

Enter query

Click to display more
search options

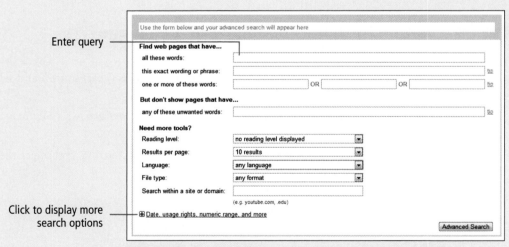

Figure 2.40 Hands-On Exercise 3, Steps 5a through 5c.

This displays additional search options.

d. Click the **Date** list arrow and select how recent the pages you want returned in your search results should be: *anytime, past 24 hours, past week, past month,* **or** *past year*.

e. Click the **Advanced Search** button.

Select date range

Click to execute search

Figure 2.41 Hands-On Exercise 3, Steps 5d and 5e.

Step 6 Search within a Numeric Range

Refer to Figures 2.42 and 2.43 as you complete Step 6.

Google also lets you search for values within a specified numeric range. For example, you might want to search for people with salaries between $50,000 and $100,000; you do this by instructing Google to search for pages that include numbers that fall within that range.

a. From the main Google search page, click the **Options** (gear) button and select **Advanced search**.

b. Enter your query into one of the three boxes in the *Find web pages that have . . .* section of the page.

c. In the *Need more tools?* section, click the **+** (plus sign) next to the *Date, usage rights, numeric range, and more* link.

Enter query

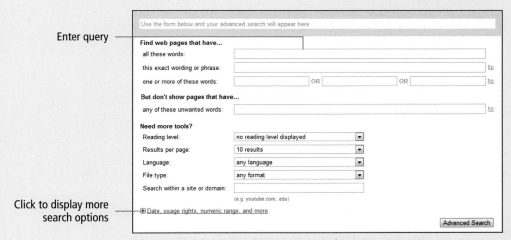

Click to display more search options

Figure 2.42 Hands-On Exercise 3, Steps 6a through 6c.

This displays additional search options.

d. Enter the lower number of the range you're searching for into the first *Numeric range* box.

e. Enter the higher number of the range you're searching for into the second *Numeric range* box.

f. Click the **Advanced Search** button.

Click to execute search

Enter lower number

Enter higher number

Figure 2.43 Hands-On Exercise 3, Steps 6d through 6f.

Step ⑦ Activate SafeSearch Filtering

Refer to Figures 2.44 and 2.45 as you complete Step 7.

You can activate SafeSearch content filtering in a number of different ways. The approach presented here activates the filter for all subsequent searches—or until SafeSearch is turned off.

a. Click the **Options** icon at the top of the page and then select **Search settings**.

Click to edit search settings

Figure 2.44 Hands-On Exercise 3, Step 7a.

This displays the *Preferences* page.

b. Scroll to the *SafeSearch Filtering* section.

c. Select the **Use strict filtering** option.

d. Click the **Save Preferences** button.

Click to enable SafeSearch filtering

Click to disable SafeSearch filtering

Click to save settings

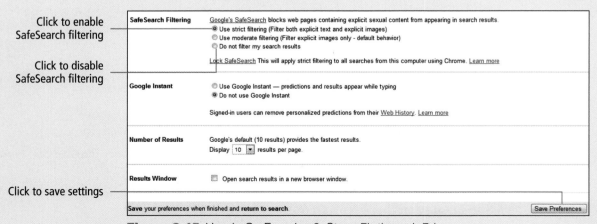

Figure 2.45 Hands-On Exercise 3, Steps 7b through 7d.

Objective 4

Search for Images

Can you use Google to search for pictures and other images?

Google offers many types of specialized searches, from news search to blog search and beyond. Among these specialized searches, the most popular is ***Google Image Search***, also known as Google Images. Google Image Search is a subset of Google's basic web search that lets you search for photos, drawings, logos, and other graphics files on the web. It's a great way to find pictures online.

How do you access Google Image Search?

There are several ways to access Google Image Search. You can click the **Images** link on the main Google search page or on any search results page, or you can go directly to **images.google.com**. And, of course, Google Image Search results appear as part of Google's universal search results when you search from the main search box.

Does Google offer advanced image search options?

When you click the **Advanced Image Search** link on the main Image Search page, you display the *Advanced Image Search* page. From here you can conduct AND/OR and exact phrase searches, as well as filter results based on image-specific criteria. For example, you can search for images that contain only faces or line drawings, files of a given size or aspect ratio, and images in black and white or full color.

 Tip **Drag and drop image search**

> You can also search for images like an existing image by dragging and dropping that image from a folder on your computer into the Google Images search box.

How does Google determine image content?

How can Google find pictures that match your search criteria? After all, pictures aren't like web pages; images don't have any text that Google can parse and index. Instead, Google analyzes the file extension, image caption, text on the host web page adjacent to the image, and other factors to try and determine what the image is a picture of. It's to Google's credit that most of the time it gets it right.

Google Image Search A subset of Google's basic web search that lets you search for photos, drawings, logos, and other graphics files on the web.

Hands-On Exercises

4 | Searching for Images

Steps: 1. Enter a Basic Query; **2.** View Image Search Results; **3.** Search by Image Size; **4.** Search by Type of Image; **5.** Search for Black and White Images.

Use Figures 2.46 through 2.54 as a guide to the exercise.

Step 1 Enter a Basic Query

Refer to Figure 2.46 as you complete Step 1.

a. Go to the Google Image Search page, located at **images.google.com**. (Alternatively, go to the main Google search page and click the **Images** link at the top of the page.)

b. Enter one or more keywords into the search box at the top of the page.

c. Click the **Search Images** button.

Click to search for images

Enter query

Figure 2.46 Hands-On Exercise 4, Step 1.

Step 2 View Image Search Results

Refer to Figures 2.47 and 2.48 as you complete Step 2.

When you click the **Search Images** button on the Google Image Search page, Google returns the first page of results. These matching images are displayed in a grid of thumbnail pictures, ranked in order of relevance.

a. To filter your search results, click an option in the left-hand sidebar.

You can opt to display images of a specific size, of a specific type (face, photo, clip art, or line drawing), or that are in black and white or have a dominant color scheme.

b. To display information about a given image, point to that image.

The image now expands and Google displays an image caption, the dimensions of the image (in pixels), the host website, and a link to the page where the image is displayed.

c. To view the original image on its host page, click the thumbnail image.

Filter image search results —

Point to image to display
more information —

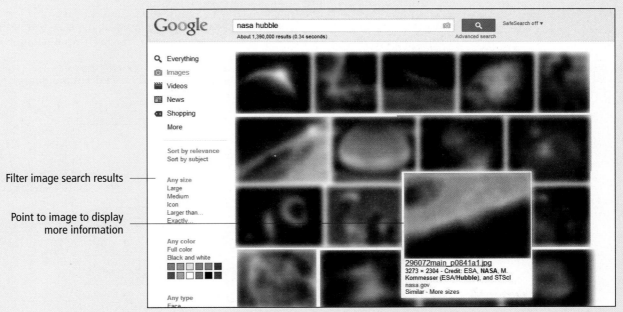

Figure 2.47 Hands-On Exercise 4, Steps 2a through 2c.

The image is now displayed in a frame that hovers above the host web page. To the right of this page is the Google Images frame, which includes information about the image and a few important links.

d. To view the host page without the Google frame, click the **Website for this image** link.

e. To view the picture full-size on its own page, without the host page, click the **Full-size image** link.

Click to view host page

Click to view full-size
image only —

File information —

Image —

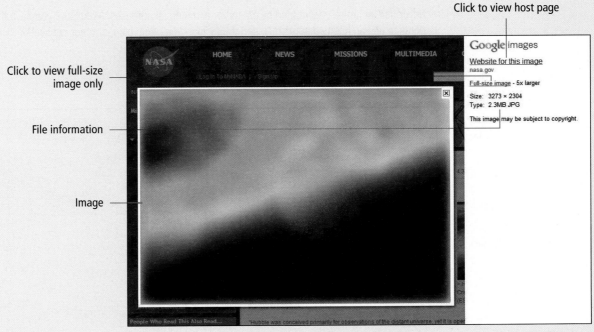

Figure 2.48 Hands-On Exercise 4, Steps 2d and 2e.

Step 3 Search by Image Size

Refer to Figures 2.49 and 2.50 as you complete Step 3.

One of the most useful options on the Advanced Image Search page is to search for images of a certain size. This lets you find a larger picture for high-resolution print purposes or a smaller picture for web use.

a. From the main *Google Image Search* page, click the **Advanced Image Search** link.

Click to display advanced
search options

Figure 2.49 Hands-On Exercise 4, Step 3a.

This displays the *Advanced Image Search* page.

b. Enter your query in the *Find results* section of the page.

c. Click the **Size** list arrow and select a sizing option.

Google lets you search for images of icon, medium, or large size, or images larger than a number of fixed dimensions or pixels.

d. Alternatively, you can enter an exact size (in pixels) into the *Width* and *Height* boxes in the *Exact size* section.

This option is good if you have an exact space to fill in a publication or on a web page.

Alert! Copyrighted Images

Never use an image copyrighted by others for commercial purposes. Make sure you have the rights to use an image before you insert it into your web page, blog, or other publication.

e. Click the **Google Search** button.

Click to execute search

Enter query

Select image size

Enter exact size (in pixels)

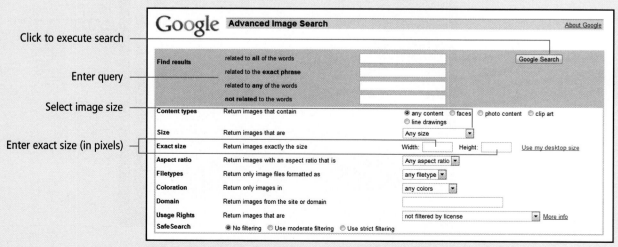

Figure 2.50 Hands-On Exercise 4, Steps 3b through 3e.

Step 4 Search by Type of Image

Refer to Figures 2.51 and 2.52 as you complete Step 4.

Google lets you search for certain types of images—faces, photos, clip art, and line drawings.

a. From the main *Google Image Search* page, click the **Advanced Image Search** link.

Click to display advanced search options

Figure 2.51 Hands-On Exercise 4, Step 4a.

This displays the *Advanced Image Search* page.

b. Enter your query in the *Find results* section of the page.

c. Go to the *Content types* section and select the desired option.

d. Click the **Google Search** button.

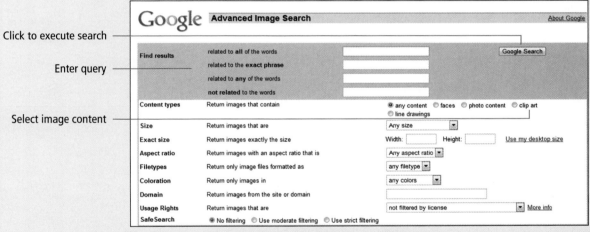

Click to execute search

Enter query

Select image content

Figure 2.52 Hands-On Exercise 4, Steps 4b through 4d.

Step 5 Search for Black and White Images

Refer to Figures 2.53 and 2.54 as you complete Step 5.

Many photographers prefer black and white images. You can use Google Image Search to search for only images in black and white.

a. From the main *Google Image Search* page, click the **Advanced Image Search** link.

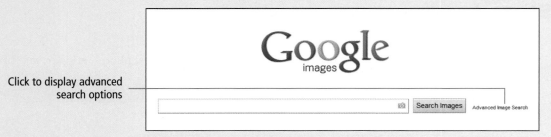

Click to display advanced
search options

Figure 2.53 Hands-On Exercise 4, Step 5a.

b. Enter your query in the *Find results* section of the page.

c. Click the **Coloration** list arrow and select **black and white**.

d. Click the **Google Search** button.

Click to execute search

Enter query

Click to select
black and white

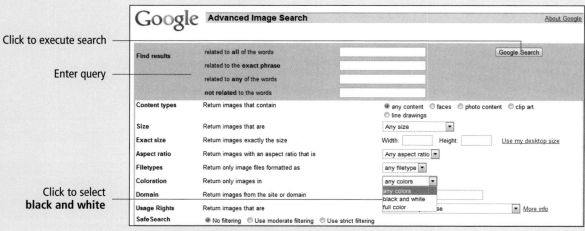

Figure 2.54 Hands-On Exercise 4, Steps 5b through 5d.

Summary

In this chapter, you visited the Google search page and conducted a basic search. You learned how to navigate a typical results page and refine your results. You fine-tuned your searches using Google's various search operators and Google's Advanced Search page. You also used Google Image Search to search for images.

Key Terms

Anchor text 32
Automatic word stemming 22
Boolean operator. 21
Cached page. 15
Crawler 13
Database 12
Domain 23
File extension 22
File type. 22
Google 12
Google Image Search 41
Google Instant. 17
GoogleBot 13
Keyword 14
OneBox 16

Organic 15
PageRank. 13
Query. 14
SafeSearch 35
Search engine 12
Search index 12
Search operator 21
Search tools 15
Stop word 21
Universal Search 17
URL 23
Usage rights. 35
Web server 12
Wildcard 22

Multiple Choice Questions

1. Which of the following is true about Google search?

   (a) Google allows full Boolean searching.

   (b) Google assumes the OR operator in its queries.

   (c) Google assumes the AND operator in its queries.

   (d) Google lets you search using wildcards.

2. To search for Adobe Acrobat PDF files about cats, enter this query:

   (a) cats pdf

   (b) cats filetype:pdf

   (c) cats

   (d) cats AND pdf

3. To search for web pages with the word "table" in their titles, enter this query:

   (a) intitle:table

   (b) inurl:table

   (c) table AND title

   (d) table

4. Moderate SafeSearch filtering

    (a) blocks pages containing adult text and images.

    (b) enables the display of all adult content.

    (c) enables pages containing adult text and images.

    (d) blocks pages containing adult images.

5. What happens when you enable Google Instant?

    (a) Google displays suggested queries as you type your query.

    (b) Google displays predicted search results as you type your query.

    (c) Google displays tweets and status updates in real time.

    (d) Google notifies you via email when it finds new matches to a query.

6. The following are examples of stop words:

    (a) a, or, the

    (b) how, what, where

    (c) 1, 4, 9

    (d) All of the above

7. To search for web pages that contain the phrase "these are the times," enter this query:

    (a) these are the times

    (b) these are + the times

    (c) "these are the times"

    (d) these times

8. To search for web pages about all birds *except* woodpeckers, enter this query:

    (a) birds +woodpeckers

    (b) birds –woodpeckers

    (c) birds NOT woodpeckers

    (d) woodpeckers OR birds

9. Thanks to automatic word stemming, a search for the keyword "step" will return pages containing the following words:

    (a) step

    (b) stepped

    (c) steps

    (d) All of the above

10. Google's software that automatically crawls the web is called

    (a) GoogleCrawler.

    (b) GoogleSpider.

    (c) GoogleBot.

    (d) GoogleIndexer.

Fill in the Blank

Write the correct word or words in the space provided.

1. Google _____ Search lets you search for pictures and photographs on the web.
2. The _____ operator lets you search for pages that include either of two keywords.
3. To perform more sophisticated searches, use Google's _____ Search page.
4. Google's massive database of web pages is called a search _____.
5. To search for words similar to a given keyword, use the _____ operator.
6. Google assumes the _____ operator between two keywords.
7. By default, Google Image Search has _____ SafeSearch enabled.
8. The URL for the main Google search page is _____.
9. The text that is associated with a web page link is called the _____ text.
10. The specialized search results found near the top of many Google search results pages are called _____ results.

Practice Exercises

1. Basic Search

(a) Search for yourself on Google.

(b) Print the first page of search results and submit to your instructor.

2. Site Search

(a) Search for people with your last name on your school website.

(b) Print the first page of search results and submit to your instructor.

3. Title Search

(a) Search for web pages with the words "daily news" in their titles.

(b) Print the first page of search results and submit to your instructor.

4. Image Search

(a) Search for images of red pickup trucks.

(b) Print the first page of search results and submit to your instructor.

5. Exclude Words

(a) Search for web pages about coffee but not about coffee cups.

(b) Print the first page of search results and submit to your instructor.

6. File Search

(a) Search for Adobe PDF documents about the Olympics.

(b) Print the first page of search results and submit to your instructor.

7. Similar Search

(a) Search for web pages similar to Google.

(b) Print the first page of search results and submit to your instructor.

8. OR Search

    (a) Search for web pages about either flowers or trees.

    (b) Print the first page of search results and submit to your instructor.

Critical Thinking

1. Google recently revamped its main search page to add a black bar at the top of the page that highlights additional search services (Images, Videos, Maps, etc.). This is Google's first significant home page redesign since its launch more than a decade ago. Write a short paper that discusses why you think Google made this change, and whether or not you think it was for the better.

2. Google displays advertisements alongside its normal search results. Many users confuse these ads with organic search results, resulting in clicks to an advertiser's website. Write a short paper discussing the ethics of Google's advertising program, and whether you find these ads confusing or helpful.

Credits

Google, Blogger, and Picasa screenshots reprinted by permission.

CHAPTER 3

Using Other Google Search Tools

Objectives

After you read this chapter, you will be able to:

1. Search for Scholarly and Legal Information
2. Search for News Articles
3. Search for Bargains

The following Hands-On Exercises will help you accomplish the chapter objectives:

Hands-On Exercises

EXERCISES	SKILLS COVERED
1. Searching for Scholarly and Legal Information	**Step 1:** Search Google Scholar **Step 2:** Conduct an Advanced Google Scholar Search **Step 3:** View Google Scholar Search Results
2. Searching for News Articles	**Step 1:** Browse News Articles **Step 2:** Search Current News Articles **Step 3:** Sign Up for Email News Alerts **Step 4:** Search the News Archive
3. Searching for Bargains	**Step 1:** Search for a Product **Step 2:** View Product Details and Make a Purchase

Objective 1

Search for Scholarly and Legal Information

What is Google Scholar?

Google Scholar A database of scholarly journals and articles.

In addition to its main search index, Google keeps a database of scholarly journals and articles, called *Google Scholar*. Google Scholar enables students and researchers to conduct their research from the comfort of their dorm rooms, homes, and offices, without having to physically visit their university or local library.

In essence, Google Scholar is a way for students and researchers to find academically appropriate and peer-reviewed literature without having to wade through all the nonprofessional information that clutters the public Internet—and Google's main search index. It's a comparable (and free) alternative to the expensive research databases offered by Elsevier, Thomson Reuters, and others.

What types of items are included in the Google Scholar database?

When you conduct a Google Scholar search, you receive a list of matching articles, journals, papers, theses, books, and the like, along with a brief summary of each item. Much of this information is available online free of charge. Some is available online only for subscribers to a particular service, while some is available online only for members of a particular library, and other information is available only in printed format.

Are Google Scholar results available from a normal Google search?

The information in the Google Scholar database is also available via a traditional Google web search, but it is often buried deep in the search results. The advantage of Google Scholar is that it focuses your search solely on the scholarly literature and returns results in a format familiar to students and researchers. The search itself is also fine-tuned for the scholarly crowd; you can confine your search to specific disciplines, authors, and publications.

How does Google identify scholarly content?

Citation A short note recognizing a source of information or of a quoted passage.

To identify content for inclusion in the Google Scholar database, Google uses an algorithm that guesses at what it thinks is scholarly content. While the Google Scholar algorithm is a closely guarded secret, we do know that Google tries to identify credentialed authors and searches for *citations* for each article. These citations are extracted and analyzed; at least in part, Google examines the connections among other documents that cite the article in question. This citation analysis is also used to help rank documents within the Google Scholar results. (Google Scholar also takes into consideration the full text of each article, the article's author, and the publication in which the article appeared to make its rankings.)

 Cited By

Another benefit of Google Scholar's citation analysis is a *Cited by* link next to each search result listing. When you click this link, you see a list of all the pages and documents that point to the current article.

Can you use Google Scholar for legal searches?

In addition to its scholarly content, Google Scholar also functions as a resource for legal content. The Google Scholar database includes rulings from both state and federal courts, along with citations and articles related to those rulings.

Hands-On Exercises

1 | Searching for Scholarly and Legal Information

Steps: 1. Search Google Scholar; **2.** Conduct an Advanced Google Scholar Search; **3.** View Google Scholar Search Results.

Use Figures 3.1 through 3.8 as a guide to the exercise.

Step **1** Search Google Scholar

Refer to Figure 3.1 as you complete Step 1.

a. From your web browser, go to the Google Scholar homepage, located at **scholar. google.com**.

b. Enter your query into the search box.

c. To search for scholarly articles, select the **Articles** option. To search for items from the legal profession, select the **Legal opinions and journals** option.

> **Note** **Patents**
>
> To include related patents in your search of scholarly articles, check the **include patents** box after you check the **Articles** option.

d. Click the **Search** button.

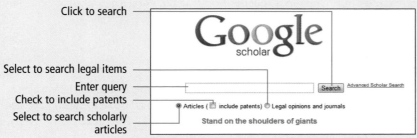

Click to search ───

Select to search legal items ───
Enter query ───
Check to include patents ───
Select to search scholarly articles ───

Figure 3.1 Hands-On Exercise 1, Step 1.

Step **2** Conduct an Advanced Google Scholar Search

Refer to Figures 3.2 through 3.4 as you complete Step 2.

You can fine-tune your Google Scholar search by using the Advanced Scholar Search page. This lets you limit your search to specific authors, publications, or topic areas.

a. From the Google Scholar homepage, click the **Advanced Scholar Search** link.

Click for advanced search

Figure 3.2 Hands-On Exercise 1, Step 2a.

This displays the *Advanced Scholar Search* page.

b. Enter the keywords of your query into the shaded *Find articles* section. You can search for articles *with all of the words*, *with the exact phrase*, *with at least one of the words*, or *without the words*. You can also select if the words appear only *in the title of the article* or *anywhere in the article*.

Note **AND/OR Searches**

By default, Google searches for pages that include all the words in a multiple-word query—the equivalent of a Boolean AND search. To search for pages that include only one or another word in a multiple-word query—the equivalent of a Boolean OR query—select the *with at least one of the words* option.

c. To find articles written by a specific author, enter the author's name into the *Author* box.

d. To find articles published in a specific publication, enter the publication's name into the *Publication* box.

Alert **Incomplete Information**

Searches by publication are often incomplete. This is due to missing or incorrect information included with many citations, which often don't mention where the article was actually published.

e. To find articles published within a specified date range, enter the starting and ending years into the *Date* boxes.

Enter an AND query
Enter an exact phrase
Enter an OR query
Enter words to exclude
Select where in article words should appear
Enter author name
Enter publication name
Enter date range

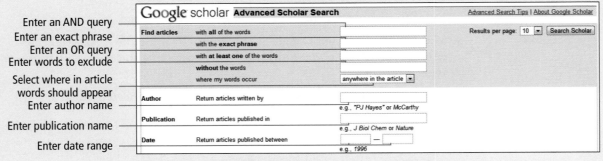

Figure 3.3 Hands-On Exercise 1, Steps 2b through 2e.

f. To limit your search to a specific subject area (biology and life sciences, business and finance, etc.), go to the *Articles and patents* section (within *Collections*) and select the **Search only articles in the following subject areas** option and then check those areas you want to search.

g. To search Google Scholar's legal database, go to the *Legal opinions and journals* section (within *Collections*) and select one of the following options:

- To search the entire database, select **Search all legal opinions and journals**.

- To search the opinions of a specific federal court, such as the United States Supreme Court or Federal Circuit court, select the first **Search opinions of** option and then select a court from the pull-down list.

- To search the opinions of a specific state court, select the second **Search opinions of** option and then select a state from the pull-down list.

 View All Courts

To view a list of all available courts, click the **Select specific courts to search** link and then check those courts you wish to search.

h. Click the **Search Scholar** button to initiate your search.

Include patents
Search all subject areas
Search specific subject areas

Search all legal opinions
Search specific federal courts
Search specific state courts
Click to view all courts
Click to search

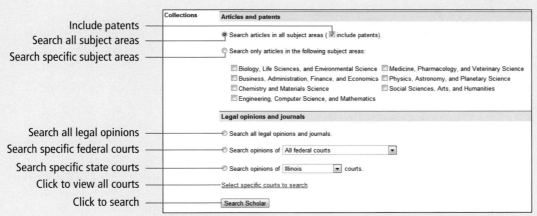

Figure 3.4 Hands-On Exercise 1, Steps 2f through 2h.

Step ③ View Google Scholar Search Results

Refer to Figures 3.5 through 3.8 as you complete Step 3.

The information you see about a particular search result depends on what type of document it is.

a. If a search result is for an article that is available for reading online, the title will be clickable. When you click the title, you're taken to either the full text of the article or (if the article itself is available only with a subscription) the article's abstract—that is, a brief description of the article. Click the **Cited by** link to view books and articles that cite the original article; click the **Related articles** link to view related articles.

Click to read article

Click to view citations
Click to read related articles

Model estimates of CO2 emissions from soil in response to **global warming**
DS Jenkinson, DE Adams... - 1991 - nature.com
ONE effect of **global warming** will be to accelerate the decomposition of soil organic matter, thereby releasing CO 2 to the atmosphere, which will further enhance the **warming** trend 1–7 . Such a feedback mechanism could be quantitatively important, because CO 2 is thought to be ...
Cited by 540 - Related articles - All 9 versions

Figure 3.5 Hands-On Exercise 1, Step 3a.

b. If a search result is for an article *not* available online, the title will *not* be a clickable link, and *[CITATION]* will appear beside the title. In this instance, you may be able to find the information you want by displaying the article's citations (click the **Cited by** link) or related articles (click the **Related articles** link).

Tip ⭐ **Search Your School Library**

Some physical books and articles may be available in your school library. If so, you'll see a **Library Search** link; click this link to check availability. If an electronic copy of an item is available from your library, you'll see a **FindIt@**_Yourlibrary_ link; click this link to see what's available.

Note 🖱 **British Library Direct**

Some articles are available for purchase only from British Library Direct. Click the **BL Direct** link, if it appears, to view ordering information and make a purchase.

Article not available for online reading

Click to view citations
Click to read related articles

[CITATION] **Global warming**: are we entering the greenhouse century?
SH Schneider - 1990 - James Clarke & Co.
Cited by 223 - Related articles - Library Search - All 8 versions

Figure 3.6 Hands-On Exercise 1, Step 3b.

c. If a search result is for a book that is available in electronic form online, *[BOOK]* will appear beside the title and the title will be a clickable link. Click the title to view either the full-text of the book or (if the book itself is available only with a subscription) the book's abstract or title page and table of contents. Click the **Cited by** link to view citations; click the **Related articles** link to view related books and articles. If the book is available for reading online in HTML format, click the **View as HTML** link.

Click to read book or abstract   Click to search for book in school library

Click to view citations
Click to read related articles

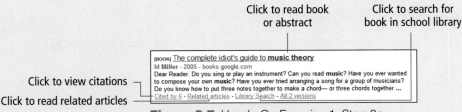

[BOOK] The complete idiot's guide to **music theory**
M Miller - 2005 - books.google.com
Dear Reader: Do you sing or play an instrument? Can you read **music**? Have you ever wanted to compose your own **music**? Have you ever tried arranging a song for a group of musicians? Do you know how to put three notes together to make a chord— or three chords together ...
Cited by 6 - Related articles - Library Search - All 2 versions

Figure 3.7 Hands-On Exercise 1, Step 3c.

d. For legal rulings, the main link is to the ruling itself. Click the **How cited** link to view a list of relevant quotes from citations of the ruling. View all citations by clicking the **Cited by** link; view articles about the ruling by clicking the **Related articles** link.

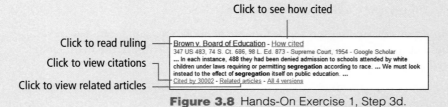

Click to see how cited

Click to read ruling

Click to view citations

Click to view related articles

Figure 3.8 Hands-On Exercise 1, Step 3d.

Objective 2

Search for News Articles

What is Google News?

Google News Google's news aggregation service.

Google News is a news-gathering service that identifies, assembles, and displays the latest news headlines from more than 4,500 different news organizations. It also offers a comprehensive news archive search.

Is Google News just for current news?

By default, Google News uses the last 30 days' worth of articles in its search results. If you want to find older news—up to 200 years old, in some cases—you can use Google's *News Archive Search*. In addition to finding recent, but not too recent, news headlines, it's also a great tool for learning about historical events.

News Archive Search Google's database of older news articles—up to 200 years old.

Where does Google News get its news?

Google News sources its articles from a variety of different newspapers, magazines, and other news-gathering organizations. Sources include the *New York Times, Washington Post, Los Angeles Times, International Herald Tribune, Wall Street Journal, USA Today, Forbes*, Bloomberg, Reuters, CBS News, ABC News, Fox News, MSNBC, BBC, CNN, and ESPN.

Hands-On Exercises

2 | Searching for News Articles

Steps: 1. Browse News Articles; **2.** Search Current News Articles; **3.** Sign Up for Email News Alerts; **4.** Search the News Archive.

Use Figures 3.9 through 3.16 as a guide to the exercise.

Browse News Articles

Refer to Figures 3.9 and 3.10 as you complete Step 1.

a. From your web browser, go to the Google News homepage, located at **news. google.com**. Alternatively, click the **News** link at the top of the main Google search page.

Google News organizes its stories by category: *Top Stories*, *World*, *U.S.*, *Business*, *Technology*, *Entertainment*, *Sports*, *Health*, *Spotlight*, and *Science*. In addition, there are often temporary categories for current news events, such as Elections. The main Google News page displays stories in the *Top Stories* category; the most recent stories are displayed in the *Recent* sidebar on the right side of the page.

b. Click a category to view a full page of stories in that category.

Figure 3.9 Hands-On Exercise 2, Steps 1a and 1b.

On each category page, Google displays the top stories within that category. For many categories, additional information and stories are displayed in the right-hand sidebar. For example, you might find Spotlight stories, Popular stories, Images, a Featured video, and a link to *Google Fast Flip*—a page that enables you to visually "flip" through the top stories in this category. For each story listed, Google News displays the article's headline, publication, date or time published, a brief synopsis, and possibly a related picture.

Google Fast Flip A visual display of the day's top stories that users can "flip" through.

c. To read a particular story in full on its originating website, click the story's headline.

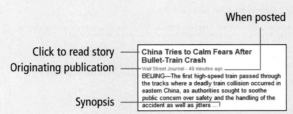

Figure 3.10 Hands-On Exercise 2, Step 1c.

Step 2 Search Current News Articles

Refer to Figures 3.11 and 3.12 as you complete Step 2.

a. From the Google News homepage, enter one or more keywords into the search box at the top of the page.

b. Click the **search (magnifying glass)** button.

Figure 3.11 Hands-On Exercise 2, Steps 2a and 2b.

Google now displays a list of stories that match your query.

c. To view the most recent stories, click one of the links in the *Any recent news* section on the left side of the page: *Past hour*, *Past day*, *Past week*, *Past month*, or (if you click the **Archives** link) a specific year or range of years.

d. To sort articles by date instead of relevance, click the **Sorted by date** link in the sidebar.

Matching articles —

Select publication date range —

Click to sort by date —

Figure 3.12 Hands-On Exercise 2, Steps 2c and 2d.

Step ③ Sign Up for Email News Alerts

Refer to Figures 3.13 and 3.14 as you complete Step 3.

To keep up-to-date on breaking news about a given subject, you can sign up to receive email *news alerts* when new stories are posted.

News alert An email notification of new stories about a given news topic.

a. Conduct a search for the topic at hand, as discussed in Step 2.

b. Scroll to the bottom of the search results page and click the **Create an email alert for (your query)** link.

Click to create news alert —

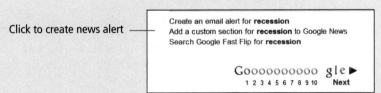

Figure 3.13 Hands-On Exercise 2, Steps 3a and 3b.

The *Google Alerts* page now appears.

c. Click the **Type** list and select what type of news items to search: *News*, *Blogs*, *Realtime* (social media), *Video*, or *Discussions*.

d. Click the **How often** list and select how often you want to be notified of new items: *as-it-happens*, *once a day*, or *once a week*.

e. Click the **Volume** list and select to receive all results or only the best results.

f. If you're currently signed in to your Google account, click the **Your email** list and select the proper email address; if you're not signed in to your Google account, enter your email address into the *Your email* box.

g. Click the **CREATE ALERT** button.

You'll now be notified of new stories according to the parameters you set.

Query

Select type of news

Select how often to email

Select all or only best results

Select email address

Click to create news alert

Figure 3.14 Hands-On Exercise 2, Steps 3c through 3g.

Step 4 Search the News Archive

Refer to Figures 3.15 and 3.16 as you complete Step 4.

You can search the Google News Archive from the main Google News page (and then restrict results to a specific date range), or from a special *News Archive Search* page—which offers additional search features.

a. From your web browser, go to the *News Archive Search* homepage, located at **www.google.com/archivesearch**.

b. Enter your query into the search box.

c. Click the **Search Archives** button.

Tip Timeline

To display news articles chronologically, click the **Show Timeline** button when conducting your search.

Click to display
timeline of articles

Enter query

Click to search archives

Figure 3.15 Hands-On Exercise 2, Steps 4a through 4c.

Google now displays a list of news stories that match your query, most relevant results first. A timeline of matching stories appears at the top of the page.

d. To view stories from a specific date range, click that time period on the timeline.

e. To search older or different dates, click the **Search other dates** link; this displays *From* and *To* boxes. Enter the start and end dates to display and then click the **Go** button.

f. To read a full article, click that article's headline.

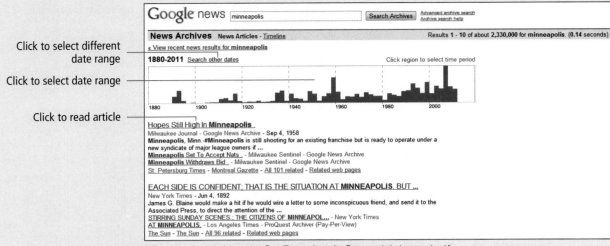

Click to select different date range

Click to select date range

Click to read article

Figure 3.16 Hands-On Exercise 2, Steps 4d through 4f.

Objective 3

Search for Bargains

What is a price-comparison site?

Price-comparison site A website that compares prices on given merchandise from multiple retailers.

If you're shopping online, you may want to use a *price-comparison site* to help you compare prices between multiple retailers. In essence, you let the price-comparison site do your shopping for you; all you have to do is evaluate the results.

What is Google Product Search?

Google Product Search Google's shopping search engine, for comparing prices from multiple retailers.

Google Product Search is Google's price-comparison site. In effect, Google Product Search functions as a shopping search engine, enabling users to search for specific products online.

 Note **Froogle**

Google Product Search was originally named Froogle (a Googlized play on the word "frugal"). Froogle became Google Product Search in April 2007.

How does Google Product Search gather price and product information?

If you've ever used a price-comparison site such as BizRate, NexTag, or Shopping.com, you might be under the impression that these sites scour the web for prices from a wide variety of online retailers. That's a false impression; instead, these sites build their price/product databases from product links submitted and paid for by participating retailers.

Google Product Search works differently from these other price-comparison sites. Google Product Search doesn't take money for its product listings; instead, it uses Google's spider software to independently scour the web for merchants and products. This makes Google's price comparisons more legitimate than those at other sites—and typically returns more results than competing price-comparison sites do.

How does Google display Product Search results?

Google Product Search displays all products that match a given query on a search results page (Figure 3.17). By default, the results are displayed in list view. If you click the **Grid view** button, you see the products displayed in a visual grid, which shows more items in the same amount of screen real estate (but with fewer immediate options for each listing).

Click to change sort order

Click to display grid view

Ads

Item

Price

Click to filter results

Figure 3.17 The results of a Google Product Search.

Also by default, Google organizes its results based on relevance, which is measured by customer demand. You can also use the pull-down list at the top of the results listing to sort products by price—either low to high or high to low.

In the left sidebar is a section of search refinements you can use to narrow the search results. These refinements differ by type of product, but typically they include filters that let you restrict your search by category, brand, price range, features, and so on. You can also filter results to show only those items in stock near you, from merchants offering Google Checkout or free shipping, or that are new (not used). Click a link or option to redisplay the results as appropriately filtered.

How can you evaluate merchants selling a product?

What do you do if you find a good price for an item on Google Product Search but have never heard of the merchant offering the item for sale? When the quality of the merchant is as important as the price of the product, you can turn to Google's seller ratings and reviews. This is a good way to steer your business toward reliable retailers and avoid those that under serve their customers.

> **Note**   **Review Sources**
>
> Google's seller ratings and reviews aren't actually provided by Google, or by Google's users. Instead, they're sourced much like all of Google's content—by spidering the web. The GoogleBot spider seeks out merchant reviews at other product-comparison sites (such as PriceGrabber.com, ResellerRatings.com, and Shopping.com) and then lists and collates them for your shopping convenience. The original reviews, in most instances, are provided by customers of that retailer.

When you search for a product, the first place you see the seller reviews is on the product detail page. Major merchants are listed with a star rating, on a scale of one to five stars. Along with the star rating is a listing of many user reviews that the merchant has received, as well as a link to view those ratings.

> **Tip**   **Weighting the Ratings**
>
> The more reviews that a seller rating has attached to it, the more weight that rating has. A one-star rating with just a handful of reviews could imply bias on the part of a few disgruntled customers.

When you click the seller's rating link, you're taken to that retailer's rating/reviews page (Figure 3.18). This page displays the seller's overall star rating, along with the most relevant reviews of that seller. (Relevance, in this instance, relates to reviews of products similar to those you searched for.)

Google displays only the first few lines of each review. To read a full review, click the **Read full review** link. This takes you to the original review on its original website.

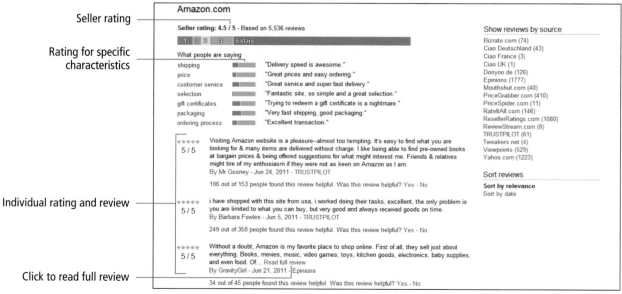

Figure 3.18 A seller review page.

Hands-On Exercises

3 │ Searching for Bargains

Steps: 1. Search for a Product; **2.** View Product Details and Make a Purchase.

Use Figures 3.19 through 3.21 as a guide to the exercise.

Step ❶ **Search for a Product**

Refer to Figures 3.19 and 3.20 as you complete Step 1.

a. From your web browser, go to the Google Product Search homepage, located at **www.google.com/products**. Alternatively, click the **Shopping** link at the top of the main Google search page.

b. Enter the name, model number, or description of the product you're shopping for into the search box.

c. Click the **Search button**.

Click to search ──────
Enter product name or
model number ──────

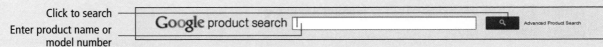

Figure 3.19 Hands-On Exercise 3, Steps 1a through 1c.

Google now returns a list of items that match your search.

d. Click an item to view more about that item.

Google now displays a product page, as discussed in the next step.

Click to display product page ──────

Figure 3.20 Hands-On Exercise 3, Step 1d.

Step 2 View Product Details and Make a Purchase

Refer to Figure 3.21 as you complete Step 2.

A Google Product Search product page displays details about a chosen item, as well as a list of merchants who offer the item for sale. The page includes a picture and description of the selected item, a summary of user star ratings (on a scale of one to five), and a list of merchants offering the item for sale. For each merchant, you see that merchant's *seller rating*, condition of the item for sale (new or used), tax and shipping charges, total price (including tax and shipping), and base price (the price of the item itself).

Seller rating In Google Product Search, a rating of a given seller, on a scale of one to five stars, as determined by that seller's customers.

a. To view only online stores offering the item, click the **Online stores** link.

b. To view nearby physical stores offering the item, click the **Nearby stores** link.

c. To view user reviews of the item, click the **Reviews** link.

d. To sort the list of merchants by seller rating, condition, total price, or base price, click that link above the given column.

e. To view the item listing at a given retailer, and perhaps to make a purchase, click that retailer's name.

> **Note** **Making a Purchase**
>
> All purchases take place on the retailer's website. Google is not involved in the purchase process.

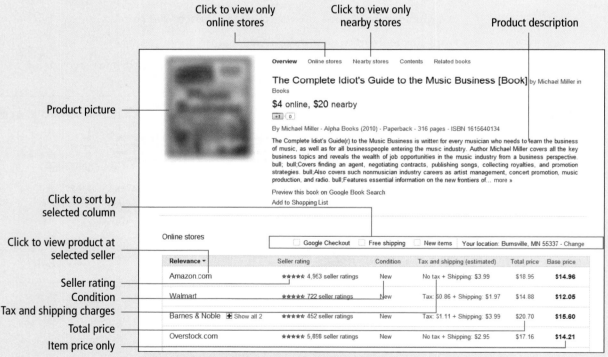

Figure 3.21 Hands-On Exercise 3, Step 2.

Summary

In this chapter, you learned how to search scholarly and legal articles with Google Scholar, search current and archived news stories with Google News, and search for bargains with Google Product Search.

Key Terms

Citation	52	News alert	60
Google Fast Flip	59	News Archive Search	57
Google News	57	Price-comparison site	62
Google Product Search	62	Seller rating	66
Google Scholar	52		

Multiple Choice Questions

1. Google Scholar lets you fine-tune your search results by the following parameters:

   (a) Date

   (b) Publication

   (c) Author

   (d) All of the above

2. The Google News archive contains articles up to how many years old?

   (a) 5 years

   (b) 10 years

   (c) 100 years

   (d) 200 years

3. Google News contains

   (a) current news articles only.

   (b) historical news articles only.

   (c) both current and historical news articles.

   (d) articles from only the top dozen news organizations.

4. The Google Scholar database does *not* contain

   (a) articles from scholarly journals.

   (b) scholarly books.

   (c) legal rulings and citations.

   (d) general web search results.

5. How does Google Scholar identify scholarly content?

   (a) Analyzes citations to a given article or web page

   (b) Searches a page's HTML code for the "academic" flag

   (c) Searches a page's content for the word "scholar"

   (d) Compares articles and pages to a database of known scholarly content

6. Google News sources its articles from approximately how many different organizations?

    (a) 100

    (b) 500

    (c) 2,500

    (d) 4,500

7. How does Google Product Search differ from other price-comparison sites?

    (a) Offers seller ratings

    (b) Doesn't accept payment for product listings

    (c) Offers items for sale directly from its own site

    (d) Displays prices from multiple retailers

8. How are advertisements labeled in Google Product Search results?

    (a) Ads

    (b) Sponsored Links

    (c) Paid Listings

    (d) Featured Results

Fill in the Blank

Write the correct word or words in the space provided.

1. The Google News homepage displays the _____ category by default.

2. Google _____ enables you to visually "flip" through top stories in a given category.

3. To view historical news articles in chronological order, select the _____ view.

4. By default, Google News keeps _____ days' worth of articles in its database; older articles can be found using News Archive Search.

5. If an article in the Google Scholar database is not available online, the word _____ appears beside the article title.

6. If a book or article in the Google Scholar database is available in your school library, you'll see a(n) _____ _____ link.

7. To receive notification of new stories about a given topic, sign up for an email _____ _____.

8. The original name of Google Product Search was _____.

9. Google's seller ratings are calculated on the basis of one to _____ stars.

Practice Exercises

1. **Google Scholar Search**

    (a) Use Google Scholar to search for scholarly articles about global warming.

    (b) Print the first page of search results and submit to your instructor.

2. **Google Scholar Legal Search**

    (a) Use Google Scholar to search for legal rulings about free speech.

    (b) Print the first page of search results and submit to your instructor.

3. **Google News Search**

   (a) Use Google News to search for articles about oil prices.

   (b) Print the first page of search results and submit to your instructor.

4. **Google News Archive Search**

   (a) Use Google News Archive Search to search for articles about the 1960 Indianapolis 500, written in that year.

   (b) Print the first page of search results and submit to your instructor.

5. **Google Product Search**

   (a) Use Google Product Search to shop for the best price on a Blu-ray disc player.

   (b) Print the first page of search results and submit to your instructor.

Critical Thinking

1. With so many different search products offered by Google, it can sometimes be challenging to select the right search for the results you need. Write a short paper that discusses when you might want to use one of the specialty search products presented in this chapter (Google Scholar, Google News, and Google Product Search) in addition to or instead of the normal Google web search.

2. The Google News Archive contains articles up to 200 years old. Explore the News Archive on your own and write a short paper discussing how you can use the News Archive to gain perspective on current news events.

Team Project

1. Different Google search products will deliver different results. For this project, assign each member of the team a different Google search product—Google web search, Google Scholar (scholarly articles), Google Scholar (legal rulings), Google News, Google News Archive Search, and Google Product Search. (If you have more or fewer team members, you may have to double up on certain search products, or have some members take more than one product.) Have each member of the team search or browse for entries matching the keyword "convertible." As a team, write a short paper that includes and compares the results returned by each search product, and why that search product returned those particular results.

Credits

Google, Blogger, and Picasa screenshots reprinted by permission.

CHAPTER 4

Using Google's Nonsearch Features

Objectives

After you read this chapter, you will be able to:

1. Customize Your iGoogle Page
2. Use Google Translate
3. Use Google for Definitions, Calculations, and Conversions

The following Hands-On Exercises will help you accomplish the chapter objectives:

Hands-On Exercises

EXERCISES	SKILLS COVERED
1. Customizing Your iGoogle Page	**Step 1:** Add Gadgets to Your iGoogle Page **Step 2:** Add RSS Feeds to Your iGoogle Page **Step 3:** Customize Individual Gadgets **Step 4:** Remove a Gadget **Step 5:** Rearrange Gadgets on the Page **Step 6:** Add New Tabs to iGoogle **Step 7:** Change iGoogle's Visual Theme
2. Using Google Translate	**Step 1:** Translate Selected Text **Step 2:** Translate an Entire Web Page **Step 3:** Translate a Document
3. Using Google for Definitions, Calculations, and Conversions	**Step 1:** Display a Single Definition **Step 2:** Display Google Dictionary Page **Step 3:** Perform a Calculation **Step 4:** Look Up the Value of a Constant **Step 5:** Convert a Unit of Measure

Objective 1

Customize Your iGoogle Page

Does Google offer more than just search?

Google is a company that offers a variety of technology-related products and services. While best known for its Google web search (**www.google.com**), the company also offers other nonsearch services, including a customized homepage (iGoogle); automated translation services (Google Translate); online definitions, calculations, and conversions; office applications (Google Docs); and an online calendar (Google Calendar), photo editing (Picasa), blog hosting (Blogger), and video sharing (YouTube). In addition, most of Google's revenues come from advertising-related activities, in the form of Google AdWords and AdSense.

What is iGoogle?

iGoogle A customizable homepage from Google.

If you've used Google search at all, you're undoubtedly familiar and comfortable with the relatively spartan Google homepage. But that's not the only way into the Google search engine; Google also offers a separate start page that you can use as a portal not just to Google, but to the entire web. This page is dubbed *iGoogle*, and it's totally customizable.

To view your iGoogle page, go to **www.google.com/ig**. (You can also access the page by clicking the **iGoogle** link from the **Options** button on the main Google search page.) You must have a Google account to create your iGoogle page; you can then log in to your account to see your iGoogle page from any computer connected to the Internet (Figure 4.1).

Figure 4.1 A customized iGoogle page.

 Tip **Make iGoogle Your Homepage**

To make iGoogle the homepage in your web browser, click the **Make iGoogle my homepage** link at the top of the iGoogle page.

What content can you add to your iGoogle page?

Gadget A content module on an iGoogle page.

iGoogle's content is offered in a series of modules called *gadgets*; select a gadget, and it appears on your iGoogle page. Google offers gadgets with content from its own network of sites, as well as feeds from other popular sites on the web. For example, you can add gadgets for news headlines, weather conditions and forecasts, sports scores, stock prices, and even daily comic strips. In addition, you can add a content module for just about any site that offers an RSS or Atom news feed.

How do you view content on iGoogle?

Most gadgets display three or more headlines related to that gadget's content. Click the + sign next to a headline to view a summary or the first sentence or so of a story. Click the headline to view the complete story on its host website in a separate tab in your browser.

How do you add gadgets to iGoogle?

The first time you access iGoogle, you are prompted to "create your own homepage in under 30 seconds," by selecting options that define your interests (news, humor, sports, etc.), a theme (how your iGoogle page will look), and your location. Make any selection in this window and then click the **See your page** button. This displays your initial iGoogle page, with content selected by Google based on the choices you made (Figure 4.2).

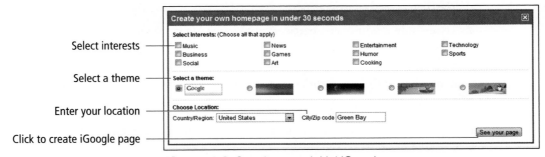

Select interests

Select a theme

Enter your location

Click to create iGoogle page

Figure 4.2 Creating your initial iGoogle page.

Once you begin using iGoogle on a regular basis, you can add more gadgets—or delete current ones—by clicking the **Add gadgets** link at the top of the page.

Can you search Google from iGoogle?

iGoogle also functions as an alternative search page for the Google search engine. To search Google, enter your query into the search box at the top of the page and then click the **Google Search** button. Google now returns a typical search results page.

Hands-On Exercises

1 | Customizing Your iGoogle Page

Steps: 1. Add Gadgets to Your iGoogle Page; **2.** Add RSS Feeds to Your iGoogle Page; **3.** Customize Individual Gadgets; **4.** Remove a Gadget; **5.** Rearrange Gadgets on the Page; **6.** Add New Tabs to iGoogle; **7.** Change iGoogle's Visual Theme.

Use Figures 4.3 through 4.16 as a guide to the exercise.

Step 1   Add Gadgets to Your iGoogle Page

Refer to Figures 4.3 and 4.4 as you complete Step 1.

The initial page that iGoogle creates is a good start, but it's probably not the ultimate page you want to create. For that, you'll need to add more content that reflects your interests, which you do by adding new gadgets to the page.

a. Go to your iGoogle page, located at **www.google.com/ig**.

> **Note**   **Log In**
>
> To access your personal iGoogle page, you need to be logged in to your Google account.

b. Click the **Add gadgets** link in the top-right corner of the page.

Click to add gadgets — Change theme from Classic | Add gadgets

Figure 4.3 Hands-On Exercise 1, Steps 1a and 1b.

This displays the *Add gadgets to your homepage* page.

c. Make sure that the **Gadgets** tab is selected.

The content on the **Gadgets** tab is organized by type (News, Tools, Communication, etc.).

d. To see only modules of a particular type, just click a category link on the left side of the page.

e. To search for a specific gadget or type of gadget, enter your query into the *Search for gadgets* box at the top-right corner of this page and then click the **Search** button.

Gadgets that match your query are displayed.

f. To view what a "live" gadget looks like (and to see more details about the content), click the gadget title.

g. To add a gadget to your iGoogle page, click the **Add it now** button, either on the main gadget listing or on the detailed content information page.

The new gadget is added to your iGoogle page, beneath existing gadgets.

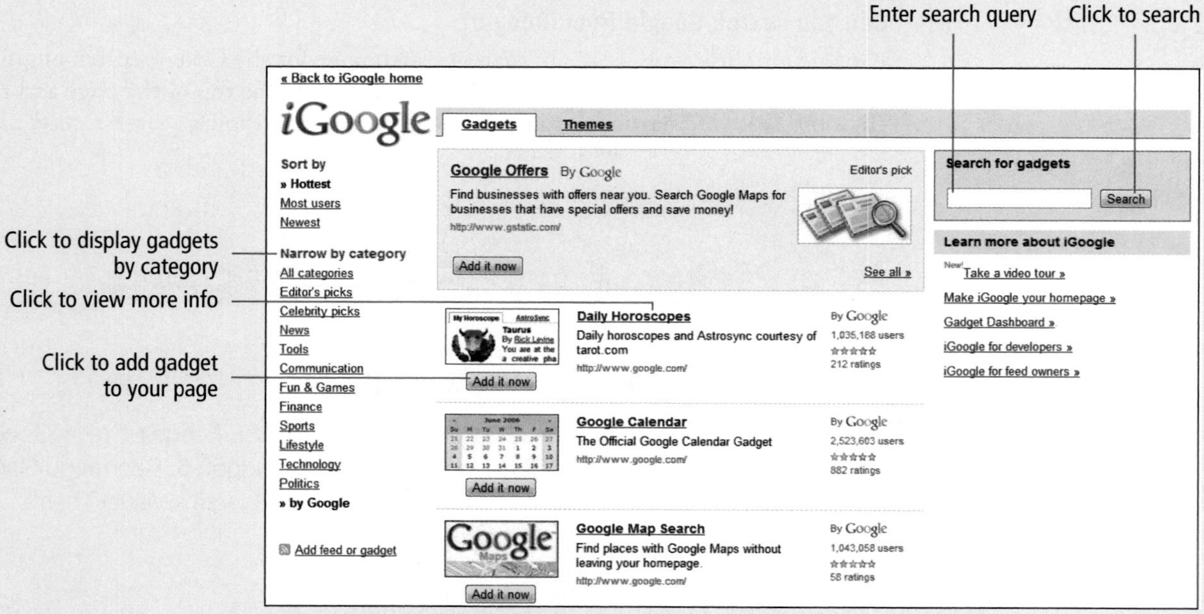

Enter search query   Click to search

Click to display gadgets by category

Click to view more info

Click to add gadget to your page

Figure 4.4 Hands-On Exercise 1, Steps 1c through 1g.

Note Additional Information

Some gadgets require additional information, such as your ZIP code, to work properly. You can add this information from the iGoogle page by editing the gadget in question, as we'll discuss later in this chapter.

Step 2 Add RSS Feeds to Your iGoogle Page

Refer to Figures 4.5 through 4.7 as you complete Step 2.

You're not limited to adding prepackaged content to your iGoogle page. You can also use iGoogle to display RSS feeds from blogs and feed-enabled websites (including major news sites). All you need to know is the URL of the RSS feed.

a. From your iGoogle page, click the **Add gadgets** link.

Click to add gadgets — Change theme from Classic | Add gadgets

Figure 4.5 Hands-On Exercise 1, Step 2a.

This displays the *Add gadgets to your homepage* page; make sure that the **Gadgets** tab is selected.

b. Click the **Add feed or gadget** link at the bottom of the left sidebar.

Click to add RSS feed

Figure 4.6 Hands-On Exercise 1, Step 2b.

The page expands to include the *Type or paste the URL below* box.

c. Enter the URL for the RSS feed into this box.

d. Click the **Add** button.

Google checks to make sure you've entered a valid URL and, if so, creates a new gadget for the feed you selected. This gadget is added beneath existing gadgets on your iGoogle page.

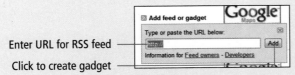

Enter URL for RSS feed —
Click to create gadget —

Figure 4.7 Hands-On Exercise 1, Steps 2c and 2d.

Step 3 Customize Individual Gadgets

Refer to Figures 4.8 through 4.10 as you complete Step 3.

After you've added a gadget to iGoogle, you may want or need to customize how it is displayed. Some gadgets let you specify the number of headlines that are displayed; others let you display information for a particular location.

a. From your iGoogle page, identify the gadget you want to customize.

b. Click the down arrow on the gadget's title bar and select **Edit settings**.

Gadget title bar
Click to edit gadget settings
Click to display actions

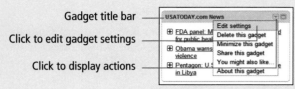

Figure 4.8 Hands-On Exercise 1, Steps 3a and 3b.

c. If a gadget lets you change the number of headlines displayed, you see a drop-down **Stories to show** list; select the number of stories from the list and then click the **Save** button.

Select number of stories to show
Click to save changes

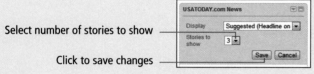

Figure 4.9 Hands-On Exercise 1, Step 3c.

d. If a gadget requires localization, you see boxes or controls for entering specific information. Enter or select the necessary information and then click the **Save** button.

Select country or region
Enter city or ZIP code
Click to save changes

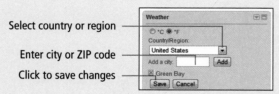

Figure 4.10 Hands-On Exercise 1, Step 3d.

Step 4 Remove a Gadget

Refer to Figure 4.11 as you complete Step 4.

You can remove gadgets you don't use from your iGoogle page at any time.

a. From your iGoogle page, identify the gadget you want to delete.

b. Click the down arrow in the gadget's title bar and select **Delete this gadget**.

Gadget title bar
Click to delete gadget
Click to display actions

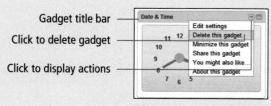

Figure 4.11 Hands-On Exercise 1, Step 4.

Step 5 Rearrange Gadgets on the Page

Refer to Figure 4.12 as you complete Step 5.

Google places gadgets on the iGoogle page pretty much in the order you add them, in a set three-column design. You can easily rearrange gadgets on the page, however, to create a customized flow of content; any gadget can appear anywhere on the page.

a. On your iGoogle page, identify the gadget you want to move.

b. Click and hold your mouse anywhere on the gadget's title bar.

The cursor changes to a four-headed arrow.

c. Drag the gadget to a new position on the page.

d. Release the mouse button to drop the gadget in place.

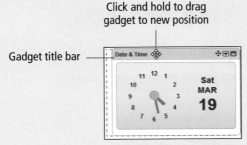

Click and hold to drag gadget to new position

Gadget title bar

Figure 4.12 Hands-On Exercise 1, Step 5.

Step 6 Add New Tabs to iGoogle

Refer to Figures 4.13 and 4.14 as you complete Step 6.

Instead of requiring you to put all your content on a single page, iGoogle lets you create multiple tabs, each of which can be filled with different content. You select different tabs from the left side of the iGoogle page, and create new tabs at any time.

a. From your iGoogle page, click the down arrow next to the currently selected tab.

b. Select **Add a tab**.

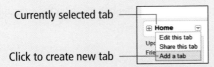

Currently selected tab

Click to create new tab

Figure 4.13 Hands-On Exercise 1, Steps 6a and 6b.

This displays the *Add a tab* dialog box.

c. Enter a name for this tab.

d. If you want Google to automatically add content based on the name of your tab, check the **I'm feeling lucky** box.

e. Click the **OK** button.

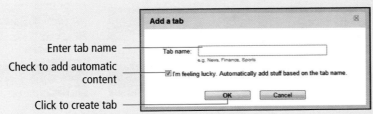

Enter tab name

Check to add automatic content

Click to create tab

Figure 4.14 Hands-On Exercise 1, Steps 6c through 6e.

Google now creates your new tab. Select the tab and then click the **Add gadgets** link to add new gadgets to the tab.

Step 7 Change iGoogle's Visual Theme

Refer to Figures 4.15 and 4.16 as you complete Step 7.

Once your gadgets are organized the way you want them, you can decide how you want iGoogle to look in terms of color and graphics. You do this through the use of predesigned themes. A theme contains a combination of text and background colors; many themes also include graphics that appear at the top of the page and behind the gadgets on the page.

Tip ★ **Themes by Tab**

You can apply different themes to different tabs on your iGoogle page.

---

a. Select the tab for which you want to change themes.

b. Click the **Change theme from** link at the top of the page.

Click to change theme ———

Figure 4.15 Hands-On Exercise 1, Steps 7a and 7b.

This displays the *Select a theme for your page* dialog box. Themes are organized by categories, which are displayed along the top of the dialog box.

c. Click the category you wish to browse.

Tip ★ **More Themes**

Find more iGoogle themes by clicking the **More options** link. This displays a dedicated *Themes* page on a new tab in your web browser. You can also search for themes by using the search box at the top of the dialog box.

---

d. When you find the theme you want, click the **Add it now** button for that theme.

e. Click the Close button (**X**) at the top-right corner of the dialog box to close the dialog box and return to your iGoogle page.

Click to display more themes   Click to close dialog box

Select theme category ———

Click to apply theme ———

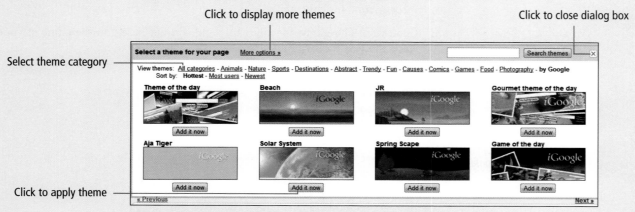

Figure 4.16 Hands-On Exercise 1, Steps 7c through 7e.

Objective 2

Use Google Translate

Google Translate Google's automatic translation service.

What is Google Translate?

Google Translate is a free translation service offered by Google. Located at **translate .google.com**, it offers automatic translation of individual words and phrases, entire web pages, and complete documents. Google Translate supports translation between more than 50 different languages, from Afrikaans to Yiddish.

How does Google Translate work?

Google Translate is a totally automated translation service, relying on machines and computer algorithms instead of human beings. Google Translate works by looking for patterns derived from hundreds of millions of previous documents; it compares the phrase or document to be translated with these previous patterns to make the best guess as to what an appropriate translation might be. (This is called *statistical machine translation*.)

Statistical machine translation Also known as SMT, an approach to language translation based on statistical models derived from the analysis of previous documents.

 Tip **Translating Web Pages**

When searching with the Google search engine, search results in other languages may display a **Translate this page** link. Click this link to translate the page without having to go to the Google Translate site.

Hands-On Exercises

2 | Using Google Translate

Steps: 1. Translate Selected Text; **2.** Translate an Entire Web Page; **3.** Translate a Document.

Use Figures 4.17 through 4.23 as a guide to the exercise.

 Step 1 **Translate Selected Text**

Refer to Figure 4.17 as you complete Step 1.

a. Go to the Google Translate page located at **translate.google.com**.

b. Enter or paste the word(s) or phrases you want to translate into the large text box.

   By default, Google Translate automatically detects the original language. You can, however, select this language manually.

c. Click the **From** button and select the source language to be translated.

d. Click the **To** button and select which language you wish to translate into.

e. Click the **Translate** button.

   Google now translates the word(s) or phrase and displays the translation on the right side of the page.

f. To listen to the proper pronunciation of the foreign word or phrase, click the appropriate **Listen** link.

Click to translate

Select destination language

Select source language

Enter word or phrase

Click to listen to pronunciation

Translation

Figure 4.17 Hands-On Exercise 2, Step 1.

Step 2 Translate an Entire Web Page

Refer to Figures 4.18 and 4.19 as you complete Step 2.

a. Go to **translate.google.com**.

b. Enter the URL for the page you want to translate into the large text box.

c. Click the **From** button and select the source language to be translated.

d. Click the **To** button and select which language you wish to translate into.

e. Click the **Translate** button.

Click to translate

Select destination language

Select source language

Enter web page URL

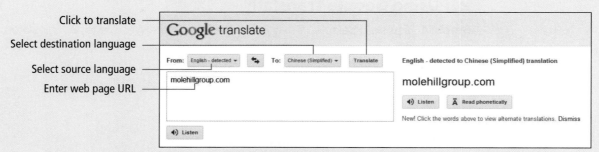

Figure 4.18 Hands-On Exercise 2, Steps 2a through 2e.

The web page, as translated, is now loaded into your web browser, along with a Google Translate frame above the translated page.

f. Select the **Original** option in the top frame to redisplay the page in its original language.

Note   **Text Translation Only**

Google Translate translates only the text elements on a web page, not images and other graphic elements. Any text appearing in an image will not be translated.

Google Translate frame

Click to view page in
original language

Translated page

Figure 4.19 Hands-On Exercise 2, Step 2f.

Step **3** Translate a Document

Refer to Figures 4.20 through 4.23 as you complete Step 3.

Google Translate also lets you translate entire documents, without having to copy and paste large blocks of text. This works for documents in the following file formats: *.doc*, *.pdf*, *.ppt*, *.rtf*, *.txt*, and *.xls*.

a. Go to **translate.google.com**.

b. Click the **To** button and select which language you wish to translate into.

c. Click the **translate a document** link.

Click to select translated
language

Click to translate document

Figure 4.20 Hands-On Exercise 2, Steps 3a through 3c.

d. When prompted, click the **Choose File** button.

Click to choose
file to translate

Figure 4.21 Hands-On Exercise 2, Step 3d.

e. When the *Open* dialog box appears, navigate to and select the file to translate and then click the **Open** button.

Select file to translate —

Click to upload document —

Figure 4.22 Hands-On Exercise 2, Step 3e.

f. Back on the Google Translate page, click the **Translate** button.

The translated document is now displayed in a new tab in your web browser.

Translated document —

Translated version of ludlow.doc

5 июля 2000

Боб и Эллен Ладлоу
154 Гринбей Серкл
Дафна, Л. 36526

Уважаемый г-н и г-жа Ладлоу:

Вот коробка WebTV Бет вам говорил. История за это, что я написал книгу WebTV около года назад, и некоторые люди на Philips получил копию и очень понравилось. Мы начали соответствующие, а потом почему-то они мне прислали около полудюжины WebTV коробки для целей оценки. (Я не знаю, почему они послали так много, они были идентичны!)

Во всяком случае, у меня были все эти коробки, и оказывается, все они пришли с бесплатным счетам. (Обычно служба проходит около $ 25/мес.) Я был передачи их на друзей и семью (дал один к Бет и ее семьи), и у меня была одна левая которых это одно.

Когда вы подключите его, вы увидите, что платежный бесплатный из Philips. Я не могу гарантировать, что это будет навсегда рода вещи, но счетов продолжаются уже около года, теперь без проблем.

Figure 4.23 Hands-On Exercise 2, Step 3f.

Objective 3

Use Google for Definitions, Calculations, and Conversions

Can you use Google to look up word definitions?

Interestingly, you can use the Google search page to do more than search the web. One of the bonus features is the option of looking up word definitions, direct from the Google search box. This is a useful feature when you need to look up the definition of a particular word, or aren't sure of a word's spelling.

Google's primary definitions come from WordNet (**wordnet.princeton.edu**), a web-based dictionary of English housed at Princeton University.

How do you look up word definitions?

Google offers two ways to look up word definitions. You can use either the **what is** or **define:** search operators in front of the word you want defined.

Can you use Google to perform calculations?

The Google search box can also be used as a calculator, to solve various types of mathematical equations. All you have to do is enter your equation or formula into the search box and then click the **Google Search** button. Just make sure you use the proper operators, as detailed in Tables 4.1 through 4.6. Also make sure you leave spaces between all numbers and operators, and separate calculations with parentheses as necessary.

What types of calculations does Google support?

Google supports both basic and advanced algebraic calculations. Table 4.1 details Google's basic calculator functions; Table 4.2 details Google's advanced mathematical functions; Table 4.3 details Google's trigonometric functions; Table 4.4 details Google's inverse trigonometric functions; Table 4.5 details Google's hyperbolic functions; and Table 4.6 details Google's logarithmic functions.

Table 4.1—Google's Basic Calculator Functions

Function	Operator	Example	Result
Addition	**+** *or* **plus** *or* **and**	2 + 1	3
Subtraction	**–** *or* **minus**	2 – 1	1
Multiplication	**X** *or* **x** *or* **times**	2 × 1	2
Division	**/** *or* **over** *or* **divided by**	2/1	2

Table 4.2—Google's Advanced Mathematical Functions

Function	Operator	Example	Result
Percent (*X* percent of *Y*)	**% of**	20% of 10	2
Square root	**sqrt**	sqrt(16)	4
Root	**nth root of**	5th root of 32	2
Exponent (raise to a power)	**^** *or* ****** *or* **to the power of**	4^2	16
Factorial	**!**	10!	3,628,800
Modulo (finds the remainder after division)	**%** *or* **mod**	15%2	1
Choose (determines the number of ways of choosing a set of *Y* elements from a set of *X* elements)	**choose**	9 choose 3	84

Table 4.3—Google's Trigonometric Functions

Function	Operator	Example	Result
Sine	**sin**	sin(100)	–0.506365641
Tangent	**tan** *or* **tangent**	tan(100)	–0.587213915
Secant	**sec** *or* **secant**	sec(100)	1.15966382
Cosine	**cos** *or* **cosine**	cos(100)	0.862318872
Cotangent	**cotangent**	cotangent(100)	–1.70295692
Cosecant	**csc** *or* **cosecant**	csc(100)	–1.97485753

Table 4.4—Google's Inverse Trigonometric Functions

Function	Operator	Example	Result
Inverse sine	**arcsin**	arcsin(1)	1.57079633
Inverse tangent	**arctan**	arctan(1)	0.785398163
Inverse secant	**arcsec**	arcsec(1)	0
Inverse cosine	**arccos**	arccos(1)	0
Inverse cotangent	**arccotangent**	arccotangent(1)	0.785398163
Inverse cosecant	**arccsc**	arccsc(1)	1.57079633

Table 4.5—Google's Hyperbolic Functions

Function	Operator	Example	Result
Hyperbolic sine	**sinh**	sinh(1)	1.17520119
Hyperbolic cosine	**cosh**	cosh(1)	1.54308063
Hyperbolic tangent	**tanh**	tanh(1)	0.761594156

Table 4.6—Google's Logarithmic Functions

Function	Operator	Example	Result
Logarithm base 10	**log**	log(100)	2
Logarithm base 2	**lg**	lg(100)	6.64385619
Logarithm base e	**ln**	ln(100)	4.60517019

What other information does Google know?

Constant A number representing a fixed value in a specified mathematical context.

In addition to performing calculations, Google knows a variety of mathematical and scientific *constants*, such as Avogadro's number and Planck's constant. Google also knows units of measure (for currency, mass, volume, area, etc.), and can convert numbers from one unit to another from the basic search box.

Hands-On Exercises

3 | Using Google for Definitions, Calculations, and Conversions

Steps: 1. Display a Single Definition; **2.** Display Google Dictionary Page; **3.** Perform a Calculation; **4.** Look Up the Value of a Constant; **5.** Convert a Unit of Measure.

Use Figures 4.24 through 4.34 as a guide to the exercise.

Step 1 Display a Single Definition

Refer to Figures 4.24 and 4.25 as you complete Step 1.

a. From Google's main search page, enter the operator **what is** into the search box, followed by the word you want to define. (No question mark is necessary.)

   For example, to look up the definition of the word "defenestrate," enter **what is defenestrate**.

b. Click the **Google Search** button.

Word to be defined

what is operator

Click to define word

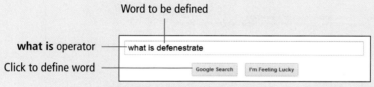

Figure 4.24 Hands-On Exercise 3, Steps 1a and 1b.

Google now returns a standard search results page, as well as a single web definition in a OneBox result at the top of the page.

Definition OneBox

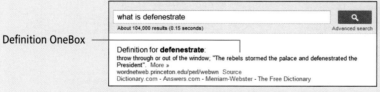

Figure 4.25 Hands-On Exercise 3, Steps 1c and 1d.

Step 2 Display Google Dictionary Page

Refer to Figures 4.26 through 4.28 as you complete Step 2.

Google also offers a Google Dictionary page, which displays additional definitions, examples of word usage, synonyms, and the like.

a. From the main Google search page, enter the **what is** operator followed by the word you want defined.

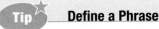
b. Click the **Google Search** button.

Word to be defined

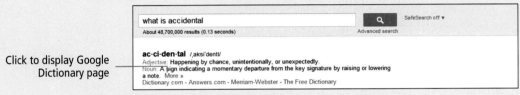

what is operator

Click to define word

Figure 4.26 Hands-On Exercise 3, Steps 2a and 2b.

Google now displays a search results page with a definition OneBox at the top.

c. Click the **More** link to view the Google Dictionary page.

Click to display Google Dictionary page

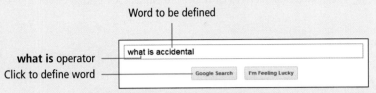

Figure 4.27 Hands-On Exercise 3, Step 2c.

d. View additional information on the Google Dictionary page for the selected word or phrase.

Pronunciation
Synonyms

Definitions

Additional definitions

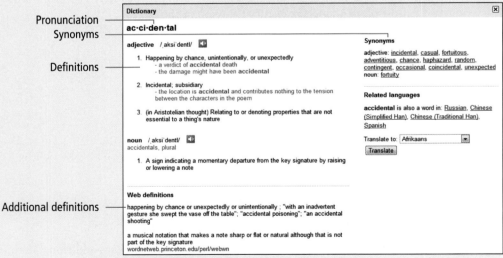

Figure 4.28 Hands-On Exercise 3, Step 2d

Step 3 Perform a Calculation

Refer to Figures 4.29 and 4.30 as you complete Step 3.

a. From Google's main search page, enter the equation into the search box.

Use the operators detailed in Tables 4.1 through 4.6. Do *not* enter an equal to sign before or after the equation.

b. Click the **Google Search** button.

Enter equation —

Click to calculate
value of expression —

Figure 4.29 Hands-On Exercise 3, Steps 3a and 3b.

The results of the calculation are shown in a Calculator OneBox listing at the top of the results page.

Original expression —

OneBox result
of calculation —

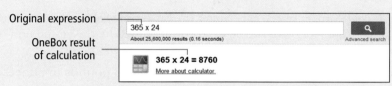

Figure 4.30 The result of a calculation.

Tip ⭐ **Multiple Operations**

Google also lets you string multiple operations together. For example, if you want to calculate 12 times 5 divided by 4, enter **12 * 5 / 4**. You can also create nesting expressions by using appropriately placed parentheses. Following mathematical rules, calculations in parentheses and those using exponents are done first and then the calculations are evaluated from left to right, multiplying and dividing first and then adding and subtracting. So, to divide the sum of 4 plus 3 by the sum of 5 plus 2, enter **(4 + 3) / (5 + 2)**.

Step 4 Look Up the Value of a Constant

Refer to Figures 4.31 and 4.32 as you complete Step 4.

a. From Google's main search page, enter the constant into the search box.

For example to display the value of Avogadro's number, enter **avogadro's number** into the search box.

b. Click the **Google Search** button.

Enter name of constant —

Click to search —

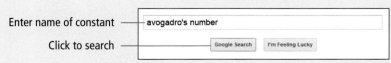

Figure 4.31 Hands-On Exercise 3, Steps 4a and 4b.

Google returns the value of the constant in a OneBox result, along with links to other search results.

Constant

Value

Figure 4.32 The value of a constant.

 Tip   **Constants in Equations**

You can include the constants that Google knows into a Google expression. For example, to divide the constant pi by 3, enter the expression: **pi / 3**.

Step 5   Convert a Unit of Measure

Refer to Figures 4.33 and 4.34 as you complete Step 5.

a. From Google's main search page, enter the value you wish to convert (in the first unit of measure), followed by the word "in," followed by the second unit of measure, into the search box.

For example, to convert 3 pounds into ounces, enter **3 pounds in ounces**.

b. Click the **Google Search** button.

Convert to
Value to convert
Click to convert

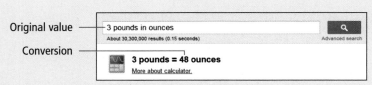

Figure 4.33 Hands-On Exercise 3, Steps 5a and 5b.

Google returns the converted value in a OneBox result, along with links to other search results.

Original value

Conversion

Figure 4.34 A value converted.

Summary

In this chapter, you learned about several of Google's nonsearch features. You learned how to create a customized homepage with iGoogle; how to translate words and web pages with Google Translate; and how to use Google to display word definitions, calculate expressions, show the value of constants, and convert values from one unit of measure to another.

Key Terms

Constant........................84   iGoogle..........................72

Gadget........................73   Statistical machine translation......79

Google Translate................79

Multiple Choice Questions

1. To display definitions of the word "cumbersome," enter this query:

   (a) word:cumbersome

   (b) dictionary:cumbersome

   (c) define:cumbersome

   (d) cumbersome

2. To calculate the value of 42 divided by the sum of 3 plus 5, enter this query:

   (a) 42 / 3 + 5

   (b) 42 / (3 + 5)

   (c) (42 / 3) + 5

   (d) = 42 / (3 + 5)

3. To convert 10 gallons to liters, enter this query:

   (a) 10 gallons in liters

   (b) 10 gallons = liters

   (c) liters = 10 gallons

   (d) how many liters in 10 gallons

4. To change the look and feel of your iGoogle page, apply a different

   (a) template.

   (b) theme.

   (c) style.

   (d) iLook.

5. To display the value of pi, enter this query:

   (a) value of pie

   (b) pi = what?

   (c) pi

   (d) define:pi

6. Google's customized homepage is called

    (a) My Google.

    (b) iGoogle.

    (c) Google Today.

    (d) Google Home.

7. How many columns does an iGoogle page have?

    (a) 1

    (b) 2

    (c) 3

    (d) As many as you like—it's totally customizable.

8. To display definitions of the word "hirsute," enter this query:

    (a) dictionary hirsute

    (b) what is hirsute

    (c) display hirsute

    (d) hirsute means what

9. Where does Google obtain its primary word definitions?

    (a) Webster's New World Dictionary

    (b) The Web Dictionary

    (c) WordNet

    (d) Google's search index

10. What can you *not* translate with Google Translate?

    (a) Individual words

    (b) Entire web pages

    (c) Word documents

    (d) Text scanned into JPG files

Fill in the Blank

Write the correct word or words in the space provided.

1. Google offers two ways to display definitions of a word: a "what is" search or the _____ operator.

2. To calculate the cotangent of 10, enter the query _____.

3. Numbers such as pi, Avogadro's number, and the speed of light are called _____.

4. Google's automatic translation service is called _____.

5. To calculate the square root of 42, enter the query _____.

6. To convert 10 furlongs into meters, enter the query _____.

7. To calculate the value of 4 times 3, enter the query _____.

8. To display the value of the mass of the sun, enter the query _____.

9. To display multiple definitions of the phrase "gross national product," enter the query _____.

10. Content modules on the iGoogle page are called _____.

Practice Exercises

Use Google to look up or calculate the answers to these questions and problems.

1. What is the speed of light?
2. What is the value of 7^3?
3. Define the word "indeterminate." (Use the first definition.)
4. Convert 70 miles per hour into kilometers per hour.
5. What is 15 percent of 475?
6. Translate the phrase "Enough is never too much" into Latin.
7. Multiply Euler's constant by the sum of pi divided by 3.
8. Convert 2 square miles into acres.
9. What is the radius of the earth?
10. Translate the Italian phrase "Il mio canoa è pieno di anguille" into English.

Critical Thinking

1. Why do you think Google offers additional nonsearch functionality as part of its search page? Write a short paper explaining your answer, as well as detailing some possible uses of this functionality.
2. Google designed iGoogle to be a homepage for web users. Write a short paper discussing the possible benefits of using iGoogle as your web browser's homepage, and how you personally might configure the page—and why.

Team Project

1. Let's play a game of "Google Translate Telephone." Follow these steps:
   (a) The first person on your team should use Google Translate to translate the following phrase from English to German: "It is a lovely day to take a walk in the rain."
   (b) The second member of the team should translate that German translation into Japanese.
   (c) The third member of the team should translate the Japanese translation into Hebrew.
   (d) The fourth member of the team should translate the Hebrew translation into Spanish.
   (e) The fifth member of the team should translate the Spanish translation into French.
   (f) The sixth member of the team should translate the French translation into Dutch.
   (g) The seventh member of the team should translate the Dutch translation into Arabic.
   (h) The eighth member of the team should translate the Arabic translation back into English.

   (If you have fewer than eight members on your team, some members may need to do more than one translation.)

   Hand in the final English translation to your instructor, along with your best guesses as to why the translation turned out as it did.

Credits

Google, Blogger, and Picasa screenshots reprinted by permission.

CHAPTER 5

Using Google Books

Objectives

After you read this chapter, you will be able to:

1. Search for Books and View Book Content

2. Review Books

3. Purchase and Download Books

4. Manage Your Library

The following Hands-On Exercises will help you accomplish the chapter Objectives:

Hands-On Exercises

EXERCISES	SKILLS COVERED
1. Searching for Books and Viewing Book Content	**Step 1:** Conduct a Basic Book Search **Step 2:** Conduct an Advanced Book Search **Step 3:** View Book Content
2. Reviewing Books	**Step 1:** Read Book Reviews **Step 2:** Write a Book Review
3. Purchasing and Downloading Books	**Step 1:** Download a Free eBook **Step 2:** Purchase an eBook **Step 3:** Purchase a Printed Book
4. Managing Your Library	**Step 1:** Add a Book to Your Library **Step 2:** View Books in Your Library

Objective 1

Search for Books and View Book Content

What is Google Books?

A lot of valuable (and often free) information is available on the web. But this pales in comparison with the amount of information available in printed books. If there were a way to create a repository of all of the world's book content, it would put the Internet to shame.

As part of its goal to be the ultimate source of information on the Internet, Google is working to create that legendary global book repository through the **Google Books** service. Imagine, if you will, every book ever published, available for searching online from your web browser. That's what Google is trying to accomplish with Google Books. If Google is successful (and there's no guarantee that it will be; the project is rather daunting), the collected wisdom of the ages will be just a mouse click away.

Google's ultimate goal with Google Books is to let users search the full text of any book ever published and then to provide the option of reading that book online (for selected books), purchasing the book (either in **eBook** format or in print from selected booksellers), or finding out where you can borrow a copy of the book (from participating libraries). To achieve this goal, Google must have the full text of all these books in its database—which is a formidable challenge.

Where does Google Books get its books?

Google Books obtains the books in its online library from two sources: book publishers (via the **Google Books Partner Program**) and libraries (via the **Google Books Library Project**). Books obtained from publishers are often books that are currently in print, even if the entire text is not always available. Books obtained from libraries are typically out-of-print or public domain books, although the entire text is often available.

How does the Google Books Partner Program work?

Publishers can submit their books for inclusion in the Google Books database via the Google Books Partner Program. This program is designed as a way for publishers to promote their books online, by means of exposure to Google's vast user base.

When a publisher signs up for a Google Books account, the company sends Google a list of the books that it wants included in Google Books. Ideally, the publisher also sends Google a printed copy of each book or the text of each book in PDF or EPUB format. (The publisher can also just have Google add the books to the Google Books database when they're scanned at a library—which we'll get into in a moment.)

Are all books in Google Books available for reading online for free?

Just because Google has the full text of a book in its database doesn't mean that users can read the entire book online for free. To protect the publisher's copyrighted content, Google only lets readers view a handful of pages online; in addition, all copy, save, and print functions are disabled, so readers can't download or print books for free. The only reason that Google archives the full text of the book is so readers can search the entire book and then read short snippets of matching text.

In other words, Google Books is not intended as a way for readers to read entire books online. Instead, you use Google Books to discover what books contain the information you're looking for; you can then either purchase the book or borrow it from a library.

This explains why many books are listed in the Google Books database without detailed content. Many publishers have opted to provide book listings only, as a kind of a pseudo-advertisement on the Google site. Click one of these listings and you

Google Books Google's searchable online repository of book content.

eBook Short for electronic book, a digital version of a traditional printed book.

Google Books Partner Program Google's program that enables book publishers to submit books to the Google Books database.

Google Books Library Project Google's program that encourages partner libraries to scan books in their collections for submission to the Google Books database.

don't see a synopsis or manuscript; instead, you're shown a list of places where you can buy the book—often accompanied by the publisher's marketing blurb.

What is the Google Books Library Project?

The other way that Google is obtaining content for its Google Books database is from participating libraries, as part of the Google Books Library Project. To date, Google has agreements with a variety of academic and public libraries across the country and around the globe:

- Austrian National Library (Austria)
- Bavarian State Library (Germany)
- Columbia University
- Committee on Institutional Cooperation (CIC)
- Cornell University Library
- Ghent University Library (Belgium)
- Harvard University
- Keio University Library (Japan)
- Lyon Municipal Library (France)
- National Library of Catalonia (Spain)
- New York Public Library
- Oxford University, Bodleian Library (UK)
- Princeton University
- Stanford University
- University of California
- University Complutense of Madrid (Spain)
- University Library of Lausanne (Switzerland)
- University of Michigan
- University of Texas at Austin
- University of Virginia
- University of Wisconsin–Madison and Wisconsin Historical Society Library

These partners are continuously scanning the books in their collections to make these books available for searching online. The result is like having all the books from these libraries available in your web browser, with Google Books serving as a kind of online card catalog to all that book content.

Of course, the library doesn't own the content of all the books in its collection. While Google may be able to scan a library's books, it can't legally distribute those books (or provide access to those books electronically) unless the books' publishers have given Google permission to do so—unless, that is, a given book is so old that its copyright has expired.

So the library collections available through Google Books contain searchable indexes of all available texts, and full-text versions of works in the *public domain*. It's not quite the same as having the full content of a library available for reading online, but it's getting close.

Public domain Any intellectual property whose rights are not held or controlled by any entity; the rights are held by the public at large.

Excluding Books

If a publisher or copyright holder doesn't want some or all of its books included in Google Books, they can ask Google not to scan selected library texts. For more information on excluding titles from the database, see **books.google.com/partner/exclusion-signup**.

Where can you find Google Books search results?

Naturally, you can search the Google Books database from the Google Books homepage, located at **books.google.com**. But you don't have to go to the Google Books page to search for book content. Google Books results can appear as the result of a standard Google web search—assuming the books in question have something to do with the query at hand. In this instance, matching books appear in OneBox results either at the top or at the bottom of the first search results page.

What viewing options are available?

When you search Google Books, the books in the search results can have four different viewing options, depending on the book's copyright status and publisher/author wishes:

- **Read**—the full text of these books is available for reading online.

- **Preview**—these books have only a limited number of pages available for reading online as a preview to the rest of the book. The full text of the book is not available for reading online.

Snippet A short excerpt from a book.

- **Snippet**—similar to preview books, these books only offer a few small snippets of text for preview. *Snippets* show a few instances of the search term in context; the full text of the book is not available for reading online.

- **No preview available**—for these books, no previews or snippets are available.

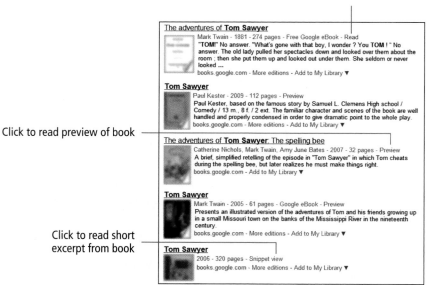

Click to read full text of book online

Click to read preview of book

Click to read short excerpt from book

Figure 5.1 Three viewing options for Google Books search results—read full text, preview, or snippet.

Hands-On Exercises

1 | Searching for Books and Viewing Book Content

Steps: 1. Conduct a Basic Book Search; **2.** Conduct an Advanced Book Search; **3.** View Book Content.

Use Figures 5.2 through 5.6 as a guide to the exercise.

Step 1   Conduct a Basic Book Search

Refer to Figure 5.2 as you complete Step 1.

a. Go to the Google Books homepage, located at **books.google.com**.

b. Enter your query into the search box.

   You can search by book title, author name, or book content.

c. Click the **Search Books** button.

Enter query

Click to search books

Figure 5.2 Hands-On Exercise 1, Step 1.

> **Tip** ⭐   **Browse the Bookshelves**
>
> You can also browse for books from the main Google Books page. Click the **Browse books and magazines** link under the search box to display the book category page. Then click a category (subject) on the left; keep clicking till you find what you're looking for.

Step 2   Conduct an Advanced Book Search

Refer to Figures 5.3 and 5.4 as you complete Step 2.

Google Books also has an *Advanced Book Search* page that offers many of the advanced search options you find on Google's regular *Advanced Search* page, as well as several book-specific search options.

a. Conduct a basic book search as described in Hands-On Exercise 1, Step 1.

b. From the search results page, click the **Advanced search** link under the search box at the top of the page.

mark twain   🔍
About 3,230,000 results (0.15 seconds)   Advanced search

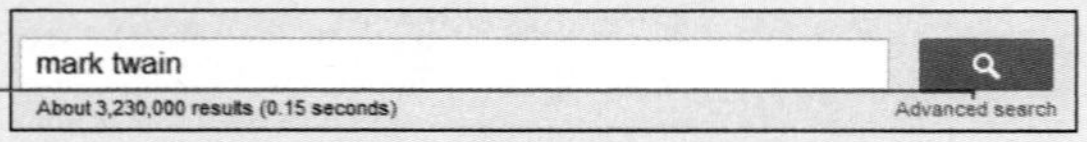

Figure 5.3 Hands-On Exercise 1, Step 2b.

This displays the *Advanced Book Search* page. The keywords from your initial search are entered in the *Find results with all of the words* box.

c. If you want to modify your search to take advantage of advanced search options (exact phrase, searching for one word or another, or word exclusion), enter your query in the appropriate boxes in the *Find results* section.

d. To limit your search to those books that offer their full text for online reading, go to the *Search* section and select the **Full view only** option. To limit your search to those books that offer either a full view or a limited preview, select the **Limited preview and full view** option. To limit your search to those books available in electronic format only, select the **Google eBooks only** option. To search all books, select the **All books** option.

e. To limit your search to books only (no magazines), go to the *Content* section and select **Books**. To search only magazines, select **Magazines**. To search both books and magazines, select **All content**.

f. To search for books written in a specific language, select a language from the **Language** drop-down list.

g. To search for a book by its title, enter your query into the *Title* box.

h. To search for works by a specific author, enter the author's name into the *Author* box.

i. To search for books by a specific publisher, enter the publisher's name into the *Publisher* box.

j. To search for books about a specific subject, enter one or more keywords that describe that subject into the *Subject* box.

k. To search for books published within a particular time frame, go to the *Publication Date* section and select the **Return content published between** option and then enter the starting and ending years (or, optionally, months and years).

l. If you know the book's *ISBN*, enter that number into the *ISBN* box.

m. If you know a magazine's *ISSN*, enter that number into the *ISSN* box.

n. Click the **Google Search** button to initiate your search.

ISBN Short for International Standard Book Number, a unique numeric identification code for commercially published books.

ISSN Short for International Standard Serial Number, a unique numeric identification code for periodical publications.

Enter or revise query   Click to initiate search

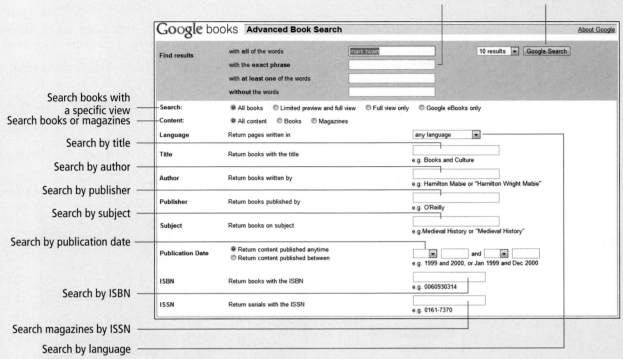

Search books with a specific view
Search books or magazines
Search by title
Search by author
Search by publisher
Search by subject
Search by publication date
Search by ISBN
Search magazines by ISSN
Search by language

Figure 5.4 Hands-On Exercise 1, Steps 2c through 2n.

 Searching by ISBN

Books that are published in different versions (both hardcover and softcover, for instance) will have a different ISBN for each version—which means that searching by ISBN might not be the best way to search for widely published books.

Step 3 View Book Content

Refer to Figures 5.5 and 5.6 as you complete Step 3.

After you initiate a Google Books search, Google returns a list of matching books. For each book in the search results, Google displays the book cover, title, author(s), publication date, page count, and short description. If the full text of the book is available for viewing online, you'll see a *Read* link under the book's title; if a preview is available, you'll see a *Preview* link; if only a short excerpt is available, you'll see a *Snippet* link.

a. To view the Google page for the book and read available book content, click the book title.

Author   Publication date   Page count   Description

Book title; click to view book page

Cover

Figure 5.5 Hands-On Exercise 1, Step 3a.

The Google book page is comprised of a large viewing pane and a smaller informational sidebar.

b. To read the available book content, click the right arrow at the top of the viewing pane to go to the next page, or the left arrow to return to the previous page.

c. To view the book's table of contents, click the **Contents** link at the top of the viewing pane; click any given section or chapter to go directly to that part of the book.

d. To search within the book, enter your query into the search box in the sidebar and then click the **Go** button.

e. To read more about this book, click the **About this book** link in the sidebar.

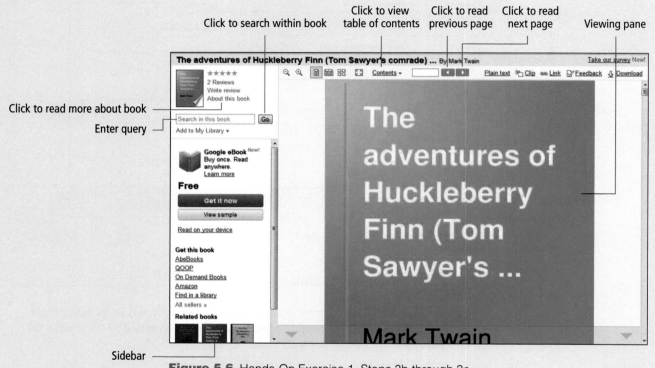

Figure 5.6 Hands-On Exercise 1, Steps 3b through 3e.

 Note   **All Books in Google Books Are Not the Same**

Not all options are available for all books; the availability of information depends mainly on copyright restrictions. Many books simply let you see a preview or snippet, some brief bibliographical information, and a link or two to purchase the book online. Other books feature full online reading privileges with additional viewing options, such as viewing full screen, viewing two pages at a time, and clipping (copying) the book's text.

Objective 2

Review Books

Can you review the books you read?

One of the social features of Google Books is the book review function. You can review any of the books you read, as well as read reviews written by other users.

Where do Google's book reviews come from?

A book's reviews come from other Google Books users, as well as other sources. These sources include Goodreads, a popular social cataloging website for book readers, Bookreport.com, a book review website, and Overstock.com, an online retailer.

Hands-On Exercises

2 | Reviewing Books

Steps: 1. Read Book Reviews; **2.** Write a Book Review.

Use Figures 5.7 through 5.10 as a guide to the exercise.

Step 1   Read Book Reviews

Refer to Figures 5.7 and 5.8 as you complete Step 1.

a. Go to the Google Books page for a given book.

   The top of the sidebar shows a book's star rating, from 1 to 5.

b. To view reviews of this book, click the **x Reviews** link (where *x* is the number of reviews).

Star rating

Click to read book reviews

Figure 5.7 Hands-On Exercise 2, Steps 1a and 1b.

This opens the book reviews page. A summary of the book's rating is displayed in the right sidebar. For most reviews, only a snippet or excerpt of the review is displayed.

c. To read a complete review, click the **Read full review** link.

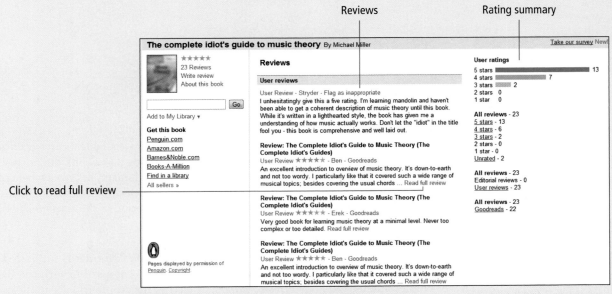

Reviews

Rating summary

Click to read full review

Figure 5.8 Hands-On Exercise 2, Step 1c.

Step 2   Write a Book Review

Refer to Figures 5.9 and 5.10 as you complete Step 2.

a. Go to the Google Books page for a given book.

b. Click the **Write review** link in the sidebar.

Click to write a review ——

Figure 5.9 Hands-On Exercise 2, Steps 2a and 2b.

This displays the book review page.

   c. Drag your mouse over the *Rating* graphic and click on a specific star to give a rating from 1 to 5 stars.

   d. Write your review in the large *Review* box.

   e. Click the **Save** button when done.

Drag and click to give
a star rating (1 to 5 stars) ——

Write book review ——

Click to save ——

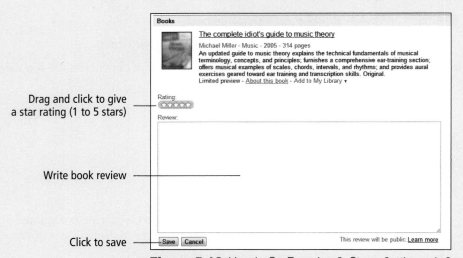

Figure 5.10 Hands-On Exercise 2, Steps 2c through 2e.

Objective 3

Purchase and Download Books

Are the books in Google Books available for downloading?

Some of the books stored in the Google Books database are available for free reading or downloading in eBook format; these books are indicated by a *Read* link under the title in the search results. These are often books in the public domain, or books where the author or publisher has authorized eBook distribution in this manner. Other books are available for purchase in eBook format, again at the discretion of the author or publisher.

Which eBook formats does Google Books support?

In many cases, the book publisher determines which eBook format is supported. Some Google eBooks are in the ***EPUB*** format, which is compatible with the Barnes & Noble NOOK and Sony ***eBook readers***, as well as the Apple iBooks application for the iPhone and iPad. Other Google eBooks are in PDF, which is compatible with most computers and eBook readers.

Can you purchase printed books via Google Books?

Many of the books in the Google Books database are still in print and available for purchase online. You can purchase these books by clicking a retailer link in the *Get this book* section in the sidebar on the Google book page.

EPUB A popular eBook format, the official standard of the International Digital Publishing Forum and compatible with most eBook readers and applications.

eBook reader A handheld device designed specifically for reading electronic books.

Hands-On Exercises

3 | Purchasing and Downloading Books

Steps: 1. Download a Free eBook; **2.** Purchase an eBook; **3.** Purchase a Printed Book.

Use Figures 5.11 through 5.15 as a guide to the exercise.

Step 1 | Download a Free eBook

Refer to Figures 5.11 and 5.12 as you complete Step 1.

eBooks that are available for free downloading have a *Read* link under the title on the search results page, and are indicated as "Free" on the Google book page.

a. Go to the Google Books page for a given book.

b. To view the book onscreen, click the **Get it now** button.

c. To download the book, click the **Read on your device** link.

Click to read onscreen ⎯⎯⎯

Click to download eBook ⎯⎯⎯

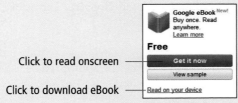

Figure 5.11 Hands-On Exercise 3, Steps 1a through 1c.

This displays the *Read on your device* page.

d. Scroll to the bottom of the page and click the appropriate **Download** button. To download in EPUB format (when available), click the **Download EPUB** button; to download in PDF, click the **Download PDF** button.

When prompted, enter the security code as displayed onscreen and then click the **Submit** button. The book is now downloaded to your computer. Follow the appropriate actions to transfer the file to your handheld eBook reader, if desired.

Click to download in EPUB format ⎯⎯⎯

Click to download in PDF format ⎯⎯⎯

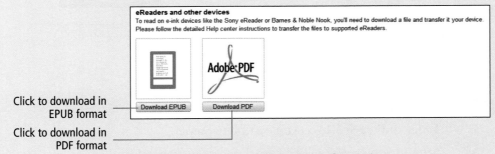

Figure 5.12 Hands-On Exercise 3, Step 1d.

Step 2 Purchase an eBook

Refer to Figures 5.13 and 5.14 as you complete Step 2.

Many books are available for purchase in eBook format. These books are indicated by a Google eBook graphic on the book page. The price of the book is listed on the *Buy now* button.

a. Go to the Google Books page for a given book.

b. Go to the *Google eBook* section in the sidebar and click the **Buy now** button.

Click to purchase eBook ———

Figure 5.13 Hands-On Exercise 3, Steps 2a and 2b.

If prompted to sign in to your Google account, do so now. You then see the *Google checkout* page for this book.

c. If you have not previously purchased via Google Checkout, enter your credit card information. If you have previously purchased via Google Checkout, select a method of payment.

d. Check the box to indicate that you've read and accepted Google's Terms of Service.

e. Click the **Complete your purchase** button.

The book is now downloaded to your computer. Follow the appropriate actions to transfer the file to your handheld eBook reader, if desired.

Check to accept Terms of Service ———
Select method of payment ———
Click to complete purchase ———

Figure 5.14 Hands-On Exercise 3, Steps 2c through 2e.

Step 3 Purchase a Printed Book

Refer to Figure 5.15 as you complete Step 3.

Most in-print books are available for purchase from selected online retailers. You can make your purchase through Google Books and have the printed book shipped to you.

a. Go to the Google Books page for a given book.

b. Go to the *Get this book* section in the sidebar and click the link for a given retailer.

You are now taken to the retailer's page for that book. Follow the retailer's instructions for completing your purchase.

Click to go to retailer's web page

Figure 5.15 Hands-On Exercise 3, Step 3.

Objective 4
Manage Your Library

What is your Google Books library?

To help you keep track of the books you read and purchase via Google Books, Google provides you with your own personal book library online. Your library enables you to organize, review, rate, and search your favorite books.

Can you share your book library with others?

Google Books enables you to share all the books in your library with friends, family, and colleagues. By default, your library is public; you share it with others by sharing the URL for your library page. (Your library's URL is located in the address bar of your web browser when you go to your library; you can copy and paste this URL into an email message.)

Hands-On Exercises

4 | Managing Your Library

Steps: 1. Add a Book to Your Library; **2.** View Books in Your Library.

Use Figures 5.16 through 5.18 as a guide to the exercise.

Step 1 Add a Book to Your Library

Refer to Figure 5.16 as you complete Step 1.

All books that you purchase are automatically added to your library. You can also manually add other books to your library.

a. Go to the Google Books page for a given book.

b. Click the **Add to My Library** link in the sidebar.

c. Check the appropriate status for this book: **My Google eBooks, Favorites, Reading now, To read,** or **Have read**.

d. Click the **Save** button.

Click to add to library

Select book status

Click to save

Figure 5.16 Hands-On Exercise 4, Step 1.

Step ② View Books in Your Library

Refer to Figures 5.17 and 5.18 as you complete Step 2.

a. Go to the Google Books main page (**books.google.com**).

b. Click the **My library** link.

Click to view your library

Figure 5.17 Hands-On Exercise 4, Steps 2a and 2b.

This displays the *My library* page, with all books organized by status or category.

c. Click a book cover or **Read Now** button to read a given book.

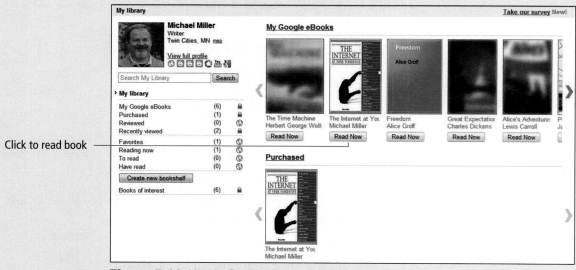

Click to read book

Figure 5.18 Hands-On Exercise 4, Step 2c.

Summary

In this chapter, you learned how to search for books in the Google Books database, and how to read books online. You also learned how to purchase and download eBooks, as well as how to purchase printed books. Finally, you learned how to review the books you read, and how to manage the books in your Google Books library.

Key Terms

eBook	94	Google Books Partner Program	94
eBook reader	102	ISBN	98
EPUB	102	ISSN	98
Google Books	94	Public domain	95
Google Books Library Project	94	Snippet	96

Multiple Choice Questions

1. When using the Advanced Book Search page, which of the following is *not* an option for searching for books?

    (a) Search by title

    (b) Search by author

    (c) Search by publisher

    (d) Search by page count

2. What types of books are typically available for free online reading and downloading?

    (a) Fiction bestsellers

    (b) Nonfiction reference

    (c) Public domain titles

    (d) Children's books

3. What books are automatically added to your Google Books library?

    (a) eBooks you've purchased

    (b) Books you've read online

    (c) Books you've searched for

    (d) Books in the public domain

4. Where does Google get books for the Google Books database?

    (a) Publishers participating in the Google Books Partner Program

    (b) Books scanned by libraries as part of the Google Books Library Project

    (c) Books submitted by Google users

    (d) Both (a) and (b)

    (e) Both (a) and (c)

5. Which of the following is *not* a viewing option for books found through Google Books?

   (a) Read (full text)

   (b) Download index only

   (c) Preview

   (d) Snippet

6. Where do Google Books' book reviews come from?

   (a) Professional book reviewers

   (b) Other Google users

   (c) Selected third-party websites

   (d) Both (a) and (b)

   (e) Both (b) and (c)

7. How do you share the books in your Google Books library?

   (a) Share the URL of your library page

   (b) Click the Share button on your library page

   (c) Copy and paste individual book titles from your library page

   (d) Click the Notify link beneath each book you wish to share

8. Which of the following eBook formats does Google Books support?

   (a) EPUB

   (b) PDF

   (c) MOBI (Kindle)

   (d) Both (a) and (b)

   (e) Both (a) and (c)

9. Which of the following statements is true regarding printed books?

   (a) Google sells printed books in its own Google Bookstore.

   (b) Printed books are available for purchase from selected online retailers.

   (c) There are no links to printed books on the Google Books site.

   (d) All books in the Google Books database are available as printed books.

10. Books obtained from book publishers are typically

    (a) out-of-print titles.

    (b) public domain titles.

    (c) in-print titles.

    (d) overstocks and remainders.

Fill in the Blank

Write the correct word or words in the space provided.

1. The unique numeric identification code for a book used in the book industry is called the _____.

2. If the full text of a book is available for online reading, Google displays a(n) _____ link on the search results page.

3. A brief excerpt from a book is called a(n) _____.
4. Books you've read or downloaded are stored in your _____.
5. A handheld device designed specifically for reading electronic books is called a(n) _____ _____.

Practice Exercises

Use Google Books to look up the answers to these questions and problems.
1. In the book *Life on the Mississippi* by Mark Twain, what is the first sentence of Chapter 1?
2. In the book *The Time Machine* by H.G. Wells, what is the title of Chapter III?
3. In what year was *The Complete Idiot's Guide to Music History* published?
4. In the book *Thomas Jefferson* by John Torrey Morse, what is the title of Chapter V?
5. Who wrote the book *At the Earth's Core?*

Critical Thinking

1. Google Books has met with opposition from some authors and publishers who claim that it deprives them of potential revenues from sales of their books. Google has countered that it provides access to out-of-print books as well as publicizes in-print books that are available for purchase.

   In 2008, Google reached a proposed settlement with publishers and authors that would enable Google to offer copyrighted books online but then compensate the copyright holders for those works. This settlement was overturned in 2011 by a federal judge who ruled that it would give Google the ability to exploit books without the permission of copyright owners, by requiring them to opt out of the Google Books library, instead of opting in.

   Research the 2008 agreement between Google, publishers, and authors and then write a short paper on this issue. Examine how the various parties might benefit from or be harmed by Google Books and the proposed 2008 settlement.

2. Google has partnered with several libraries to scan the books in their collections for inclusion in Google Books. Write a short paper examining why a library may or may not want to participate in the Google Books Library Project. Discuss what potential benefits a library might see from participation in this program.

Credits

Google, Blogger, and Picasa screenshots reprinted by permission.

CHAPTER 6

Using Google Groups and Google Reader

Objectives

After you read this chapter, you will be able to:

1. Search Google Groups

2. Visit and Participate in Groups

3. Create a New Group

4. Use Google Reader

The following Hands-On Exercises will help you accomplish the chapter objectives:

Hands-On Exercises

EXERCISES	SKILLS COVERED
1. Searching Google Groups	**Step 1:** Browse through Groups **Step 2:** Search for Groups **Step 3:** Search for Posts across All Groups
2. Visiting and Participating in Groups	**Step 1:** Join a Group **Step 2:** Read and Reply to Posts **Step 3:** Create a New Message Thread
3. Creating a New Group	**Step 1:** Set Up a New Group **Step 2:** Invite Members to Your Group **Step 3:** Manage Your Group
4. Using Google Reader	**Step 1:** Search for Blogs, News Feeds, and Twitter Feeds **Step 2:** Read Posts, Articles, and Tweets

Objective 1

Search Google Groups

What is Google Groups?

Google Groups is a collection of web-based special interest discussion groups or message forums, like online clubs for specific topics. Google Groups hosts its own topic-specific groups, and also functions as a newsreader for groups hosted on a part of the Internet called *Usenet*.

What is Usenet?

Usenet is a network that piggybacks on the larger Internet. It predates the World Wide Web, while still using the Internet's underlying infrastructure.

Today, Usenet is a collection of more than 30,000 online discussion groups, called *newsgroups*, organized by topic. In essence, a Usenet newsgroup is an electronic gathering place for people with similar interests. Within a newsgroup, users post messages (called *articles*) about a variety of topics; other users read these articles and, when so disposed, respond. The result is a kind of ongoing, free-form discussion in which dozens—or hundreds—of interested users can participate.

> **Note** **No Moderation**
>
> Unlike some web-based discussion forums or blogs, most Usenet newsgroups are not moderated, meaning that no one monitors the message content to ensure that subject discussions stay on track. The result is slightly organized chaos, typically including a lot of off-topic messages and thinly concealed advertisements mixed in with the on-topic and useful messages.

How does Google Groups incorporate and go beyond Usenet?

Over the years, there have been several attempts to archive historical Usenet postings. The most successful of these archives was DejaNews (later called Deja.com), which Google purchased in 2001. Google subsequently turned DejaNews into Google Groups, which continues to function as both an archive of historical Usenet articles and a web-based newsreader for current Usenet newsgroups. You can use Google Groups to search the newsgroup archives or to browse the current messages in any Usenet newsgroup.

Google expanded beyond Usenet by introducing its own user-created discussion groups. These native Google groups do not exist on Usenet, but are still accessed via the Google Groups service.

Google Groups A collection of web-based special interest discussion groups, both based on Google and hosted on Usenet.

Usenet A subset of the Internet comprised of tens of thousands of online discussion groups.

Newsgroup A topic-specific discussion group on Usenet.

Article A message posted on a Usenet newsgroup.

Hands-On Exercises

1 | Searching Google Groups

Steps: 1. Browse through Groups; **2.** Search for Groups; **3.** Search for Posts across All Groups.

Use Figures 6.1 through 6.6 as a guide to the exercise.

Step 1 Browse through Groups

Refer to Figures 6.1 and 6.2 as you complete Step 1.

a. Use your web browser to go to the Google Groups homepage, located at **groups. google.com**, and click **Home** in the sidebar.

b. Click the **Browse all** button.

Click to browse groups

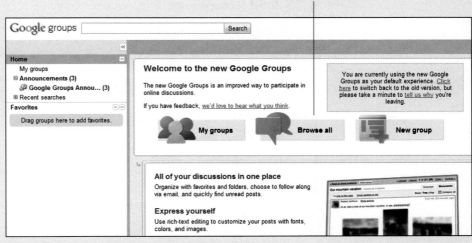

Figure 6.1 Hands-On Exercise 1, Steps 1a and 1b.

This displays the *Browse Groups* page.

c. Click any major category to view additional subcategories.

d. Keep clicking through the various subcategories until you find the specific group you want.

Click to view subcategories

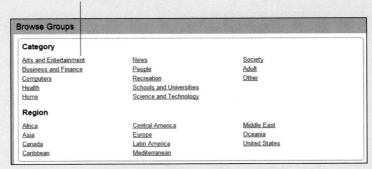

Figure 6.2 Hands-On Exercise 1, Steps 1c and 1d.

Step 2 Search for Groups

Refer to Figures 6.3 and 6.4 as you complete Step 2.

You can also search for specific groups.

a. From the Google Groups homepage, enter the name of the group or topic into the search box at the top of the page.

b. Click the **Search** button.

Enter search query   Click to search for groups

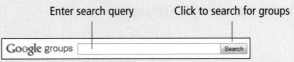

Figure 6.3 Hands-On Exercise 1, Steps 2a and 2b.

Post Another word for a message or article in a group.

The search results page is now displayed. At the top of this page is a short list of groups that match your query; below that are individual *posts* that match the query.

c. Click the **Groups matching <query>** link.

The search results page now changes to display only matching groups.

d. To visit a specific group, click that group's name in the search results.

Click to display all matching groups

Click to view group

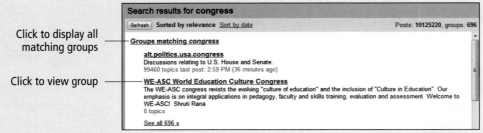

Figure 6.4 Hands-On Exercise 1, Steps 2c and 2d.

> **Note**   **Identifying Groups**
>
> For each group on the search results page, Google lists the group name, the group's activity level, and the time or date of the most recent post. If it's a Usenet group, the title reflects the Usenet hierarchy, such as alt.music.topic or rec.arts.topic.

Step 3 Search for Posts across All Groups

Refer to Figures 6.5 and 6.6 as you complete Step 3.

You can also search for individual posts about a given topic, across all groups.

a. From the Google Groups homepage, enter your query into the search box.

b. Click the **Search** button.

Enter search query   Click to search for posts

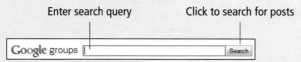

Figure 6.5 Hands-On Exercise 1, Steps 3a and 3b.

The search results page displays a handful of groups that match your query at the top of the page, with individual posts that match your query below that. Each result displays the message title, the group where the message was posted, a snippet (short excerpt) of the message text, the date of the post, the author of the post, and the number of authors writing about this topic.

c. Click any header to view the complete post.

d. To view the hosting group for a post, click the group name beside the post title.

Hosting group; click to view group page

Post title; click to read post

> Saltwater Reef Aquarium - Reduced price Group: ba.market.misc
> Here are the details: 45 gallon **reef aquarium**: Solid Oak stand and hood. Hood includes one 100 watt Metal Halide and two 20 watt actinic bulbs. Built in trickle filter with Hagen 402 power-head, heater, and protein skimmer. Also Mini-jet 404 for circulation. I aquired it from my daughter when she moved out. ...
> 12/5/97 by David Anderson - 1 post by 1 author
>
> For sale -200 gal. Oceanic Reef Aquarium Group: milw.general
> ... with bio-filter material Sandpoint RO unit 20gal. a day capacity Plus-miscellaneous odds and ends $2000, best offer or trade for computer hardware (over $5K invested) I also have a 100 gal. All Glass **aquarium** and stand for sale w/glass tops,a large quantity of red gravel and petrified wood and other misc. parts.
> 7/13/96 by Don Beaulieu - 1 post by 1 author
>
> [email] Hydroponic and Reef Aquarium Interest.....hpjXYG--851qyfkwcbs Group: news.admin.net-abuse.sightings
> Derrick Der...@folertrazt.net news admin net-abuse sightings Return-path: <hydr...@excite.com> Received: from mta1.srv.hcvlny.cv.net (mta1.srv.hcvlny.cv.net [167.206.5.4]) by mstr5.srv.hcvlny.cv.net (iPlanet Messaging Server 5.2 HotFix 1.05 (built Nov 6 2002)) with ESMTP id ...
> 4/29/03 by Derrick - 1 post by 1 author

Figure 6.6 Hands-On Exercise 1, Steps 3c and 3d.

Objective 2

Visit and Participate in Groups

What does Google Groups look like?

Both Google-created groups and Usenet newsgroups are accessible via Google Groups.

 Note **Joining Groups**

You may need to join some Google-created groups before you can view the pages for those groups.

Discussion In Google Groups, a collection of messages on a specific topic.

Thread On Usenet, a collection of posts on a specific topic.

When you visit the page for a Google-created group, you see a list of the most recent *discussions* on the right side of the page. Groups can also contain specialized pages (on the *Pages* tab) and files for downloading (on the *Files* tab).

The page for a Usenet newsgroup looks similar to a Google group page. A list of the most recent topics (in Usenet terminology, *threads*) appears on the left side of the page, with a snippet of the most recent post in each thread. A list of older topics is displayed in the right column. If you like, you also can search the messages within this group by using the search box at the top of the page and clicking the **Search this group** button.

What is a message thread?

In Usenet newsgroups, a thread is a collection of all posts on a given topic. In Google Groups, a thread is called a discussion.

Do you need to join a group?

Restricted group A Google group that requires members to join before viewing or posting messages.

Some Google-created groups are *restricted groups* that require you to join the group before you can access the group page. Other groups do not require you to join and their pages can be viewed by anyone.

That said, if you want to keep up-to-date on all the new messages in a group, you may want to join that group. When you join a group, you're automatically notified of new messages posted to the group via email; you don't have to visit the group page to read messages.

Hands-On Exercises

2 | Visiting and Participating in Groups

Steps: 1. Join a Group; **2.** Read and Reply to Posts; **3.** Create a New Message
Thread.

Use Figures 6.7 through 6.13 as a guide to the exercise.

 Step 1 Join a Group

Refer to Figures 6.7 and 6.8 as you complete Step 1.

a. Go to the main page for a group.

b. Click the **Join group** or **Join group to post** link at the top of the page.

Click to join this group

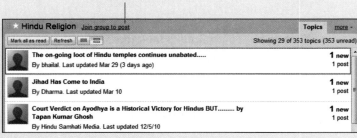

Figure 6.7 Hands-On Exercise 2, Steps 1a and 1b.

This displays the *Join group* dialog box.

c. Select how you want to be notified of new group messages:

- **No Email**—you aren't informed of new messages; you have to go to the Google
  Groups site to read the group's messages.

- **Abridged Email**—you get one email a day that summarizes all the new
  messages.

- **Digest Email**—you get one or more emails a day containing the full text of
  up to 25 messages. If a group has more than 25 messages in a day, you receive
  additional digest emails containing the excess messages.

- **Email**—each new message in the group is sent to you via email as it is posted.

d. To display information from your Google account profile, check the **Link to my
  Google profile and show my photo on posts** box.

e. To use the name listed on your Google profile, check the **Use the full name
  from my Google profile** option. To use a different nickname, select the **Use this
  nickname:** option and enter the desired nickname.

f. Click the **Join this group** button.

Select how you wish to
receive email notification

Click to link to Google profile

Click to use Google
profile name

Click to use another nickname

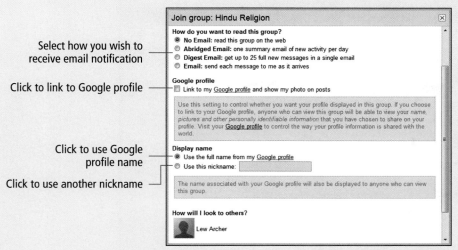

Figure 6.8 Hands-On Exercise 2, Steps 1c through 1e.

 Tip **Unsubscribing**

To unsubscribe from a group, go to that group's page, click the **My membership** link, and then click the **Leave group** button when the *About group* dialog box appears.

Step 2 Read and Reply to Posts

Refer to Figures 6.9 through 6.11 as you complete Step 2.

a. On the group's page, click the title of the thread or discussion you want to read.

Click to view discussion

Figure 6.9 Hands-On Exercise 2, Step 2a.

This displays the message page. Posts are listed in chronological order (the first post at the top and the last at the bottom).

b. Go to the specific message you want to reply to and click the **Post reply** link.

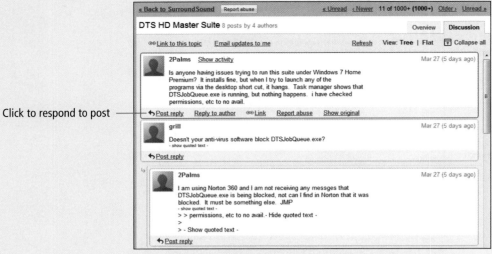

Click to respond to post

Figure 6.10 Hands-On Exercise 2, Step 2b.

This displays a reply pane beneath the current post.

c. Enter your message into the reply pane.

d. To include ("quote") the original post, click the **Quote original** link.

e. Format the message as desired, using the controls on the Formatting toolbar.

f. Click the **Post** button.

Your reply is added beneath the selected post.

Formatting toolbar

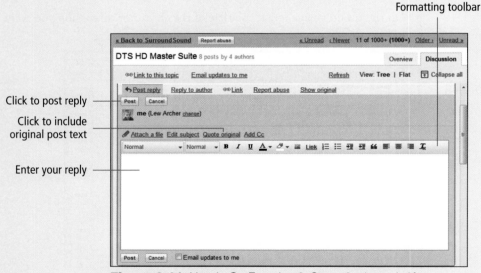

Click to post reply

Click to include
original post text

Enter your reply

Figure 6.11 Hands-On Exercise 2, Steps 2c through 2f.

Step ❸ Create a New Message Thread

Refer to Figures 6.12 and 6.13 as you complete Step 3.

You're not limited to replying to existing posts. You can also start a new message thread, called a discussion, with a new post about a new topic.

a. Go to the main page for the group.

b. Click the **New topic** button at the top of the page.

Click to create new post on a new topic

Figure 6.12 Hands-On Exercise 2, Steps 3a and 3b.

This displays the *New topic* page.

c. Enter a name for the new discussion into the *Subject* box.

d. Enter the text of your post into the large message box.

e. Format the message as desired, using the controls on the Formatting toolbar.

f. To be notified of replies to this post, check the **Email updates to me** box.

g. Click the **Post** button.

In unmoderated groups, your message is immediately posted to the group. In moderated groups, all posts have to be approved by the group's moderators before they are publicly posted.

Enter message subject   Formatting toolbar

Enter message text

Click to be notified of replies

Click to post message

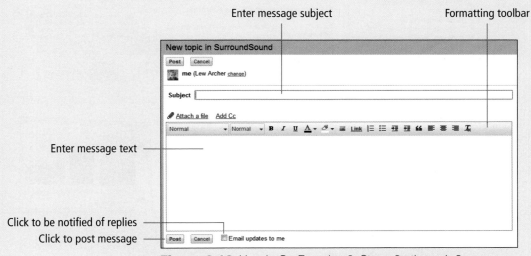

Figure 6.13 Hands-On Exercise 2, Steps 3c through 3g.

Objective 3

Create a New Group

Can you create your own Google group?

With the tens of thousands of groups available on Google Groups, it's still possible that no group is available for a given topic in which you're interested. If this is the case, you can start your own Google group, on just about any topic you want.

 Note   **Google-Created Groups Only**

User-created groups are not Usenet newsgroups, and they are available only to users of the Google Groups website.

Hands-On Exercises

3 | Creating a New Group

Steps: 1. Set Up a New Group; **2.** Invite Members to Your Group; **3.** Manage Your Group.

Use Figures 6.14 through 6.18 as a guide to the exercise.

 Set Up a New Group

Refer to Figures 6.14 through 6.16 as you complete Step 1.

a. From the main Google Groups page, click the **New group** button.

Click to create new group

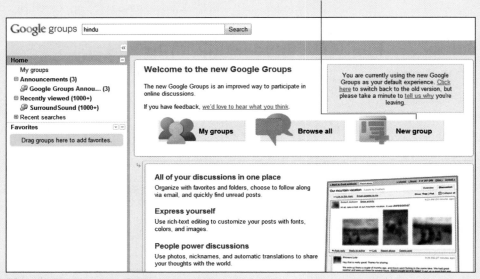

Figure 6.14 Hands-On Exercise 3, Step 1a.

This displays the *Create a group* page.

b. Enter a name for your group into the *Name your group* box.

c. Enter an email address for your group, in the form of *groupname*@googlegroups. com, into the *Create a group email address* box.

d. Enter a brief description of your group into the *Write a group description* box.

e. If the group is likely to contain adult content or language, check the **This group may contain adult content...** box.

f. Select the desired access level for the group:

- **Public** (anyone can join, but only members can read messages)

- **Announcement-only** (anyone can join, but only managers—moderators—can post messages)

- **Restricted** (only the people you invite can join)

g. Click the **Create my group** button.

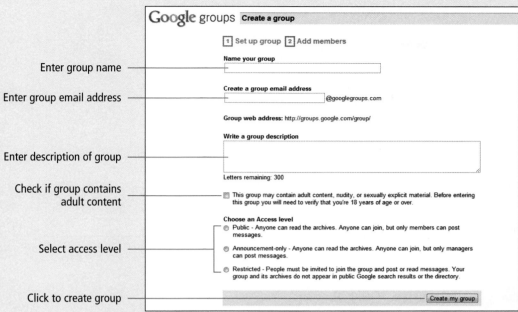

Enter group name

Enter group email address

Enter description of group

Check if group contains adult content

Select access level

Click to create group

Figure 6.15 Hands-On Exercise 3, Steps 1b through 1g.

You now see the verification page.

h. Enter the verification characters into the box and click the **Create my group** button.

Enter verification characters

Click to create group

Figure 6.16 Hands-On Exercise 3, Step 1h.

Step 2 Invite Members to Your Group

Refer to Figure 6.17 as you complete Step 2.

After you've created your group, you need to invite others to join the group. You do this during the group creation process. After you click the **Create my group** button, as described in Hands-On Exercise 3, Step 1, the *Add members* page appears.

 Google Groups Directory

If you created a Public or Announcement-only group, your group will appear in the public Google Groups directory. Any user who finds your group in the directory can join at that point.

a. Enter the email addresses of those people you want to invite to your group into the *Enter email addresses of people to invite* box; separate multiple addresses with commas.

b. Enter an invitation message into the *Write an invitation message* box to send to each person you signified.

c. Click the **Invite members** button.

Enter email addresses ———

Enter invitation message ———

Click to invite new members ———

Figure 6.17 Hands-On Exercise 3, Step 2.

 Manage Your Group

Refer to Figure 6.18 as you complete Step 3.

After you've created your group, you can manage it on a day-to-day basis.

a. Open your group page.

As the group owner, you see a special group page; all visitors see the normal group page.

b. To start a new discussion topic, click the **New topic** button.

c. To change the visual appearance of your group page, click the **more** link, select **Settings**, select the **Appearance** tab, and then make the necessary changes.

d. To invite more members, click the **more** link, select **Settings**, and then click the **Invite members** link.

e. To display all group members, click the **Members** tab.

Click to start new discussion   Click to view group members   Click to configure settings and invite new members

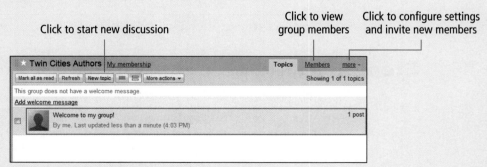

Figure 6.18 Hands-On Exercise 3, Step 3.

Objective 4

Use Google Reader

What is a blog?

Blog A diary-like website that features commentary about a given topic.

A *blog*—short for web log—is a personal website that is updated frequently with commentary, links to other sites, and anything else the author might be interested in. Many blogs also let visitors post comments in response to the owner's postings, resulting in a community that is very similar to that of a message board. It's a 21st-century version of self-publishing, enabled by the Internet.

What is a news feed?

News feed Also known as a site feed, an automatically updated stream of contents for a blog or news site.

RSS Short for Really Simple Syndication, a popular format for news feeds.

A *news feed* or site feed is an automatically updated stream of a blog's contents, enabled by a special file format called *RSS* (Really Simple Syndication). When a blog has an RSS feed enabled, any updated content is automatically published as a special file that contains the RSS feed. The syndicated feed is then normally picked up by RSS feed reader programs and RSS aggregators for websites.

 Atom Feeds

Atom is another feed format similar to RSS, with a few extra features.

What is a newsreader?

Newsreader A software program or website that aggregates news feeds.

When you want to read the postings from your favorite blogs or news sites, you need some sort of feed-reading mechanism. That can be a *newsreader* software program, or a website that aggregates feeds from a variety of sources.

What is Google Reader?

Google Reader A Google site that aggregates news feeds from blogs, news sites, and Twitter feeds.

Google Reader is a newsreader website that aggregates news feeds from a variety of blogs, news sites, and Twitter feeds. You can use Google Reader to display the latest news headlines from popular news sites, as well as to catch the latest ponderings from your favorite bloggers and Twitterers. All you need to do is know which feed you want to subscribe to; Google Reader automatically displays the latest content, all in one place.

 Sign In to Use

To use Google Reader, you must have a Google account and be signed in to that account.

Hands-On Exercises

4 | Using Google Reader

Steps: 1. Search for Blogs, News Feeds, and Twitter Feeds; **2.** Read Posts, Articles, and Tweets.

Use Figures 6.19 through 6.22 as a guide to the exercise.

Step 1 Search for Blogs, News Feeds, and Twitter Feeds

Refer to Figures 6.19 through 6.21 as you complete Step 1.

a. Use your web browser to go to the Google Reader homepage, located at **www. google.com/reader**, and sign in to your Google account.

b. Click the **Add a subscription** button in the left panel.

Click to search for a blog or feed

Figure 6.19 Hands-On Exercise 4, Steps 1a and 1b.

This displays an *Add a subscription* box.

c. Enter one or more keywords to search for blogs about a given topic.

If you know the URL for a blog or blog feed, you can enter that URL into the *Add a subscription* box.

d. Click the **Add** button.

Click to search for blogs or feeds

Enter search query

Figure 6.20 Hands-On Exercise 4, Steps 1c and 1d.

Google Reader returns a list of matching blogs and feeds.

e. Click the **Subscribe** button for a given blog or feed to add that subscription to Google Reader.

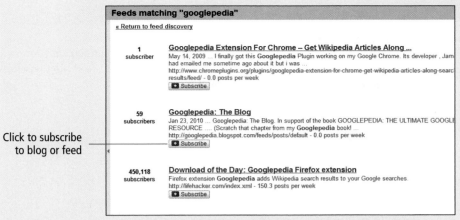

Figure 6.21 Hands-On Exercise 4, Step 1e.

Click to subscribe
to blog or feed

Step ❷ Read Posts, Articles, and Tweets

Refer to Figure 6.22 as you complete Step 2.

a. Go to **www.google.com/reader**.

The news feeds you've subscribed to are displayed in the left sidebar. Feeds with new (unread) postings are displayed in bold. The latest postings from the feeds to which you are subscribed are displayed in the main (right) pane.

b. To read the latest postings for a given feed, click the feed name in the sidebar.

The postings for that feed are displayed in the main window on the right side of the page. Use the scroll bar or the **Previous item/Next item** buttons to move through the postings.

 Tip Read on Original Page

If you'd prefer to read a posting on the original blog or news site, rather than in Google Reader, click the title of the blog entry. The selected post on the original site opens in a new browser window.

Click to view post on original blog   Posts for selected blog

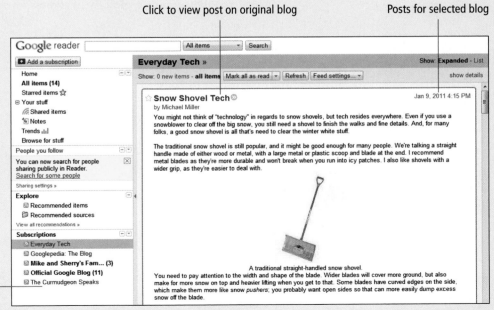

Blogs to which you
are subscribed

Figure 6.22 Hands-On Exercise 4, Step 2.

Summary

In this chapter, you learned how to join, participate in, and create your own Google groups. You also learned how to subscribe to blog feeds and read blog postings with Google Reader.

Key Terms

Article	112	Newsreader	123
Blog	123	Post	114
Discussion	115	Restricted group	115
Google Groups	112	RSS	123
Google Reader	123	Thread	115
News feed	123	Usenet	112
Newsgroup	112		

Multiple Choice Questions

1. Which part of the Internet hosts thousands of discussion forums?

    (a) World Wide Web

    (b) FTP

    (c) Usenet

    (d) Gopher

2. Which of the following statements about Usenet is *not* true?

    (a) Usenet predates the World Wide Web.

    (b) Most Usenet newsgroups are not moderated.

    (c) Usenet newsgroups are devoted to and organized by specific topics.

    (d) There are more than a half million individual Usenet newsgroups.

3. Which of the following is a typical email address for a Google group?

    (a) mygroup@google.com

    (b) mygroup@gmail.com

    (c) mygroup@googlegroups.com

    (d) mygroup@usenet.net

4. One of the first Usenet archives was called

    (a) ArchiveNet.

    (b) NewsArchive.

    (c) The Official Usenet Archive.

    (d) DejaNews.

5. To receive a daily email that summarizes all new messages in a group, choose this delivery option:

   (a) No Email

   (b) Abridged Email

   (c) Digest Email

   (d) Email

6. In a Google group, posts are arranged in which order?

   (a) Newest messages first

   (b) Oldest messages first

   (c) Alphabetical order (A–Z)

   (d) By author name, alphabetically

7. Which of the following statements about Google Groups is true?

   (a) All Google Groups are Usenet newsgroups.

   (b) Google Groups users can create new Usenet newsgroups.

   (c) Usenet newsgroups are accessible via Google Groups.

   (d) Google Groups users cannot post to Usenet newsgroups.

8. To create a moderated Google group that anyone can join, select this option:

   (a) Public

   (b) Announcement-only

   (c) Restricted

   (d) Open

9. RSS stands for

   (a) Real Simple Subscription.

   (b) Runtime Super Syndication.

   (c) Really Simple Syndication.

   (d) Relatively Simplified Service.

10. A program that aggregates news feeds is called a

   (a) subscription aggregator.

   (b) newsreader.

   (c) feed summarizer.

   (d) blog master.

Fill in the Blank

Write the correct word or words in the space provided.

1. In Usenet, a discussion is called a(n) _____.

2. In Usenet, a message is called a(n) _____.

3. An automatically updated stream of blog contents is called a(n) _____ _____.

4. The word "blog" is short for _____ _____.

5. In Google Reader, to view automatic updates via a blog's feed, you must _____ to that blog.

Practice Exercises

1. **Google Groups**

   Create your own Google group, on any topic you like. Start at least one discussion in the group. Invite your instructor to join the group.

2. **Google Reader**

   Search for and subscribe to the Official Google Blog. Write down the titles of the five most recent posts to this blog and submit to your instructor.

Critical Thinking

1. Google Groups incorporate both Google-created groups and Usenet newsgroups. Explore a given topic in both types of groups and then write a short paper discussing the differences between Google-created groups and Usenet newsgroups, and why you might prefer one over the other.

2. Google Reader lets you subscribe to feed from blogs, news sites, and Twitter feeds. Write a short paper discussing why you might want to consolidate all your feed reading in a single application, as opposed to reading posts on their native sites.

Credits

Google, Blogger, and Picasa screenshots reprinted by permission.

CHAPTER 7

Using Google Maps and Google Earth

Objectives

After you read this chapter, you will be able to:

1. Map a Location
2. Search for a Nearby Business
3. Create a Custom Map
4. Generate Turn-by-Turn Directions
5. Navigate Google Earth
6. Use Layers
7. Generate Google Earth Driving Directions

The following Hands-On Exercises will help you accomplish the chapter objectives:

Hands-On Exercises

EXERCISES	SKILLS COVERED
1. Mapping a Location	**Step 1:** Generate a Google Map **Step 2:** Navigate a Google Map **Step 3:** View Live Traffic Conditions **Step 4:** Display Street View Photos **Step 5:** Display Satellite Images **Step 6:** Display Google Earth View **Step 7:** Display Overlay Data **Step 8:** Print a Map
2. Searching for a Nearby Business	**Step 1:** Search for a Local Business **Step 2:** View Business Information
3. Creating a Custom Map	**Step 1:** Save a Map to My Places **Step 2:** View Your Custom Maps **Step 3:** Add a Placemark to a Map **Step 4:** Share a Custom Map
4. Generating Turn-by-Turn Directions	**Step 1:** Generate Driving Directions **Step 2:** Generate Multiple-Stop Directions **Step 3:** Reverse Your Directions **Step 4:** Print Your Directions
5. Navigating Google Earth	**Step 1:** Navigate with the Onscreen Navigation Controls **Step 2:** Navigate with the Mouse **Step 3:** Search for Places
6. Using Layers	**Step 1:** Display a Layer **Step 2:** Display Places of Interest
7. Generating Google Earth Driving Directions	**Step 1:** Generate Directions **Step 2:** Tour Your Route **Step 3:** Print Directions

Objective 1

Map a Location

What is Google Maps?

Google Maps Google's online mapping service.

Google Maps is an online mapping service offered by Google. Google Maps has been a pioneer in online mapping functionality; it continues to evolve its maps and other offerings.

Like competing online mapping services, such as MapQuest and Bing Maps, Google Maps offers many useful features packed into an easy-to-use interface. You can generate maps for any given address or location; you can also click and drag the maps to view adjacent sections, overlay the map info on satellite images of the given area, view local traffic conditions, display nearby businesses as a series of pinpoints on the map, view street-level photos of a given location, and even plot driving directions to and from one location to any other location.

Google Maps does all its mapping from the familiar Google search box. Unlike other map sites, there are no forms to fill out; just enter what you want to see into the search box, and let Google Maps do the rest. If you're used to using Google for web searches, using it for mapping isn't a whole lot different.

What is the difference between Google Maps and Google Local?

Google announced its online mapping service in February 2005, following the acquisition of mapping technology from a company named Where2 Technologies. Google's mapping service was originally part of the Google Local product, which offered local business listings. In April 2006, Google changed the name from Google Local to Google Maps, with online mapping its primary focus.

What map views are available with Google Maps?

When you create a map with Google Maps, the default view is that of a traditional street map. Google also offers a number of other map views, including the following:

- **Traffic view**, which displays real-time traffic information on the street map.

- **Satellite view**, which displays a bird's-eye view of a given location.

 Aerial Photography

Although it's called Satellite view, many of these images are actually high-resolution aerial photographic images taken from airplanes.

- **Street View**, which displays street-level photos of the map's location.

- **Google Earth view**, which provides a 3D (three-dimensional) version of the traditional Satellite view that lets you fly through and around a map's location.

What is Google Maps Street View?

Street View A Google Maps view that displays street-level photos of a given location.

Google Maps **Street View** displays panoramic photos of most major streets and locations. Street View photos are taken with a special revolving camera fitted on the top of a moving car that snaps one photo each second. Multiple photos are sewn together digitally to give the panoramic view.

What is Google Maps Earth view?

Earth view A Google Maps view that displays a 3D version of a satellite photo.

Google Maps' special *Earth view* is essentially a 3D version of the traditional Satellite view. In Satellite view, you're limited to looking down from straight above; in Earth view, you can zoom in, around, and through all the maps you create. In essence, Google Maps' Earth view is a subset of what you get in the separate Google Earth software.

What is a map overlay?

Overlay A layer of data displayed on top of a Google map.

Google offers other interesting data that you can display on your maps, via the use of *overlays*. That is, this information is overlaid on the normal map display. Table 7.1 details the overlays available; note that not all overlays are available for all mapped areas.

Table 7.1—Google Maps Overlays	
Overlay	**Description**
Traffic	Displays live traffic conditions
Transit	Displays mass transit routes
Photos	Displays photos taken within the map area
Terrain	Changes the normal map to a topographical map
Webcams	Displays webcams operating in the map area
Videos	Displays videos taken within the map area
Wikipedia	Displays Wikipedia entries having to do with items or locations in the map area
Bicycling	Displays bicycling routes in the map area
Buzz	Displays users of Google Buzz who are currently in the map area
45°	Displays 45° imagery in Satellite view
Labels	Displays street and location labels in Satellite view

Hands-On Exercises

1 | Mapping a Location

Steps: 1. Generate a Google Map; **2.** Navigate a Google Map; **3.** View Live Traffic Conditions; **4.** Display Street View Photos; **5.** Display Satellite Images; **6.** Display Google Earth View; **7.** Display Overlay Data; **8.** Print a Map.

Use Figures 7.1 through 7.14 as a guide to the exercise.

Step 1 Generate a Google Map

Refer to Figure 7.1 as you complete Step 1.

a. Go to the Google Maps homepage located at **maps.google.com**.

b. Enter a street address or general location into the search box.

Table 7.2 details the various ways you can enter an address or location.

Table 7.2—Google Maps Address Formats	
Address Format	**Example**
City, state	san jose, ca
Zip	95113
Address, city, state	170 s market street, san jose, ca
Address, city, zip	170 s market street, san jose, 95113
Street intersection, city, state	e san Fernando and s 3rd, san jose, ca
Street intersection, zip	e san Fernando and s 3rd, 95113
Latitude, longitude	37.385, −121.897
Airport code	SJC
Subway station	graham avenue station

 Tip **Don't Spell It Out**

In most instances, you don't need to spell out words like "east," "street," or "drive"; common abbreviations are okay, and you don't need to put a period after the abbreviation. In addition, when entering a street intersection, you can use the ampersand (&) instead of the word "and."

 Tip **Smart Searching**

As you start typing a street name, city, and so on, a drop-down list beneath the search box offers suggestions that match what you've entered; you can then point to one of these suggestions to make that your search. For example, as you start to type "mi," Google might suggest Michigan, Milwaukee, Minneapolis, Miami, and any locations you've recently searched for that include the letters "mi."

c. Click the **Search Maps** button.

Enter address or location   Click to generate map

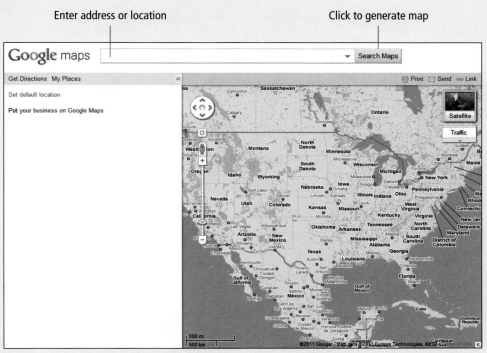

Figure 7.1 Hands-On Exercise 1, Step 1.

 Step 2 **Navigate a Google Map**

Refer to Figure 7.2 as you complete Step 2.

When you map an address, Google displays a map of that address in the right side of the browser window. The address itself is listed in the search results pane on the left side of the window; information about the address is displayed in a balloon overlaid on the main map. Navigation controls display along the left side of the map.

> **Tip** ★ **Full-Width Display**
>
> To display the map the full width of your browser window, click the left arrow at the top of the left-hand pane. This hides the entire left-hand pane and expands the map to fill the space.

a. To pan left (west), click the **left-arrow pan** button, or press the left-arrow key on your keyboard.

b. To pan right (east), click the **right-arrow pan** button, or press the right-arrow key on your keyboard.

c. To pan up (north), click the **top-arrow pan** button, or press the up-arrow key on your keyboard.

d. To pan down (south), click the **bottom-arrow pan** button, or press the down-arrow key on your keyboard.

e. To zoom out and display a wider area, click the − button on the Zoom slider or drag the Zoom slider down. Alternatively, you can press the − key on your keyboard.

f. To zoom in and display a smaller area, click the + button on the Zoom slider or drag the Zoom slider up. Alternatively, you can press the + key on your keyboard.

g. To drag the map in any direction, position the cursor on the map, click and hold the mouse button, and then drag the map around.

h. To center the map on a new location, position the cursor over that location and then double-click the mouse, or click the **Show My Location** button in the navigation controls.

> **Note** **Zoom Detail**
>
> The closer you zoom in, the more detail is displayed on the map. You won't see specific road information until you're fairly zoomed in; even then, major roads are displayed first and then minor roads are displayed on more extreme zoom levels.

Pan control —

Click to show current location —

Click to zoom in —
Zoom slider —

Click to zoom out —

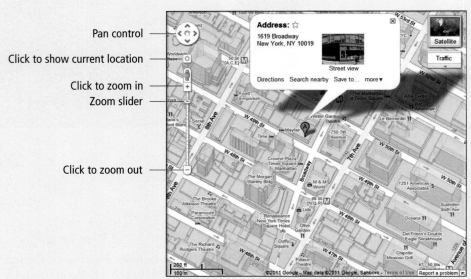

Figure 7.2 Hands-On Exercise 1, Step 2.

Step View Live Traffic Conditions

Refer to Figure 7.3 as you complete Step 3.

Google Maps displays live traffic conditions for many major cities around the world.

a. Generate a map for a given location.

b. Click the **Traffic** button.

Traffic for major roads appears as green (smoothly flowing traffic), yellow (busy), or red (congested). Road construction is indicated by a separate icon, as are road closures. And on interstate highways, you get the green/yellow/red separately for lanes in both directions.

> **Note** **Turn Off Traffic**
>
> To hide the traffic display, click the **Traffic** button again.

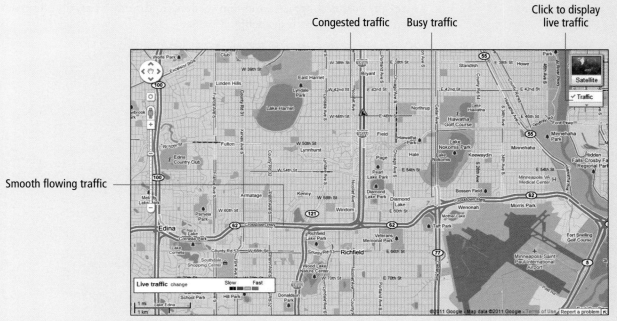

Congested traffic **Busy traffic** Click to display live traffic

Smooth flowing traffic

Figure 7.3 Hands-On Exercise 1, Step 3.

Step 4 Display Street View Photos

Refer to Figures 7.4 through 7.6 as you complete Step 4.

a. Generate a map of a given location.

b. Click and drag the **Street View** icon (the little man above the *Zoom* control) to a location on your map, but do not yet release the mouse button.

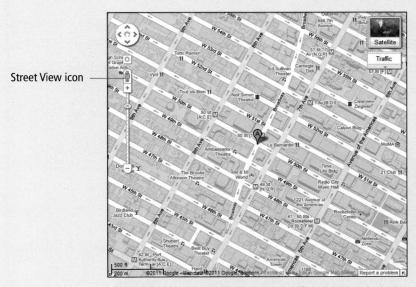

Street View icon

Figure 7.4 Hands-On Exercise 1, Steps 4a and 4b.

Note **Street View Availability**

If Street View is available for a location, the street on the map will turn blue when you start to drag the Street View icon. If Street View is not available for a given location, the Street View icon will not be present.

c. Hover the cursor above a location on the map to display a pop-up photo of the specific location if one is available.

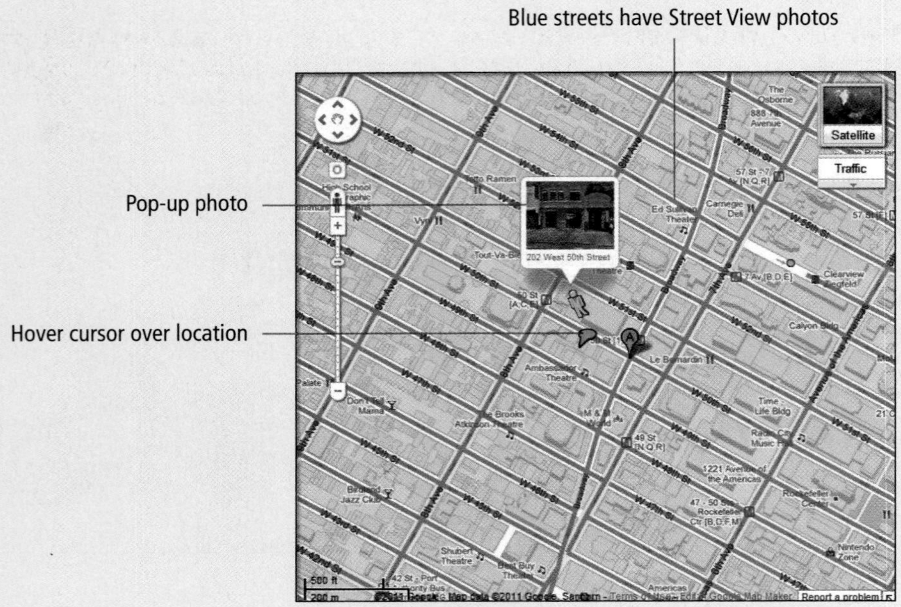

Blue streets have Street View photos

Pop-up photo

Hover cursor over location

Figure 7.5 Hands-On Exercise 1, Step 4c.

d. Release the mouse button to drop the icon onto the street and display a panoramic Street View photo of that location.

e. To pan left, right, up, or down the photo, click and drag a location on the map. Alternatively, you can use the *Pan* control in the navigation controls to pan around the photo.

f. To zoom in or out of the photo, use the *Zoom* control in the navigation controls.

g. To move up or down the street, click the direction arrows overlaid on the road.

h. To center on another location in the photo, double-click that location.

i. To switch back to regular map view, click the **x** at the top-right corner of the photo window.

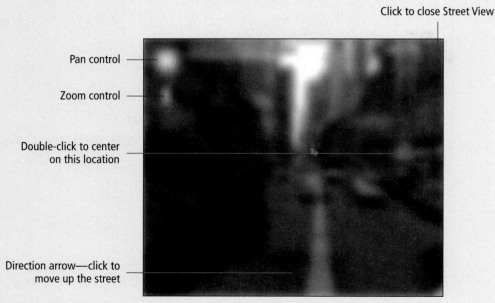

Click to close Street View

Pan control

Zoom control

Double-click to center on this location

Direction arrow—click to move up the street

Figure 7.6 Hands-On Exercise 1, Steps 4d through 4i.

Step 5 Display Satellite Images

Refer to Figures 7.7 and 7.8 as you complete Step 5.

By default, Google Maps displays a standard map of any location you enter. But that's not the only way you can view a location. Google Maps also incorporates satellite images, which let you get a bird's eye view of the actual location.

a. Generate a map of a given location.

b. Click the **Satellite** button at the top-right corner of the map.

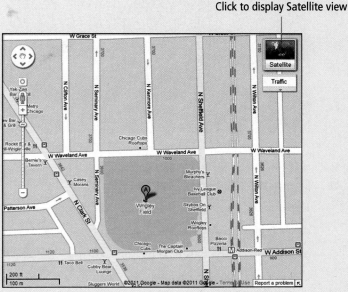

Click to display Satellite view

Figure 7.7 Hands-On Exercise 1, Steps 5a and 5b.

This displays the satellite map. The *Satellite* button changes to a *Map* button.

c. Use the standard navigation and *Zoom* controls to pan around and zoom in or out of the satellite image.

d. To display names on your satellite map, hover over the **Map** button and check the **Labels** option; uncheck this option for a less cluttered satellite map.

e. To display live traffic data in Satellite view, click the **Traffic** button; click the button again to turn off the display of traffic data.

f. To return to standard map view, click the **Map** button.

> **Note** **Not So Current**
>
> Google's satellite images are often less current than its map data, meaning that you could be looking at an image that was taken several months ago.

Click to display map view   Click to overlay traffic data

Pan control —

Zoom control —

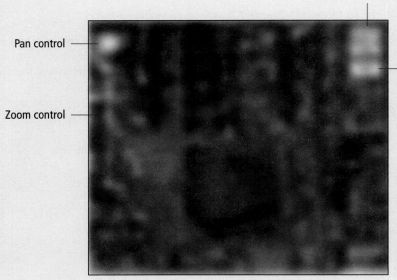

Figure 7.8 Hands-On Exercise 1, Steps 5c through 5f.

Step 6 Display Google Earth View

Refer to Figures 7.9 and 7.10 as you complete Step 6.

a. Generate a map of a given location.

b. Hover over the **Satellite** button to display the *Earth* button.

c. Click the **Earth** button.

> **Note** **Download Plug-in**
>
> The first time you access Google Earth view, you'll be prompted to download the Google Earth plug-in for your web browser. Follow the onscreen instructions to do so.

Click to switch   Hover over to display
to Earth view   Earth button

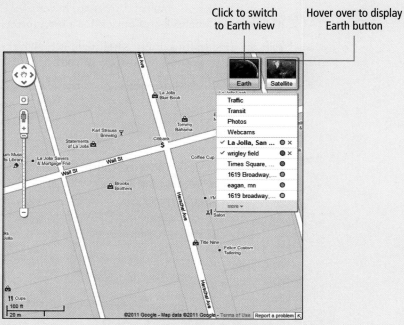

Figure 7.9 Hands-On Exercise 1, Steps 6a through 6c.

Google Maps now switches to Earth view.

d. To shift the viewing angle up, down, left, or right, use the *Look Around* control.

e. To move the location forward, backward, to the left, or to the right, use the *Move Around* control.

f. To zoom in or out of a location, use the *Zoom* control.

g. To return to standard map view, click the **Map** button.

> **Tip** ★ **Click and Drag**
>
> You can also click and drag the map itself to fly around the landscape.

Click to return to map view

Look Around control – use to shift viewing angle

Move Around control – use to move location

Zoom control – use to zoom in or out of location

Figure 7.10 Hands-On Exercise 1, Steps 6d through 6g.

Step 7 Display Overlay Data

Refer to Figure 7.11 as you complete Step 7.

a. Generate a map of a given location.

b. Hover over the **Satellite** button to display the pop-up menu.

c. Check one of the available overlays or click **More** to select additional overlays; uncheck those overlays you don't want displayed.

> **Note** **Multiple Overlays**
>
> You can display more than one overlay at the same time.

Hover over to display menu

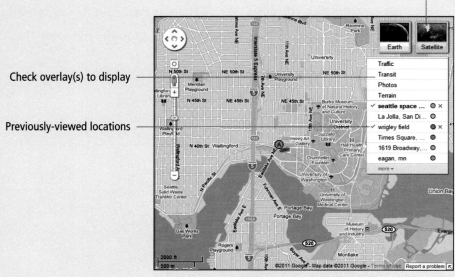

Check overlay(s) to display

Previously-viewed locations

Figure 7.11 Hands-On Exercise 1, Step 7.

Step ⑧ Print a Map

Refer to Figures 7.12 through 7.14 as you complete Step 8.

a. Generate a map of a given location.

b. Click the **Print** link above the map.

Click to print

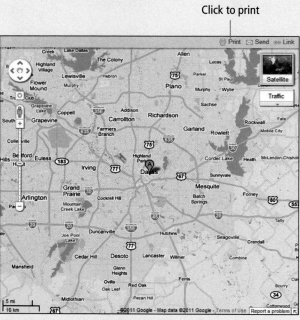

Figure 7.12 Hands-On Exercise 1, Steps 8a and 8b.

Google now displays a printable version of the map.

c. Click the **Print** link above the printable map.

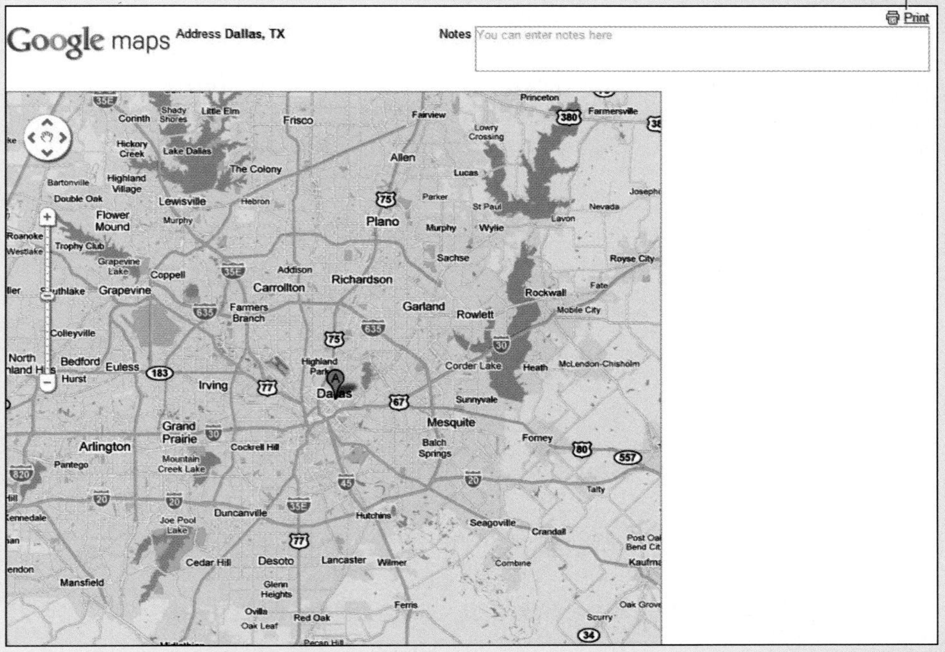

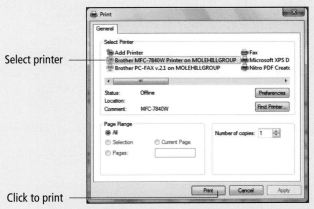

Click to print

Figure 7.13 Hands-On Exercise 1, Step 8c.

Your web browser's *Print* dialog box is now opened.

d. Select the desired printer and click the **Print** button.

Select printer

Click to print

Figure 7.14 Hands-On Exercise 1, Step 8d.

Objective 2

Search for a Nearby Business

Can you use Google Maps to find local businesses?

As part of its Google Maps service, Google hosts a large database of local businesses. This lets you use Google Maps to search for various types of companies within any area or neighborhood, or near any address.

Google Places A program, supplemental to Google Maps, that gathers information about local businesses.

Place page A page of information about a given business, as compiled by Google.

What is Google Places?

Google Maps gathers the bulk of its local retailer information from various Yellow Pages directories; it then supplements that with information submitted by individual businesses and reviews from customers. This information is part of the *Google Places* program, which feeds useful information to Google Maps. This information is displayed on a *Place page* for a given business; a Google Maps user views a Place page when he or she clicks the **more info** link for that business.

Hands-On Exercises

2 | Searching for a Nearby Business

Steps: 1. Search for a Local Business; **2.** View Business Information.

Use Figures 7.15 through 7.18 as a guide to the exercise.

Step 1 | Search for a Local Business

Refer to Figures 7.15 and 7.16 as you complete Step 1.

a. Generate a map of a given location.

b. Enter the name of a business or a type of business into the search box.

   If you're looking for a specific business, it's best to enter the full name of the business. For example, if you're looking for a Starbucks location, enter **starbucks** into the search box.

   If you're looking for any business of a given type, enter the category of business into the search box. For example, to look for all nearby coffeehouses, enter **coffee** into the search box.

c. Click the **Search Maps** button.

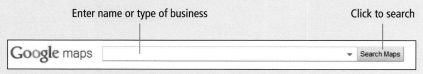

Figure 7.15 Hands-On Exercise 2, Steps 1a through 1c.

Pinpoint A specific location or business marked on a Google map.

Google now displays a map of the specified location with matching businesses displayed as *pinpoints* on the map and listed on the left side of the page.

d. To display businesses over a wider area, zoom out of the map. To view businesses closer to the location, zoom in to the map.

   By default, Google Maps lists ten businesses per page.

e. To display the next page of results, scroll down to the bottom of the information pane and click the **Next** link.

   The map will change (zoom in or out) to display this next batch of businesses; Google Maps typically lists the closest businesses first and then expands its results geographically.

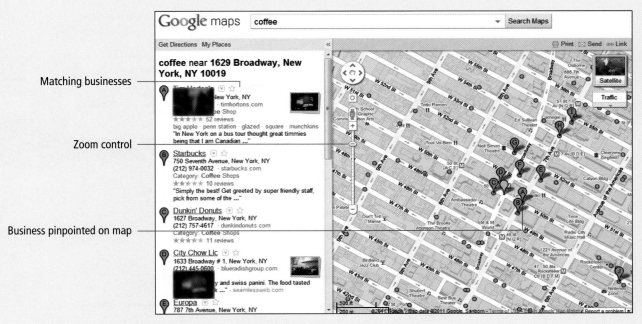

Matching businesses

Zoom control

Business pinpointed on map

Figure 7.16 Hands-On Exercise 2, Steps 1d and 1e.

Step 2 View Business Information

Refer to Figures 7.17 and 7.18 as you complete Step 2.

a. Generate a map and search for a given business or a type of business, as detailed in Hands-On Exercise 2, Step 1.

Each business displayed on the map is identified with a letter. Each business is also listed in the information pane, with more information about each business.

b. Click a business name on a pinpoint.

This displays an information balloon about the business.

c. To rate the business, click on the appropriate star, from 1 (lowest) to 5 (highest).

d. To read user reviews of the business, click the **Reviews** link.

e. To go to the business' website, click the website address.

f. To view directions to this business, click the **Directions** link.

g. To search near this business, click the **Search nearby** link.

h. To save this business to a list of your favorite maps, click the **Save to** link.

i. To view the business' *Place* page, click the **more info** link.

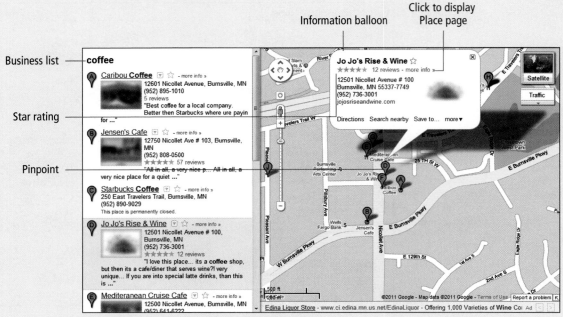

Figure 7.17 Hands-On Exercise 2, Step 2.

The Place page displays all the information Google knows about the business, including user reviews and photos.

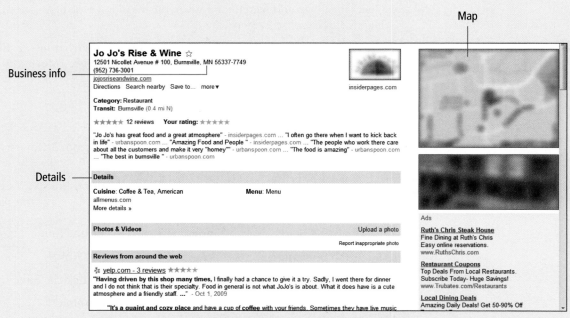

Figure 7.18 A typical Google Place page for a business.

Objective 3

Create a Custom Map

What is a map mashup?

Mashup A custom map that includes personal data overlaid on a Google map.

A *mashup* is a custom map created with Google Maps. This name is derived because you're mashing together a Google map with your own personal data. That data might simply be a set of coordinates so that you map a specific location, or they might be a collection of locations that you want to display on a map.

What is My Places?

My Places A subset of Google Maps that lets you create, save, and share custom maps.

My Places is a subset of Google Maps that lets you create, save, and share your own custom map mashups. A custom map can be as simple as a street map of a given location, or can include sophisticated features such as text annotations, location placemarks, and embedded photos and videos.

How can you highlight a location on a custom map?

Placemark A marker on a map that pinpoints a specific location.

The easiest way to highlight a location on a custom map is to mark that location with a *placemark*. A placemark is simply a little pinpoint graphic attached to a given point on the map.

Google offers dozens of these predesigned markers. In addition to somewhat generic icons in various colors, there are also custom markers for bars, restaurants, gas stations, webcams, and the like.

What can you do with a custom map?

Once you create a custom map with My Places, you can save it for future access from your Google Maps page. You can also share your map with others, embed it in a website or blog, or view the map in Google Earth. You can even collaborate with others to create group maps.

The following are some suggestions as to why you might want to create a custom map mashup.

- If you work for a business, you can use My Places to create a map of your company's headquarters, so that visitors can see where you are.

- If your company has multiple locations, you can map them all on a single custom map, and embed that map on your website.

- If you're in real estate, you can map all your properties for sale or rent in a given area.

- If you're in government or property planning, you can use My Places to create maps of a given area or jurisdiction, complete with boundary lines and markers.

- If you're an individual planning a vacation, you can map all the locations you want to visit during your trip.

Hands-On Exercises

3 | Creating a Custom Map

Steps: 1. Save a Map to My Places; **2.** View Your Custom Maps; **3.** Add a Placemark to a Map; **4.** Share a Custom Map.

Use Figures 7.19 through 7.27 as a guide to the exercise.

Step ❶ Save a Map to My Places

Refer to Figures 7.19 and 7.20 as you complete Step 1.

a. Generate a map of your desired location.

b. Click the **My Places** link in the left-hand pane.

> **Note First-Time Use**
>
> The first time you access the My Places feature, Google offers the option of viewing a tutorial on how to use My Places. View this if you like, or proceed to use My Places.

c. Click the **Create new map** link.

Click to display My Places pane

Click to create new map

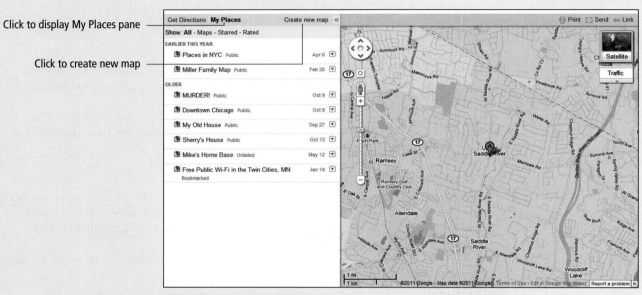

Figure 7.19 Hands-On Exercise 3, Steps 1a through 1c.

The Navigation pane now changes to display *Title* and *Description* boxes.

d. Enter a title for your map into the *Title* box.

e. Enter a brief description of your map into the *Description* box.

f. If you want your map to be shared with everyone, click the **Public** option. If you want your map to remain private, click the **Unlisted** option.

g. Click the **Save** button.

h. Click the **Done** button.

Your map is now saved to My Places.

Click when done
Enter map title
Enter map description
Click to save map
Click to make map public
Click to make map private

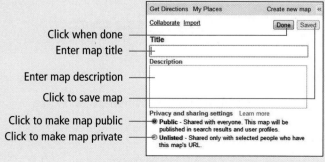

Figure 7.20 Hands-On Exercise 3, Steps 1d through 1h.

Step 2 View Your Custom Maps

Refer to Figure 7.21 as you complete Step 2.

All your custom maps are listed on the *My Places* tab in the Navigation pane.

a. Go to the main Google Maps page (**maps.google.com**).

b. Click the **My Places** tab in the Navigation pane.

c. Click a map name to display that specific custom map.

Click to display My Places pane

Click to display custom map

Figure 7.21 Hands-On Exercise 3, Step 2.

Step 3 Add a Placemark to a Map

Refer to Figures 7.22 through 7.25 as you complete Step 3.

a. From the Google Maps page, click the **My Places** tab to display your list of custom maps.

b. Click the link for the map you want to edit.

Click to display My Places tab

Click to edit custom map

Figure 7.22 Hands-On Exercise 3, Steps 3a and 3b.

The selected map is now displayed in the viewing pane.

c. Click the **Edit** button in the information pane.

Click to edit custom map

Figure 7.23 Hands-On Exercise 3, Step 3c.

This displays three editing buttons on the map itself: *Select/edit map features*, *Add a placemark*, and *Draw a line*.

d. Click the **Add a placemark** button.

e. Position your cursor on the map and click the location you want to highlight.

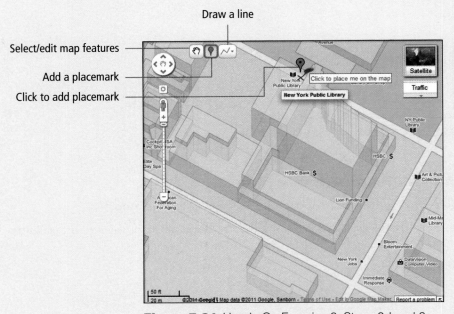

Figure 7.24 Hands-On Exercise 3, Steps 3d and 3e.

This places a placemark on the map and opens an information balloon for editing.

f. Enter the name of the placemark into the *Title* box.

g. Enter a description for the placemark into the *Description* box.

You can enter plain text, rich text, or HTML code.

h. To change the color or shape of the placemark, click the **Placemark** icon in the placemark balloon; this displays a menu of choices. Click a new icon to select it.

i. When done creating the placemark, click the **OK** button in the placemark balloon.

Repeat steps 3d through 3i to create additional placemarks.

j. When you're done adding placemarks, click the **Save** button in the left-hand pane.

Click to save changes   Enter placemark name   Click to change placemark shape or color

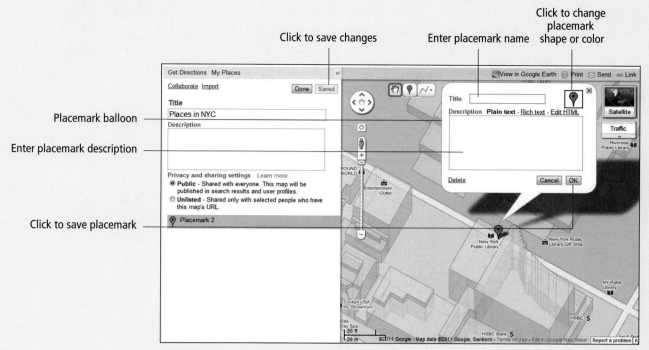

Placemark balloon

Enter placemark description

Click to save placemark

Figure 7.25 Hands-On Exercise 3, Steps 3f through 3j.

Step 4   Share a Custom Map

Refer to Figures 7.26 and 7.27 as you complete Step 4.

One of the nice things about My Places is that you can share them with others. For example, if you're an apartment owner, you might want to create a map of all your properties and then share it with potential renters via email. Google enables you to send a link to any custom map to others via Gmail.

a. Go to your My Places page and display the map you want to share.

b. Click the **Send** link on the right side above the map.

Click to send email

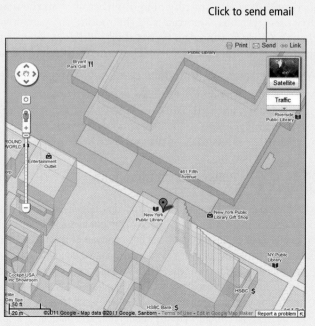

Figure 7.26 Hands-On Exercise 3, Steps 4a and 4b.

This displays the *Send to: Email* dialog box.

c. Enter the recipient's email address into the *To:* box.

d. If your email address is not entered automatically, enter it into the *From:* box.

e. Accept or edit the subject line in the *Subject:* box.

f. Enter a personal message into the *Message:* box.

g. Click the **Send** button to send the My Places link via Gmail.

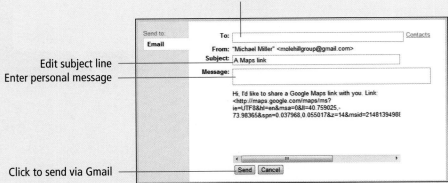

Figure 7.27 Hands-On Exercise 3, Steps 4c through 4g.

Objective 4

Generate Turn-by-Turn Directions

Can you use Google Maps to generate driving directions?

Google Maps does more than just display maps; it can also generate driving directions from one location to another. It's a simple matter of entering two locations, and letting Google get you directions from point A to point B (and even to points C and D).

How easy is it to modify your route?

If you don't like the specific directions that Google suggests, you can easily change your driving directions—just by dragging the route on the map. Start by generating your driving directions as normal and then locate the part of your route that you want to change. Click that location on the map, hold down your left mouse button, and then drag the route to a different location. The route readjusts to include the changes you've made.

What other types of directions can Google Maps generate?

Most people use Google Maps to generate driving directions; we are a nation of automobile travel, after all. But you can also use Google Maps to generate directions for travel via bicycle, public transit, and even walking. Just click the **By public transit**, **Walking**, or **Bicycling** buttons above the *Get Directions* pane.

 Public Transit Directions

When you generate public transit directions, Google will incorporate a variety of transportation methods, if that's what's necessary. You might find a route that tells you to walk to a bus stop, ride the bus, change buses, get off the bus and walk to a subway station, take the subway, and then walk the remaining distance to your destination. Google will also display the scheduled arrival and departure times for each type of public transportation used, as well as the names of each station or stop you need to use. It will also tell you how many stops there are along the route, and how much time you have between stops to make each transfer or change. This will help you determine the best possible route, in terms of both time and number of stops.

Hands-On Exercises

4 | Generating Turn-by-Turn Directions

Steps: 1. Generate Driving Directions; **2.** Generate Multiple-Stop Directions;
3. Reverse Your Directions; **4.** Print Your Directions.

Use Figures 7.28 through 7.32 as a guide to the exercise.

Step 1 Generate Driving Directions

Refer to Figure 7.28 as you complete Step 1.

a. Go to the Google Maps main page (**maps.google.com**).

b. Click the **Get Directions** tab in the left-hand pane.

  The left-hand pane now changes to include two search boxes.

c. Enter your starting location into the first *(A)* box.

d. Enter your ending location into the second *(B)* box.

e. Make sure the *By car* button, below the *Get Directions* tab, is selected.

f. Click the **Get Directions** button.

  Google now generates turn-by-turn driving directions for the given route and
  displays those directions beneath the *Get Directions* panel. The route itself is
  mapped in the map pane.

> **Tip** ☆ **Fine-Tune Your Route**
>
> You can, if you like, tell Google how you'd prefer to travel to your destination. Click the **Show options** link, below the *(B)* box. You can then check either the **Avoid highways** or **Avoid tolls** options. (You can also opt to display your route in miles or kilometers.)

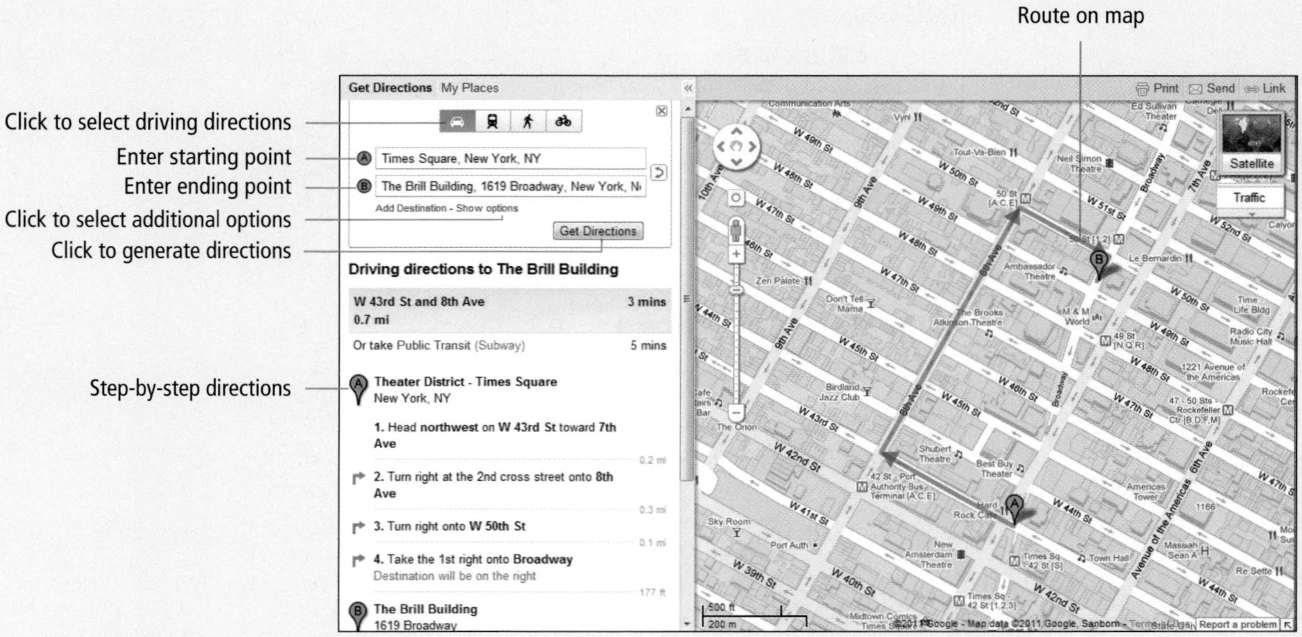

Route on map

Click to select driving directions
Enter starting point
Enter ending point
Click to select additional options
Click to generate directions

Step-by-step directions

Figure 7.28 Hands-On Exercise 4, Step 1.

Step 2   Generate Multiple-Stop Directions

Refer to Figure 7.29 as you complete Step 2.

By default, Google generates point-to-point directions. You can, however, add other stops to your route.

a. Generate directions from the starting point to your first stop, as described in Hands-On Exercise 4, Step 1.

b. Click the **Add Destination** link.

This extends the *Get Directions* panel to include a third *(C)* address box.

c. Enter your second stop into the *(C)* address box.

To enter additional stops, repeat steps 2b and 2c.

d. When you're done adding destinations, click the **Get Directions** button.

Enter new destination ———
Click to add another destination ———
Click to generate directions ———

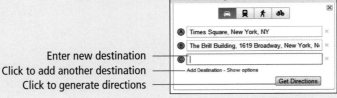

Figure 7.29 Hands-On Exercise 4, Step 2.

Step 3   Reverse Your Directions

Refer to Figure 7.30 as you complete Step 3.

a. Generate your initial driving directions.

b. Click the **Get reverse directions** button.

Google now swaps boxes *(A)* and *(B)* and then generates the appropriate reverse driving instructions to get you from your original end location back to your original start location.

Click to reverse directions ———

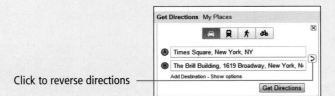

Figure 7.30 Hands-On Exercise 4, Step 3.

Step 4   Print Your Directions

Refer to Figures 7.31 and 7.32 as you complete Step 4.

a. Generate your driving directions.

b. Click the **Print** link above the map.

Click to print directions

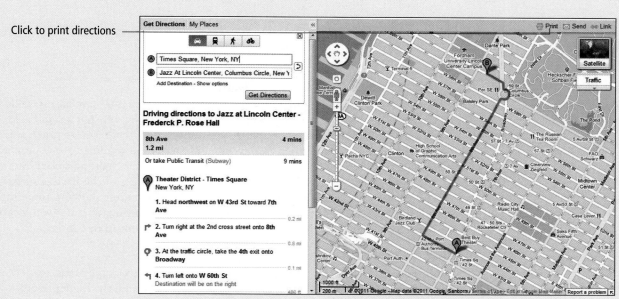

Figure 7.31 Hands-On Exercise 4, Steps 4a and 4b.

Google now generates a page of printable directions.

c. To display a small map of each individual step, click the **Maps** link.

d. To display a Street View photo of each individual step, click the **Street View** link.

e. To include a large overview map of your entire route, check the **Include large map** box.

f. Click the **Print** button.

Click to display photos for each step Click to display route map Click to print directions

Click to display maps for each step

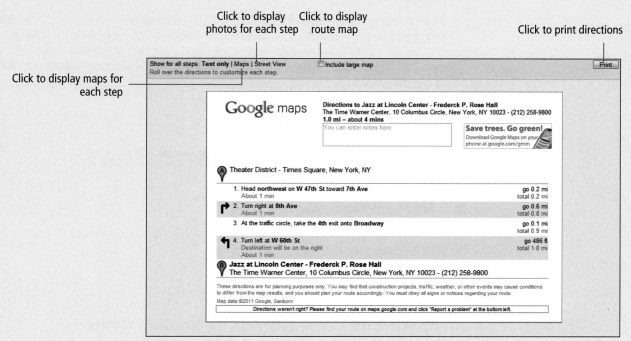

Figure 7.32 Hands-On Exercise 4, Steps 4c through 4f.

Objective 5

Navigate Google Earth

Google Earth A software program that generates high-resolution, 3D flybys of any location on the planet.

What is Google Earth?

Google Earth is a software program that lets you create, view, and save high-resolution, 3D flybys of any location on the planet. Unlike Google Maps, which is a web-based application, Google Earth is a traditional software application that retrieves much of its data from the web. That is, you run it from your computer as you would a normal program, but you need to be connected to the Internet to use some of its more advanced features.

Google Earth displays detailed satellite or aerial images of the Earth's surface. These images can be tilted to provide a 3D perspective, better showing topography, buildings, and the like. You can enter the address or coordinates of a given location, or use the program's navigation controls to fly to and zoom in to a location.

How can you use Google Earth?

Many people use Google Earth the same ways that they use Google Maps, to view a given location, plot driving directions, and the like. That said, the higher resolution of Google Earth photography, along with the 3D display, allows a more realistic viewing experience than what you get with Google Maps. And the ability to fly through the terrain in real time adds a kind of video-game perspective to the whole endeavor.

How do you download and install Google Earth?

To download and install Google Earth on your computer, go to **www.google.com/earth** and follow the onscreen instructions. There are three versions of Google Earth available: Google Earth (free), Google Earth Pro ($399), and Google Earth Enterprise (pricing varies by installation, but runs in the tens of thousands of dollars). Most users choose the free Google Earth version.

> **Note** **Requirements**
>
> Google Earth runs on computers running Windows 2000 and above (including Windows XP, Windows Vista, and Windows 7—both 32- and 64-bit versions), Mac OS X 10.3.9 and above, Linux Kernel 2.3 or above, and FreeBSD. On a Windows system, you'll need a minimum of 400MB free hard disk space (2GB space recommended) and a 3D-capable graphics card with at least 16MB of video RAM.

Hands-On Exercises

5 | Navigating Google Earth

Steps: 1. Navigate with the Onscreen Navigation Controls; **2.** Navigate with the Mouse; **3.** Search for Places.

Use Figures 7.33 and 7.34 as a guide to the exercise.

Step 1 Navigate with the Onscreen Navigation Controls

Refer to Figure 7.33 as you complete Step 1.

When you first launch Google Earth, you see a large view of the planet Earth, as well as surrounding navigation and display controls. The major parts of the screen include three panes on the left side of the screen (*Search*, *Places*, and *Layers*), the main view display, and the navigation controls. You start your journey through Google Earth from this 3D view of the globe. You can zoom in on any location on the planet, and navigate from place to place around the planet, using the onscreen navigation controls.

a. Go to the Google Earth main page (**www.google.com/earth**) to launch Google Earth.

b. Use the *Zoom* control to zoom in or out of the map. Move the slider up or click the + button to display a closer, more detailed view; move the slider down or click the − button to display a further away, less detailed view.

c. Click and hold anywhere on the outside edge of the **Move** control to move around the globe.

d. Click and hold anywhere on the outside edge of the **Look** control to move around from a single vantage point, as if you're turning your head.

e. Click and drag the **Rotate** control (the outer ring of the *Look* control) to rotate the view.

Rotating clockwise moves north to the right; rotating counterclockwise moves north to the left.

f. Double-click the **North** button (the *N* at the top of the *Rotate* control) to return north to the straight-up position.

> **Tip** ⭐ **Just Like a Joystick**
>
> Both the *Look* and *Move* controls work like a joystick—that is, you can use your mouse to click and hold each control and then drag your mouse to move or look in the designated direction.

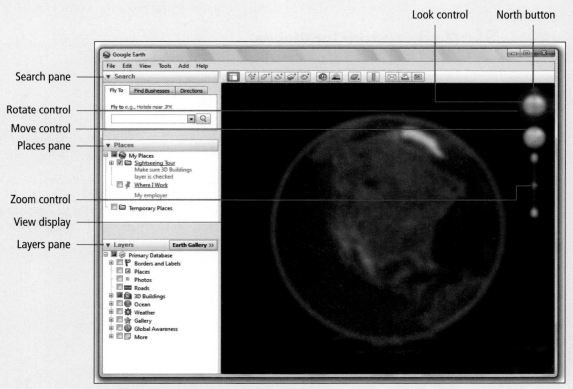

Figure 7.33 Hands-On Exercise 5, Step 1.

Step 2 Navigate with the Mouse

If you're handy with your mouse, you can use it alone (without the onscreen navigation controls) to zoom around Google Earth.

a. To zoom in to a specific point, double-click on that point on the map.

b. To generally zoom in, use your mouse's scroll wheel (if it has one) to scroll away from you.

You can also generally zoom in by clicking and holding the right mouse button and then moving your mouse down (towards you).

c. To generally zoom out, use your mouse's scroll wheel to scroll toward you.

You can also click and hold the right mouse button and then move your mouse up (away from you).

d. To zoom continuously in or out, hold down the right mouse button, briefly move the mouse down (to zoom in) or up (to zoom out), and then quickly release the mouse button.

To stop the zoom, click once in the viewer.

e. To move the map in any direction, click and hold the left mouse button and then drag your mouse in the desired direction.

f. To drift continuously in any direction, hold down the left mouse button, briefly move the mouse in the desired direction, and then quickly release the mouse button.

To stop the drift, click once in the viewer.

g. To tilt the view, hold down the **Shift** key on your keyboard and then move the mouse's scroll wheel up or down.

Alternatively, if your mouse has a depressible scroll wheel or middle button, depress the scroll wheel or middle button and then move the mouse up or down.

h. To rotate the view, hold down the **Ctrl** key on your keyboard, click the left mouse button, and then move the mouse either left or right.

Alternatively, if your mouse has a depressible scroll wheel or middle button, depress the scroll wheel or middle button and then move the mouse either left or right.

Step ③ Search for Places

Refer to Figure 7.34 as you complete Step 3.

a. Select the **Fly To** tab in the *Search* pane.

b. Enter the desired location into the search box.

c. Click the **Search** (magnifying glass) button.

Google Earth now zooms into the location you entered.

> **Note** **Multiple Matches**
>
> If you enter a general location that could have multiple matches, Google Earth displays those matches at the bottom of the *Search* pane. Click a specific location to zoom to that place.

Fly To tab ⎯
Enter location ⎯
Click to search ⎯

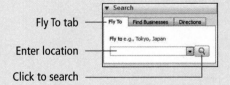

Figure 7.34 Hands-On Exercise 5, Step 3.

Objective 6

Use Layers

What is a layer?

Layer In Google Earth, a set of data overlaid on the basic map.

One of the things that makes Google Earth so useful is its capability to overlay other data on top of its maps. This data is added in the form of *layers*; Google Earth includes layers for borders, labels, places, roads, and much, much more.

Each layer in Google Earth adds a level of detail to the underlying map. The map itself is nothing more than the satellite or aerial photo; every piece of information on the map, every road and label and location marked, is part of a layer that is overlaid on top of that basic map.

What layers are available in Google Earth?

Google Earth supplies a variety of layers in what it calls its "primary database." Additional layers are supplied by third parties and other users. Table 7.3 details those layers that are available in the primary database.

Table 7.3—Google Earth Primary Layers	
Layer	**Description**
Borders and Labels	Layers that describe physical and virtual borders and coastlines, including country names; also includes labels for various places
Places	Displays major points of interest—hotels, restaurants, and so forth
Photos	Displays photos of the selected area taken by users of the Panoramio photo-sharing service
Roads	Displays road names
3D Buildings	For many major cities, displays 3D buildings, in either Photorealistic or Gray representations
Ocean	Includes a number of separate layers regarding features of the oceans and marine life
Weather	Consists of several weather-related layers, including Clouds, Radar, Conditions and Forecasts, and Information
Gallery	Consists of individual layers submitted by third parties
Global Awareness	Contains several layers regarding environmental issues
More	Includes a variety of different layers, including Park/Recreation Areas, Geographic Features, Place Categories, Transportation, Traffic, Wikipedia, GeoEye Featured Imagery, Spot Image, DigitalGlobe Coverage, and U.S. Government

Places of interest Specific locations overlaid on a Google Earth map.

What are places of interest?

Many of the layers available in Google Earth contain what are known as *places of interest* (POIs). These are specific locations overlaid on a map, such as ATMs, restaurants, and gas stations.

Hands-On Exercises

6 | Using Layers

Steps: 1. Display a Layer; **2.** Display Places of Interest.

Use Figures 7.35 and 7.36 as a guide to the exercise.

Step 1 Display a Layer

Refer to Figure 7.35 as you complete Step 1.

a. Go to the *Layers* pane.

Layers are organized into categories and subcategories.

b. Check the desired layer(s) to display.

To hide a layer, uncheck it in the *Layers* pane.

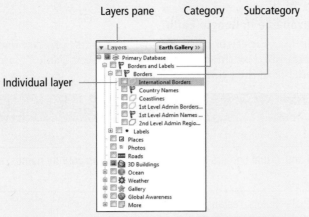

Figure 7.35 Hands-On Exercise 6, Step 1.

Step 2 Display Places of Interest

Refer to Figure 7.36 as you complete Step 2.

Many layers display individual POIs on the underlying map.

a. Display the desired layer.

POI are now displayed on the map.

b. Click a POI to display an information balloon for that item.

Within this info box is information about this location, as well as links to other information.

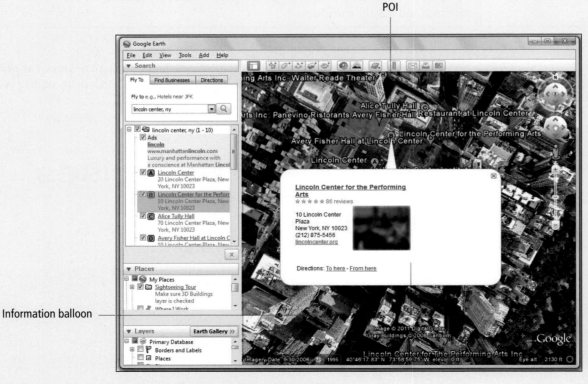

Figure 7.36 Hands-On Exercise 6, Step 2.

Objective 7

Generate Google Earth Driving Directions

Can Google Earth display driving directions?

Google Earth is great for looking at places and finding information about those places. But you can also use Google Earth to map driving directions, just as you can with Google Maps.

How do Google Earth driving directions differ from those in Google Maps?

The big difference in using Google Earth for driving directions is that your directions are mapped in a 3D view, so you can get more of a bird's-eye view of where you'll be driving. In addition, and even more fun, Google Earth actually lets you "drive" your route—in full 3D glory.

Hands-On Exercises

7 | Generating Google Earth Driving Directions

Steps: 1. Generate Directions; **2.** Tour Your Route; **3.** Print Directions.

Use Figures 7.37 through 7.40 as a guide to the exercise.

Step 1 Generate Directions

Refer to Figure 7.37 as you complete Step 1.

a. Go to the *Search* pane and select the **Directions** tab.

b. Enter your starting location into the *From* box.

c. Enter your ending location into the *To* box.

d. Click the **Begin Search** button.

Your route is mapped onscreen, with each turn marked on the map. Turn-by-turn directions are also listed in the *Search* pane.

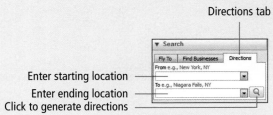

Figure 7.37 Hands-On Exercise 7, Step 1.

Step 2 Tour Your Route

Refer to Figure 7.38 as you complete Step 2.

Once you have your route displayed onscreen, you can use Google Earth's tour feature to "fly" the complete route in the viewer.

a. Generate the directions, as described in Hands-On Exercise 7, Step 1.

b. Select the **Route** item at the end of the directions listing.

c. Click the **Play Tour** button.

Google Earth now zooms you through your route, as if you were flying through it.

> **Tip** ★ **Playback Controls**
>
> During the course of the ride through your route, Google Earth displays playback controls in the map view window. You can pause or resume the playback at any point, or click the fast forward or reverse buttons to speed your way through (or back through) the route. You can also use the slider control to go to a specific location on the route. Click the **Repeat** button to continuously play the tour, or click the **Save** button to save this tour in your *Places* folder.

Click to display tour controls ⎯

Click to play tour ⎯

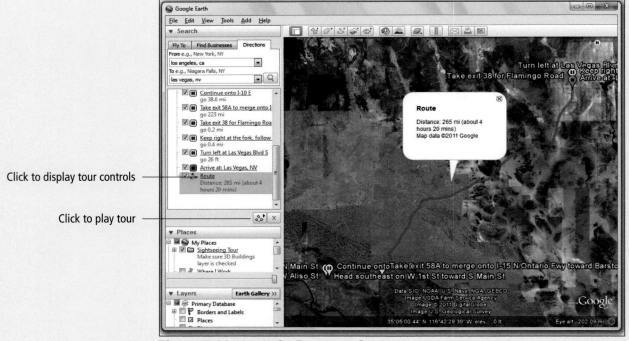

Figure 7.38 Hands-On Exercise 7, Step 2.

Step 3 Print Directions

Refer to Figures 7.39 and 7.40 as you complete Step 3.

a. Click the **Printable view** link in the directions listing.

Click to display printable view
in your web browser

Figure 7.39 Hands-On Exercise 7, Step 3a.

This opens a Google Maps web page in a new browser window, with the directions displayed in that window.

b. Click the **Print** link to print the directions.

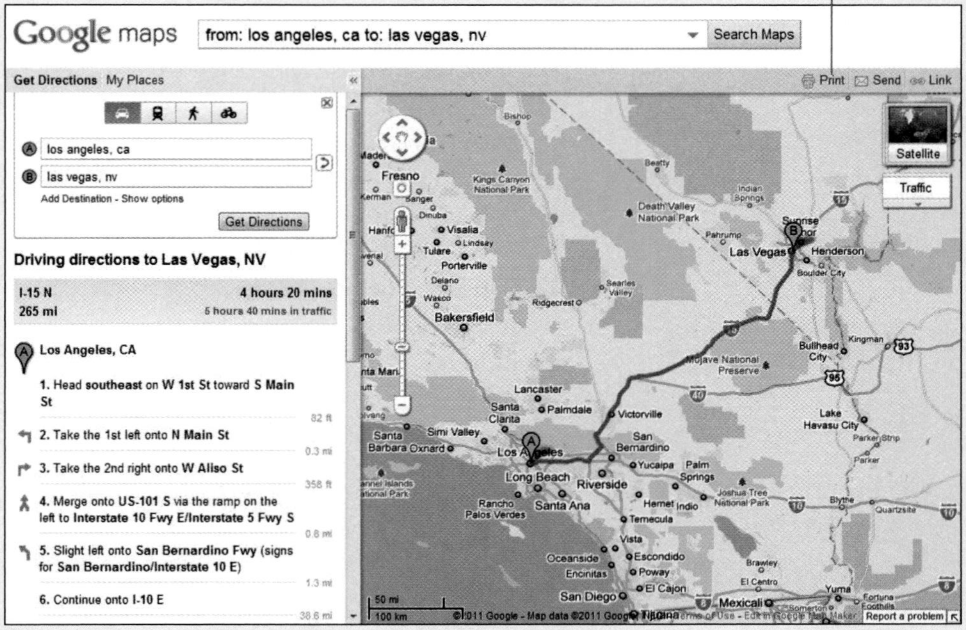

Click to print directions

Figure 7.40 Hands-On Exercise 7, Step 3b.

Summary

In this chapter, you learned how to use Google Maps to generate maps and directions. You also learned how to create and share your own custom maps. Finally, you learned how to use Google Earth to display detailed 3D maps and driving directions.

Key Terms

Earth view 131
Google Earth 154
Google Maps 130
Google Places 142
Layer 156
Mashup 145
My Places 145

Overlay. 131
Pinpoint. 142
Place page 142
Placemark 145
Places of interest 157
Street View .130

Multiple Choice Questions

1. Which of the following is *not* a Google Maps view?

    (a) Map view

    (b) Street View

    (c) Bird's-eye view

    (d) Satellite view

2. How are Google Maps Street View photos obtained?

    (a) From volunteers in local neighborhoods, using their own cameras

    (b) From a special revolving camera fitted on the top of a moving car

    (c) From official photographs submitted by local towns and cities

    (d) From public domain photos uploaded to the Flickr photo-sharing site

3. Where do Google Maps Satellite view photos come from?

    (a) Satellites (satellite photography)

    (b) Airplanes (aerial photography)

    (c) Blimps

    (d) Both (a) and (b)

    (e) Both (a) and (c)

4. Which of the following is *not* an available Google Maps overlay?

    (a) MP3s

    (b) Traffic

    (c) Photos

    (d) Terrain

5. Which of the following is *not* a valid address format for Google Maps?

   (a) new york, ny

   (b) 1619 broadway, new york, ny

   (c) 1619 broadway, new york, 10019

   (d) broadway and 50th, 10019

   (e) All of these are valid address formats.

6. When viewing live traffic conditions on a Google Map, what does the color yellow indicate?

   (a) Smooth flowing traffic

   (b) Busy traffic

   (c) Congested traffic

   (d) Use caution when driving

7. Where does the information on a Place page come from?

   (a) Yellow Pages directories

   (b) Google searches

   (c) Information submitted by individual businesses

   (d) Both (a) and (b)

   (e) Both (a) and (c)

8. To modify a route generated in Google Maps, do the following:

   (a) Click and drag the route on the map.

   (b) Click the Modify route link.

   (c) Go to the Advanced options pane and enter specific instructions.

   (d) You can't change a route in Google Maps.

9. Google Maps *cannot* generate the following type of directions:

   (a) Public transit

   (b) Biking

   (c) Flying

   (d) Walking

10. What is one of the major differences in driving directions generated by Google Earth vs. Google Maps?

   (a) Google Earth lets you add multiple stops.

   (b) Google Earth lets you drag a route to modify it.

   (c) Google Earth lets you generate walking and biking directions.

   (d) Google Earth lets you take a 3D fly through your route.

Fill in the Blank

Write the correct word or words in the space provided.

1. Google Maps was originally launched as part of the _____ _____ product.

2. The Google Maps view that displays street-level photographs of a location is called _____ _____.

3. A(n) _____ is a custom map that includes personal data overlaid on a Google map.

4. _____ _____ is a subset of Google Maps that lets you create and save custom maps.

5. In Google Maps, detailed information about a business is displayed on that business' _____ page.

6. To highlight a location on a custom map, create a(n) _____.

7. To display more data in Google Earth, activate a(n) _____.

8. In Google Earth, specific locations on a map are known as _____ _____ _____.

9. The free version of Google Earth is called _____ _____.

10. In Google Earth, to move around a single vantage point, as if you're turning your head, use the _____ control.

Practice Exercises

1. **Custom Map**
Create a custom map of your hometown. Use placeholders to place several of your favorite locations on the map. Email the link to your map to your instructor.

2. **Driving Directions**
Generate driving directions from your home to campus. Print the directions and hand them in to your instructor.

Critical Thinking

1. Google has been very aggressive in taking Street View photos to add to Google Maps. Many individuals and localities have objected to Google taking these pictures, even though they're of public locations, charging that they are an invasion of privacy. Write a short paper discussing this situation, and state your opinion on who's right—Google or the privacy-minded individuals and localities.

2. You can use both Google Maps and Google Earth to generate maps and driving directions. Write a short paper discussing why and when you might want to use one application over another; discuss the pros and cons of each application for both maps and driving directions.

Credits

Google, Blogger, and Picasa screenshots reprinted by permission.

CHAPTER 8

Using Gmail

Objectives

After you read this chapter, you will be able to:

1. Sign Up for a Gmail Account

2. Manage Your Inbox

3. Send and Receive Email Messages

4. Protect against Spam and Viruses

5. Manage Your Contacts

6. Customize Gmail

The following Hands-On Exercises will help you accomplish the chapter objectives:

Hands-On Exercises

EXERCISES	SKILLS COVERED
1. Signing Up for a Gmail Account	**Step 1:** Sign Up for a Gmail Account **Step 2:** Sign In to Gmail
2. Managing Your Inbox	**Step 1:** Search Your Inbox **Step 2:** Use Gmail's Advanced Search Options **Step 3:** Star an Important Message **Step 4:** Flag a Message as Important **Step 5:** Assign a Label to a Message **Step 6:** View Messages with a Common Label **Step 7:** Archive Old Messages **Step 8:** Filter Incoming Messages **Step 9:** Delete Messages from the Inbox
3. Sending and Receiving Email Messages	**Step 1:** Read an Email Message **Step 2:** View a Gmail Conversation **Step 3:** Reply to a Message **Step 4:** Forward a Message **Step 5:** Create a New Email Message **Step 6:** Add a Signature to Your Messages **Step 7:** Attach a File to a Message **Step 8:** View or Download an Attached File
4. Protecting against Spam	**Step 1:** Report a Message as Spam **Step 2:** Remove a Legitimate Message from Your Spam List **Step 3:** Permanently Delete Messages from Your Spam List
5. Managing Your Contacts	**Step 1:** Create a New Contact **Step 2:** Display Your Contacts **Step 3:** Delete a Contact **Step 4:** Create a Contact Group **Step 5:** Send a Message to a Contact or Contact Group
6. Customizing Gmail	**Step 1:** Change Gmail's Visual Theme **Step 2:** Activate Vacation Mode **Step 3:** Change the Contents of a Priority Inbox Section **Step 4:** Delete a Priority Inbox Section **Step 5:** Add a New Priority Inbox Section

Objective 1

Sign Up for a Gmail Account

Gmail Google's web-based email service.

Email Electronic mail, a way of delivering messages over the Internet.

POP email A type of email service where messages are stored on an email server and delivered directly to users' computers via email client software. (POP stands for Post Office Protocol, the protocol used to retrieve email messages from the server.)

What is Gmail?

Gmail is a web-based **email** service, part of Google's suite of online applications. You can use Gmail to send and receive email from any computer with Internet access. Your messages are stored on Google's servers, so they're always accessible no matter where you are.

How does Gmail differ from other email services?

Gmail differs from traditional **POP email** in that it is web-based, and does not require the use of a dedicated email application. With web-based email, all messages are delivered via and stored in the cloud; in the case of Gmail, messages are stored on Google's servers. Gmail messages can be read and sent from any computer connected to the Internet; no special software is required.

How much does it cost to use Gmail?

Gmail is a free service; anyone can establish an account for no charge. Because it's web-based, there's no software to download. When you sign up for your Gmail account, you get assigned your email address (in the form of *name*@gmail.com) and you get access to the Gmail inbox page. As of summer 2011, Gmail offered more than 7.5GB of storage for users.

Hands-On Exercises

1 │ Signing Up for a Gmail Account

Steps: 1. Sign Up for a Gmail Account; **2.** Sign In to Gmail.

Use Figures 8.1 through 8.4 as a guide to the exercise.

Sign Up for a Gmail Account

Refer to Figures 8.1 through 8.3 as you complete Step 1.

If you already have a Google account, that account serves as your Gmail account. If you don't yet have a Google account, you can create a new account from the Gmail page.

a. From your web browser, go to **mail.google.com**.

b. Click the **Create an account** button.

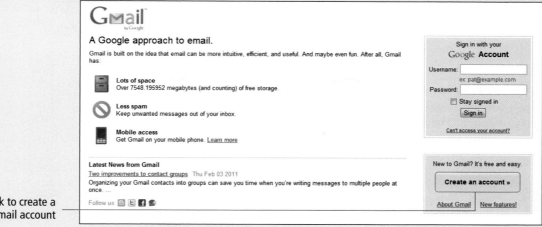

Click to create a new Gmail account

Figure 8.1 Hands-On Exercise 1, Steps 1a and 1b.

c. When the *Create an Account* page appears, enter your first name and last name into the *First name* and *Last name* boxes.

d. Enter the username you'd like to use (at least six characters) into the *Desired Login Name* box and then click the **check availability!** button.

   If your chosen username is available, Google tells you so, and you can proceed to the next step. If that name isn't available, Google suggests some options; select one of the options or enter a new username.

e. Enter your desired password into the *Choose a password* box and then enter it again into the *Re-enter password* box.

 Create a Strong Password

> To create a stronger password, create a longer password. You can also strengthen your password by including letters, numbers, and special characters. (Google will tell you how strong your password is as you type it.)

f. Check the **Stay signed in** box only if you are using a private computer; do not check this if you are using a shared or lab computer.

Alert! **Don't Stay Signed In**

> If you're using a public computer, selecting the **Stay signed in** option could enable strangers to access your account after you've left the computer, thus compromising your account.

g. If you want Google to track your online activities to better fine-tune your search results, check the **Enable Web History** box.

h. Select a security question from the **Security Question** list and then enter the answer to that question into the *Answer* box.

i. Enter a secondary email address (your home or school address) into the *Recovery email* box, to be used in case you ever have problems accessing your Gmail account.

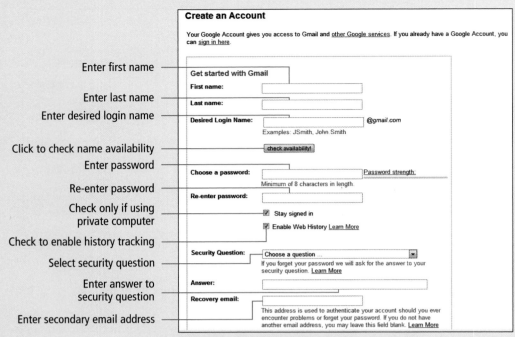

Enter first name

Enter last name

Enter desired login name

Click to check name availability

Enter password

Re-enter password

Check only if using
private computer

Check to enable history tracking

Select security question

Enter answer to
security question

Enter secondary email address

Figure 8.2 Hands-On Exercise 1, Steps 1c through 1i.

j. Select your country from the *Location* list.

k. Enter your date of birth, in the form of MM/DD/YYYY, into the *Birthday* box.

l. Type the appropriate characters into the *Word Verification* box; this helps to prevent automated software from signing up for accounts (typically for spam purposes).

m. Read the *Terms of Service* and then click the **I accept. Create my account.** button.

Google now creates your account and assigns you the requested email address, in the form of *username*@gmail.com.

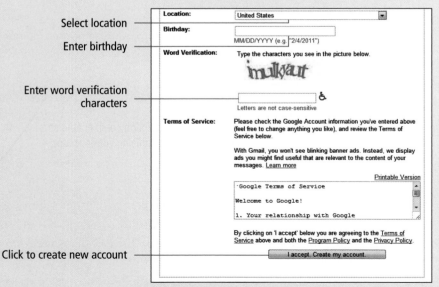

Select location

Enter birthday

Enter word verification
characters

Click to create new account

Figure 8.3 Hands-On Exercise 1, Steps 1j through 1m.

Sign In to Gmail

Refer to Figure 8.4 as you complete Step 2.

You can sign in to your Gmail account with a dedicated Gmail username and password, or with an existing Google account username and password.

a. Go to **mail.google.com**.

b. Enter your username into the *Username* box.

c. Enter your password into the *Password* box.

d. To stay signed in for the day, without having to re-enter your username and password, check the **Stay signed in** box.

e. Click the **Sign in** button.

Enter username
Enter password
Check to stay signed in
Click to sign in

Figure 8.4 Hands-On Exercise 1, Step 2.

Objective 2

Manage Your Inbox

How are messages organized in Gmail?

Inbox The main storage area for new incoming email messages.

As with most email services, Gmail stores all incoming messages in a common *inbox*. Unlike other services, however, Gmail doesn't use folders to organize messages. Instead, Gmail pushes search as the way to find the messages you want—that is, all messages are stored in the inbox, but you can search for specific messages you want to read.

Label A keyword or tag that describes an email message.

Gmail does, however, let you "tag" each message with one or more *labels*. This has the effect of creating virtual folders, as you can search and sort your messages by any of these labels.

What is the Priority Inbox?

Priority Inbox A special Gmail inbox that organizes messages in order of importance.

In addition to the traditional inbox, which stores all incoming messages, Gmail also offers a *Priority Inbox.* If the Priority Inbox is not displayed by default, you can activate it by clicking the **Settings** link on the Gmail homepage (or clicking **Options** and selecting **Mail settings**), then selecting the **Priority Inbox** tab. Go to the *Show Priority Inbox* section and select **Show Priority Inbox** and click the **Save Changes** button. Return to the Priority Inbox tab of the *Settings* page and select **Priority Inbox** from the *Default inbox* list.

The Priority Inbox differs from the regular inbox, in that it tries to organize your messages in order of importance. The first section of the Priority Inbox is for **Important and unread** messages; next is a section for **Starred** messages; the final section, where all other messages reside, is labeled **Everything else.**

How are messages displayed in the inbox?

Snippet A short excerpt from an email message.

Each message in the Gmail inbox is listed with the message's sender, the subject of the message, a short *snippet* or excerpt from the message itself, and the date or time the message was sent (Figure 8.5). (The snippet is typically the first line of the message text.) If you've assigned a label to a message, the label appears in green before the message subject.

Unread messages are listed in bold against the white page background. After a message has been read, it's displayed in normal, nonbold text with a blue shaded background.

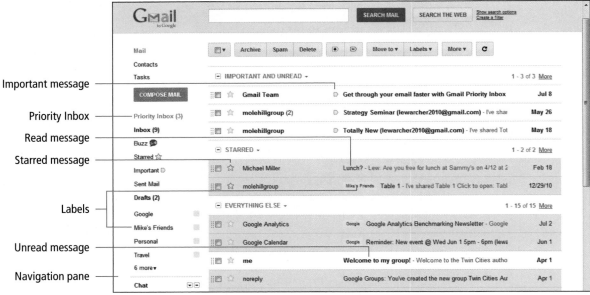

Figure 8.5 The Gmail homepage and Priority Inbox.

What other views are available?

By default, Gmail displays the Priority Inbox. You can, however, select other views by clicking the appropriate link in the Navigation pane on the left side. For example, to display sent messages only, click the **Sent Mail** link.

How can you work with messages in the inbox?

To perform an action on a message or group of messages, put a check mark by the message(s) and then click one of the buttons at the top or bottom of the list. Additional actions are available by clicking the **More actions** list; this displays a menu of options that let you mark a message as read or unread, add or remove a star from a message, and so forth.

What is a starred message?

Star A means of flagging important email messages.

If you find a message that you think is more important than other messages, you can *star* that message. In effect, Gmail "starring" is the same as the "flagging" feature you find in competing email services and programs.

Is there any other way to flag important messages?

Gmail's Priority Inbox lets you mark selected messages as "important." Messages marked as important get displayed first in the Priority Inbox, in the Important and unread section. Gmail also learns from the messages you mark as important to flag similar messages the same way going forward.

Do all old messages stay in the inbox?

If you're a frequent emailer, chances are your Gmail inbox will get very large very quickly. This is particularly true with Gmail, as you can't move messages from the inbox into folders.

Archive A means of storing older or inactive email messages.

Fortunately, when your inbox becomes too cluttered with messages, Gmail lets you *archive* older messages. When you archive a message, it moves out of the inbox into a larger area called All Mail. Because all your Gmail searches search the All Mail messages, one strategy is to archive all messages after you've read them, thus freeing up the inbox for only your most recent messages.

Can you filter incoming messages?

Filter A means of applying one or more actions to incoming messages that meet specific criteria.

Another way to organize your email messages—specifically, to manage what happens to them when they arrive in your inbox—is to apply *filters* to all incoming messages. Gmail lets you create up to 20 filters that identify certain types of incoming messages and then handle them in a specified manner.

For example, you might want to create a filter that applies a label to all messages with certain words in the subject line. Or you could star all messages that come from a particular person. Or forward all messages from one sender to another recipient. Or just automatically delete all messages from a particular sender or on a particular subject.

What types of filter actions are available?

Gmail lets you choose from nine different actions for your filters:

- Skip the inbox (automatically archive the message)
- Mark as read
- Star it
- Apply the label (choose from a list or create a new label)
- Forward it to (a specified email address)
- Delete it
- Never send it to the Spam folder
- Always mark it as important
- Never mark it as important

 Archiving vs. Deleting

Given Gmail's 7.5GB storage capacity, Google recommends archiving old messages rather than deleting them—just in case you ever need them. It's kind of a pack-rat approach to email management, but that's what happens when storage is virtually unlimited and search tools are fairly effective.

Hands-On Exercises

2 | Managing Your Inbox

Steps: 1. Search Your Inbox; **2.** Use Gmail's Advanced Search Options; **3.** Star an Important Message; **4.** Flag a Message as Important; **5.** Assign a Label to a Message; **6.** View Messages with a Common Label; **7.** Archive Old Messages; **8.** Filter Incoming Messages; **9.** Delete Messages from the Inbox.

Use Figures 8.6 through 8.19 as a guide to the exercise.

Step **Search Your Inbox**

Refer to Figures 8.6 and 8.7 as you complete Step 1.

Keyword A word included as part of a search query.

a. Enter your search query, in the form of one or more *keywords*, into the search box at the top of any Gmail page.

> **Note** **No Automatic Matching**
>
> Unlike Google's web search, Gmail search doesn't recognize matches to partial strings, plurals, misspellings, and the like. If you search for **dog**, for example, Gmail won't recognize **dogs**, **dogged**, or **doggy**.

b. Click the **Search Mail** button.

Enter search query   Click to search

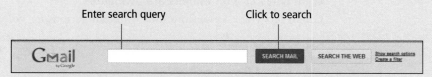

Figure 8.6 Hands-On Exercise 2, Steps 1a and 1b.

Gmail now returns a search results page. This page lists messages in which the keywords you entered appear anywhere in the email—in the subject line, in the message text, or in the sender or recipient lists.

c. Click a message to read it.

Click to read
Search results

Figure 8.7 Hands-On Exercise 2, Step 1c.

Step ② Use Gmail's Advanced Search Options

Refer to Figures 8.8 and 8.9 as you complete Step 2.

The more messages in your inbox, the more you'll need to fine-tune your email searches. Fortunately, Gmail makes this easy with an advanced *Search Options* pane.

a. From any Gmail page, click the **Show search options** link near the search box.

Click to display
advanced search options

Figure 8.8 Hands-On Exercise 2, Step 2a.

This expands the top of the page to display the *Search Options* pane. You can use any or all the options presented here for your search.

b. To search only for messages from a selected person, enter that person's name (or part of his or her name) into the *From:* field.

c. To search only for messages to a selected person or email address, enter that person's name or address into the *To:* field.

d. To search only in the *Subject* field of messages, enter one or more keywords into the *Subject:* field.

e. To limit your search to certain types of messages, click the **Search** drop-down list and make a selection.

You can search within All Mail, Inbox, Starred, Sent Mail, Drafts, and so forth. You can also limit your search to messages with a specific label.

f. To search for messages that include specific keywords, enter those keywords into the *Has the words:* field.

g. To exclude messages that contain one or more specific words, enter those words into the *Doesn't have:* field.

h. To search only for messages with files attached, check the **Has attachment** box.

i. To search for messages by date, select a timeframe (1 day, 3 days, 1 week, 2 weeks, 1 month, 2 months, 6 months, 1 year) from the **Date within:** list and then enter a specific date into the related box.

j. Click the **Search Mail** button to initiate your search.

Search by label   Search for messages   Include   Exclude
or message type   with attachments   these words   these words

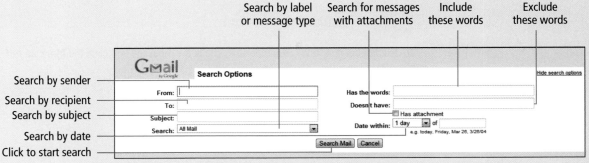

Search by sender
Search by recipient
Search by subject
Search by date
Click to start search

Figure 8.9 Hands-On Exercise 2, Steps 2b through 2j.

Step ③ Star an Important Message

Refer to Figure 8.10 as you complete Step 3.

a. In the Gmail Priority Inbox, click the empty star next to the message.

Once clicked, the star appears in solid colors (a shade of gold or yellow with a blue border).

b. To display only starred messages, click the **Starred** link in the Navigation pane.

> **Tip** **Unstarring a Message**
>
> To "unstar" a message, click the solid yellow star next to the message.

Click to star the message

Starred message

Click to display only starred messages

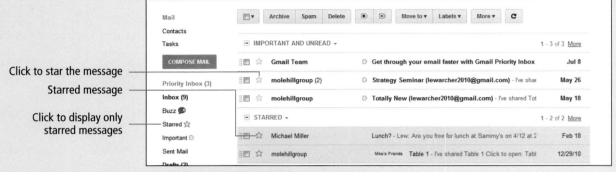

Figure 8.10 Hands-On Exercise 2, Step 3.

Step ④ Flag a Message as Important

Refer to Figure 8.11 as you complete Step 4.

Messages marked as important get displayed first in the Priority Inbox, in the Important and unread section. (The "important" option is not available in the normal inbox.) Gmail learns from the messages you mark as important to flag similar messages the same way going forward.

a. In the Gmail inbox, check those messages you want to mark as important.

b. Click the **Mark as important** (+) button.

> **Tip** **Mark as Unimportant**
>
> To designate a message as unimportant, check the message and click the **Mark as not important** (–) button.

Click to mark as unimportant

Click to mark as important

Check to select message

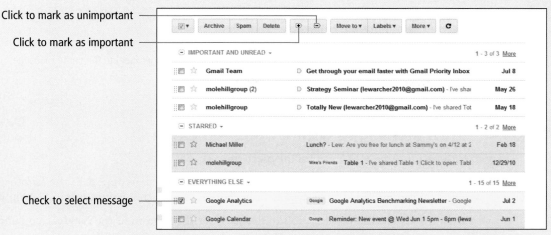

Figure 8.11 Hands-On Exercise 2, Step 4.

Step 5 Assign a Label to a Message

Refer to Figures 8.12 and 8.13 as you complete Step 5.

a. In the Gmail inbox, check those messages you want to share the same label.

b. Click the **Labels** button.

Gmail displays a list with all existing labels included.

c. Select a label from the list.

Click to display labels

Click to assign label

Click to create a new label

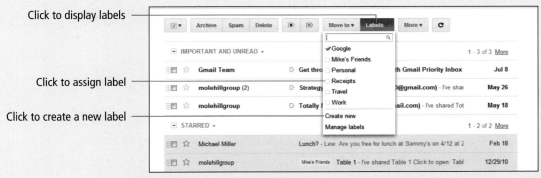

Figure 8.12 Hands-On Exercise 2, Steps 5a through 5c.

d. To create a new label, click **Create new**. When the *New Label* dialog box appears, enter the name of the new label and click **Create**.

Enter new label name

Click to assign label

Figure 8.13 Hands-On Exercise 2, Step 5d.

After you assign a label, that label appears before the message's subject line.

> ### Tip ⭐ Multiple Labels
>
> You can apply multiple labels to a single message. To apply another label to the same message, just repeat the procedure for assigning a label.

Step 6 View Messages with a Common Label

Refer to Figure 8.14 as you complete Step 6.

After you've assigned labels to your messages, all these labels appear in the *Labels* list. You can use this list to display only those messages that have a specific label.

a. In the Gmail inbox, scroll to the *Labels* list at the bottom of the Navigation pane.

b. Click the desired label.

Gmail now displays all the messages designated with that label.

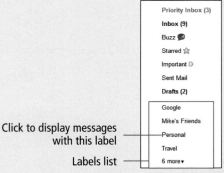

Click to display messages with this label
Labels list

Figure 8.14 Hands-On Exercise 2, Step 6.

Step 7 Archive Old Messages

Refer to Figure 8.15 as you complete Step 7.

a. From the Gmail inbox, check those messages you want to archive.

b. Click the **Archive** button.

The messages you marked are now removed from the inbox, but remain accessible whenever you perform a Gmail search.

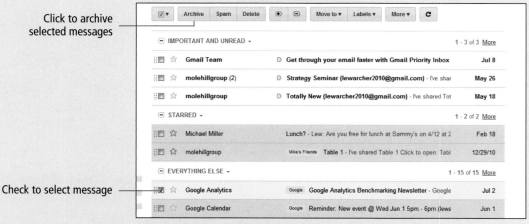

Click to archive selected messages
Check to select message

Figure 8.15 Hands-On Exercise 2, Step 7.

Step 8 Filter Incoming Messages

Refer to Figures 8.16 through 8.18 as you complete Step 8.

a. From the Gmail inbox, click the **Create a filter** link (beside the search box).

Click to create a new filter ──────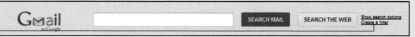

Figure 8.16 Hands-On Exercise 2, Step 8a.

The *Create a Filter* panel now appears at the top of the inbox page.

b. To filter by message sender, enter one or more names or addresses into the *From:* box.

c. To filter by message recipient, enter one or more names or addresses into the *To:* box.

d. To filter by words in the subject line, enter those words into the *Subject:* box.

e. To filter messages that contain certain words in the message text, enter those words into the *Has the words:* box.

f. To filter messages that do not contain specific words, enter those words into the *Doesn't have:* box.

g. To filter messages that have a file attached, check the **Has attachment** box.

h. To see which messages will be filtered based on the selected criteria, click the **Test Search** button.

i. When you have selected all your filter criteria, click the **Next Step** button.

Filter by file attachment   Filter by included words   Filter by excluded words

Filter by sender ──────
Filter by recipient ──────
Filter by subject ──────
Click to proceed ──────

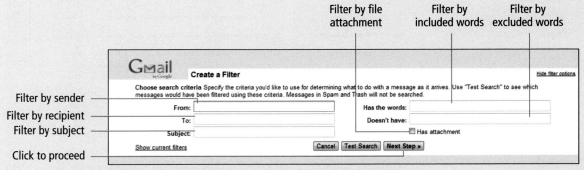

Figure 8.17 Hands-On Exercise 2, Steps 8b through 8i.

Gmail displays a list of possible actions for this filter.

j. Check one or more actions you want applied to this filter.

k. If you want this filter applied to existing messages, check the **Also apply filter to** *x* **conversations below** box.

l. Click the **Create Filter** button.

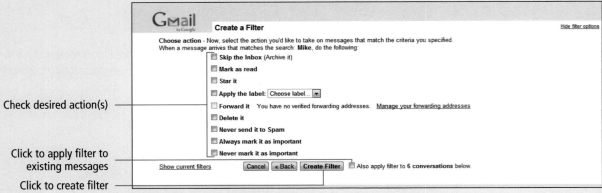

Check desired action(s)

Click to apply filter to existing messages

Click to create filter

Figure 8.18 Hands-On Exercise 2, Steps 8j through 8l.

All future messages that match your defined criteria will now have the specified action performed on them.

 Viewing and Editing Filters

To view all your current filters, as well as to edit or delete selected filters, click the **Settings** link at the top of the Gmail inbox page (or click **Options** and then select **Mail settings**) and then select the **Filters** tab.

Step 9 Delete Messages from the Inbox

Refer to Figure 8.19 as you complete Step 9.

a. From the Gmail inbox, check those messages you want to delete.

b. Click the **Delete** button.

Deleted messages are moved to the *Trash*.

Click to delete selected messages

Check message(s) to delete

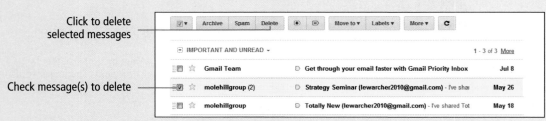

Figure 8.19 Hands-On Exercise 2, Step 9.

 Viewing Your Trash

To view the messages in the *Trash*, click the **more** link below the *Labels* section of the Navigation pane and then click the **Trash** link. You can then undelete any message by checking it, clicking the **Move to** button, and selecting **Inbox**.

Objective 3

Send and Receive Email Messages

What is a conversation?

Conversation A grouping of related email messages.

Gmail groups together related email messages in what Google calls ***conversations.*** A conversation might be an initial message and all the replies (and replies to replies) to that message; a conversation might also be all the daily emails from a single source that have a common subject, such as messages from subscribed-to mailing lists.

A conversation is noted in the inbox list by a number in parentheses after the sender name(s). If a conversation has replies from more than one person, more than one name is listed.

Can you add a signature to your Gmail messages?

Signature Personalized text that appears at the bottom of an email message.

A ***signature*** is personalized text that appears at the bottom of an email message (Figure 8.20). Signatures typically include the sender's name and contact information, or some personal message. Gmail lets you create a single signature and apply it to all your outgoing email messages.

Signature —

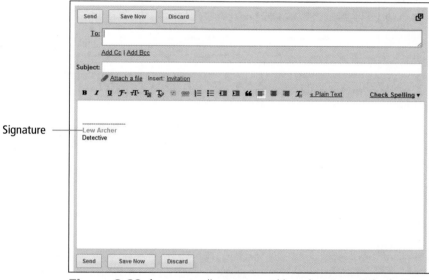

Figure 8.20 A new email message with a signature at the bottom.

Can you attach files to a Gmail message?

Gmail lets you attach most application files to outgoing email messages. You can send Word documents, Excel spreadsheets, MP3 music files, JPG picture files, and the like as ***attachments***.

Attachment A file that is attached to a normal text email message.

 No Program Files

While Gmail lets you attach application files to outgoing email messages, it won't let you attach ***executable program files*** (files that have an *.exe* extension). You can't even send *.exe* files when they're compressed into *.zip* files. Gmail blocks the transmittal of all *.exe* files, in an attempt to prevent potential computer viruses.

Executable program file A computer file that contains a software program.

Hands-On Exercises

3 | Sending and Receiving Email Messages

Steps: 1. Read an Email Message; **2.** View a Gmail Conversation; **3.** Reply to a Message; **4.** Forward a Message; **5.** Create a New Email Message; **6.** Add a Signature to Your Messages; **7.** Attach a File to a Message; **8.** View or Download an Attached File.

Use Figures 8.21 through 8.37 as a guide to the exercise.

 Step 1 **Read an Email Message**

Refer to Figures 8.21 and 8.22 as you complete Step 1.

a. From the Gmail inbox, select the message you want to read and click that message's title.

Click to read message ───

Figure 8.21 Hands-On Exercise 3, Step 1a.

The full text of the message is displayed on a new page.

 Tip **Display in New Window**

To display the selected message in its own window, click the **New window** icon at the top-right corner of the message.

b. To return to the inbox, click the **back arrow** button.

Click to return to inbox ───

Click to display message in a separate window ───

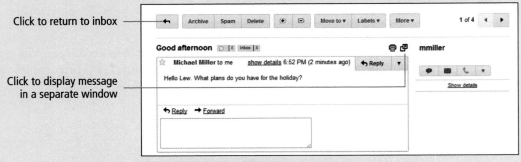

Figure 8.22 Hands-On Exercise 3, Step 1b.

 Step 2 **View a Gmail Conversation**

Refer to Figures 8.23 and 8.24 as you complete Step 2.

a. From the Gmail inbox, click the message title for the conversation you want to view. (Conversations have a number in parentheses, indicating the number of messages in the conversation.)

Click to read conversation ────

Number of messages ────
in conversation

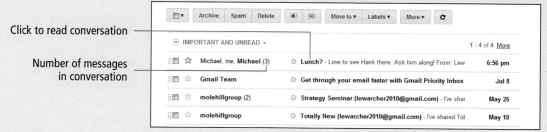

Figure 8.23 Hands-On Exercise 3, Step 2a.

The conversation now appears in your web browser, with only the most recent message displayed in full.

b. To view the text of any previous message in the conversation, click that message's subject.

c. To expand *all* the messages in a conversation, click the **Expand all** icon at the top-right corner of the message.

All the messages in the conversation are now stacked on top of each other, with the text of the newest message fully displayed.

Click to expand all ────
messages in conversation

Click to expand message ────
within conversation

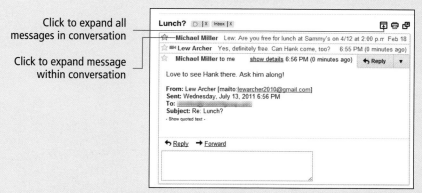

Figure 8.24 Hands-On Exercise 3, Steps 2b and 2c.

> **Tip** ⭐ **Turning Off Conversation View**
>
> If you don't like Gmail's conversation view, you can disable it and display messages in regular order. Click the **Settings** link at the top of any Gmail page, or click **Options** and select **Mail settings**. When the *Settings* page appears, select the **General** tab. Scroll to the *Conversation View* section and select the **Conversation view off** option.

Step ❸ Reply to a Message

Refer to Figures 8.25 and 8.26 as you complete Step 3.

a. In the original message, click the **Reply** button.

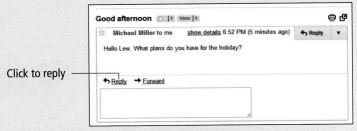

Figure 8.25 Hands-On Exercise 3, Step 3a.

Click to reply

This expands the message to include a reply box. The text of the original message is already quoted in the reply, and the original sender's address is automatically added to the *To:* line.

b. Add your new text above the original text.

c. Click the **Send** button to send the message.

Sender of original message

Enter new text here

Text of original message

Click to send reply

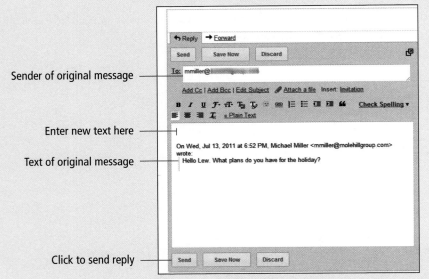

Figure 8.26 Hands-On Exercise 3, Steps 3b and 3c.

 Reply to All

If a conversation has multiple participants, you can reply to all of them by clicking the down arrow next to the **Reply** button and selecting **Reply to all**.

 Step 4 **Forward a Message**

Refer to Figures 8.27 and 8.28 as you complete Step 4.

a. In the original message, click the **Forward** link.

Click to forward message

Figure 8.27 Hands-On Exercise 3, Step 4a.

This expands the message to include a forward box.

b. Add the recipient's email address to the *To:* box.

c. Enter your own message into the main message box.

d. Click the **Send** button to send the message.

Add recipient's address

Enter your message

Click to send

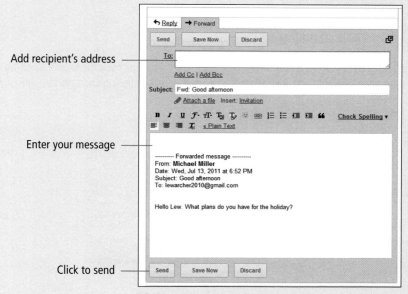

Figure 8.28 Hands-On Exercise 3, Steps 4b through 4d.

Step 5 Create a New Email Message

Refer to Figures 8.29 and 8.30 as you complete Step 5.

a. From any Gmail page, click the **COMPOSE MAIL** button in the Navigation pane.

This displays the new message page.

Click to create new message

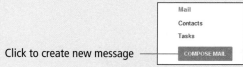

Figure 8.29 Hands-On Exercise 3, Step 5a.

b. Enter the recipient's email address into the *To:* box.

Separate multiple recipients with commas.

Cc Carbon copy; sends a message to additional recipients.

Bcc Blind carbon copy; sends a message to additional recipients without displaying their addresses.

c. To *Cc* (carbon copy) or *Bcc* (blind carbon copy) additional recipients, click the **Add Cc** or **Add Bcc** links. This expands the message to include *Cc* or *Bcc* boxes, into which you enter the recipients' email addresses.

> **Note** Cc and Bcc
>
> A Bcc sends the message to the intended recipients, but hides their addresses from the main recipients; this is useful for sending email to people who don't necessarily know each other, or to those who don't need to know the other recipients. A Cc displays the recipients' addresses, and lets people know that others are reading the message.

d. Enter a subject for the message into the *Subject:* box.

e. Enter the text of your message into the large text box. Use the buttons on the Formatting toolbar (bold, italic, font, etc.) to enhance your message as desired.

f. When you're done composing your message, click the **Send** button.

> **Tip** Spell-checking
>
> Gmail provides spell-checking for all your outgoing messages. Just click the **Check Spelling** link on the right of your toolbar and then accept or reject suggested spelling changes throughout your message.

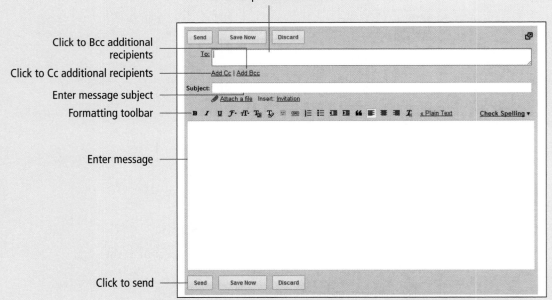

Enter recipients' addresses

Click to Bcc additional recipients

Click to Cc additional recipients

Enter message subject

Formatting toolbar

Enter message

Click to send

Figure 8.30 Hands-On Exercise 3, Steps 5b through 5f.

Step 6 Add a Signature to Your Messages

Refer to Figures 8.31 and 8.32 as you complete Step 6.

Before you can add a signature to your outgoing messages, you first have to create a signature.

a. Click the **Options** (gear) button at the top right of the Gmail page and select **Mail settings**.

Click to display
Settings page

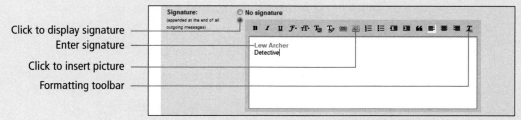

Figure 8.31 Hands-On Exercise 3, Step 6a.

b. When the *Settings* page appears, select the **General** tab.

c. Scroll to the *Signature* section and check the second option (the one below *No signature*).

d. Enter your signature into the large text box.

e. Use any of the formatting controls to format the text in your signature.

f. To add a picture to your signature, click the **Insert Image** button on the Formatting toolbar and then select the image file to insert.

g. When done, click the **Save Changes** button at the bottom of the *Settings* page.

Your new signature will now appear at the bottom of all new messages you create.

Click to display signature
Enter signature
Click to insert picture
Formatting toolbar

Figure 8.32 Hands-On Exercise 3, Steps 6b through 6g.

Tip ★ **No Signature**

If you prefer not to include a signature, select the **No signature** option on the *Settings* page.

Step ⑦ Attach a File to a Message

Refer to Figures 8.33 through 8.35 as you complete Step 7.

a. Use Gmail to compose a new message, as discussed previously.

b. From the new message page, click the **Attach a file** link.

Click to attach a file

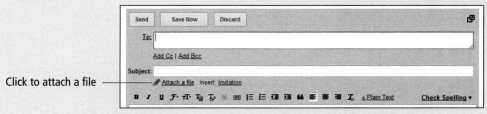

Figure 8.33 Hands-On Exercise 3, Steps 7a and 7b.

This displays the *Choose File to Upload* or *Open* dialog box.

c. Navigate to and select the file you want to attach and then click the **Open** button.

Select file to attach —

Click to attach file —

Figure 8.34 Hands-On Exercise 3, Step 7c.

The file you selected now appears under the *Subject:* box on the new message page.

d. To attach another file to this same message, click the **Attach another file** link; otherwise, continue composing and then send your message as normal.

Click to send message —

Attached file —

Click to attach another file —

Figure 8.35 Hands-On Exercise 3, Step 7d.

Step 8 View or Download an Attached File

Refer to Figures 8.36 and 8.37 as you complete Step 8.

a. From the Google inbox, click a message with an attachment to open the message. (Messages with attachments have a paperclip icon in the inbox.)

Click to open message —

Message with attachment —

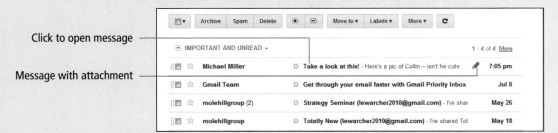

Figure 8.36 Hands-On Exercise 3, Step 8a.

The message now opens. If the attached file is a picture, it is displayed below the message text; otherwise, the filename appears below the message text.

b. To view the attached file, click the **View** link.

This opens the file in a new window.

c. To save the file to your computer's hard disk, click the **Download** link. Follow your browser's instructions to save the file to a specific location on your computer.

Attached picture file

Click to view attachment

Click to download attached file

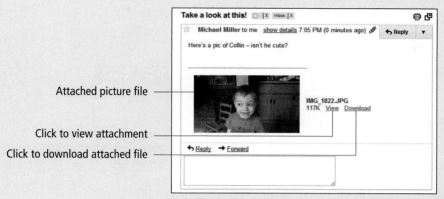

Figure 8.37 Hands-On Exercise 3, Steps 8b and 8c.

Objective 4

Protect against Spam and Viruses

What is spam?

Spam Unsolicited commercial email.

Spam, also known as junk email or unsolicited commercial email (UCE), is any commercial email message that you didn't request or opt into. In this definition, emails from a merchant you previously purchased from are not spam, while unwanted advertisements selling herbal remedies and financial "get rich quick" schemes are.

How does Gmail guard against spam?

Google applies a variety of internal spam filters to identify spam as it enters the Gmail system, and thus block it from appearing in users' inboxes. In most cases, you never see the spam; Google blocks it before it ever gets to you.

Does spam ever make it to your computer?

Sometimes spam makes it past Google's main filter but then is caught on the receiving end. When this happens, the spam message appears in the *Spam* section of your Gmail inbox. You can view purported spam messages by clicking the **more** link in the *Labels* section of the Navigation pane and then clicking **Spam**.

Does Gmail protect against computer viruses?

Computer virus A malicious computer program capable of reproducing itself and causing harm to files or programs on a computer system.

Gmail takes steps to protect you from email-borne *computer viruses*. These viruses typically come as file attachments, even more typically as EXE files attached to email messages.

So, Gmail automatically blocks the sending and receiving of all EXE files. It's a fairly extreme approach, but it works; there's no way around the system to send a legitimate EXE file.

Google also scans all the attached files you send and receive via Gmail, no matter what the file extension. If a virus is found in an attachment, Gmail tries to clean the file (remove the virus); if the virus can't be removed, you won't be able to download or send the file.

Hands-On Exercises

4 | Protecting against Spam

Steps: 1. Report a Message as Spam; **2.** Remove a Legitimate Message from Your Spam List; **3.** Permanently Delete Messages from Your Spam List.

Use Figures 8.38 through 8.42 as a guide to the exercise.

 Report a Message as Spam

Refer to Figure 8.38 as you complete Step 1.

If you inadvertently receive a spam message in your Gmail inbox, you can help train Google's spam filters by reporting it.

a. From the Gmail inbox, check the suspected spam message.

b. Click the **Spam** button.

This action both removes the spam message from your inbox and sends information about the message back to Google.

Click to remove and report selected message(s)

Check to select spam message

Figure 8.38 Hands-On Exercise 4, Step 1.

 Remove a Legitimate Message from Your Spam List

Refer to Figures 8.39 and 8.40 as you complete Step 2.

If Google happens to route a legitimate message to your spam list (it happens sometimes), you can move that message back to your regular Gmail inbox.

a. Click the **more** link in the *Labels* section of the Gmail Navigation pane and then click **Spam**.

This displays all stored spam messages.

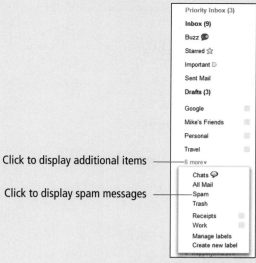

Click to display additional items ——
Click to display spam messages ——

Figure 8.39 Hands-On Exercise 4, Step 2a.

b. Check the non-spam message.

c. Click the **Not spam** button.

This moves the selected message out of the spam list and back into your general inbox.

Click to move message to inbox ——
Check non-spam message ——

Figure 8.40 Hands-On Exercise 4, Steps 2b and 2c.

Step ③ Permanently Delete Messages from Your Spam List

Refer to Figures 8.41 and 8.42 as you complete Step 3.

a. Click the **more** link in the *Labels* section of the Gmail Navigation pane and then click **Spam**.

This displays all stored spam messages.

Click to display additional items ——
Click to display Spam messages ——

Figure 8.41 Hands-On Exercise 4, Step 3a.

b. To permanently delete an individual message from the spam list, check the message and then click the **Delete forever** button.

c. To permanently delete all messages in the spam list, click the **Delete all spam messages now** link above the spam list.

Click to delete selected spam message(s)

Check to select message

Click to delete all spam messages

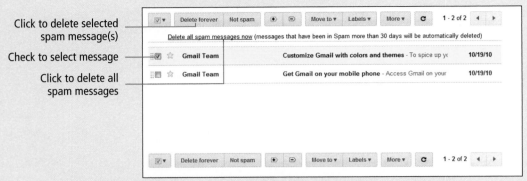

Figure 8.42 Hands-On Exercise 4, Steps 3b and 3c.

Objective 5

Manage Your Contacts

Does Gmail let you store the names and email addresses of people you email frequently?

Contact A person to whom you send email messages.

Most email programs and services offer some sort of address book, a list of your most-frequent *contacts*. Gmail's contacts list lets you store contact information (including but not limited to email addresses) for thousands of people.

What is a contact group?

Contact group A group of contacts, typically used to send email mailing lists.

Most email programs let you create mailing lists that contain multiple email addresses, which makes it easier to send bulk mailings to groups of people. Gmail also offers a mailing list-like feature, which it calls *contact groups*. When you want to send a message to all members of a group, you only have to select the group name—not every contact individually.

Hands-On Exercises

5 | Managing Your Contacts

Steps: 1. Create a New Contact; **2.** Display Your Contacts; **3.** Delete a Contact; **4.** Create a Contact Group; **5.** Send a Message to a Contact or Contact Group.

Use Figures 8.43 through 8.51 as a guide to the exercise.

Step 1 Create a New Contact

Refer to Figures 8.43 through 8.45 as you complete Step 1.

a. Click **Contacts** in the Gmail Navigation pane.

This displays the *Contacts* page. All your existing contacts are listed here.

b. Click the **NEW CONTACT** button.

This displays a new contact page.

Click to display contacts ──────

Click to create new contact ──────

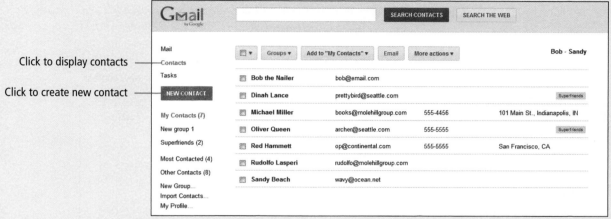

Figure 8.43 Hands-On Exercise 5, Steps 1a and 1b.

c. Click the **Add name** box and enter the contact's first and last names.

 Adding Names

To add a new name, you can also click the **Details** button next to the *Add name* box. This displays the *Edit name* dialog box; from here, enter the contact's prefix, first name, middle initial, last name, and suffix.

d. Enter the contact's email address into the *Email* box and then click the down arrow to the left of this box to select which address this is—*Home, Work,* or *Custom.*

 Optional Information

All the information requested for a contact is optional—including name and email address. You can add as much or as little information as you like about any of your contacts.

e. Enter the person's phone number into the *Phone* box and then click the down arrow to the left of this box to select which number this is—*Mobile, Work, Home,* and so forth.

f. Enter the person's street address, city, state, and ZIP code into the *Address* box and then click the down arrow to the left of this box to select which address this is—*Home, Work,* or *Custom.*

g. Enter the person's birthday, if you know it, into the *Birthday* box.

You can also click the down arrow to the left of this box to select and enter this individual's anniversary or other custom date.

h. If this person has a website or blog, enter that address into the *URL* box and then click the down arrow to the left of this box to select what type of address this is—*Profile, Blog, Home Page, Work,* or *Custom*.

i. Add any free-form notes about this person into the *Notes* box.

j. To include additional information about this contact, click the **Add** button and select what type of field to add: *Phonetic name, Nickname, Title and company, File As, Email, Phone, Address, Birthday, URL, Relationship, Instant messaging, Internet call,* or *Custom*.

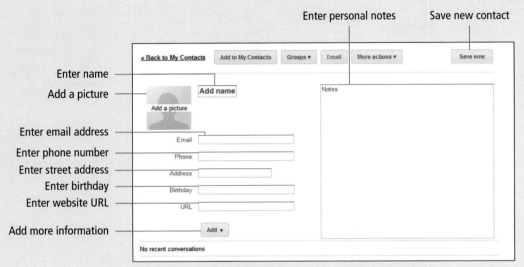

Figure 8.44 Hands-On Exercise 5, Steps 1c through 1j.

k. To add this person's picture to his or her contact information, click **Add a picture**. When the *Upload a picture* dialog box appears, click the **Browse** or **Choose File** button to display the *Choose File to Upload* or *Open* dialog box; navigate to and select the image file and click the **Open** button. The *Upload a Picture* dialog box now changes to a *Crop this picture* dialog box. Drag the box corners to enlarge or shrink the image area and drag the box itself to reposition the viewable area of the image. Click the **Apply Changes** button when done.

Figure 8.45 Hands-On Exercise 5, Step 1k.

l. If the **Save Now** button appears, click the button to create the contact.

Tip **Adding a Contact from an Email**

You can also add a sender's email address to your contacts list whenever you receive a new email message. All you have to do is click the down arrow next to the **Reply** button at the top-right corner of the message and select **Add Sender to Contacts list**.

Step 2 Display Your Contacts

Refer to Figure 8.46 as you complete Step 2.

The most obvious use of Gmail's contacts list is to send email messages to your contacts. But you can also view the information about a contact at any time, even if you're not sending email.

 Tip **Contact Groups**

The *Contacts* page also displays all contact groups you've created. To view the contacts in a specific group, select that group from the navigation pane.

a. Click **Contacts** in the Gmail Navigation pane.

The *Contacts* page now appears, with your contacts shown in the main panel. By default, you view your entire contacts list, or what's labeled *My Contacts* in the Navigation pane. You can, however, filter your contacts by selecting other options in the Navigation pane, such as *Most Contacted*. You can also create your own contacts list, which we'll discuss momentarily.

b. Hover over a contact to display that person's basic contact information.

c. To display more detailed information about a contact, click that contact's name in the contacts list.

Click to display contacts

Click to display more detailed information

Hover to display basic contact information

Figure 8.46 Hands-On Exercise 5, Step 2.

 Tip **Editing Contact Information**

You can edit information for a selected contact by displaying the contact's detailed information page, selecting an information field, and then entering new data as necessary.

Step 3 Delete a Contact

Refer to Figure 8.47 as you complete Step 3.

a. From the contacts list, check the contact(s) you want to delete.

b. Click the **More actions** drop-down list and select **Delete contact**.

Figure 8.47 Hands-On Exercise 5, Step 3.

Step 4 Create a Contact Group

Refer to Figures 8.48 through 8.50 as you complete Step 4.

a. From the contacts list, click **New Group** in the Navigation pane.

Figure 8.48 Hands-On Exercise 5, Step 4a.

b. When the *New group* dialog box appears, enter a name for the new group and click the **OK** button.

Figure 8.49 Hands-On Exercise 5, Step 4b.

The Navigation pane of the *Contacts* page is now updated with the new group.

c. Select the group name in the Navigation pane.

The *Contacts* page changes to show any current contacts in this group.

d. To add a contact to this group, click the **Add to "Group"** button and enter that person's name into the search box; Gmail now lists matching contacts. Select the contact you want to add to the group.

Click to add contact to group →

Enter contact name →

Click to add contact →

Click to select new group →

Figure 8.50 Hands-On Exercise 5, Steps 4c and 4d.

 Tip **Adding to a Group**

You can also add contacts to a group from your master *My Contacts* list. Just check the contacts you want to add, click the **Groups** button, and select the name of the destination contact group.

Step 5 Send a Message to a Contact or Contact Group

Refer to Figure 8.51 as you complete Step 5.

a. Click the **Compose mail** button from any Gmail page.

b. When the compose mail page appears, begin typing the name of the contact or contact group into the *To:* list.

As you type, Gmail will display a list of matching contacts.

c. Click the name of the contact or contact group you want to email.

When you select a contact group, the *To:* box is automatically filled with the email addresses of all the individual contacts in that group.

d. Complete your email message as normal and click the **Send** button.

Click to send →

Type contact name →

Select contact from list →

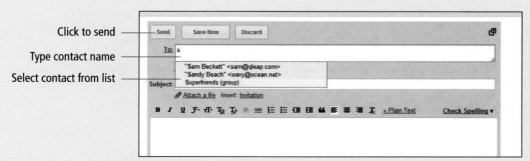

Figure 8.51 Hands-On Exercise 5, Step 5.

Objective 6

Customize Gmail

How can Gmail be customized?

There are many facets of the Gmail application that you can personalize to your own tastes and needs. Most Gmail configuration options are available by clicking **Options** (gear) and selecting **Mail options**. The resulting *Settings* page contains various tabs, each of which contains associated settings, as detailed in Table 8.1.

Table 8.1—Gmail Configuration Settings	
Tab	**Configuration Settings**
General	Language
	Maximum page size
	Keyboard shortcuts (on/off)
	External content (displays/doesn't display images in email messages)
	Browser connection (uses/doesn't use https)
	Conversation View (enables/disables conversation threading of email messages)
	Desktop Notifications (enables/disables notification when you receive new email or chat messages)
	My picture (enables/disables display of your profile picture and lets you change your picture)
	Contacts' pictures (displays/doesn't display pictures for your contacts)
	Create contacts for auto-complete (automatically creates new contacts for any message to a new person, or not)
	Importance signals for ads (use message information to show more relevant ads at top of page)
	Signature (lets you create a signature for your new messages)
	Personal level indicators (helps you determine whether you're the only recipient of a message or whether the message was sent to all members of a mailing list)
	Snippets (displays/doesn't display snippets of message contents)
	Vacation responder (lets you forward all messages while you're on vacation)
	Outgoing message encoding (determines text encoding for outgoing messages)
	Attachments (activates/deactivates advanced file attachment features)
Labels	Lets you show or hide all available email labels on a label-by-label basis

Tab	Configuration Settings
Table 8.1—continued	
Accounts	Change account settings (links to the settings page for your Google account)
	Import mail and contacts (lets you import from your other email accounts)
	Send mail as (lets you display another email address when sending messages)
	Check mail using POP3 (lets you view email from other accounts in Gmail)
	Using Gmail for work? (links to an advertisement for the Premier Edition of Google Apps)
	Grant access to your account (allows others to read and send email on your behalf)
	Add additional storage (lets you purchase additional storage for your Gmail messages)
Filters	Displays and lets you edit or delete all the filters you've set up for your email messages
Forwarding and POP/IMAP	Forwarding (lets you forward Gmail messages to another email address)
	POP Download (lets you send Gmail messages to a POP email account)
	IMAP Access (lets you send Gmail messages to an iPhone or other smartphone)
Chat	Lets you configure various Google Talk chat settings (learn more in Appendix A, "Using Google Talk")
Web Clips	Determines which information clips are displayed above the Gmail message list
Labs	Displays experimental Gmail features from Gmail Labs
Priority Inbox	Default inbox (determines whether you see the normal inbox or Priority Inbox when Gmail opens)
	Priority Inbox sections (determines which sections are displayed)
	Filtered mail (lets Priority Inbox override existing email filters)
	Importance markers (shows or hides yellow "important mail" flags)
	Show Priority Inbox (enables/disables the Priority Inbox feature)
Offline	No longer functional
Themes	Lets you change Gmail's visual theme
Buzz	Contains configuration settings for Google Buzz (Google's social networking service)

What is a Gmail theme?

If you want to change the way Gmail looks and feels, you can apply a predesigned theme. Themes define Gmail's color scheme and, depending on the scheme, apply background graphics and change the look of various onscreen elements (Figure 8.52).

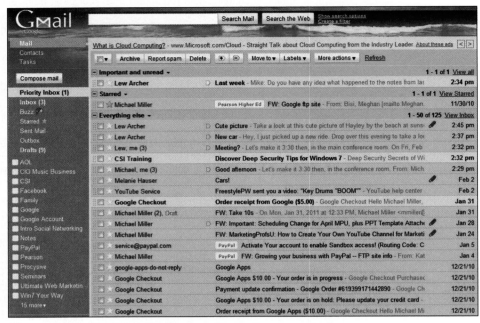

Figure 8.52 Gmail with the Summer Ocean theme applied.

What is vacation mode?

Vacation mode When enabled, puts a Gmail account on hold while the user is on vacation.

Gmail has a dedicated *vacation mode* that essentially lets you put your account on "hold" while you're away. When you activate vacation mode, anyone who sends you a message automatically gets a response that you're on vacation.

Hands-On Exercises

6 | Customizing Gmail

Steps: 1. Change Gmail's Visual Theme; **2.** Activate Vacation Mode; **3.** Change the Contents of a Priority Inbox Section; **4.** Delete a Priority Inbox Section; **5.** Add a New Priority Inbox Section.

Use Figures 8.53 through 8.58 as a guide to the exercise.

Step 1 — Change Gmail's Visual Theme

Refer to Figure 8.53 as you complete Step 1.

a. Click the **Options** (gear) button at the top of any Gmail page and select **Mail settings**.

b. When the *Settings* page appears, select the **Themes** tab.

c. Click the theme you want to use.

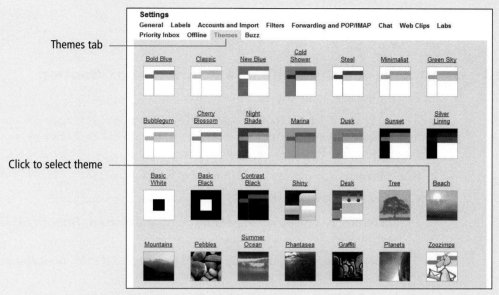

Figure 8.53 Hands-On Exercise 6, Step 1.

Step 2 — Activate Vacation Mode

Refer to Figure 8.54 as you complete Step 2.

a. Click the **Options** (gear) button at the top of any Gmail page and select **Mail settings**.

b. When the *Settings* page appears, select the **General** tab.

c. Scroll to the *Vacation responder* section.

d. Select the **Vacation responder on** option.

e. Enter the first day of your vacation into the *First day* box.

f. If you know when you're returning, enter that date into the *Ends* box (and check the **Ends** option).

g. Enter a subject for the message you want the responder to automatically send out, something along the lines of, "I'm on vacation."

h. Enter the text of your vacation message.

i. If you want only your contacts to receive this vacation message, check the **Only send a response to people in my Contacts** box.

j. Click the **Save Changes** button at the bottom of the page.

With the vacation responder activated, anyone who sends you a message while you are on vacation automatically receives your vacation message in reply. When you return from vacation, return to the *Settings* page and select the **Vacation responder off** option.

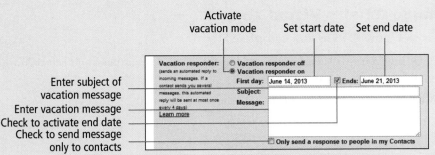

Activate vacation mode   Set start date   Set end date

Enter subject of vacation message
Enter vacation message
Check to activate end date
Check to send message only to contacts

Figure 8.54 Hands-On Exercise 6, Step 2.

Step 3 Change the Contents of a Priority Inbox Section

Refer to Figure 8.55 as you complete Step 3.

You can accept the default configuration of Gmail's Priority Inbox, or customize the contents of any existing section. For example, you could opt to display only unread messages instead of important and unread ones.

a. Select **Priority Inbox** from the Gmail Navigation pane.

b. Click the down arrow next to the section you want to reconfigure.

c. Select one of the available options: **Important and unread, Important, Unread,** or **Starred**.

d. To create a section containing only labeled messages, select **More options** and then check the desired label.

e. To determine how many messages are displayed in a section, select an option in the **Show up to** section.

Click to configure Priority Inbox section
Select contents
Click to display only labeled messages
Display selected number of messages

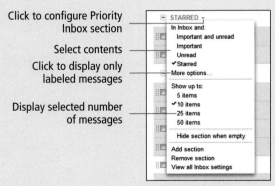

Figure 8.55 Hands-On Exercise 6, Step 3.

Step 4 Delete a Priority Inbox Section

Refer to Figure 8.56 as you complete Step 4.

You can delete any *Priority Inbox* section except the *Everything Else* section.

a. Select **Priority Inbox** from the Gmail Navigation pane.

b. Click the down arrow next to the section you want to delete.

c. Click **Remove section**.

Click to delete section ⎯⎯

Figure 8.56 Hands-On Exercise 6, Step 4.

> **Tip** ⭐ **Hide a Section**
>
> Instead of completely deleting a section, you can opt to hide it if it contains no messages. Just click the down arrow next to that section and select **Hide section when empty**.

Step 5 Add a New Priority Inbox Section

Refer to Figures 8.57 and 8.58 as you complete Step 5.

a. Select **Priority Inbox** from the Gmail Navigation pane.

b. Click the down arrow next to the section above where you want the new section to appear.

c. Select **Add section**.

A new blank section is added.

Click to add new section
below current section ⎯⎯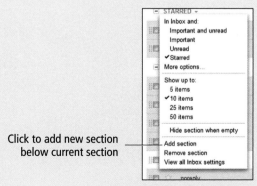

Figure 8.57 Hands-On Exercise 6, Step 5c.

d. Click the down arrow next to the **CLICK TO CONFIGURE** link for the new section.

e. Select one of the available options: **Important and unread**, **Important**, **Unread**, or **Starred**, or click **More options** to display labeled messages.

Click to configure new section ————

Select section content ————

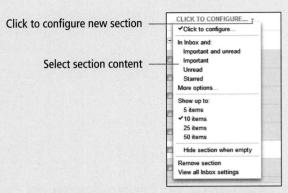

Figure 8.58 Hands-On Exercise 6, Steps 5d and 5e.

Summary

In this chapter, you learned how to sign up for and log in to a Gmail account. You learned how to manage the messages in your Gmail inbox, as well as how to read, reply to, and create new email messages. You learned how Gmail protects against spam and computer viruses, and how to manage your Gmail contacts. Finally, you learned how to customize Gmail—including how to change Gmail's visual theme.

Key Terms

Archive	171	Gmail	166
Attachment	179	Inbox	169
Bcc	184	Keyword	172
Cc	184	Label	169
Computer virus	187	POP email	166
Contact	190	Priority Inbox	169
Contact group	190	Signature	179
Conversation	179	Snippet	170
Email	166	Spam	187
Executable program file	179	Star	170
Filter	171	Vacation mode	198

Multiple Choice Questions

1. Which of the following is true?

    (a) Gmail is a feature of Microsoft Outlook.

    (b) Gmail is a web-based email service.

    (c) Gmail costs $9.95/month.

    (d) Gmail requires you to download a software program.

2. Gmail uses _____ to organize email messages.

    (a) Labels

    (b) Folders

    (c) Hierarchical directories

    (d) All of the above

3. A conversation is

    (s) an instant message session saved as an email message.

    (b) a message sent to a contact group.

    (c) a private message sent to a single member of a contact group.

    (d) a series of related messages grouped together.

4. "Bcc" stands for

    (a) blind carbon copy.

    (b) blind copy contact.

    (c) before content copy.

    (d) bring cranberry cake.

5. Which of the following file types *cannot* be attached to a Gmail message?

   (a) .jpg

   (b) .doc

   (c) .exe

   (d) .pdf

6. Which of the following is true?

   (a) Gmail never permanently deletes old messages.

   (b) Spam messages are automatically deleted.

   (c) You can delete only the message you're reading.

   (d) Deleted messages are stored in the Trash.

7. Which of the following is *not* an action you can apply to an email filter?

   (a) Star the message

   (b) Mark the message as spam

   (c) Apply a label to the message

   (d) Delete the message

8. Which of the following is mandatory information for a new contact?

   (a) Name

   (b) Email address

   (c) Phone number

   (d) None of the above

9. Which of the following is *not* true about spam in Gmail?

   (a) Gmail applies spam filters before messages arrive in your inbox.

   (b) Messages in your spam list can be restored to your normal inbox.

   (c) Gmail is 100% effective in blocking spam messages.

   (d) You can permanently delete messages in your spam list.

10. To send an existing message to a different recipient, use the following function:

    (a) Reply

    (b) Forward

    (c) Cc:

    (d) Star

Fill in the Blank

Write the correct word or words in the space provided.

1. A(n) _____ is a block of personalized text that appears at the bottom of an email message.

2. Unsolicited commercial email is called _____.

3. To send a file via email, you _____ the file to a message.

4. Unlike other email applications, Gmail does not use _____ to organize received messages.

5. To help identify like messages, you can assign unique _____ to your email messages.

6. A(n) _____ is a collection of contacts, like a mailing list.

7. Archived email messages are stored in the _____ list.

8. A(n) _____ identifies specific messages and applies an action to those messages.

9. To permanently delete messages from the Spam list, click the _____ button.

10. To perform an advanced search of your Gmail inbox, click the _____ link.

Practice Exercises

1. **Basic Email**

   For our first exercise, we'll assume you have a Gmail account. If you do not yet have an account, create one now as part of this exercise.

   (a) Create a new email message.

   (b) Enter your instructor as the message recipient.

   (c) Enter as the subject line **Class Assignment 1**.

   (d) For the message text, describe this project.

   (e) Send the email to your instructor.

2. **Fancy Email**

   In this exercise, you learn how to format the text in an email message.

   (a) Create a Gmail signature that includes your name, the name of the class, and the name of your school, on three separate lines.

   (b) Create a new email message.

   (c) Enter your instructor as the message recipient.

   (d) Enter as the subject line **Class Assignment 2**.

   (e) For the message text, write a short paragraph describing some of the formatting options available in Gmail. Make sure the paragraph has at least three sentences.

   (f) Format the first sentence with Wide font, large size, red.

   (g) Format the second sentence with Comic Sans MS font, normal size, blue.

   (h) Format the third sentence with Tahoma font, normal size, bold, green.

   (i) Send the email to your instructor.

3. **Email with Attachment**

   In this exercise, you learn how to attach an image file to an email message.

   (a) Create a new email message.

   (b) Enter your instructor as the message recipient.

   (c) Enter as the subject line **Class Assignment 3**.

   (d) For the message text, enter **Here's a picture I thought you'd like!**

   (e) Attach to the message a digital photo of yourself, a family member, or a friend.

   (f) Send the email to your instructor.

4. **Email with Bcc**

   In this exercise, you learn how to use Gmail's Bcc function to copy other people on a message.

   (a) Create a new email message.

   (b) Enter one of your classmates as the message recipient.

   (c) Enter as the subject line **Class Assignment 4**.

   (d) For the message text, write a general greeting of goodwill. (It doesn't have to be long.)

   (e) Bcc your instructor on the message.

   (f) Send the email.

Critical Thinking

1. Google lets you create multiple Gmail accounts. For that matter, you can create multiple accounts on different web-based email services, such as Windows Live Hotmail and Yahoo! Mail, as well as web-based email accounts separate from your school email account. Discuss reasons why you might want to have multiple email accounts—under what circumstances multiple accounts might be beneficial.
2. Gmail's Cc and Bcc functions are similar, in that they let you send an email message to people beyond the main recipients. The main difference between the two is that Bcc hides the names and email addresses of additional recipients, whereas Cc displays the additional recipients' names and addresses. Discuss why you might use the Cc or Bcc function, and when it might be beneficial to use Bcc to hide recipient names.

Team Projects

1. Each member of the team should enter the other team members as contacts, and add those contacts to a new contact group. You should also add your instructor to your contacts list and to this contact group. Each team member should then send an email message to the entire contact group, introducing himself or herself to the team.
2. The first member of the team should send an email message to the other team members, discussing a topic of interest to the group. The other members should each respond to the initial email, using the Reply to all function; responses to the responses are also encouraged. The goal is to create a robust conversation thread in Gmail. When the exchange of emails has ended, the first team member should then forward the entire conversation to the instructor.

Credits

Google, Blogger, and Picasa screenshots reprinted by permission.

CHAPTER 9

Using Google Calendar

Objectives

After you read this chapter, you will be able to:

1. Create a New Calendar
2. View Your Calendars
3. Add New Events
4. Share a Public Calendar
5. Create and Manage a To-Do List

The following Hands-On Exercises will help you accomplish the chapter objectives:

Hands-On Exercises

EXERCISES	SKILLS COVERED
1. Creating a New Calendar	**Step 1:** Set Up a Basic Calendar **Step 2:** Set Up Additional Calendars **Step 3:** Activate a Holiday or Sports Calendar
2. Viewing Your Calendars	**Step 1:** Display Different Calendar Views **Step 2:** Create a Customized Calendar View **Step 3:** View Multiple Calendars **Step 4:** Print a Calendar
3. Adding New Events	**Step 1:** Add an Event Directly to Your Calendar **Step 2:** Add an Event with the Create Event Button **Step 3:** Add an Event using Quick Add **Step 4:** Add an Event from Gmail **Step 5:** Invite Others to an Existing Event
4. Sharing a Public Calendar	**Step 1:** Make an Existing Calendar Public **Step 2:** Share a Calendar with Specific People **Step 3:** Receive Event Notifications
5. Creating and Managing a To-Do List	**Step 1:** Create Multiple Task Lists **Step 2:** Add a New Task from the Calendar **Step 3:** Add a New Task from the Tasks Pane **Step 4:** Mark a Task as Completed **Step 5:** Manage Your Task List

Objective 1

Create a New Calendar

Google Calendar Google's
web-based calendar application.

What is Google Calendar?

Google Calendar is a web-based calendar application accessible from any web browser, using any computer that is connected to the Internet. It enables you to keep track of your schedule and appointments wherever you are, even if you're away from home, school, or work.

How does Google Calendar differ from other calendar applications?

Google Calendar is unique because it stores your schedule on Google's servers, not on your own computer. The advantage is that you can open your calendar from any computer with Internet access anywhere in the world. Just log in to the Google Calendar page, and your calendar and all events are there.

Because Google Calendar is web-based, you can use it to create not only a private calendar for yourself but also public calendars for your company or organization. Create a public calendar and all employees or attendees can access it via the web. In addition, special event invitation features make it easy to invite others to an event—public or private.

Can you create more than one calendar in Google Calendar?

Google Calendar enables you to create several different calendars for different uses. For example, you can create one calendar for home, another for school, and yet another for extracurricular activities and then you can view all your calendars from the same Google Calendar page.

Does Google Calendar come with any specialty calendars?

Google also includes a number of built-in calendars you can add to your calendar display. Some of these are holiday calendars, which add national and religious holidays to a basic calendar. Others are major league sports calendars, which include the dates of all games for a given team. There are also calendars that display phases of the moon, Star Trek stardates, and birthdays and events from your Gmail contacts.

Hands-On Exercises

1 | Creating a New Calendar

Steps: 1. Set Up a Basic Calendar; **2.** Set Up Additional Calendars; **3.** Activate a Holiday or Sports Calendar.

Use Figures 9.1 through 9.5 as a guide to the exercise.

 Google Account

In order to use Google Calendar, you must have a Google account.

Step 1 Set Up a Basic Calendar

Refer to Figure 9.1 as you complete Step 1.

Setting up your first calendar is easy. In fact, there's really nothing to set up; Google creates your first calendar automatically the first time you visit the Google Calendar site.

a. Use your web browser to go to the Google Calendar main page (**calendar.google.com**).

b. If prompted, sign in to your Google account.

> **Note** **First-Time Use**
>
> The first time you access Google Calendar, you may be prompted to supply some basic information about yourself—your name, location, and time zone. Enter the appropriate information and then click the **Continue** button to go to your Google Calendar page.

Google Calendar now displays your default calendar. The name of this calendar, typically your Google account name or email address, is shown in the *My calendars* pane on the left of the page.

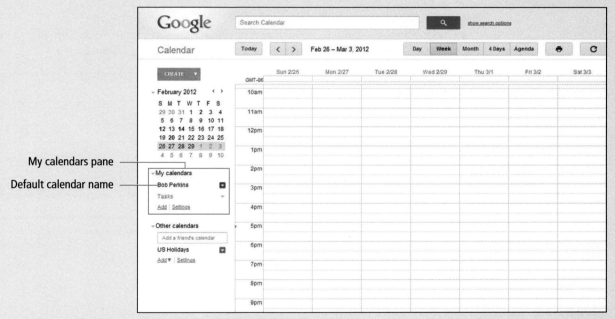

Figure 9.1 Hands-On Exercise 1, Step 1.

Step 2 Set Up Additional Calendars

Refer to Figures 9.2 and 9.3 as you complete Step 2.

a. From the main Google Calendar page, go to the *My calendars* pane and click the **Add** link.

Click to add new calendar

Figure 9.2 Hands-On Exercise 1, Step 2a.

This displays the *Create New Calendar* page.

b. Enter a name for the calendar into the *Calendar Name* box.

c. Enter a short description of the calendar into the *Description* box.

d. Enter your location (city and state) into the *Location* box.

e. Select your country from the **Country** list.

f. Select your time zone from the **Now select a time zone** list.

g. If you want to make this calendar public to everyone on the Internet, check the **Make this calendar public** option. To leave it as a private calendar (default), don't check this option.

h. If you want to share this calendar with others, enter their email addresses (separated by commas) into the *Person* box in the *Share with specific people* section. Click the **Permission Settings** drop-down list to determine what that person can see.

> **Note** **Permission Settings**
>
> When sharing a new calendar, you can opt to have each person see all event details, see only free/busy time (hide event details), make changes to events, or make changes and manage sharing.

i. Click the **Create Calendar** button.

Your new calendar is now listed in the *My calendars* pane on the left side of the Google Calendar page under the name of your default calendar.

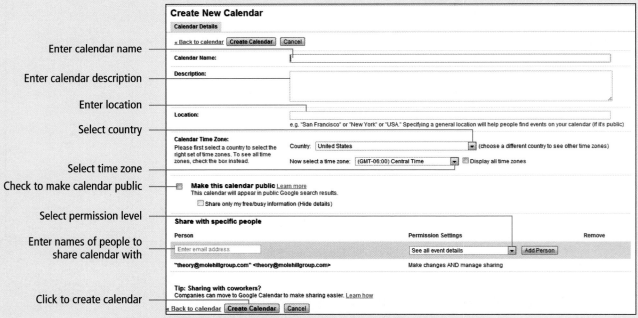

Figure 9.3 Hands-On Exercise 1, Steps 2b through 2i.

Step ❸ Activate a Holiday or Sports Calendar

Refer to Figures 9.4 and 9.5 as you complete Step 3.

a. In the *Other calendars* pane on your Google Calendar page, click the **Add** drop-down list and select **Browse Interesting Calendars**.

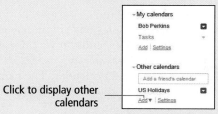

Click to display other calendars

Figure 9.4 Hands-On Exercise 1, Step 3a.

This displays the *Interesting Calendars* page.

b. Select the tab for the type of calendar you want to add—**Holidays, Sports,** or **More.**

c. Find the calendar you wish to add.

d. To preview a calendar, click the **Preview** link.

e. To add a calendar, click the **Subscribe** link.

f. Click **Back to calendar** to return to the Google Calendar page.

The selected calendar now displays in your *Other calendars* pane.

Click to return to main calendar page

Select calendar type

Click to preview calendar

Click to add calendar

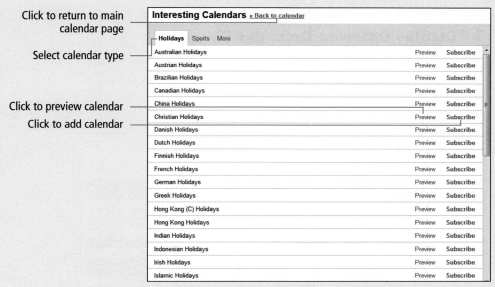

Figure 9.5 Hands-On Exercise 1, Steps 3b through 3f.

Objective 2

View Your Calendars

How can you view your calendars?

The main Google Calendar page is where you view all your calendars. You can view your calendar in several different ways—by day, week, month, or the next four days. Google Calendar even offers a special events-only agenda view.

How do you display multiple calendars?

The main calendar on the Google Calendar page can display any single calendar individually, or multiple calendars simultaneously. It all depends on which—and how many—calendars you select in the *My calendars* and *Other calendars* panes.

Every calendar that is selected is displayed in the main calendar. The name of each selected calendar displays with a colored background in the pane; events for that calendar are displayed in the same color.

Hands-On Exercises

2 | Viewing Your Calendars

Steps: 1. Display Different Calendar Views; **2.** Create a Customized Calendar View; **3.** View Multiple Calendars; **4.** Print a Calendar.

Use Figures 9.6 through 9.16 as a guide to the exercise.

Step 1 Display Different Calendar Views

Refer to Figures 9.6 through 9.12 as you complete Step 1.

a. Use your web browser to go to the Google Calendar main page.

b. To view a daily calendar, click the **Day** button.

Click to display daily calendar ——

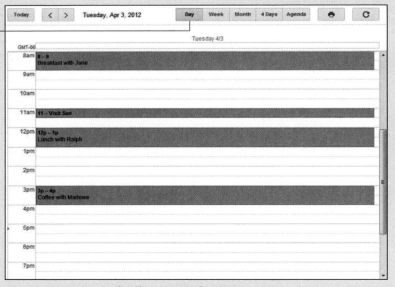

Figure 9.6 Hands-On Exercise 2, Step 1b.

c. To view a weekly calendar, click the **Week** button.

Click to display
weekly calendar

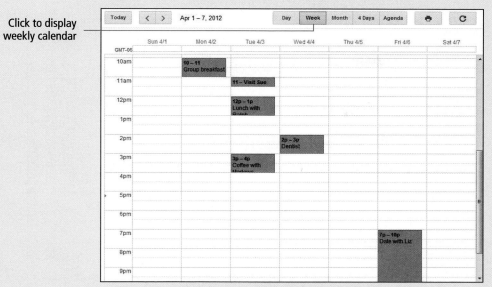

Figure 9.7 Hands-On Exercise 2, Step 1c.

d. To view a full-month calendar, click the **Month** button.

Click to display
monthly calendar

Figure 9.8 Hands-On Exercise 2, Step 1d.

e. To view a calendar for the next four days, click the 4 **Days** button.

Click to display
next four days

Figure 9.9 Hands-On Exercise 2, Step 1e.

f. To view a list of upcoming events, click the **Agenda** button.

Click to display
agenda of events

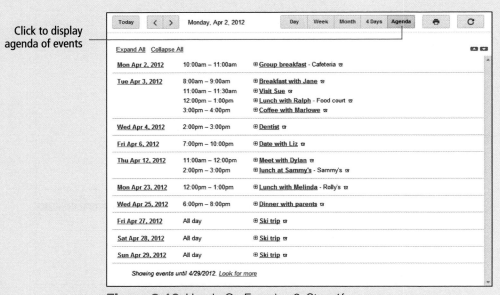

Figure 9.10 Hands-On Exercise 2, Step 1f.

g. To move backward and forward in time in any view, click the left and right arrow buttons at the top left of the calendar.

h. To display the current day on your calendar click the **Today** button.

Note **Today**

The **Today** option is not available for all calendar views.

Click to display current day on calendar

Click to move back in time

Click to move forward in time

Figure 9.11 Hands-On Exercise 2, Steps 1g and 1h.

i. To view details about a specific event, click that event in the calendar.

To close the pop-up balloon, click the **x** in the top-right corner of the balloon.

To display the event details page instead, click the link for the name of the event in the calendar.

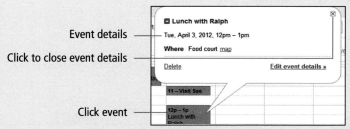

Event details

Click to close event details

Click event

Figure 9.12 Hands-On Exercise 2, Step 1i.

Step 2 Create a Customized Calendar View

Refer to Figure 9.13 as you complete Step 2.

a. From the Google Calendar main page, go to the mini-calendar on the left side of the page.

b. Click the first day you wish to view and hold down the left mouse button.

c. Drag the cursor across the calendar to the last day you wish to view and then release the mouse button.

The main calendar view changes to reflect the days you've selected. (If you select more than seven days, the calendar defaults to displaying entire weeks.)

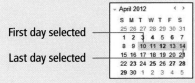

First day selected

Last day selected

Figure 9.13 Hands-On Exercise 2, Step 2.

Step 3 View Multiple Calendars

Refer to Figure 9.14 as you complete Step 3.

a. From the Google Calendar main page, go to either the *My calendars* or the *Other calendars* pane.

b. Click the name of the first calendar you want to display.

c. To view events from another calendar, click that calendar name.

All the events from the selected calendars are displayed on the main calendar, color coded appropriately.

Selected calendars

Figure 9.14 Hands-On Exercise 2, Step 3.

> **Tip** ⭐ **Change Calendar Color**
>
> To change the color for a given calendar, click the down arrow next to that calendar in the *My calendars* or *Other calendars* pane and select a different color.

Step ▶ 4 Print a Calendar

Refer to Figures 9.15 and 9.16 as you complete Step 4.

a. Configure your calendar to display the view you want to print.

For example, to display a monthly calendar, select the *Month* view and navigate to display the month you want to print.

b. Click the **Print** icon above the calendar.

Click to print current
calendar view

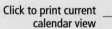

Figure 9.15 Hands-On Exercise 2, Steps 4a and 4b.

This opens the *Calendar Print Preview* window. The calendar to be printed is previewed here.

c. Click the **Print Range** drop-down list and select the date range to print.

d. Click the **Font Size** drop-down list to select a smaller or larger font for the calendar.

e. Click the **Orientation** drop-down list to select a different display orientation (portrait or landscape).

f. To hide events that you've declined, uncheck the **Show events you have declined** box.

g. To print the calendar in black and white (which can save ink on a color printer), check the **Black & White** box.

h. Click the **Print** button.

Calendar preview

Select date range

Change font size

Change orientation

Uncheck to hide declined events

Check to print in black and white

Click to print

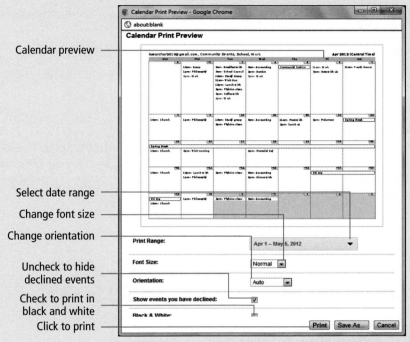

Figure 9.16 Hands-On Exercise 2, Steps 4c through 4h.

Objective 3

Add New Events

How do you maintain your schedule with Google Calendar?

Event An item scheduled with Google Calendar.

All the items scheduled on your calendar are called *events*. An event can be a meeting, an appointment, or anything else you do in the course of a day.

How do you add an event to your calendar?

You can create an event by adding it directly to the calendar itself, by using the *Create event* button, or by using Google Calendar's *Quick Add* feature. Quick Add is quite intelligent; for example, if you enter *Lunch with George at noon Monday at McDonald's*, Quick Add translates the text and enters the appropriate event at the specified date and time.

Quick Add An "intelligent" feature that lets you quickly add an event to a Google calendar.

What information can you enter about an event?

An event can include all manner of information, including the following:

- Title
- Start and stop times and dates
- Whether it's an all-day event
- Whether the event repeats

- Location

- Which of your calendars the event should be added to

- A brief description

- How much in advance you want to be reminded of the event, and how you want to be reminded

- Whether you should be shown as available or busy, for anyone viewing a public calendar

- Whether the event is private or public

- Guest list and whether those guests can modify the event, invite others to the event, or see the guest list

Does Google Calendar integrate with Gmail?

Because both applications are part of the same Google online empire, Google Calendar integrates smoothly with Gmail. Google Calendar can scan your email messages for dates and times and, with a few clicks of your mouse, create events based on the content of your Gmail messages.

Hands-On Exercises

3 │ Adding New Events

Steps: 1. Add an Event Directly to Your Calendar; **2.** Add an Event with the Create Event Button; **3.** Add an Event using Quick Add; **4.** Add an Event from Gmail; **5.** Invite Others to an Existing Event.

Use Figures 9.17 through 9.27 as a guide to the exercise.

Step 1 Add an Event Directly to Your Calendar

Refer to Figure 9.17 as you complete Step 1.

a. From the main Google Calendar page, click the hour or the day on your calendar for which you'd like to create the event. If you want to add an event to a daily or weekly calendar, click and drag your cursor over the entire timeframe of the event.

This opens a new event balloon.

b. Enter the name of the event into the *What* box.

c. If you've created multiple calendars, click the **Calendar** drop-down list and select which calendar you want to add the event to.

d. Click the **Create event** button.

 Add More Details

To add more information about the event, click the **Edit event details** link to open the event details page, discussed in Step 2. Enter the appropriate information and then click the **Save** button.

Enter event name
Select calendar
Click to create event
Click to add more information

Figure 9.17 Hands-On Exercise 3, Step 1.

Step 2 — Add an Event with the Create Event Button

Refer to Figures 9.18 through 9.21 as you complete Step 2.

To create an event with more details included, use the **CREATE** button.

a. From the main Google Calendar page, click the **CREATE** button.

Click to create
new event

Figure 9.18 Hands-On Exercise 3, Step 2a.

This opens the event details page.

b. Enter the title of the event.

c. Enter the start and end times and dates for the event.

d. If the event is an all-day event, check **All day**.

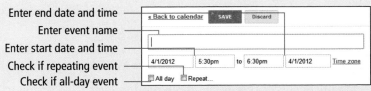

Enter end date and time
Enter event name
Enter start date and time
Check if repeating event
Check if all-day event

Figure 9.19 Hands-On Exercise 3, Steps 2b through 2d.

e. To add a repeating event, check **Repeat** on the event details page to display the *Repeat* dialog box. Select how (daily, weekly, monthly, etc.) and how often the event repeats and then choose when or if the repeating ends. Click the **Done** button to return to the event details page.

Select how
the event repeats

Select how often
the event repeats

Select how (or if)
event ends

Click to return to
event details page

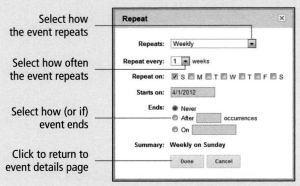

Figure 9.20 Hands-On Exercise 3, Step 2e.

f. Make sure the *Event details* tab is selected and then enter the location of the event into the *Where* box.

 Event Map

When you include location information about an event, Google Calendar includes a **map** link in that event's information. Click the **map** link to view a Google Map of that event's location.

g. Select which calendar the event should be added to.

h. To set a color for the event, check one of the color boxes in the *Event color* section.

i. Select how you want to receive reminders (via email or browser pop-up— or, if you've added your mobile phone number to your Google account, via SMS text messaging) and how long before the event you want to be reminded.

j. For shared calendars, select whether you want to be shown as available or busy for this event.

k. To make this a public event, select **Public**. To keep this a private event on your own schedule, select **Private**.

l. To invite a person to this event, enter that person's email address into the *Add guests* box and then click the **Add** button. Repeat to add multiple guests.

m. To let guests modify details of this event, check **modify event**. To let guests invite other guests, check **invite others**. To let guests see other guests invited to this event, check **see guest list**.

n. Click the **SAVE** button to add this event to your calendar.

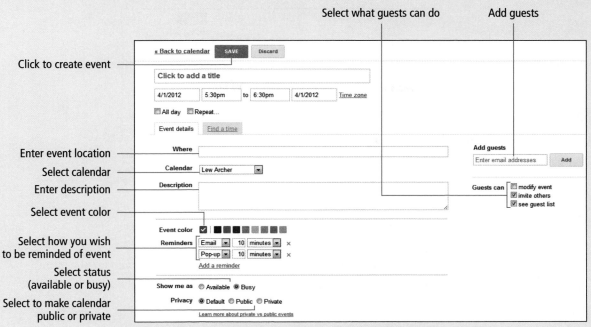

Select what guests can do   Add guests

Click to create event

Enter event location

Select calendar

Enter description

Select event color

Select how you wish
to be reminded of event

Select status
(available or busy)

Select to make calendar
public or private

Figure 9.21 Hands-On Exercise 3, Steps 2f through 2n.

Step ③ Add an Event using Quick Add

Refer to Figure 9.22 as you complete Step 3.

a. From the main Google Calendar page, click the **CREATE** arrow (or type the letter **q**).

This displays the *Quick Add* entry box.

b. Enter information about the event, such as the event's date, time, and location.

For example, to add an event for a study group meeting on November 12 at 9:00 a.m., enter *Study group meeting 11/12 9am*. You don't have to enter commas between items.

c. Click the **Add** button or press **Enter** on your computer keyboard.

The event is now added to your default calendar at the specified date and time.

Click to display Quick Add box

Enter information about event

Click to add event

Figure 9.22 Hands-On Exercise 3, Step 3.

Step ④ Add an Event from Gmail

Refer to Figures 9.23 and 9.24 as you complete Step 4.

When you're reading a Gmail message that contains information pertaining to a possible event, such as date, time, and location, you can quickly add that event to Google Calendar. Google uses artificial intelligence to parse the event information from the text of your message and then uses that information to create a new event.

a. From within the Gmail message, click the **More** drop-down list and select **Create event**.

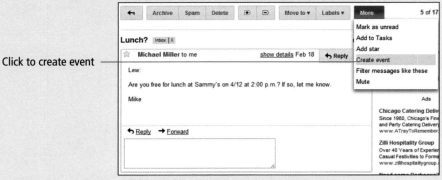

Click to create event

Figure 9.23 Hands-On Exercise 3, Step 4a.

This opens a new event window. Google fills in as much information as it can figure out about the event.

b. Correct or fill in any incorrect or missing information about the event.

c. Click the **SAVE** button.

The event is added to Google Calendar.

Click to add event to Google Calendar

Correct or complete necessary information

Figure 9.24 Hands-On Exercise 3, Steps 4b and 4c.

Step 5 Invite Others to an Existing Event

Refer to Figures 9.25 through 9.27 as you complete Step 5.

When you first create an event, you have the option of inviting guests to that event. You can also invite guests to an event after it's been created.

a. Double-click the event on your calendar.

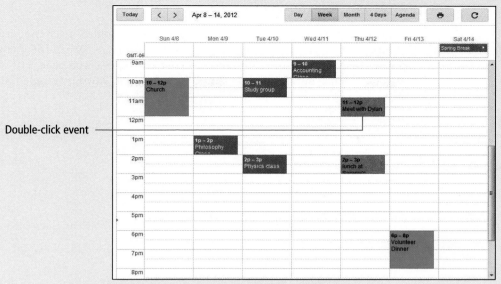

Double-click event

Figure 9.25 Hands-On Exercise 3, Step 5a.

This opens the event details page.

b. Go to the *Add guests* pane and enter the email addresses of your guests into the text box; separate multiple addresses with commas.

c. Click the **Add** button to add the guests you've entered.

d. If you want your guests to modify details of the event, check the **modify event** option. If you don't want them to have this level of access, uncheck this option.

e. If you want your guests to be able to invite other guests to the event, check the **invite others** option. If you don't want additional guests to be invited, uncheck this option.

f. If you want your guests to see who else was invited to the event, check the **see guest list** option. If you want your guest list to remain private, uncheck this option.

g. Click the **SAVE** button.

Click to save changes

Enter email addresses

Click to add guests

Check if guests can modify event

Check if guests can invite others

Check if guests can see guest list

Figure 9.26 Hands-On Exercise 3, Steps 5b through 5g.

Google Calendar now displays the *Send invitations?* dialog box.

h. Click the **Send** button.

Google sends email invitations to all the guests you added. Each invitation includes links for the guest's response—*Yes*, *No*, or *Maybe*. When the guest clicks
one of these links, he or she is taken to a *Submit Response* web page. His or her
response is then automatically entered into the event in your Google Calendar, as
shown in the *Guests* section of the event page.

Click to send invitations ——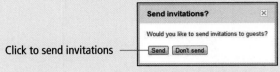

Figure 9.27 Hands-On Exercise 3, Step 5h.

Objective 4

Share a Public Calendar

What is a public calendar?

By default, a Google calendar is private—that is, it can be viewed only by the person
who created it. You can, however, make a calendar public, so that it can be viewed by
anyone on the web. When a calendar is public, anyone can search for it via Google's
web search, and it can appear in Google's search results. It's a great way to dissemi-
nate information about public events, such as sports teams or community groups.

Can you create a calendar that is shared only with specific people?

When you make a calendar public, by default anyone can search for it via Google's web
search. If you'd rather share your calendar with a select group of people, Google Calendar offers that option—and you can even let them add or edit events on the calendar.

How do you make a calendar public?

You can make a calendar public when you first create the calendar, by checking the
Make this calendar public option. You can also edit any existing private calendar
to make it public.

Hands-On Exercises

4 | Sharing a Public Calendar

Steps: 1. Make an Existing Calendar Public; **2.** Share a Calendar with Specific
People; **3.** Receive Event Notifications.

Use Figures 9.28 through 9.34 as a guide to the exercise.

Step 1 Make an Existing Calendar Public

Refer to Figures 9.28 through 9.30 as you complete Step 1.

a. In the *My calendars* pane of the Google Calendar page, click the down arrow next to the calendar you want to make public and select **Share this Calendar**.

Selected calendar ———

Click to share calendar ———

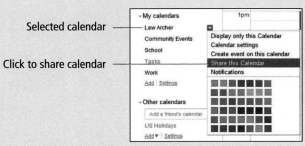

Figure 9.28 Hands-On Exercise 4, Step 1a.

This displays the details page for the calendar, with the *Share this Calendar* tab selected.

b. Check the **Make this calendar public** box.

c. If you want to hide the details of your calendar (to show only your free/busy status), check the **Share only my free/busy information (Hide details)** box. Otherwise, your entire calendar will be visible.

d. Click the **Save** button.

Check to make calendar public ———

Check to hide calendar details ———

Click to save changes ———

Figure 9.29 Hands-On Exercise 4, Steps 1b through 1d.

e. If a *Warning* dialog box appears, click the **Yes** button.

Click to confirm public calendar ———

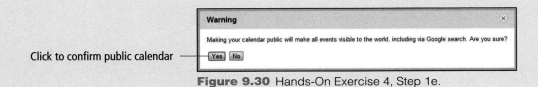

Figure 9.30 Hands-On Exercise 4, Step 1e.

Step 2 Share a Calendar with Specific People

Refer to Figures 9.31 and 9.32 as you complete Step 2.

a. In the *My calendars* pane of the Google Calendar page, click the down arrow next to the calendar you want to share and select **Share this Calendar**.

Selected calendar

Click to share calendar

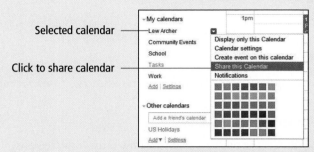

Figure 9.31 Hands-On Exercise 4, Step 2a.

This displays the details page for the calendar, with the *Share this Calendar* tab selected.

b. Go to the *Share with specific people* section and enter the email address of the first person you want to have access to your calendar into the *Person* box.

c. Click the **Permission Settings** drop-down list and specify what type of access you want this person to have: *Make changes AND manage sharing* (add and edit events, and invite others to share the calendar), *Make changes to events* (add and edit events, but not invite others to share), *See all event details* (but not add or edit events), or *See only free/busy (hide details)*.

d. To share with another person, click the **Add Person** button and repeat steps 2b and 2c.

e. Click the **Save** button.

Each person you've added will receive an email with the URL of your calendar. Each person can then access the calendar with the permission level you selected.

Click to add another collaborator

Select permission level

Enter email address

Click to save changes

Figure 9.32 Hands-On Exercise 4, Steps 2b through 2e.

> **Note** **Google Accounts**
>
> Everyone sharing your calendar must have a Google account. If they don't currently have an account, you're prompted to invite them to create one.

Step 3 Receive Event Notifications

Refer to Figures 9.33 and 9.34 as you complete Step 3.

If you're sharing a public calendar with another person, you may want to be notified when that person adds a new event to the calendar. It's a good way to keep track of new events in which you may be interested.

a. In the *My calendars* pane of the Google Calendar page, click the down arrow next to the selected calendar and select **Notifications**.

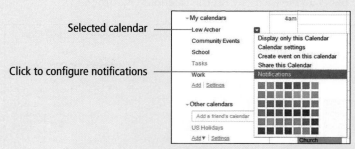

Selected calendar

Click to configure notifications

Figure 9.33 Hands-On Exercise 4, Step 3a.

This displays the details page for the calendar, with the *Notifications* tab selected.

b. Check the **Email** box for each type of action for which you'd like to be notified— *New invitations*, *Changed invitations*, *Canceled invitations*, *Invitation replies*, or *Daily agenda*.

c. If you'd prefer to be notified via text message on your mobile phone, check the **SMS** box for each action for which you'd like to be notified.

d. Click the **Save** button.

You'll now receive notifications of each new or changed event, as you've determined.

Check to receive notification via email

Check to receive notification via text message

Click to save changes

Figure 9.34 Hands-On Exercise 4, Steps 3b through 3d.

Objective 5

Create and Manage a To-Do List

Can you use Google Calendar to manage a to-do list?

Task list A to-do list of up-coming tasks managed in Google Calendar.

Google Calendar isn't just about scheduling events. Like Microsoft Outlook before it, Google Calendar also functions as a task manager to help you manage your to-do list, or what Google calls a *task list*. In fact, Google Calendar lets you keep multiple to-do lists, which is useful if you have more than one project you want to track.

How do you display the task list?

In Google Calendar, tasks are treated as a separate type of calendar. You display your task list in much the same way you display a calendar.

To display all pending tasks, go to the *My calendars* pane and click the **Tasks** item to activate that item. This displays all pending (noncompleted) tasks on the current calendar, in the panel above each day on the calendar (Figure 9.35).

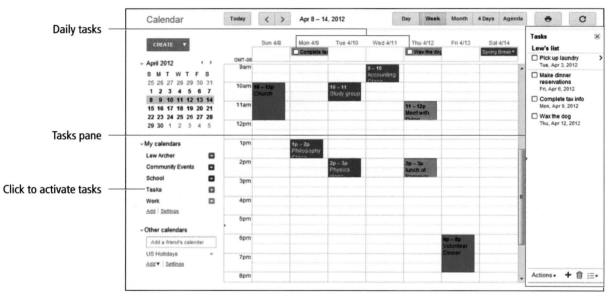

Figure 9.35 Displaying tasks in Google Calendar.

Activating the *Tasks* item also opens a *Tasks* pane on the right side of the Google Calendar pane. All current tasks are listed here, along with controls for adding, deleting, and managing tasks.

Hands-On Exercises

5 | Creating and Managing a To-Do List

Steps: 1. Create Multiple Task Lists; **2.** Add a New Task from the Calendar; **3.** Add a New Task from the Tasks Pane; **4.** Mark a Task as Completed; **5.** Manage Your Task List.

Use Figures 9.36 through 9.42 as a guide to the exercise.

Step 1 Create Multiple Task Lists

Refer to Figures 9.36 and 9.37 as you complete Step 1.

a. From the *Tasks* pane, click the **Switch list** button and select **New list**.

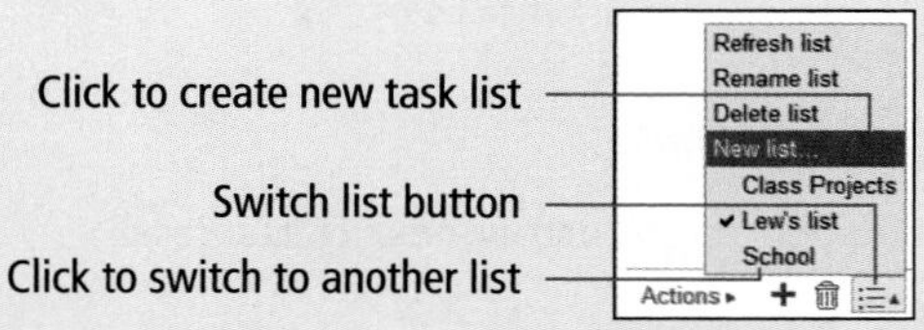

Click to create new task list —

Switch list button —

Click to switch to another list —

Figure 9.36 Hands-On Exercise 5, Steps 1a and 1c.

b. When the dialog box appears, enter a name for the new list and click **OK**.

Enter list name —

Click to create list —

Figure 9.37 Hands-On Exercise 5, Step 1b.

c. To switch to a different list, click the **Switch list** button and select that list.

Step 2 Add a New Task from the Calendar

Refer to Figure 9.38 as you complete Step 2.

You can add new tasks to a task list from the *Tasks* pane or from the calendar. The calendar method lets you easily create a task due on a certain date.

a. On the calendar, navigate to the day the new task will be due and click in the panel above that day. (If you're in *Month* view, click in the block for that day.)

This displays a new event/task balloon.

b. Click the **Task** link.

c. Enter the name of the task into the *Task* box.

d. Enter any necessary descriptive notes into the *Note* box.

e. Click the **Create task** button.

Click on task due date —

Click for task —

Enter task name —

Enter task details —

Click to create task —

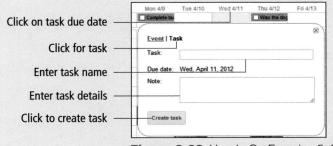

Figure 9.38 Hands-On Exercise 5, Step 2.

Step **3** Add a New Task from the Tasks Pane

Refer to Figures 9.39 and 9.40 as you complete Step 3.

a. From the *Tasks* pane, click the **Add task** (+) button—or just click in a blank area of the *Tasks* list.

A new task is now highlighted in the *Tasks* list.

b. Enter the name of the task into the highlighted area.

c. To enter more details about this task, click the right arrow next to the task.

Enter task name ⎯⎯

Click to enter more details ⎯⎯

Click to create new task ⎯⎯

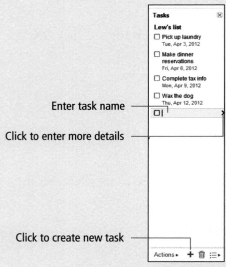

Figure 9.39 Hands-On Exercise 5, Steps 3a through 3c.

This opens the task within the *Tasks* pane.

d. Click the calendar icon to select a due date for the task.

e. Enter any notes about the task into the *Notes* box.

f. Click the **Back to list** link when done.

Click to display calendar ⎯⎯

Enter due date ⎯⎯

Enter task details ⎯⎯

Click to return to Task list ⎯⎯

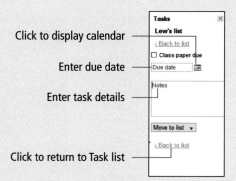

Figure 9.40 Hands-On Exercise 5, Steps 3d through 3f.

Step 4 Mark a Task as Completed

Refer to Figure 9.41 as you complete Step 4.

When you complete a task, you want to mark it as completed.

a. From the *Tasks* pane, check the box next to that task.

or

b. From the calendar, check the box next to that task.

Check to mark as completed ⎯⎯⎯

Completed task ⎯⎯⎯

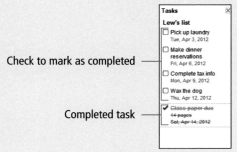

Figure 9.41 Hands-On Exercise 5, Step 4.

Step 5 Manage Your Task List

Refer to Figure 9.42 as you complete Step 5.

There are many actions you can take to manage the tasks in your to-do list, such as changing the task order and clearing completed tasks. You can apply any of these actions to any individual task from within the *Tasks* pane.

a. From the *Tasks* pane, highlight the task you wish to manage.

b. Click the **Actions** button and then select one of the following actions:

- **Indent**, which helps to identify a less important or subsidiary task by indenting it in the list

- **Un-indent**, which unindents any previously indented task

- **Move up**, which moves a task one position higher in the list

- **Move down**, which moves a task one position lower in the list

- **Edit details**, which displays the full task in the *Tasks* pane for editing

c. To apply an action to the entire *Tasks* list, click the **Actions** button and select one of the following:

- **Print task list**, which prints a copy of your task list

- **View completed tasks**, which displays those tasks previously marked as completed

- **Sort by due date**, which sorts the list by date due instead of date entered

- **View in my order**, which re-sorts the list by the date entered when you've sorted by due date

- **Reverse sort order**, which reverses the order of the task list if the tasks have been previously sorted

- **Clear completed tasks**, which removes all completed tasks from the list

d. To delete an individual task, without first marking it as complete, select the task in the *Tasks* list and then click the **Delete task** (trashcan) button.

Click to delete selected task ————
Click to display actions ————

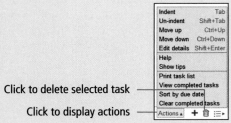

Figure 9.42 Hands-On Exercise 5, Step 5.

Summary

In this chapter, you learned how to create multiple calendars in Google Calendar and how to view those calendars in different ways. You also learned how to add events to a calendar and invite others to those events. In addition, you learned how to make a calendar public and share that calendar with others. Finally, you learned how to use Google Calendar to manage your to-do lists.

Key Terms

Event 217   Quick Add. .217

Google Calendar 208   Task list 228

Multiple Choice Questions

1. Which of the following is true?

   (a) Google Calendar is stored on your computer's hard disk.

   (b) Google Calendar is accessible from any computer with Internet access.

   (c) Google Calendar is only for office use.

   (d) All of the above

2. By default, the Google calendars you create are

   (a) private.

   (b) public.

   (c) shared with your Gmail contacts list.

   (d) None of the above

3. Google Calendar's Quick Add feature lets you

   (a) quickly invite a person to share your calendar.

   (b) quickly create a new calendar.

   (c) quickly display holidays on your calendar.

   (d) quickly create a new event with a line of descriptive text.

4. Tasks to be completed are displayed

   (a) in the Google Calendar Tasks pane.

   (b) in a special Tasks pop-up window.

   (c) in the pane above the task's due date in Google Calendar Day or Week view.

   (d) Both (a) and (b)

   (e) Both (a) and (c)

5. Google calendars can be displayed by

   (a) day.

   (b) week.

   (c) month.

   (d) All of the above

6. When you select a calendar in the Calendars list, the following happens:
    (a) Events for that calendar are displayed in the main calendar.
    (b) The calendar name is displayed as a text link.
    (c) The calendar name is displayed with a colored background.
    (d) Both (a) and (c)
    (e) Both (b) and (c)

7. You can sort the tasks in a Tasks list in the following order:
    (a) Alphabetical
    (b) By the order entered
    (c) By due date
    (d) Both (a) and (b)
    (e) Both (b) and (c)

8. Which of the following is true?
    (a) When you include location information for an event, a Map link is displayed.
    (b) When you include a hotel or restaurant name for an event, a logo for that hotel or restaurant is displayed.
    (c) When you invite others to an event, those people's photos are displayed.
    (d) When you include location information for an event, driving directions are displayed.

9. When you invite someone to an event, which of the following happens?
    (a) The event automatically appears on that person's Google Calendar.
    (b) The person receives an invitation to the event via email.
    (c) The person is automatically added to your Gmail contacts list.
    (d) A special calendar is created in your Google Calendar just for that person.

10. Which of the following is *not* an option for sharing a calendar?
    (a) See all event details only—cannot edit or add events
    (b) Edit events only—cannot add new events
    (c) Make changes to events—can add and edit events
    (d) Make changes and manage sharing—can add and edit events *and* invite others to share

Fill in the Blank

Write the correct word or words in the space provided.

1. To shift a calendar view to center around the current date, click the _____ button.
2. An appointment on your calendar is called a(n) _____.
3. People can search for a(n) _____ calendar via Google's web search.
4. To add an event via a short text description, click the _____ link.
5. In Google Calendar, a to-do list is called a(n) _____ list.
6. To view a list of upcoming events, select the _____ button.
7. When creating an event, enter location information into the _____ box on the event details page.

8. To specify a recurring event, check the _____ box.

9. When you invite someone to an event, he or she receives notice of the event via _____.

10. Events for each calendar you create are assigned their own unique _____.

Practice Exercises

1. **Holiday Calendar**

   In this exercise, you add a holiday calendar to Google Calendar.

   (a) From the Google Calendar page, click the Add button in the Other calendars pane and select Browse Interesting Calendars.

   (b) Select the Holidays tab and subscribe to the US Holidays calendar.

   (c) Return to your calendar page and make sure that only the US Holidays calendar is selected.

   (d) Select the Month view and display only this calendar for the current month.

   (e) Print this calendar view and hand it in to your instructor.

2. **Community Calendar**

   In this exercise, you create a calendar for community events.

   (a) Create a new calendar named Community Events.

   (b) Add several upcoming events to this calendar. You can use real school or community events, or make some up. Make sure the calendar has at least a half-dozen or so events scheduled.

   (c) Select the Month view and display the calendar for the current month.

   (d) Print this calendar view and hand it in to your instructor.

3. **Custom View**

   In this exercise, you create a custom view for the Community Events calendar you created in the previous exercise.

   (a) Select the Community Events calendar you previously created.

   (b) Create a custom view starting today and going forward the next five days, for six days total. (For example, if today is the fifth of the month, you'd create a view that showed the days from the fifth through the tenth.)

   (c) Print this calendar view and hand it in to your instructor.

4. **Class Task List**

   In this exercise, you create a to-do list for upcoming class projects and assignments.

   (a) Create a new task list titled Class Projects.

   (b) Enter all upcoming class assignments and projects into the to-do list, using the due dates supplied by your instructor.

   (c) As you create the list, mark any assignments you've already completed as such.

   (d) Print a copy of this task list and submit it to your instructor.

Critical Thinking

1. Google Calendar is a web-based application, meaning that you can access your calendars from any computer or mobile device connected to the Internet. Write a short paper describing the benefits of using a web-based calendar, focusing on how you personally might use Google Calendar.

2. Google Calendar lets you create multiple calendars for multiple purposes. Write a short paper discussing how you personally might use multiple calendars, and why this feature might be useful for you.

Team Project

1. As a team, create a new public calendar and make sure each team member has access to that calendar. This calendar should be for upcoming school or class events. Each member of the team should add at least one event to the calendar, including his or her name within the event description. When the calendar is complete, use Google Calendar's sharing options to share the calendar with your instructor.

Credits

Google, Blogger, and Picasa screenshots reprinted by permission.

CHAPTER 10

Using the Google Chrome Browser

Objectives

After you read this chapter, you will be able to:

1. Navigate the Web with Google Chrome

2. Manage Tabs and Homepages

3. Add and Manage Bookmarks and History

4. Use Google Chrome with Google Apps

The following Hands-On Exercises will help you accomplish the chapter objectives:

Hands-On Exercises

EXERCISES	SKILLS COVERED
1. Navigating the Web with Google Chrome	**Step 1:** Launch Google Chrome **Step 2:** Navigate to a Web Page **Step 3:** Search the Web **Step 4:** Print a Web Page **Step 5:** Browse Anonymously in Incognito Mode
2. Managing Tabs and Homepages	**Step 1:** Open a New Tab **Step 2:** Set Chrome's Homepage
3. Adding and Managing Bookmarks and History	**Step 1:** Bookmark a Web Page **Step 2:** Organize Your Bookmarks **Step 3:** Import Bookmarks and Settings **Step 4:** Synchronize Bookmarks and Settings **Step 5:** View Your Browsing History **Step 6:** Delete Your Browsing History
4. Using Google Chrome with Google Apps	**Step 1:** Create an Application Shortcut **Step 2:** Run a Google App in a Chromeless Window

Objective 1

Navigate the Web with Google Chrome

What is Google Chrome?

Google Chrome Google's web browser.

Web browser An application designed to view HTML-based pages on the web.

Google Chrome is Google's *web browser*. Chrome is similar to all the other web browsers available today, but it is a bit sleeker, with no Menu bar, search bar, or Status bar. This difference makes the web page bigger in the window. In essence, it moves the business of the browser out of the way so that you can pay more attention to the web page itself.

> **Note** **Minimizing the Chrome**
>
> According to Google, the name Chrome derives from the "chrome," or bells and whistles, that accompany a typical user interface. Google sought to minimize the chrome, which led to the browser's name.

How does Google Chrome work?

Omnibox The combination address box and search box at the top of the Chrome web browser window.

The Google Chrome interface resembles that of Internet Explorer and other modern web browsers, complete with tabs for different web pages (Figure 10.1). To go to a web page, type the URL into what looks like a standard address box at the top of the browser window. This box is more than an address box—Google calls it the *Omnibox*, and you can also use it to enter search queries. When you start typing in the Omnibox, Google suggests both likely queries and web pages you are likely to visit. Just select what you want from the list or finish typing your URL or query and then press Enter.

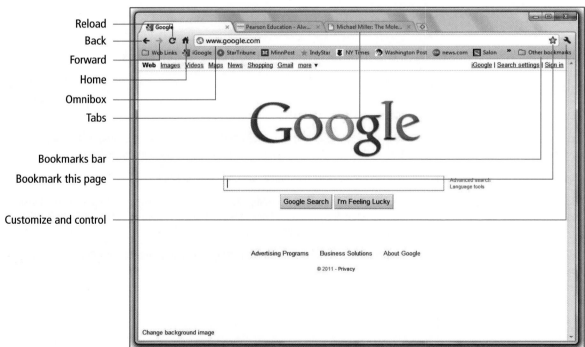

Figure 10.1 The Google Chrome interface.

Why would you use Google Chrome instead of Internet Explorer?

Google Chrome is, first and foremost, a web browser, that's similar to Internet Explorer, Firefox, Opera, and Safari. That said, Chrome is actually more than a web browser; some people have compared it to a web-based operating system or, at the very least, an operating container for web-based applications—especially when running web-based applications, such as Google Docs or Google Calendar.

Select the right options within Google Chrome and any web-based application appears in a window that resembles a traditional desktop application window rather than a browser; the tabs and the toolbars fade away so that all you see is the application itself. Even better, web-based applications run much faster in Chrome than they do in competing web browsers—more than 50 times faster than with Internet Explorer. (That's what Google's engineers claim, in any case.)

> **Note** **A Faster Engine**
>
> Chrome's speed is due partly to its stripped-down interface, but is more likely a result of the modern JavaScript engine used to run the browser. Chrome's engine, dubbed "V8," is designed to improve the performance of complex applications just like the web-based applications that Google serves up to its millions of users.

How do you configure Google Chrome's settings?

Chrome lets you configure several key program settings—but not too many. When it comes to configuration settings, Google Chrome is definitely lean and mean.

To configure Chrome's settings, click the **Customize and control Google Chrome** (wrench) button in the top-right corner and then select **Options**. This opens the *Google Chrome Options* page, in a new browser tab. This page has three tabs, each with its own related configuration settings. Settings on this page are changed as you select them; there's no *Save* button to click (Figure 10.2). Table 10.1 details the configuration settings found on each tab of the *Options* page.

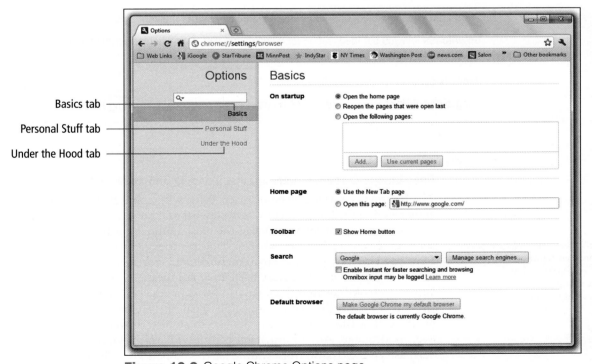

Basics tab

Personal Stuff tab

Under the Hood tab

Figure 10.2 Google Chrome Options page.

Table 10.1—Google Chrome Configuration Options	
Tab	**Settings**
Basics	**On startup** determines what you see when you launch Google Chrome—the homepage, last-opened pages, or pages you select.
	Home page determines what Google Chrome uses for its homepage—the New Tab page or a page you select.
	Toolbar determines whether Chrome displays a Home button.
	Search determines which search engine Google Chrome uses by default.
	Default browser lets you set Chrome as your default web browser.
Personal Stuff	**Sync** lets you use the same bookmarks and settings in any version of Google Chrome on any computer.
	Passwords lets you store passwords to specific websites.
	Form autofill lets you store form data to automatically fill in forms the next time you visit specific sites.
	Browsing data lets you import bookmarks and settings from other web browsers.
	Themes lets you change the visual look and feel of Google Chrome.
Under the Hood	**Privacy** offers various privacy-related settings and controls, including **Content settings** (cookies, images, JavaScript, plug-ins, pop-ups, location, and notifications) and **Clear browsing data**.
	Web Content helps you configure how content appears on a page.
	Network lets you change your network proxy settings.
	Translate, when enabled, offers to translate pages in a different language.
	Downloads lets you set the location for downloaded files, and whether certain types of files will automatically open when downloaded.
	Security controls various security-related settings.
	Google Cloud Print lets you sign in to and use Google's web-based printing service.

Does Google Chrome protect against phishing and malware?

The Internet can be a dangerous place, filled with scams and frauds and illicit activities designed to separate you from what you hold dear—either your personal information or your money. One of the most common forms of online scams involves something called *phishing*, where a fraudster tries to extract valuable information from you via a series of fake email messages and websites.

Most phishing scams start with an email message. A phishing email is designed to look like an official email, but is in reality a clever forgery, down to the use of the original firm's logo. The goal of the email is to get you to click an enclosed link that purports to take you to an official website. That website, however, is also fake. Any information you provide to that website is then used for various types of fraud, from simple username/password theft to credit card and identity theft.

Phishing A type of web-based scam that typically involves an official-looking (but fake) website designed to solicit your personal information.

Because phishing sites are designed to look like official sites, it's often difficult to tell a fraudulent site from the real thing. Fortunately, Google Chrome includes antiphishing technology that can detect most phishing websites. If you navigate to a known phishing website, or one known to contain computer viruses or spyware, Chrome displays a warning message instead of the suspect web page. When you see this warning message in the Chrome browser, navigate away from the troublesome web page as quickly as possible.

Chrome also includes advanced antimalware technology to protect against the inadvertent downloading of malicious software (***malware***). This phishing and malware detection is enabled by default.

Malware Any type of malicious software, including computer viruses and spyware.

Is it possible to browse anonymously?

All web browsers keep a record of every web page you visit, in the background, without your knowledge or explicit approval. That's fine, but every now and then, you might browse some web pages that you don't want tracked.

If you want or need to keep your browsing private, Google Chrome offers what it calls ***Incognito mode***. In this special mode (actually, a separate browser window), the pages you visit aren't saved to your browser's history file, ***cookies*** aren't saved, and your activity is basically done without any record being kept.

Incognito mode A form of anonymous browsing offered in Google Chrome.

Cookie A small text file, stored on your computer, used to track your web browsing behavior.

 Dual Mode

Chrome lets you run both normal and incognito windows simultaneously.

How do you download and install Google Chrome?

Like Internet Explorer and Firefox, Google Chrome is free for anyone to use. You can download and install your copy of Chrome from **www.google.com/chrome**. Click the **Download Google Chrome** button and then follow the onscreen instructions to complete the installation.

 System Requirements

As of summer 2011, Chrome works with computers running Windows 7, Windows Vista, or Windows XP (Service Pack 2 or above). There are also versions of Chrome for the Mac (OS X 10.5.6 or later) and Linux (Ubuntu 8.04 or later, Debian 5, OpenSuse 11.1, or Fedora Linux 10).

 Versions

This chapter covers Google Chrome version 11.0.696.71. It is likely that you will be using a newer version than this, which means that some of the features discussed in this chapter may be slightly different than those on your version of Google Chrome. Likewise, some of the screenshots of Chrome in this chapter may differ slightly from what you see onscreen.

Hands-On Exercises

1 | Navigating the Web with Google Chrome

Steps: 1. Launch Google Chrome; **2.** Navigate to a Web Page; **3.** Search the Web; **4.** Print a Web Page; **5.** Browse Anonymously in Incognito Mode.

Use Figures 10.3 through 10.9 as a guide to the exercise.

Step 1 Launch Google Chrome

Refer to Figure 10.3 as you complete Step 1.

a. Launch Google Chrome from either your desktop or the Windows *Start* menu.

   By default, Chrome displays the *New Tab* page when launched. This page shows your eight most visited web pages, along with a list of recently closed pages.

b. Click one of the pages on the *New Tab* page, or enter the address of another page into the Omnibox.

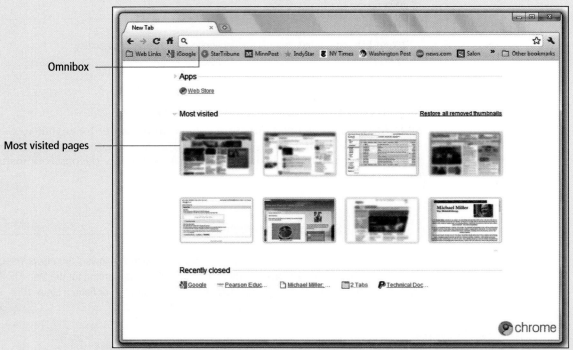

Omnibox

Most visited pages

Figure 10.3 Hands-On Exercise 1, Step 1.

Step 2 Navigate to a Web Page

Refer to Figure 10.4 as you complete Step 2.

You can use Google Chrome's Omnibox as an address box to navigate to specific web pages.

URL Uniform resource locator, the address of a specific web page.

a. Type a web page's *URL* into the Omnibox at the top of the browser window.

   As you start typing in the Omnibox, Google suggests both likely queries and web pages you are likely to visit.

b. Select the page you want from the drop-down list or finish typing your URL.

c. Press **Enter** (if you entered the full URL).

Google Chrome now navigates to and displays the page you entered.

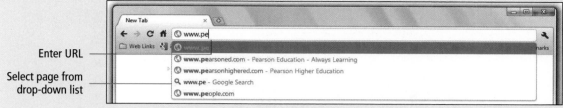

Enter URL

Select page from drop-down list

Figure 10.4 Hands-On Exercise 1, Step 2.

 Tip ⭐ **Reload a Page**

To "refresh" or reload the current web page, click the **Reload this page** button to the left of the address bar.

Step ③ Search the Web

Refer to Figure 10.5 as you complete Step 3.

As mentioned previously, Google Chrome's Omnibox functions not only as an address box but also as a search box for searching the web. That is, you can use the Omnibox to enter a web page's URL or to enter a search query.

a. Enter your search query into the address box.

As you start typing in the Omnibox, Google suggests both likely queries and web pages you are likely to visit.

b. Select the query you want from the drop-down list or finish typing your query.

c. Press **Enter** (if you entered the complete search term).

Your search results are now displayed in the browser window.

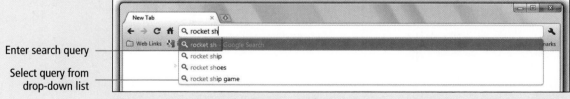

Enter search query

Select query from drop-down list

Figure 10.5 Hands-On Exercise 1, Step 3.

 Tip ⭐ **Change Search Providers**

By default, Google Chrome uses Google for all of its browser-based searches. You can, however, change the search provider. Click the **Customize and control Google Chrome** (wrench) button at the top right of the browser window and then select **Options**. When the *Options* page appears, select the **Basics** tab and then pull down the list in the *Search* section and select a provider: Google, Yahoo!, or Bing. To choose from additional search providers, click the **Manage search engines** button; when the *Search Engine* screen appears, click the desired search provider and then click the **Make default** button.

Step 4 Print a Web Page

Refer to Figures 10.6 and 10.7 as you complete Step 4.

a. Navigate to the page you want to print.

b. Click the **Customize and control Google Chrome** button and select **Print**.

Click to print the current page

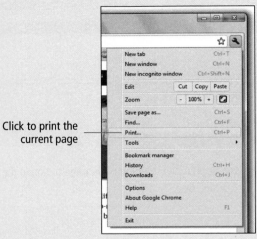

Figure 10.6 Hands-On Exercise 1, Steps 4a and 4b.

This opens the *Print* dialog box.

c. Make sure that the desired printer is selected in the *Select Printer* section.

d. In the *Page Range* section, select how much of the web page you want to print. To print the entire page, select **All**. To print just part of a page, select the **Pages** option and enter a page number or page range.

e. Click the **Print** button.

Select printer

Enter print range
Click to print entire page
Click to print part of the page

Click to print

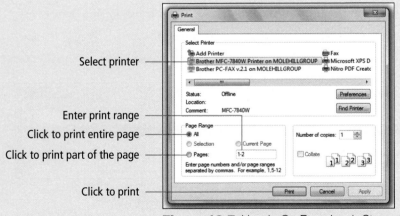

Figure 10.7 Hands-On Exercise 1, Steps 4c through 4e.

Step 5 Browse Anonymously in Incognito Mode

Refer to Figures 10.8 and 10.9 as you complete Step 5.

a. Click the **Customize and control Google Chrome** button.

b. Select **New incognito window**.

Click to open
incognito window —

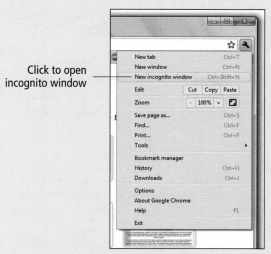

Figure 10.8 Hands-On Exercise 1, Step 5.

This opens a new window with a little spy icon in the upper-left corner next to the first tab. When you're done with your private browsing, just close the incognito window and no one will be the wiser.

Incognito logo —

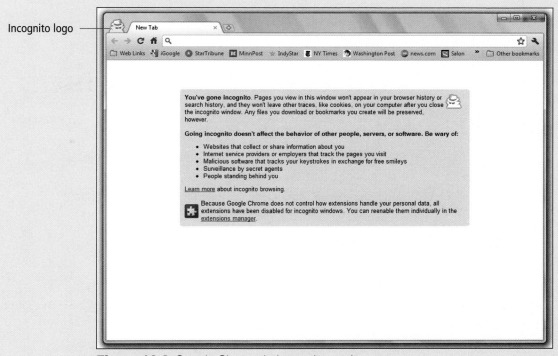

Figure 10.9 Google Chrome in Incognito mode.

Objective 2

Manage Tabs and Homepages

What is tabbed browsing?

Tab In Google Chrome, a means of displaying multiple web pages within a single browser window.

If you've used Internet Explorer and similar web browsers, you may already be familiar with the concept of tabbed browsing. With tabbed browsing, you can open different web pages in different *tabs*, instead of displaying one page after another or using multiple browser windows.

Google Chrome makes good use of tabbed browsing. You can display multiple web pages in multiple tabs, all located in a tab row at the top of the browser window. To switch to a different tab, simply click that tab.

How do you manage open tabs in Google Chrome?

To display the contents of an open tab, simply click it. To cycle through all open tabs, press **Ctrl+Tab**. To change the order of open tabs, click and drag a tab into a new location in the tab row.

Detachable Tabs

To detach a tab and open it in a new browser window, click and drag the tab outside the current browser window; this opens a new browser window. You can add that page back to the original browser window, again by dragging and dropping.

What is a homepage?

In a web browser, the homepage is the page that opens when you first launch the browser. By default, Chrome displays its *New Tab* page as its homepage, although you can specify any other web page as the browser's home.

Hands-On Exercises

2 | Managing Tabs and Homepages

Steps: 1. Open a New Tab; **2.** Set Chrome's Homepage.

Use Figures 10.10 through 10.12 as a guide to the exercise.

Step 1 Open a New Tab

Refer to Figure 10.10 as you complete Step 1.

a. Click the + button at the far right of the row of open tabs. (Alternatively, you can click the **Customize and control Google Chrome** button and select **New tab**, or press **Ctrl+T**.)

A new tab opens to the right of the currently open tabs.

Click to open new tab —————

Figure 10.10 Hands-On Exercise 2, Step 1.

Open a Link as a Tab

You can open any web page link in a new tab by right-clicking the link and selecting **Open link in new tab**.

Step 2 Set Chrome's Homepage

Refer to Figures 10.11 and 10.12 as you complete Step 2.

To set a given page as Google Chrome's home, you need to know the URL of the page you want to go to.

a. From within Chrome, click the **Customize and control Google Chrome** button at the top right of the browser window and then select **Options**.

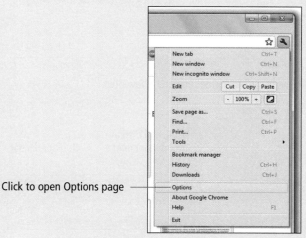

Click to open Options page

Figure 10.11 Hands-On Exercise 2, Step 2a.

This opens the *Options* page in the browser window.

b. Click the **Basics** tab.

c. Go to the *Home page* section and select the **Open this page** option.

d. Enter the URL for the desired homepage into the *Open this page* box.

e. Make sure that **Show Home button** on the *Toolbar* section is selected.

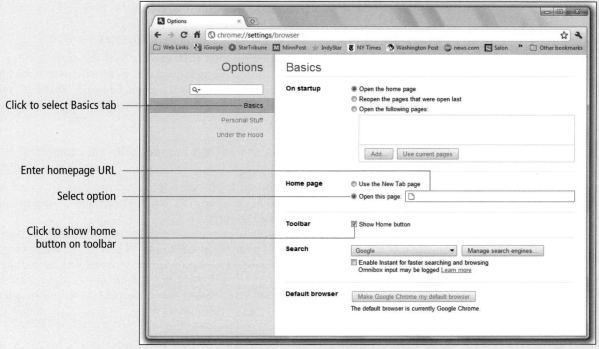

Click to select Basics tab

Enter homepage URL

Select option

Click to show home button on toolbar

Figure 10.12 Hands-On Exercise 2, Steps 2b through 2e.

Objective 3

Add and Manage Bookmarks and History

What is a bookmark?

Bookmark A means of storing links to favorite web pages for quick recall.

In Google Chrome, you keep track of your favorite web pages via the use of *bookmarks*. You can bookmark the pages you want to return to in the future and display your bookmarks in a bookmarks bar that appears just below Google Chrome's address bar (Figure 10.13).

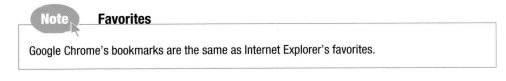

Note   Favorites

Google Chrome's bookmarks are the same as Internet Explorer's favorites.

Click to display more bookmarks   Bookmarks bar

Click to open bookmarked page

Figure 10.13 Google Chrome's bookmarks bar.

How do you display the bookmarks bar?

The bookmarks bar should be displayed by default. If it isn't displayed, click the **Customize and control Google Chrome** button, select **Tools**, and then select **Always show bookmarks bar**. Uncheck this option to hide the bookmarks bar.

If you have more bookmarks than can fit in the width of the browser window, the bookmarks bar displays a double arrow on the far right side. Click this double arrow to display the additional bookmarks in a drop-down menu.

Can you import your existing bookmarks into Google Chrome?

For many people, Google Chrome is not the first web browser they use. If you already have bookmarks (favorites) and settings configured in another web browser, you can import these bookmarks and settings into Google Chrome. This lets you get started with Chrome without having to abandon everything you've built in your current browser.

Can you synchronize bookmarks and settings between different computers?

Google Chrome is part of Google's web-based, cloud computing architecture. Therefore, if you use Google Chrome on multiple computers, you can keep the same bookmarks and settings for each of those computers. There's no copying of files necessary; synchronization is done online via the Internet.

This synchronization is possible because, once enabled, Google saves all your bookmarks and settings online in your Google account. Whenever or wherever you launch Chrome and connect to your Google account, the settings you see will be the same ones you saved previously. Any changes you make from any computer are also saved online, and those changes are visible from other computers you use to access the Internet.

Hands-On Exercises

3 | Adding and Managing Bookmarks and History

Steps: 1. Bookmark a Web Page; **2.** Organize Your Bookmarks; **3.** Import Bookmarks and Settings; **4.** Synchronize Bookmarks and Settings; **5.** View Your Browsing History; **6.** Delete Your Browsing History.

Use Figures 10.14 through 10.28 as a guide to the exercise.

Step 1 Bookmark a Web Page

Refer to Figures 10.14 and 10.15 as you complete Step 1.

There are several ways to bookmark a web page. We'll examine the fastest method.

a. Navigate to the web page you want to bookmark.

b. Click the **Bookmark this page** (star) icon in the Omnibox.

Click to bookmark current page

Figure 10.14 Hands-On Exercise 3, Steps 1a and 1b.

Chrome now bookmarks the page and displays an information bubble.

c. Edit the name of the bookmark if you want and then pull down the *Folder* list to determine where you want to save this bookmark.

d. Click the **Done** button to save the bookmark.

Edit bookmark name

Select bookmark location

Click to save bookmark

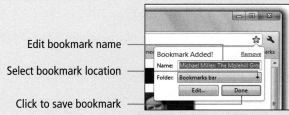

Figure 10.15 Hands-On Exercise 3, Steps 1c and 1d.

Step 2 Organize Your Bookmarks

Refer to Figures 10.16 and 10.17 as you complete Step 2.

Google Chrome lets you organize your bookmarks into folders and subfolders that branch off from the bookmarks bar, as well as in other folders on the same level as the bookmarks bar. You do it by using Chrome's *Bookmark Manager*.

a. Click the **Customize and control Google Chrome** button in the top right of the browser window and then select **Bookmark manager**.

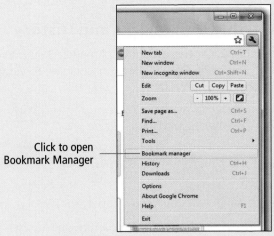

Click to open
Bookmark Manager

Figure 10.16 Hands-On Exercise 3, Step 2a.

This displays the Bookmark Manager in a new browser tab. The folders and sub-folders of bookmarks are displayed in the left Navigation pane; the individual bookmarks are displayed in the right pane.

b. To display the contents of a folder or subfolder, select that folder in the Navigation pane.

c. To change the order of bookmarks in a folder, click and drag that bookmark to a new position.

d. To list a folder's bookmarks in alphabetical order, select the folder, click **Organize** on the Menu bar, and then select **Reorder by title**.

e. To move a bookmark to a different folder, drag and drop that bookmark onto the new folder.

f. To create a new folder or subfolder, click **Organize** on the Menu bar and select **Add folder**. Then type the folder name and press **Enter**.

g. To rename a folder, select that folder, click **Organize** on the Menu bar, select **Rename**, and then enter a new name for the folder.

h. To edit information about a specific bookmark, select the bookmark, click **Organize** on the Menu bar, and then select **Edit**.

You can then edit the bookmark's name and URL from within the URL list.

i. To delete a bookmark, select that bookmark, click **Organize** on the Menu bar, and then select **Delete**.

Click to manage bookmarks

Click to display folder contents

Click to display subfolders

Bookmark

Figure 10.17 Hands-On Exercise 3, Steps 2b through 2i.

Step ③ Import Bookmarks and Settings

Refer to Figures 10.18 through 10.20 as you complete Step 3.

Google Chrome lets you import bookmarks and settings from Internet Explorer, Firefox, and other web browsers.

a. Click the **Customize and control Google Chrome** button and select **Options**.

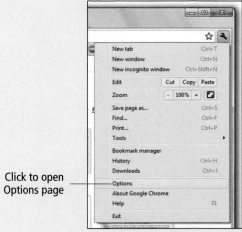

Click to open Options page

Figure 10.18 Hands-On Exercise 3, Step 3a.

This displays the *Options* page.

b. Select the **Personal Stuff** tab.

c. In the *Browsing data* section, click the **Import data from another browser** button.

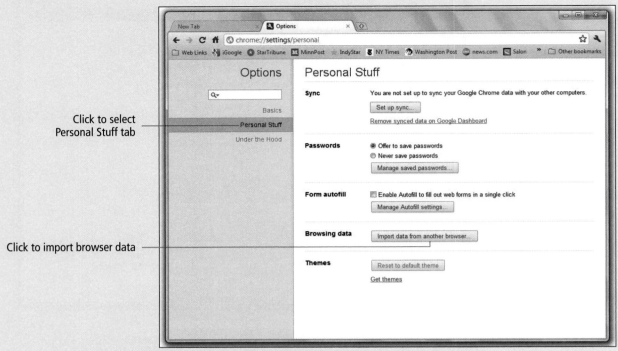

Click to select Personal Stuff tab

Click to import browser data

Figure 10.19 Hands-On Exercise 3, Steps 3b and 3c.

This displays the *Import Bookmarks and Settings* dialog box.

d. Pull down the *From* list and select the browser you're importing from.

e. Check which items you want to import: *Browsing history*, *Favorites/Bookmarks*, *Saved passwords*, or *Search engines*.

f. Click the **Import** button.

Your bookmarks and settings from the selected browser are now imported into Google Chrome.

Click to select other browser

Check items to import

Click to import items

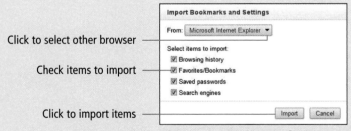

Figure 10.20 Hands-On Exercise 3, Steps 3d through 3f.

 Synchronize Bookmarks and Settings

Refer to Figures 10.21 through 10.24 as you complete Step 4.

You can configure Chrome to use the same bookmarks and settings when you open Chrome on other computers. To do so, you have to enable Chrome's sync function.

a. Click the **Customize and control Google Chrome** button and select **Options**.

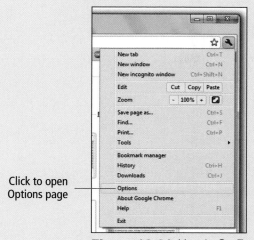

Click to open
Options page

Figure 10.21 Hands-On Exercise 3, Step 4a.

This opens the *Options* page.

b. Select the **Personal Stuff** tab.

c. In the *Sync* section, click the **Set up sync** button.

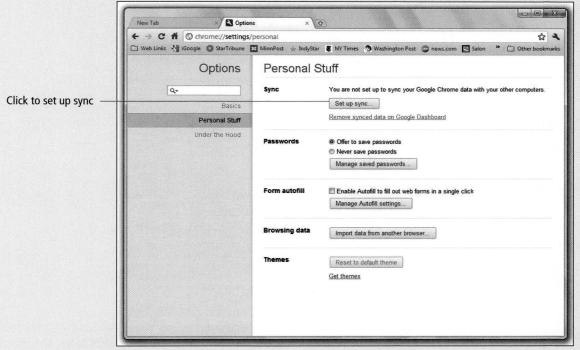

Click to set up sync

Figure 10.22 Hands-On Exercise 3, Steps 4b and 4c.

This displays the *Set up sync* dialog box.

d. Enter your Google account email address and password and click the **Sign in** button.

Enter Google account email address

Enter password

Click to sign in

Figure 10.23 Hands-On Exercise 3, Step 4d.

This displays a new version of the *Set up sync* dialog box, with the **Data Types** tab selected.

e. Select what you want to sync: *Keep everything synced, Apps, Autofill, Bookmarks, Extensions, Passwords, Preferences,* or *Themes.*

f. Click the **OK** button.

Click to sync everything

Click to sync specific items

Click to start syncing

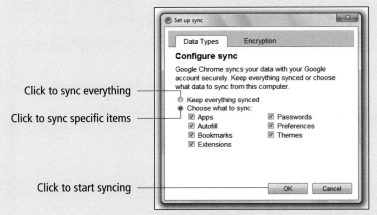

Figure 10.24 Hands-On Exercise 3, Steps 4e through 4g.

g. When the *Success!* dialog box appears, click **OK**.

 Stop Synchronizing

You may find that you don't want to synchronize all your settings across all the computers you use. To deactivate the sync function, click the **Customize and control Google Chrome** button and select **Options**; when the *Options* page appears, select the **Personal Stuff** tab. In the *Sync* section, click the **Stop syncing this account** button. When prompted, click the **Stop syncing** button.

 View Your Browsing History

Refer to Figures 10.25 and 10.26 as you complete Step 5.

Another way to revisit web pages you have viewed in the past is to use Google Chrome's history feature. Chrome keeps track of your history for up to ten weeks.

a. Click the **Customize and control Google Chrome** button and select **History**.

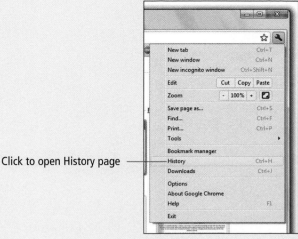

Figure 10.25 Hands-On Exercise 3, Step 5a.

Click to open History page

The *History* page is now displayed in a new tab.

b. To revisit any particular page, click that page's link.

c. To view additional pages in your history, scroll to the bottom of the page and click the **Older** link.

d. To search for a particular page you've visited, enter that page's name or URL into the search box and click the **Search history** button.

Click to search history

Enter query

Click to re-open visited page

Figure 10.26 Hands-On Exercise 3, Steps 5b through 5d.

Step 6 Delete Your Browsing History

Refer to Figures 10.27 and 10.28 as you complete Step 6.

You may not want your entire browsing history visible to others using your web browser. So, you can delete your browsing history.

a. Click the **Customize and control Google Chrome** button and then point to **Tools** and select **Clear browsing data**.

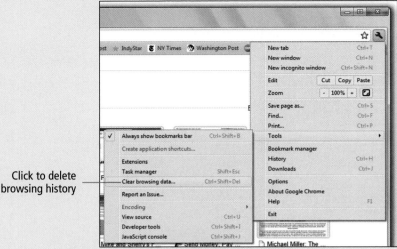

Click to delete browsing history

Figure 10.27 Hands-On Exercise 3, Step 6a.

This displays the *Clear Browsing Data* dialog box.

b. Check those items you want to delete: *Clear browsing history*, *Clear download history*, *Empty the cache*, *Delete cookies and other site data*, *Clear saved passwords*, or *Clear saved Autofill form data*.

c. Pull down the *Obliterate the following items from* list and select how much data to delete: *the past hour, the past day, the past week, the last 4 weeks,* or *the beginning of time*.

d. Click the **Clear browsing data** button.

Click to select how much data to delete

Select which items to delete

Click to delete selected items

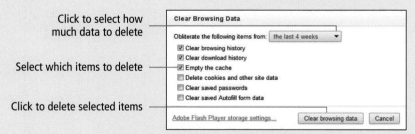

Figure 10.28 Hands-On Exercise 3, Steps 6b through 6d.

Alert! **What Not to Delete**

You may not want to select all the options in the *Clear Browsing Data* dialog box. Clearing browsing and download data erases your browsing history, so those are probably good choices. Emptying the *cache* is sometimes necessary, in and of itself, to clear out old versions of pages and enable you to see the most recent versions of some web pages. Deleting cookies is generally not advised, however, as this will get rid of tracking data that make some sites easier to access. And clearing saved passwords and *Autofill* form data might also make it less convenient to revisit pages where you've previously entered information.

Cache A temporary storage area on your hard disk where recently visited web pages are stored.

Autofill A feature in Google Chrome that lets you save frequently entered form data for future entry.

Objective 4

Use Google Chrome with Google Apps

How does Google Chrome work with Google applications?

If you use Google apps, such as Google Docs or Google Calendar, one of the best things about Google Chrome is how it runs these web-based applications. Not only does Google Chrome run these applications fast, it also lets you make a web-based application look and feel like a traditional desktop application by running the app in a "chromeless" window (Figure 10.29).

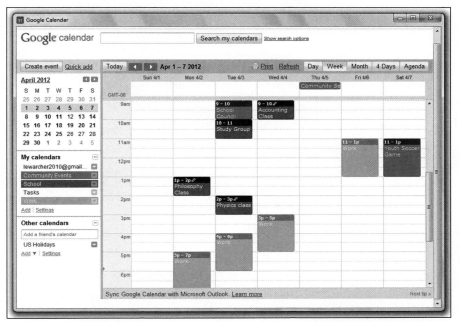

Figure 10.29 Google Calendar running in a chromeless Google Chrome window.

This window doesn't look like a traditional web browser window; instead, it looks and functions like any traditional desktop application window. It can be resized and, when you next open the application, the window opens to the previously saved size.

Hands-On Exercises

4 | Using Google Chrome with Google Apps

Steps: 1. Create an Application Shortcut; **2.** Run a Google App in a Chromeless Window.

Use Figures 10.30 through 10.32 as a guide to the exercise.

Step 1 Create an Application Shortcut

Refer to Figures 10.30 and 10.31 as you complete Step 1.

To make a web-based application function like a desktop application in Google Chrome, you have to create a *shortcut* for that application.

Shortcut A small file, often appearing as a desktop icon, that points to and opens an associated application or document.

a. From within Google Chrome, open the web page for the application.

b. Click the **Customize and control Google Chrome** button and then point to **Tools** and select **Create application shortcuts**.

Click to create shortcut

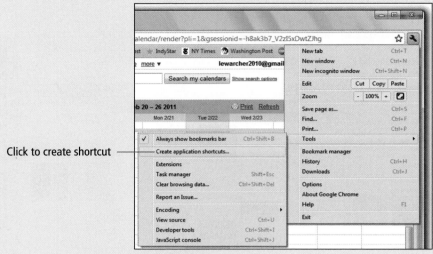

Figure 10.30 Hands-On Exercise 4, Steps 1a and 1b.

This displays the *Create application shortcuts* dialog box.

c. Select what types of shortcuts to create: *Desktop*, *Start menu*, or (in Windows 7) *Pin to Taskbar*.

> **Note** **Shortcuts**
>
> The shortcut options offered by Google Chrome depend on the operating system you're using. For example, if you're using Windows Vista, you'll see the option to create a shortcut on the *Quick Launch* bar.

d. Click the **Create** button.

Select type of shortcut to create

Click to create shortcuts

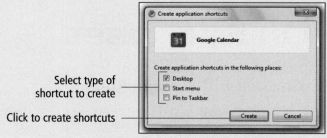

Figure 10.31 Hands-On Exercise 4, Steps 1c and 1d.

Google Chrome now creates the application shortcuts you specified. In the future, you won't have to navigate to the application's page on the web to use the application. Instead, you open the application by clicking the shortcut you just created, just like a traditional desktop application.

Step 2 Run a Google App in a Chromeless Window

Refer to Figure 10.32 as you complete Step 2.

To run a web-based application in a chromeless window, you must open the application from the shortcut you created.

a. Click or double-click the shortcut for the application.

The application opens in a new chromeless Google Chrome window. You can now use the application as you would normally.

Application shortcut on desktop

Application shortcut on Windows Start menu

Figure 10.32 Hands-On Exercise 4, Step 2.

Summary

In this chapter, you learned how to use Google Chrome to browse the web. You learned how to navigate to a web page, search the web, and browse anonymously in Incognito mode. You also learned how to use tabbed browsing, set Chrome's homepage, bookmark your favorite pages, and view and delete your browsing history. Finally, you learned how to use Google Chrome to run Google applications in a chromeless window—just like a traditional desktop application.

Key Terms

Autofill	256	Omnibox	238
Bookmark	248	Phishing	240
Cache	256	Shortcut	258
Cookie	241	Tab	245
Google Chrome	238	URL	242
Incognito mode	241	Web browser	238
Malware	241		

Multiple Choice Questions

1. Which of the following is *not* true about tabbed browsing in Google Chrome?

    (a) You can detach a tab to open it in a new window.

    (b) You can right-click on web links to open in a new tab.

    (c) You're limited to just five open tabs at any time.

    (d) You can press **Ctrl+Tab** to cycle through all open tabs.

2. What can you enter into Google Chrome's Omnibox?

    (a) Web page addresses

    (b) Search queries

    (c) Form data

    (d) Both (a) and (b)

    (e) Both (a) and (c)

3. To bookmark a page, do the following:

    (a) Click the Bookmark button on the toolbar

    (b) Click the Customize and control Google Chrome button and select Bookmark

    (c) Click the Bookmark this page star in the Omnibox

    (d) Right-click the page and select Bookmark

4. To print a web page in Google Chrome, do the following:

    (a) Click the Print button on the toolbar

    (b) Click the Print button on the bookmarks bar

    (c) Click the Options menu and select Print

    (d) Click the Customize and control Google Chrome button and select Print

5. To open a Google application in a chromeless window, you must do the following:

    (a) Configure Chrome to open in Application mode

    (b) Create an application shortcut

    (c) Download the desktop version of the application

    (d) Right-click the open application and select Full Screen from the pop-up menu

6. Google Chrome's default homepage is

    (a) the Google search page (www.google.com).

    (b) Wikipedia (www.wikipedia.org).

    (c) the New Tab page.

    (d) the last page you visited.

7. URL stands for

    (a) universal resource location.

    (b) uniform resource locator.

    (c) unidentified research lead.

    (d) universal rendering landscape.

8. Which of the following is *not* true?

    (a) Google Chrome is available for Windows 7.

    (b) Google Chrome is available for Windows NT.

    (c) Google Chrome is available for Mac.

    (d) Google Chrome is available for Linux.

9. What does Google Chrome's Incognito mode let you do?

    (a) Visit web pages under an assumed name

    (b) Browse anonymously

    (c) Sign in to Gmail with a different identity

    (d) Open multiple browser windows, each with a different homepage

10. Most of Chrome's settings are found by clicking which button?

    (a) Home

    (b) Favorites

    (c) Options and settings

    (d) Customize and control Google Chrome

Fill in the Blank

Write the correct word or words in the space provided.

1. You use a web _____ to view pages on the web.

2. The bells and whistles that often clutter an application interface, such as toolbars and Menu bars, is called the _____.

3. Google Chrome's combination address box and search box is called the _____.

4. In Google Chrome, a favorite site is called a(n) _____.

5. A web page address is called a(n) _____.

6. Computer viruses and spyware are collectively known as _____.

7. Google Chrome uses _____ to display multiple web pages in a single window.

8. To organize your bookmarks, open Chrome's _____.

9. To use the same bookmarks and settings when using Google Chrome on different computers, you need to _____ these items.

10. Google Chrome's default search engine is _____.

Practice Exercises

1. **Navigating the Web**

   In this exercise, you use Google Chrome to navigate the web.

   (a) If you haven't yet downloaded and installed Google Chrome on your computer, do so now.

   (b) Navigate to **www.pearsoned.com**.

   (c) Click the Higher Ed link.

   (d) Print this page and hand it in to your instructor.

2. **Bookmarks**

   In this exercise, you create a series of bookmarks.

   (a) Navigate back to the **www.pearsoned.com** page and bookmark the page.

   (b) Navigate to **www.whitehouse.gov** and bookmark the page.

   (c) Navigate to **www.google.com** and bookmark the page.

   (d) Open Google Chrome's Bookmark Manager and print the Bookmark Manager page. (It prints just like any other web page.) Hand in this page to your instructor.

3. **Searching**

   In this exercise, you search within Google Chrome.

   (a) Use Google Chrome's Omnibox to search for "nasa."

   (b) From the search results, click on the homepage for NASA.

   (c) Print NASA's homepage and hand it in to your instructor.

4. **Google Applications**

   In this exercise, you use Google Chrome to open Google Calendar as a chromeless application.

   (a) Use Google Chrome to open your Google Calendar page.

   (b) Create an application shortcut for Google Calendar. Save this shortcut to your desktop.

   (c) Launch Google Calendar from the desktop shortcut. (It should launch in a chromeless application window.)

   (d) At your instructor's request, show him or her your desktop with the chromeless Google Calendar window open.

Critical Thinking

1. Google Chrome is just one of several web browsers available today. Write a short paper discussing the advantages of Google Chrome over competing browsers, and why you personally might switch to Google Chrome.

2. Google Chrome includes an Incognito mode for anonymous web browsing. Write a short paper discussing for what purposes you might want to use incognito mode.

Credits

Google, Blogger, and Picasa screenshots reprinted by permission.

CHAPTER 11

Using Google Buzz

Objectives

After you read this chapter, you will be able to:

1. Configure Google Buzz
2. Follow and Post to Google Buzz

The following Hands-On Exercises will help you accomplish the chapter objectives:

Hands-On Exercises

EXERCISES	SKILLS COVERED
1. Configuring Google Buzz	**Step 1:** Show Buzz in Gmail **Step 2:** Put Buzz in Your Inbox **Step 3:** Connect Sites to Buzz
2. Following and Posting to Google Buzz	**Step 1:** Find People to Follow **Step 2:** View and Comment on Friends' Posts **Step 3:** Make a New Post **Step 4:** Make a Private Post

Objective 1

Configure Google Buzz

What is a social network?

Social network A website or service, such as Facebook or MySpace, where users can form communities with like-minded people and share details of their lives with friends, family, fellow students, and coworkers.

A *social network* is a web-based service that hosts a community of users and facilitates public and private communication between those users. Social networks enable users to share experiences and opinions with each other via short posts or status updates.

Some social networks, such as school or alumni, are devoted to a specific topic or community. Other social networks, such as Facebook and Twitter, are more broad-based, which allows for communities within the overall network devoted to specific topics.

What is Google Buzz?

Google Buzz A social networking tool that integrates data from a variety of social networks, including Twitter, Blogger, and FriendFeed. Google Buzz was launched in 2010, and integrates with Gmail, Google's web-based email service.

Google Buzz is a relatively new social networking tool from Google that exists within Gmail, Google's web-based email application. (Buzz was launched in 2010.) You do all your buzzing from the Gmail homepage, and all incoming status updates appear in your Gmail inbox.

Buzz lets you post short status updates, hyperlinks, and images to your friends, as you do with Twitter and similar social networking services. Buzz also lets you import your activity from other social networking sites; when you follow friends on these sites, their posts show up in the Buzz section of your Gmail inbox.

 Note **Gmail Account**

To use Google Buzz, you must have a Gmail account. To sign up for a free account, go to **mail.google.com**.

What social media can you consolidate with Google Buzz?

Google Buzz lets you read posts and messages posted to Twitter, Flickr, Picasa Web Albums, and Google Reader. Google is likely to add other services in the future.

How does Google Buzz differ from Twitter?

At its most basic, Google Buzz lets you broadcast status messages to a group of followers, much the same way you do with Twitter. The big difference between Buzz and Twitter is that you assemble your Buzz followers from your Gmail contacts.

Why use Google Buzz?

Google Buzz is a useful tool if you frequent more than one of the social networks integrated into the Buzz service. For example, if you follow several people on Twitter, a particular Blogger blog, and someone who uses Flickr, you can consolidate all those posts in Google Buzz. You can read all the new posts from these people on a single page and don't have to visit each of the sites individually—except to post.

Google Buzz is also convenient in that it operates as part of Gmail. If you're a Gmail user, this places all your incoming Buzz posts in your Gmail inbox, along with your normal email messages. When you check your email, you see your most recent Buzz posts.

Hands-On Exercises

1 | Configuring Google Buzz

Steps: 1. Show Buzz in Gmail; **2.** Put Buzz in Your Inbox; **3.** Connect Sites to Buzz.

Use Figures 11.1 through 11.6 as a guide to the exercise.

Step 1 Show Buzz in Gmail

Refer to Figures 11.1 and 11.2 as you complete Step 1.

You configure Google Buzz as part of your Gmail configuration.

a. Go to the Gmail homepage (**mail.google.com**) and log in to your Gmail account.

b. Click the **Options** (gear) icon and select **Mail settings**.

Click to configure
Gmail settings

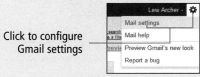

Figure 11.1 Hands-On Exercise 1, Steps 1a and 1b.

This displays the *Settings* page.

c. Click the **Buzz** tab.

d. Scroll down the page to the *Show Buzz in Gmail:* section and then select the **Show Google Buzz in Gmail** option.

e. Click the **Save Changes** button at the bottom of the page.

A Buzz item will now appear in the Navigation pane of your Gmail page.

Click to display Buzz tab

Select to display Buzz
in Gmail

Click to save changes

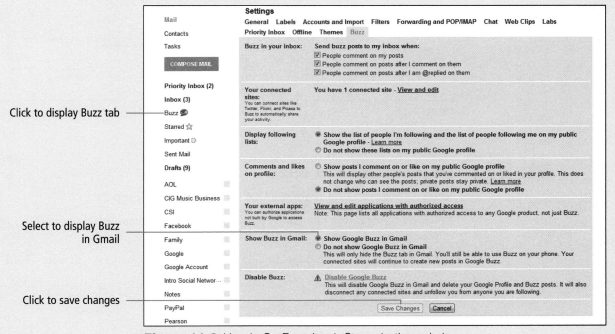

Figure 11.2 Hands-On Exercise 1, Steps 1c through 1e.

Step 2 Put Buzz in Your Inbox

Refer to Figure 11.3 as you complete Step 2.

You can configure what types of Buzz messages appear in your Gmail inbox.

a. Go to the Gmail homepage and click the **Options** (gear) icon and select **Mail settings**.

b. Click the **Buzz** tab.

c. Go to the *Buzz in your inbox:* section.

d. To display comments on your posts, check the **People comment on my posts** box.

e. To display comments on your comments, check the **People comment on posts after I comment on them** box.

f. To display comments on posts sent to you via the *@replies* function, check the **People comment on posts after I am @replied on them** box.

g. Scroll to the bottom of the page and click the **Save Changes** button.

@replies In Google Buzz, a way to direct a buzz to a particular contact, by putting an @ sign in front of a contact's name.

Check to display comments on posts

Check to display comments on comments

Check to display comments via @replies

Click to save changes

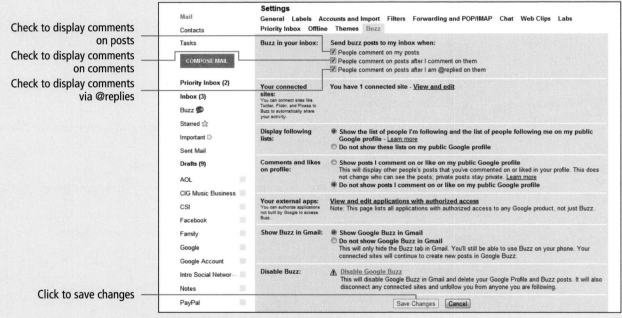

Figure 11.3 Hands-On Exercise 1, Step 2.

Step 3 Connect Sites to Buzz

Refer to Figures 11.4 through 11.6 as you complete Step 3.

You have to configure Google Buzz in order to link to those social networking sites to which you subscribe.

a. Go to the Gmail homepage and click the **Options** (gear) icon and select **Mail settings**.

b. Click the **Buzz** tab.

c. Go to the *Your connected sites:* section.

d. Click the **View and edit** link.

Click to add sites —

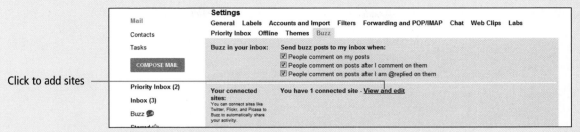

Figure 11.4 Hands-On Exercise 1, Steps 3a through 3d.

This displays the *Connected sites* dialog box.

e. Find a site you wish to connect to and then click the **Add** button for that site.

Click to add site —

Figure 11.5 Hands-On Exercise 1, Step 3e.

For some sites, this opens a site panel.

f. If necessary, enter your username and password for the selected site.

g. Repeat steps 3e and 3f to connect additional sites.

h. Click the **Save** button when you are done.

Enter username for site —

Click to save —

Figure 11.6 Hands-On Exercise 1, Steps 3f through 3h.

Objective 2

Follow and Post to Google Buzz

How does Google Buzz work?

To use Google Buzz, you first have to create a list of people you wish to follow. These people need to have a Google or Gmail account, or subscribe to one of the services that consolidates with Buzz. Posts from these people will then appear in the Buzz section of your Gmail page.

Other Buzz users may opt to follow you, as well. Posts you make will appear on your followers' Gmail pages.

Can you use Google Buzz to post to other social networks?

While you can use Google Buzz to view messages posted on compatible social networks, you cannot post from Buzz to those networks. The posts you make in Google Buzz are sent only to those followers who use Google Buzz.

What can you attach to a Buzz message?

Google lets you attach hyperlinks, digital photos uploaded from your computer, and photos stored in Picasa Web Albums to any Buzz message.

Are all Buzz posts public?

By default, Buzz posts are publicly viewable by anyone online. You can, however, opt to make private posts; when you select the private option, you then determine which group receives the post.

Hands-On Exercises

2 | Following and Posting to Google Buzz

Steps: 1. Find People to Follow; **2.** View and Comment on Friends' Posts; **3.** Make a New Post; **4.** Make a Private Post.

Use Figures 11.7 through 11.15 as a guide to the exercise.

Step 1 | Find People to Follow

Refer to Figures 11.7 through 11.9 as you complete Step 1.

a. Go to the Gmail homepage (**mail.google.com**).

b. Click the **Buzz** link in the sidebar.

> **Note** **Profile**
>
> The first time you use Google Buzz you may be asked to set up a profile. If so prompted, follow the onscreen instructions to do so.

Click to display
Google Buzz page

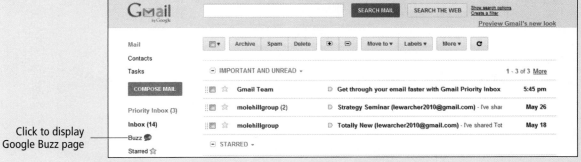

Figure 11.7 Hands-On Exercise 2, Steps 1a and 1b.

Google displays the main Google Buzz page.

c. Click the **Find people** link at the top of the Buzz feed.

> **Tip** **Follow Back**
>
> Once someone has chosen to follow you on Google Buzz, you can follow them back. Open the Google Buzz page and go to the **x followers** link to see how many people have started following you section. Click the **Follow back** button to follow any given person who is following you.

Click to find people
to follow

Figure 11.8 Hands-On Exercise 2, Step 1c.

This opens the *<Your name> is following* dialog box.

d. Enter the name or email address of the person you want to follow into the *Follow more people* box and then press **Enter**.

Google displays a list of people who match your query.

e. Click the **Follow** link next to the person you want to follow.

f. Click the **Done** button to close the dialog box.

Enter name or
email address

Click to follow

Click when done

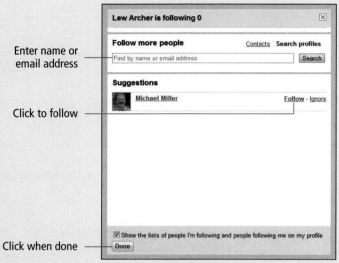

Figure 11.9 Hands-On Exercise 2, Steps 1d through 1f.

Step 2 View and Comment on Friends' Posts

Refer to Figure 11.10 as you complete Step 2.

a. Go to the Gmail homepage (**mail.google.com**).

b. Click the **Buzz** link in the sidebar.

c. Scroll down the page to the *Buzz* section.

The most recent posts from the people you're following are displayed here.

 Like a Post

To express approval of a post, click the **Like** link.

d. To comment on a post, click **Comment**.

e. When the post expands, enter your comment into the text box.

f. When you're done writing, click the **Post comment** button.

Click to display Buzz page →
Click to comment on post →
Enter comment →
Click to post comment →
Click to "like" a post →

Figure 11.10 Hands-On Exercise 2, Step 2.

Step ③ Make a New Post

Refer to Figure 11.11 as you complete Step 3.

a. Go to the Gmail homepage (**mail.google.com**).

b. Click the **Buzz** link in the sidebar.

c. Type the text of your message into the text box at the top of the page.

d. To attach a hyperlink to your post, click **Link**. When the posting area expands, enter the URL into the *Add a link to this post* box and then click the **Add link** button.

e. To attach a photo to this post, click **Photo**. When the *Add photos to post* window appears, click the **Choose photos to upload** button. When the *Add photos to post* dialog box appears, navigate to and select the photos you wish to attach and then click the **Open** button. When you're returned to the *Add photos to post* window, click the **Add Photos to post** button.

f. To post your update, click the **Post** button.

Enter message text →
Click to attach photo →
Click to attach link →
Click to post update →
Click to display Buzz page →

Figure 11.11 Hands-On Exercise 2, Step 3.

Step ④ Make a Private Post

Refer to Figures 11.12 through 11.15 as you complete Step 4.

a. Create a new Buzz post as described in Hands-On Exercise 2, Step 3.

b. Type the text of your message into the text box at the top of the page.

c. Click **Public on the web** (beneath the text box) and select **Private**.

Enter message text ———

Click and select Private ———

Figure 11.12 Hands-On Exercise 2, Steps 4a through 4c.

d. Click the **Post to a group** link.

Click to select who can
view the message ———

Figure 11.13 Hands-On Exercise 2, Step 4d.

e. Select the group to post to, or click **Create a new group** to create a new group of recipients.

Click to post update ———

Click group to receive message ———

Click to create new group ———

Figure 11.14 Hands-On Exercise 2, Step 4e.

This displays a new dialog box.

f. Enter the name of the group into the *Group name* box.

g. To select recipients from the *Suggestions* list, click **Add** to add a recipient to the group.

h. To search for new recipients from your Gmail contacts, enter a name or email address into the *Find by name or email address* box. Matching contacts will appear as you type; click a name and then click the **Add** button to add that recipient.

i. Click the **Done** button to close the dialog box and return to the previous screen.

j. Click the **Post** button to post your update.

Figure 11.15 Hands-On Exercise 2, Steps 4f through 4j.

Summary

In this chapter, you learned how to configure and use Google Buzz. You also learned how to follow new friends with Buzz, and how to read and comment on their posts. Finally, you learned how to make your own new posts.

Key Terms

@replies 266   Social network 264

Google Buzz 264

Multiple Choice Questions

1. Which of these social networking services can you connect to Google Buzz?

    (a) Facebook

    (b) Twitter

    (c) MySpace

    (d) LinkedIn

2. Where do Google Buzz messages appear?

    (a) On the main Google search page

    (b) In the Google Buzz application

    (c) In your Gmail inbox

    (d) In your Twitter feed

3. Which of the following statements about Google Buzz is true?

    (a) All Buzz messages are posted publicly.

    (b) All Buzz messages are also posted to Twitter.

    (c) All Buzz messages are private and viewable only to selected followers.

    (d) Any Buzz message can be posted privately to a group of people you select.

4. How do you post a Buzz message to Facebook?

    (a) Create a new message and then click the Post button. The message will automatically be posted to Facebook and other connected networks.

    (b) Create a new message and then click the Facebook icon.

    (c) Click the Post to Facebook button and then create and post the message.

    (d) You can't post Buzz messages to Facebook.

5. Which of the following *cannot* be attached to a Buzz message?

    (a) Word documents

    (b) Hyperlinks

    (c) Photos uploaded from your computer

    (d) Photos stored in a Picasa Web Album

Practice Exercises

Create a Buzz Feed

Google Buzz lets you post status updates to those who follow your posts. You can invite anyone to become a follower.

    (a) If you do not yet have a Gmail account, create one.

    (b) Invite your instructor to become a follower.

    (c) Once your instructor is following your posts, make a new post announcing that you've completed this exercise.

Critical Thinking

1. Google is using Buzz to enter the social networking space. That said, Buzz lacks many of the community features of other social networks such as Facebook and LinkedIn—profile/wall pages, photo storage/sharing, and the like. Discuss how Google Buzz differs from Facebook and similar social networks, why you might choose to use Buzz in addition to or in place of Facebook, and what Google might do to improve Buzz's social usability.

Credits

Google, Blogger, and Picasa screenshots reprinted by permission.

CHAPTER 12

Using Blogger

Objectives

After you read this chapter, you will be able to:

1. Create a New Blog

2. Create New Blog Posts

3. Customize Your Blog

4. Manage Blog Comments

The following Hands-On Exercises will help you accomplish the chapter objectives:

Hands-On Exercises

EXERCISES	SKILLS COVERED
1. Creating a New Blog	**Step 1:** Sign Up for Blogger **Step 2:** Create Your Blog
2. Creating New Blog Posts	**Step 1:** Post from the Blogger Dashboard **Step 2:** Format Your Blog Post **Step 3:** Add a Link to Your Post **Step 4:** Add a Photo to Your Post **Step 5:** Add a Video to Your Post **Step 6:** Add Labels to Your Post
3. Customizing Your Blog	**Step 1:** Choose a Different Template **Step 2:** Change Other Page Elements **Step 3:** Add a Gadget to the Sidebar **Step 4:** Rearrange Elements on the Page
4. Managing Blog Comments	**Step 1:** Limit Blog Comments **Step 2:** Disable All Blog Comments **Step 3:** Enable Comment Moderation **Step 4:** Moderate Blog Comments

Objective 1

Create a New Blog

What is a blog?

Blog A personal or professional journal on the web, consisting of multiple short posts made over time.

A *blog*—short for "web log"—is a personal or professional journal that is hosted on the web. Individual messages posted to the blog are called blog *posts*.

A blog post can contain commentary, links to other sites, and anything else the author might be interested in. Many blogs also let visitors post comments in response to the owner's postings, resulting in a community that is very similar to that of a message board. It's a 21st-century version of self-publishing, enabled by the Internet.

Post A message posted to a blog.

Why do people blog?

The question of why people blog has many different answers. Some people create blogs as a kind of personal-yet-public scrapbook—an online diary to record their general thoughts for posterity. Other blogs have some sort of focus; you can find blogs devoted to hobbies, to sports teams, to local events, to particular industries, and so on. Bloggers write about music or video games or travel or cooking or whatever they're interested in.

Many people blog for a cause, political or otherwise. The most serious of these issues-oriented bloggers are like columnists in the traditional media; they write with a passion, a point of view, and a personal sensibility that makes their blogs extremely interesting to read.

Other blogs are more professional, or even commercial. Many companies offer their own company or product blogs, blogging about their own products and important issues in their industries.

Blogosphere The entire universe of blogs.

The bottom line is that the *blogosphere* consists of blogs of all shapes and sizes, both professional and personal. Any individual, company, or organization can create a blog; there are no rules dictating or prohibiting blog content.

What does a blog look like?

A typical blog has the title of the blog at the top of the page, often with a subtitle or description just below that (Figure 12.1). Blog posts take up the balance of the page, with more static information located in a sidebar column to the right or left of the postings.

Blog title —

Sidebar —

Blog post —

Figure 12.1 A typical blog.

How do you create your own blog?

Creating a blog is surprisingly easy. You can use blogging software to create a blog on your own website, using your own web-hosting service, or you can create a blog at one of the many *blog-hosting services*.

Using a blog-hosting service is the easiest, and thus the most popular, option. Creating your own blog on one of these sites is as simple as clicking a few buttons and filling out a few forms. After your blog is created, you can update it as frequently as you like, again by clicking a link or two.

Blog-hosting service A website that offers easy-to-use tools to build, host, and maintain a blog—typically for free.

What is Blogger?

Blogger (www.blogger.com), also known as Google Blogs, is the most popular blog-hosting service on the web today. Launched in 1999 as a freestanding service, Blogger was purchased by Google in 2003 and is now part of the Google family of websites. Blogger is host to more than 8 million individual blogs, more than any other blog-hosting service.

Blogger Google's blog-hosting service.

How much does Blogger cost to use?

Blogger is completely free to use. To use Blogger, you must have an existing Google account or create a new one.

Hands-On Exercises

1 | Creating a New Blog

Steps: 1. Sign Up for Blogger; **2.** Create Your Blog.

Use Figures 12.2 through 12.5 as a guide to the exercise.

 Step 1 Sign Up for Blogger

Refer to Figures 12.2 and 12.3 as you complete Step 1.

a. Go to www.blogger.com.

b. Enter your Google account email address into the *Email:* box.

c. Enter your Google account password into the *Password:* box.

d. Click the **Sign in** button.

Note   Create a New Account

If you do not yet have a Google account, click the **Get started** link to create a new one.

Enter email address

Enter password

Click to sign in to your account

Figure 12.2 Hands-On Exercise 1, Steps 1a through 1d.

Google now displays the *Sign up for Blogger* page.

e. Enter the name you wish displayed on your blog posts into the *Display name* box.

f. If you want Google to send you Blogger-related promotional announcements, check the **Email notifications** box. Otherwise, leave this box unchecked.

g. Check the **I accept the Terms of Service** box.

h. Click **CONTINUE**.

Google now prompts you to create your first blog.

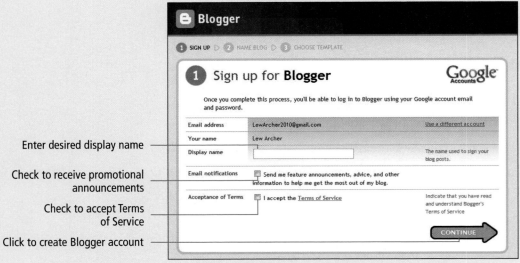

Enter desired display name

Check to receive promotional announcements

Check to accept Terms of Service

Click to create Blogger account

Figure 12.3 Hands-On Exercise 1, Steps 1e through 1h.

Step 2 | Create Your Blog

Refer to Figures 12.4 and 12.5 as you complete Step 2.

You're prompted to create your first blog as the second step in the Blogger sign-up process. When you click **CONTINUE** on the *Sign up for Blogger* page, Blogger displays the *Name your blog* page. (If Blogger displays the Dashboard again, click the **Create a Blog** link.)

> **Note** **Creating a Blog from the Dashboard**
>
> You can also create a new blog from the Blogger Dashboard, which is where you manage all your Blogger blogs. Sign in to Blogger to open the Dashboard and then click the **Create a Blog** link.

a. When the *Name your blog* page appears, enter the desired name for your blog into the *Blog title* box.

b. Enter the desired web address for your blog into the *Blog address (URL)* box.

> *Blog address* For Blogger blogs, the part of the blog's URL that appears before the blogspot.com domain.

The ***blog address*** is the part of the blog's URL that appears before Blogger's **blogspot.com** domain. Your blog will have a complete address in the form of ***blogname***.blogspot.com. Click the **Check Availability** link to make sure the desired name/address is available.

c. Click **CONTINUE**.

Enter desired blog name
Enter desired blog address
Click to check blog address availability
Click to continue

Figure 12.4 Hands-On Exercise 1, Steps 2a through 2c.

This displays the *Choose a starter template* page.

d. Click the template you want to use for your blog.

> **Note** **Blogger Templates**
>
> A Blogger template is a predesigned combination of page layout, colors, and fonts. The templates presented on the *Choose a starter template* page are just a subset of the larger number of available templates; you can choose from additional templates after you've created your blog.

e. Click **CONTINUE**.

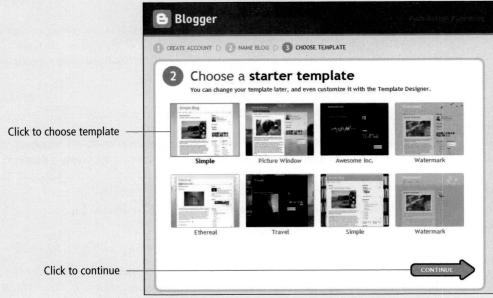

Click to choose template

Click to continue

Figure 12.5 Hands-On Exercise 1, Steps 2d and 2e.

Blogger now creates your blog and displays the *Your blog has been created!* page. Click **START BLOGGING** if now is a good time to write your first blog post. Otherwise, you can create posts later.

 Note **View Your Blog**

You can view your blog by entering the previously assigned URL, or by going to the Blogger Dashboard (**www.blogger.com**), clicking the blog name, and then clicking the **View Blog** link.

Objective 2

Create New Blog Posts

How often should you post to your blog?

You can post to your blog as frequently as you like. Many bloggers post weekly, some daily, and some several times a day.

How long should a blog post be?

Blog posts can be as short as a word or two or as long as you like; there are no rules. However, frequent short posts are more common than infrequent long posts. Blog readers seem to favor shorter, more concise posts; they tend to graze rather than read.

How can you categorize your posts?

Label In a Blogger blog, a keyword that helps describe or categorize a specific blog post.

After you've made a number of posts to your blog, it becomes increasingly difficult for readers to find any particular post. You can make this easier for your blog visitors by using *labels* to categorize your posts. Visitors can then click a label in the label list to view all posts related to that particular topic.

Can you add nontext items to a blog post?

Blog posts can include more than just plain text. You can turn your blog into a virtual multimedia theater by including photos and videos in your posts.

For example, you can create a blog consisting of nothing but digital photos. (This type of blog is called a *photoblog*.) This is a nice way to share pictures with family and friends, and it takes only a few minutes each week to post your latest pictures.

Photoblog A blog consisting primarily or solely of photographs.

What is the Blogger Dashboard?

The Blogger *Dashboard* is your gateway to all your blog activity; it's where you manage all your Blogger blogs.

The Blogger Dashboard is located at **www.blogger.com**, after you've signed in to Blogger and created your first blog. From here you can change each blog's settings and layout, create new blog posts, and view the contents of each blog. You can also use the Dashboard to create new blogs, manage your Blogger account and profile, and access Blogger's help system.

Dashboard In Blogger, the page that enables you to manage all your blogs and blog-related activities.

Hands-On Exercises

2 | Creating New Blog Posts

Steps: 1. Post from the Blogger Dashboard; **2.** Format Your Blog Post; **3.** Add a Link to Your Post; **4.** Add a Photo to Your Post; **5.** Add a Video to Your Post; **6.** Add Labels to Your Post.

Use Figures 12.6 through 12.21 as a guide to the exercise.

Step 1 Post from the Blogger Dashboard

Refer to Figures 12.6 and 12.7 as you complete Step 1.

> **Note**
>
> All the screenshots in this chapter reflect Blogger's latest update. If you have not yet received this update, you can access it and other upcoming new features via Blogger in Draft (**draft.blogger.com**).

a. Go to **www.blogger.com** and sign in to Blogger to display the Dashboard.

b. From the Blogger Dashboard, click the **New Post** (pencil) button for a particular blog.

Click to create new post for a blog

Figure 12.6 Hands-On Exercise 2, Step 1b.

This displays the *Post* page.

c. Enter a title for your post into the *Post title:* box.

d. Enter the text for your post into the large text box.

If you like, you can format the text (bold, italic, colors, etc.) using the formatting toolbar above this text box.

e. To preview your post in a new tab, click the **Preview** button.

f. When you finish writing and formatting, click the **Publish** button.

Blogger now publishes your post and displays the Blogger Dashboard for this blog, with all posts listed. Click the **View blog** button to view your blog, with the new post at the top of the page.

Enter post title

Enter post text

Click to post to blog

Click to preview post

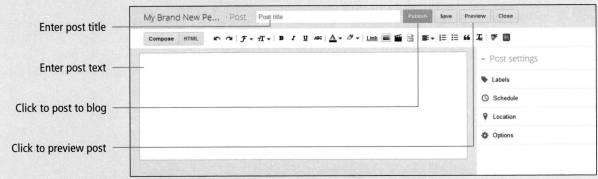

Figure 12.7 Hands-On Exercise 2, Steps 1c through 1f.

Step 2 Format Your Blog Post

Refer to Figure 12.8 as you complete Step 2.

The *Post* page includes many formatting options for your blog post, all available from the Formatting toolbar located above the text entry box.

a. To change the text font, select a block of text, click the **Font** button, and select a new font family—*Arial*, *Courier*, *Georgia*, *Helvetica*, *Times*, *Trebuchet*, or *Verdana*.

b. To change the text size, select a block of text, click the **Font size** button, and select a new size—*Smallest*, *Small*, *Normal*, *Large*, or *Largest*.

c. To bold selected text, select a block of text and click the **Bold** button.

d. To italicize selected text, select a block of text and click the **Italic** button.

e. To underline selected text, select a block of text and click the **Underline** button.

f. To strike through selected text, select a block of text and click the **Strikethrough** button.

g. To change the text color, select a block of text, click the **Text color** button, and make a choice from the color chooser.

h. To add a color highlight behind text, select a block of text, click the **Text background color** button, and make a choice from the color chooser.

i. To change the text alignment, position your cursor within a paragraph, click the **Alignment** button, and then select *Align left*, *Align center*, *Align right*, or *Justify*.

j. To start a numbered list, position your cursor at the first list item and click the **Numbered list** button.

k. To start a bulleted list, position your cursor at the first list item and click the **Bullet list** button.

l. To indent a block of text, position your cursor within the paragraph and click the **Quote** button.

> ### Tip ⭐ Remove Formatting
>
> To undo all formatting you've applied, click the **Remove formatting** button on the toolbar.

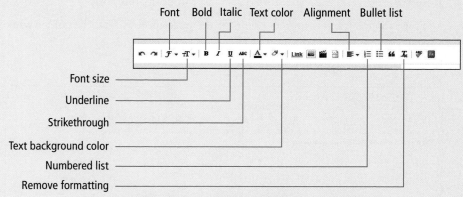

Figure 12.8 Hands-On Exercise 2, Step 2.

Step 3 Add a Link to Your Post

Refer to Figures 12.9 and 12.10 as you complete Step 3.

You can include links to other web pages in your blog posts.

a. From the *Post* page, highlight the text that you want to link.

b. Click the **Link** button on the Formatting toolbar.

Figure 12.9 Hands-On Exercise 2, Steps 3a and 3b.

This displays the *Edit Link* dialog box.

c. Make sure the **Web address** option is selected.

d. Enter the URL you want to link to into the *To what URL should this link go?* box.

e. Click **OK**.

f. Continue with your post as usual.

Select to link to Web address

Enter URL to link to

Click to insert link

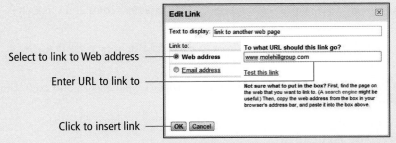

Figure 12.10 Hands-On Exercise 2, Steps 3c through 3f.

Step ④ Add a Photo to Your Post

Refer to Figures 12.11 through 12.15 as you complete Step 4.

a. From the *Post* page, enter any text for the post and position the cursor where you want the picture to appear.

b. Click the **Insert image** button on the formatting toolbar.

Click to insert photo(s)

Position insertion point for photo(s)

Figure 12.11 Hands-On Exercise 2, Steps 4a and 4b.

This displays the *Add Images* dialog box.

c. To upload an image from your computer, select the **Upload** option.

> **Note** **Other Options**
>
> In addition to uploading photos stored on your computer, you can also add photos you've previously uploaded to the blog (*From this blog*), photos stored on Picasa Web Albums (*From Picasa Web Albums*), and photos hosted on another website (*From a URL*).

d. Click the **Choose files** or **Browse** button.

Click to upload photos from your computer

Click to choose photos

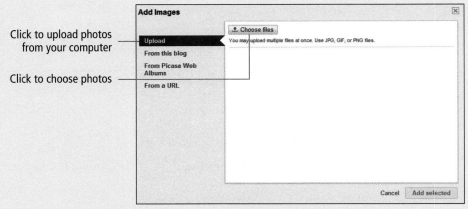

Figure 12.12 Hands-On Exercise 2, Steps 4c and 4d.

This displays the *Open* or *Choose File to Upload* dialog box.

e. Navigate to and select the image file(s) you want to upload.

To select more than one photo, hold down the **Ctrl** key while clicking each file.

f. Click the **Open** button.

Select pictures to upload

Click to choose photos

Figure 12.13 Hands-On Exercise 2, Steps 4e and 4f.

This adds the selected image file(s) to the queue in the *Add Images* dialog box. To add other files to the list, repeat steps steps 4c through 4f.

g. In the *Add Images* dialog box, select the photo(s) you want to insert.

h. Click the **Add selected** button.

Select photos to insert

Click to add photos to blog post

Figure 12.14 Hands-On Exercise 2, Steps 4g and 4h.

The selected images are now added to your blog post. You can now format the appearance of these photos in your post.

i. Click the photo to display the image formatting menu at the top of the browser window.

j. To select the size of the picture in the post, click **Small**, **Medium**, **Large**, **X-Large**, or **Original size**.

k. To specify the alignment of the picture, click **Left**, **Center**, or **Right**.

l. To delete this photo from your post, click **Remove**.

m. Continue with the rest of your post as usual.

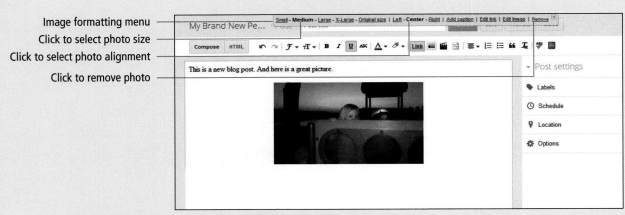

Image formatting menu
Click to select photo size
Click to select photo alignment
Click to remove photo

Figure 12.15 Hands-On Exercise 2, Steps 4i through 4m.

> **Note**   **Photo Storage**
>
> The pictures you upload to your blog are stored in a special album on Google's Picasa Web Albums site (**http://picasaweb.google.com**). Picasa creates an album with the same name as your blog; you can view, edit, and print the pictures on Picasa Web Albums by clicking the album cover.

Step 5   Add a Video to Your Post

Refer to Figures 12.16 through 12.20 as you complete Step 5.

a. From the *Post* page, enter any text for the post and position the cursor where you want the video to appear.

b. Click the **Insert a video** button on the formatting toolbar.

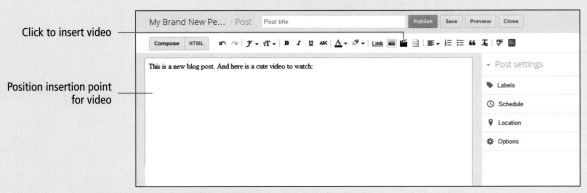

Click to insert video

Position insertion point
for video

Figure 12.16 Hands-On Exercise 2, Steps 5a and 5b.

This displays the *Add a Video* dialog box.

c. To upload a video from your computer, click the **Upload** option.

d. Click the **Choose a video to upload** or **Browse** button.

Click to upload video from your computer

Click to choose video

Figure 12.17 Hands-On Exercise 2, Steps 5c and 5d.

This displays the *Open* or *Choose File to Upload* dialog box.

e. Navigate to and select the video file you want to upload.

f. Click the **Open** button.

Select video to upload

Click to upload video

Figure 12.18 Hands-On Exercise 2, Steps 5e and 5f.

You are now returned to the *Add a Video* dialog box.

g. Click the **Upload** button.

Click to upload video file ——

Figure 12.19 Hands-On Exercise 2, Step 5g.

You now see an *Uploading video...* image in your post. This image displays while the video is being uploaded; once the video is uploaded, you'll see the regular video player and thumbnail for this video, instead.

h. Once the video is uploaded, continue with your post as usual.

Video uploading ——

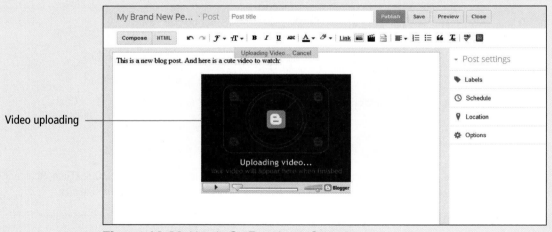

Figure 12.20 Hands-On Exercise 2, Step 5h.

Step 6 Add Labels to Your Post

Refer to Figure 12.21 as you complete Step 6.

a. On the *Post* page, click **Labels** in the right sidebar.

   This expands the *Labels* section and opens a new text box there.

b. Enter one or more labels into the text box; separate labels with commas.

c. Alternatively, click any existing label in the *Labels* list to add that label to this post.

d. Click the **Done** button.

e. Complete your post as usual.

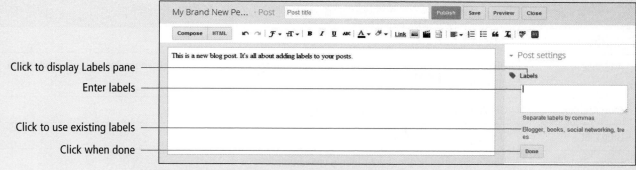

Click to display Labels pane
Enter labels
Click to use existing labels
Click when done

Figure 12.21 Hands-On Exercise 2, Step 6.

Objective 3

Customize Your Blog

Can you personalize the look and feel of your blog?

Blogger offers various ways to customize your blog. You can apply different templates, change color schemes, and even edit the blog's underlying HTML code. Most of this customization is done using Blogger's *Template Designer*, a web-based application with various formatting options.

Template Designer Blogger's web-based application for formatting the look and feel of a blog.

Can you add gadgets to your blog?

One of Blogger's most useful features is the ability to add subsidiary page elements, called *gadgets*, typically displayed in the sidebar. Each gadget has a dedicated function; some are fun, some are practical, some are merely decorative. You can use gadgets to add descriptive text, pictures, links, lists, and the like to your blog.

Gadget In Blogger, a small application module that displays in your blog's sidebar.

What Blogger gadgets are available?

Blogger has developed more than a dozen different gadgets that let you display labels, lists, photos, and even videos in your blog's sidebar. In addition, third-party developers have created thousands of gadgets you can add to your blog.

Table 12.1 describes the Blogger-created gadgets that can be added to your blog.

 Third-Party Gadgets

Additional gadgets are available from third-party developers. These third-party gadgets are available in the *Featured*, *Most Popular*, and *More Gadgets* categories of the *Add a Gadget* window—and can be added to your blog in the same manner you add Google-developed gadgets.

Table 12.1—Basic Blogger Gadgets

Gadget	Description
AdSense	Displays Google AdSense ads on your blog—an easy way to generate revenue for your blog, based on click-throughs from your blog visitors
Blog Archive	Displays links to older posts in your blog
Blog List	Displays links to your favorite blogs
Blog's Stats	Displays statistics about your blog's viewership
Feed	Displays up-to-the-minute content from another blog or news feed on the web; all you have to do is enter the feed's URL
Follow by Email	Adds a link that readers can click to receive email notification of new posts to your blog
Followers	Displays a list of users who follow your blog
HTML/JavaScript	Enables you to add snippets of HTML or JavaScript code to your blog, which you can use to incorporate additional functionality from third-party sites
Labels	Displays a list of all the labels you use to categorize your blog posts
Link List	Displays a list similar to a text list, except that each list item has a hyperlink to another web page. Use the Link List element to create lists of favorite websites
List	Displays a simple text list you can use to create lists of CDs, books, and the like. Use the List element to list any item that doesn't have a link or a picture
Logo	Displays a Blogger logo on your page
Newsreel	Displays current headlines from Google News. You supply one or more keywords and then headlines (with short synopses) that match that keyword search are displayed in a list
Page Header	Displays your blog title and description; typically goes at the top of your blog page
Pages	Displays a list of all the pages on your blog
Picture	Adds a single picture to your blog page. You can upload the picture from your PC or link to it on another site on the web
Poll	Enables you to conduct visitor polls on your blog
Popular Posts	Displays a list of the most-read posts on your blog
Profile	Displays your Blogger profile
Search Box	Displays a Google search box on your blog. You can choose to search your blog, pages you've linked to from your blog posts, or the entire web
Slideshow	Displays an automatic slideshow of selected photos
Subscription Links	Enables visitors to subscribe to a site feed for your blog
Text	Adds a block of text anywhere on your blog page. The text block can have a title and description; you can format the text itself with bold, italic, and colored text
Video Bar	Displays selected video clips from YouTube. You supply one or more keywords and then thumbnails for matching videos are displayed in a stack in your blog's sidebar

Hands-On Exercises

3 | Customizing Your Blog

Steps: 1. Choose a Different Template; **2.** Change Other Page Elements; **3.** Add a Gadget to the Sidebar; **4.** Rearrange Elements on the Page.

Use Figures 12.22 through 12.36 as a guide to the exercise.

Step 1 Choose a Different Template

Refer to Figures 12.22 through 12.25 as you complete Step 1.

a. From the Blogger Dashboard, click the **Dashboard** arrow and select **Template** for the blog you want to edit.

Click to customize your blog ——————

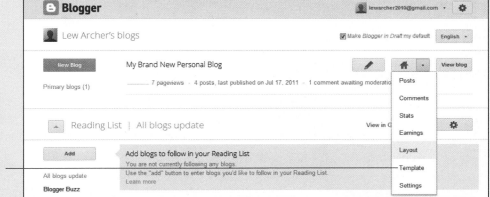

Figure 12.22 Hands-On Exercise 3, Step 1a.

This displays the *Template* page, with a thumbnail version of your current blog shown in the *Live on Blog* section.

All of Blogger's templates are displayed on the *Templates* page. This is a larger selection of templates than was visible when you first created your blog.

b. Click the template you want.

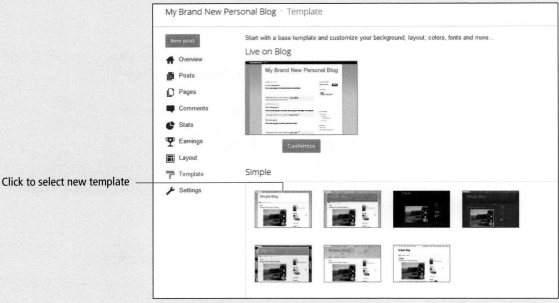

Click to select new template

Figure 12.23 Hands-On Exercise 3, Step 1b.

Blogger now displays a copy of your blog, with the new template applied, in a large window.

c. Click the left or right arrow buttons to cycle through other templates.

d. Click the **Customize** button.

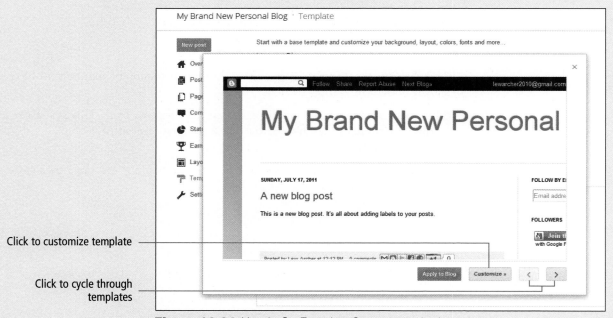

Click to customize template

Click to cycle through templates

Figure 12.24 Hands-On Exercise, Steps 1c and 1d.

This displays the *Blogger Template Designer* pane. When you select a master template in the *Template Designer*, available variations are displayed beneath.

e. Select a master template.

f. Select the desired template variation.

g. To accept a selected template, click **APPLY TO BLOG.**

Click to choose a new template —

Master templates —

Click to display more templates —

Template variations —

Copy of your blog —

Click to apply new template —

Figure 12.25 Hands-On Exercise, Steps 1e through 1g.

 Note   Switching Templates

When you switch to a different template, all your blog content remains—but adapts to the new look. Any customization you've made to your previous template will be lost, however.

Step 2 Change Other Page Elements

Refer to Figures 12.26 through 12.29 as you complete Step 2.

The *Template Designer* also enables you to customize other elements of your blog.

a. Open the *Template Designer* for your blog.

b. To change your blog's color scheme, select the **Background** tab and then click one of the suggested themes.

Click to change color scheme —

New color schemes —

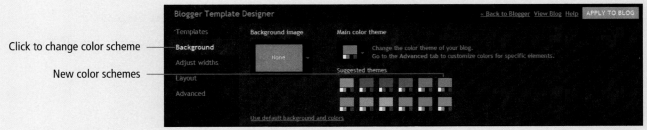

Figure 12.26 Hands-On Exercise 3, Step 2b.

c. To adjust the width of your blog page or sidebar, select the **Adjust widths** tab. Use the *Entire blog* slider to change the width of the entire blog page, or use the *Right sidebar* slider to change the width of the sidebar.

Adjust slider to change blog width

Click to adjust blog width

Adjust slider to change sidebar width

Figure 12.27 Hands-On Exercise 3, Step 2c.

d. To change the overall layout of your blog, select the **Layout** tab and then click the desired page layout.

New layouts

Click to change page layout

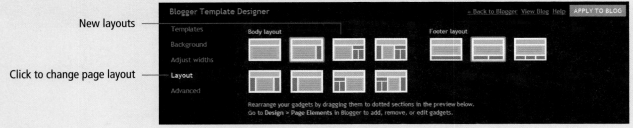

Figure 12.28 Hands-On Exercise 3, Step 2d.

e. To change the color and font of individual page elements, select the **Advanced** tab, select the element to change, and then select the desired font, font size, color, and the like.

f. When done, click **APPLY TO BLOG**.

Click to apply changes

Select page element
Select font

Select color
Click to adjust colors and fonts
Select formatting
Select font size

Figure 12.29 Hands-On Exercise 3, Steps 2e and 2f.

Step 3 Add a Gadget to the Sidebar

Refer to Figures 12.30 through 12.34 as you complete Step 3.

a. From the Blogger Dashboard, go to the blog you want to edit, then click the **Dashboard** arrow and select **Layout**.

Click to customize blog design

Figure 12.30 Hands-On Exercise 3, Step 3a.

This displays the *Layout* page.

b. Click the **Add a Gadget** link in the right column.

> **Tip** ★ **Gadgets Above and Below**
>
> Some templates also let you add gadgets above and beneath your blog posts. To do so, go to the top or the bottom of the *Page Elements* page and click the **Add a Gadget** link there.

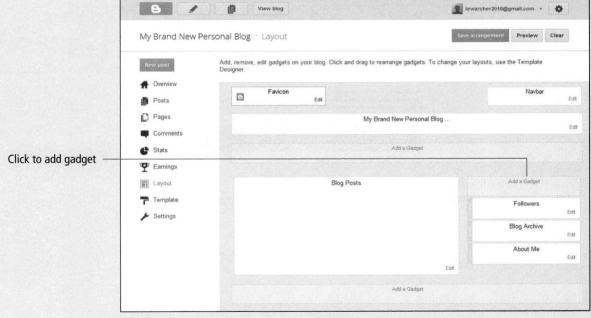

Click to add gadget

Figure 12.31 Hands-On Exercise 3, Step 3b.

This displays the *Add a Gadget* window.

c. To add a Blogger-developed gadget, click the **Basics** category on the left.

d. Scroll to the gadget you wish to add and then click that gadget's + button.

Click to display Blogger gadgets

Click to add gadget

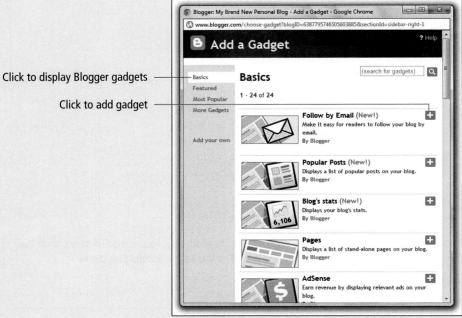

Figure 12.32 Hands-On Exercise 3, Steps 3c and 3d.

You now see a window specific to the gadget you selected.

e. Enter or select the information required in the gadget window and then click **Save**.

Enter gadget-specific information

Click to add gadget to blog

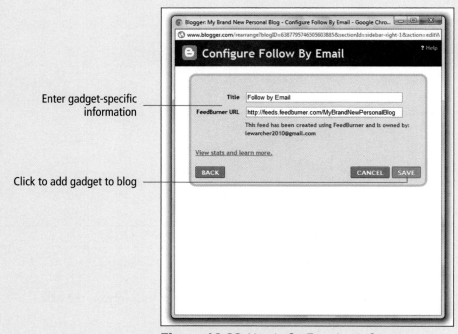

Figure 12.33 Hands-On Exercise 3, Step 3e.

The gadget you selected is now added to the *Layout* page, at the top of the blog's sidebar. You can then decide where on the page that element will appear—which we discuss in Hands-On Exercise 3, Step 4.

f. Click the **Save arrangement** button to save your blog with the new gadget.

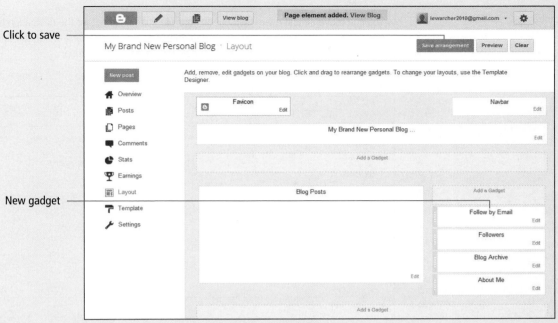

Figure 12.34 Hands-On Exercise 3, Step 3f.

Step ④ Rearrange Elements on the Page

Refer to Figures 12.35 and 12.36 as you complete Step 4.

Blogger gives you total control over where gadgets appear on your blog page. Rearranging your blog's content is as easy as using your mouse to drag and drop individual page elements.

a. From the Blogger Dashboard, go to the blog you want to edit, then click the **Dashboard** arrow and select **Layout**.

Figure 12.35 Hands-On Exercise 3, Step 4a.

This displays the *Layout* page.

b. To move an item, click and drag it with your mouse into a new position.

c. Click the **Preview** button to see what your rearranged page looks like.

d. When you're done making changes, click the **Save arrangement** button.

> **Note** 👆 **Moving Elements**
>
> You can move almost every element on your blog page, except for the navigation bar (Navbar), page header, and blog posts sections. In addition, you can move any element in the sidebar to a new position in the sidebar, or above or below the blog posts section.

Click to save changes ⎯⎯

Click and drag element to new position ⎯⎯

Figure 12.36 Hands-On Exercise 3, Steps 4b through 4d.

Objective 4

Manage Blog Comments

Can readers comment on your blog posts?

It's up to the individual blogger whether readers can comment on posts to that blog. That said, most bloggers let readers comment on their blog posts; it's a great way to develop a community of regular commenters.

Is there any way to block or limit comments on your posts?

By default, Blogger lets anyone post comments to your blog postings. If you'd rather not have all readers comment on your blog, you can limit comments to either registered Blogger users or members of your blog. It's a good way to eliminate unwanted comments from people you don't know.

You can also limit blog comments by enabling *comment moderation*. This requires you to manually accept a comment before it is posted to your blog. If you reject a comment, it does not appear on the blog.

Comment moderation
A means of blocking unwanted blog comments by requiring the owner's approval of all comments before they are displayed.

What is comment spam and how can you block it?

Without any moderation, blog comments can be used for spamming purposes. This is done by using automated spamming software to seed blog postings with unwanted spam messages. These spam messages are posted as comments to legitimate blog postings.

Comment spam Unsolicited commercial messages (spam) placed in the comments section of a blog post.

There's an easy way to defeat this automated *comment spam*. All you have to do is require some sort of human input for posting a comment. Blogger does this by adding a word verification section to the comments posting page on your blog. Readers have to enter the word verification code before posting their comments; because robots can't read graphic images like this, they can't enter the word verification code, and thus cannot leave spam.

Hands-On Exercises

4 | Managing Blog Comments

Steps: 1. Limit Blog Comments; **2.** Disable All Blog Comments; **3.** Enable Comment Moderation; **4.** Moderate Blog Comments.

Use Figures 12.37 through 12.44 as a guide to the exercise.

 Step 1 **Limit Blog Comments**

Refer to Figures 12.37 and 12.38 as you complete Step 1.

One way to discourage unwanted comments on your blog posts is to limit those people who can post comments.

a. From the Blogger Dashboard, go to the blog you want to edit, then click the **Dashboard** arrow and select **Settings**.

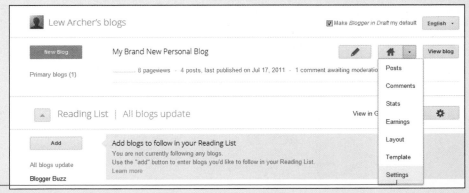

Click to configure blog comments

Figure 12.37 Hands-On Exercise 4, Step 1a.

This displays the *Settings* page.

b. Click **Posts and comments** in the left sidebar.

This displays the *Posts and comments* tab.

c. Go to the *Who can comment?* section and select from the following options:

- **Anyone,** which accepts comments from literally anyone, including anonymous readers and non-Blogger members

- **Registered User,** which accepts comments only from registered Blogger users

- **User with Google Accounts,** which accepts comments only from users with Google accounts

- **Only members of this blog,** which accepts comments only from users you've accepted as blog members

d. Click the **Save Settings** button.

Click to save settings ———

Select who can comment on your blog ———

Click to display *Posts and comments* tab ———

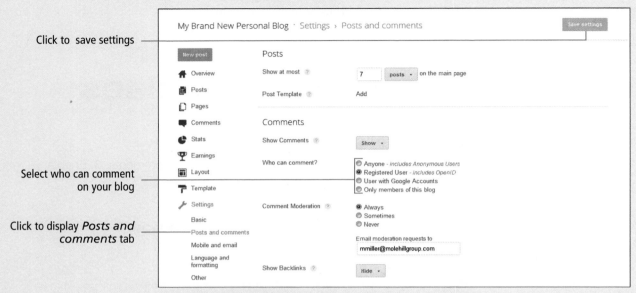

Figure 12.38 Hands-On Exercise 4, Steps 1b through 1d.

Step ② Disable All Blog Comments

Refer to Figures 12.39 and 12.40 as you complete Step 2.

You can totally eliminate unwanted comments on your blog by disabling Blogger's comments feature.

a. From the Blogger Dashboard, go to the blog you want to edit, then click the **Dashboard** arrow and select **Settings**.

Click to configure blog comments ———

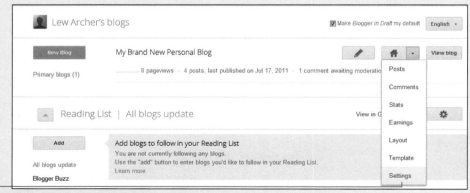

Figure 12.39 Hands-On Exercise 4, Step 2a.

This displays the *Settings* page.

b. Click **Posts and comments** in the left sidebar.

This displays the *Posts and comments* tab.

c. Click the **Show Comments** button and select **Hide**.

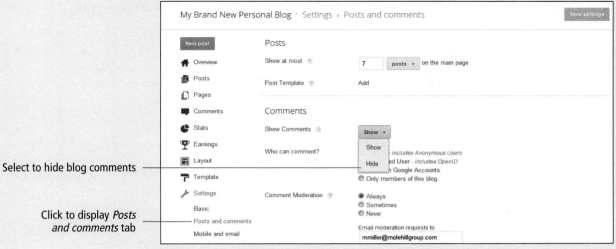

Select to hide blog comments ————

Click to display *Posts and comments* tab ————

Figure 12.40 Hands-On Exercise 4, Steps 2b and 2c.

d. Click the **Save settings** button.

Step 3 Enable Comment Moderation

Refer to Figures 12.41 and 12.42 as you complete Step 3.

Another way to discourage unwanted comments is to enable comment moderation. When you choose to moderate comments, you must approve any comments to your blog before the user can post them.

a. From the Blogger Dashboard, go to the blog you want to edit, then click the **Dashboard** arrow and select **Settings**.

Click to configure blog comments ————

Figure 12.41 Hands-On Exercise 4, Step 3a.

This displays the *Settings* page.

b. Click **Posts and comments** in the left sidebar.

This displays the *Posts and comments* tab.

c. In the *Comment Moderation* section, select from the following options:

- **Always,** which requires your approval for all comments.

- **Sometimes,** which requires your approval for older posts, which are more prone to comment spam, whereas newer posts can be commented on without your approval. Enter the specific number of days into the text box, or opt to moderate posts for non-authors.

- **Never,** which disables comment moderation.

d. Enter your email address into the *Email moderation requests to* box.

Blogger will email all comments to this address for your approval.

e. Click the **Save settings** button.

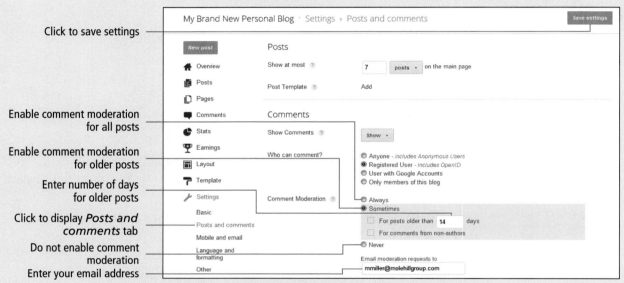

Click to save settings

Enable comment moderation for all posts

Enable comment moderation for older posts

Enter number of days for older posts

Click to display *Posts and comments* tab

Do not enable comment moderation

Enter your email address

Figure 12.42 Hands-On Exercise 4, Steps 3b through 3e.

Step 4 Moderate Blog Comments

Refer to Figures 12.43 and 12.44 as you complete Step 4.

Once you've activated comment moderation, Blogger displays a new *Awaiting moderation* tab on the *Comments* page. All user-written comments appear here, awaiting your approval or rejection.

a. From the Blogger Dashboard, go to the blog you want to edit, then click the **Dashboard** arrow and select **Comments**.

Click to view blog comments

Figure 12.43 Hands-On Exercise 4, Step 4a.

This displays the *Comments* page.

b. Click **Awaiting moderation** in the left sidebar.

This displays the *Awaiting moderation* tab.

c. Check the comment you wish to moderate.

d. To approve and publish the comment, click **Publish**.

e. To delete the comment, click **Delete**.

f. To report the comment as spam, click **Spam**.

Figure 12.44 Hands-On Exercise 4, Steps 4b through 4f.

Summary

In this chapter, you learned how to sign up for Blogger and create a blog. You also learned how to post to your blog, and how to include links, photos, and videos in your blog posts. Finally, you learned how to configure various aspects of your blog—including blog comments.

Key Terms

Blog 278

Blog address 281

Blog-hosting service 279

Blogger 279

Blogosphere. 278

Comment moderation. 300

Comment spam 301

Dashboard .283

Gadget 291

Label 282

Photoblog .283

Post 278

Template Designer 291

Multiple Choice Questions

1. What is Blogger?

    (a) A directory of blogs on the web

    (b) A blog-hosting community

    (c) A software program for creating blogs

    (d) An add-on program for Twitter that turns tweets into blog posts

2. The word "blog" is short for

    (a) best log.

    (b) Blogger site.

    (c) web log.

    (d) beneath the legal operating grid.

3. You manage all your Blogger blogs from

    (a) the Blogger Dashboard.

    (b) your Gmail inbox.

    (c) the Google Settings page.

    (d) Google Reader.

4. The default domain assigned to all new Blogger blogs is

    (a) blogger.com.

    (b) google.com.

    (c) googleblogs.com.

    (d) blogspot.com.

5. How often should you post to your blog?

    (a) Daily

    (b) Weekly

    (c) Monthly

    (d) There is no set rule for posting frequency.

6. Which of the following items can you *not* add to a blog post in Blogger?

    (a) Word document

    (b) Digital photograph

    (c) Video

    (d) Hyperlink

7. Blogger's Template Designer lets you do all of the following *except*

    (a) change your blog's template.

    (b) customize individual elements on your blog page.

    (c) add gadgets to your blog.

    (d) change the blog page layout.

8. Most gadgets are displayed

    (a) in a blog's sidebar.

    (b) between blog posts.

    (c) above all blog posts.

    (d) at the very bottom of the blog page.

9. What happens when you enable comment moderation?

    (a) All comments are blocked.

    (b) Only comments from your friends are allowed.

    (c) You must approve all comments before they appear on your blog.

    (d) Blogger must approve all comments to your blog.

10. Why do people blog?

    (a) To create an online personal diary

    (b) To comment on important issues

    (c) Because they can

    (d) All of the above

Fill in the Blank

Write the correct word or words in the space provided.

1. Individual messages within a blog are called _____.

2. The part of your blog's URL that appears before the blogspot.com domain is called the _____.

3. A blog devoted exclusively or primarily to photographs is called a(n) _____.

4. You categorize your blog posts by adding _____ to each post.

5. To personalize the look and feel of your blog, choose a new _____.

6. A(n) _____ is a small application module that adds functionality to your blog.

7. A person responding to a blog post makes a(n) _____.

8. An unsolicited commercial message posted in response to a blog post is called _____.

9. Static information on a blog post is typically displayed in the blog's _____.

10. The universe of blogs is called the _____.

Practice Exercises

1. **Create a Blog**
   (a) Sign up for Blogger.
   (b) Create a new blog on the topic of your choice. Choose your own name and template for the blog.
   (c) Customize the blog with at least two sidebar gadgets of your choosing.
   (d) Make at least three posts to your blog, one of which should include a photograph of some sort.
   (e) Email the address of your blog to your instructor.

Critical Thinking

1. Many businesses incorporate blogs as part of their online marketing strategy. They use these company or product blogs to post news and information to their customers, and to help personalize their company or products. Locate such a company or product blog online and write a short paper describing why, in your opinion, this particular blog works or doesn't work in terms of establishing a bond with the company's customers. Describe what the blog is doing right and what it might improve upon.

2. The number of personal blogs is declining, with many individuals choosing instead to post blog-like messages to social networks such as Facebook and Twitter. Write a short paper describing how and when a blog might be preferable to posting to a social network, and when the reverse might be true. Explain your own personal decision to host a blog or post to social networks.

Credits

Google, Blogger, and Picasa screenshots reprinted by permission.

CHAPTER 13

Using Picasa

Objectives

After you read this chapter, you will be able to:

1. Organize Your Photographs

2. Edit Your Photographs

3. Print and Share Your Photographs

4. Share Your Photographs with Picasa Web Albums

The following Hands-On Exercises will help you accomplish the chapter objectives:

Hands-On Exercises

EXERCISES	SKILLS COVERED
1. Organizing Your Photographs	**Step 1:** Filter Photos **Step 2:** Sort Photos **Step 3:** Create a New Photo Album **Step 4:** Move Photos
2. Editing Your Photographs	**Step 1:** Adjust Contrast and Brightness **Step 2:** Adjust Color **Step 3:** Remove Red Eye **Step 4:** Crop a Picture **Step 5:** Save an Edited File
3. Printing and Sharing Your Photographs	**Step 1:** Print a Photo on Your Personal Printer **Step 2:** Print Photos to an Online Printing Service **Step 3:** Email Photos
4. Sharing Your Photographs with Picasa Web Albums	**Step 1:** Upload Your Photos from Picasa **Step 2:** Upload Your Photos from Your Web Browser **Step 3:** View Photos Online **Step 4:** Share Your Photos Online

Objective 1

Organize Your Photographs

Picasa Google's photo-editing application.

What is Picasa?

Picasa is a software application by Google that helps you organize and edit digital photographs. It offers much of the same functionality as similar photo-editing programs, such as Adobe Photoshop Elements, but is free of charge.

How do you download and install Picasa?

Unlike most of Google's other applications, which are web-based, Picasa is a traditional computer software program. The program is free to download and use.

To download Picasa, go to **picasa.google.com** and click the **Download Picasa** button. The download will start automatically; follow the onscreen instructions to finish the download and install the program.

 System Requirements

Picasa is available only for computers running Windows XP, Windows Vista, or Windows 7. Picasa does not run on older versions of Windows or on Apple Macintosh computers.

How does Picasa work?

Once installed, you launch Picasa by opening the Windows Start menu and selecting **All Programs > Picasa 3 > Picasa 3**.

The first time you launch the program, Picasa scans your computer for picture files. When prompted, select where Picasa should search—your entire computer or only the My Documents, My Pictures, and Desktop folders. Obviously, it takes less time to scan these selected folders than it does to scan your entire hard disk; if you're well organized, select this option. If your photos are spread over additional folders, have Picasa search your entire computer for picture files.

The picture files that Picasa finds are used to create an index within the Picasa program. This picture index is used to organize your photos into visual albums. Most users find that it's easier to locate pictures from within Picasa's albums than it is to use the My Pictures or Pictures folder in Windows.

 Picasa 3.8

This chapter is based on Picasa version 3.8. If you're using another version of the program, certain screenshots and operations may differ from those shown and described in this book.

Library The main view in Picasa that displays photos stored on your computer.

By default, Picasa displays your photos in the *Library* view. The individual folders in your Library are displayed in the left folders pane; the photos within the selected folder are displayed in the main window. You can also use the scroll bars to scroll up and down through all the photos in Picasa's index (Figure 13.1).

Toolbar
Photo albums

Selected folder

Pictures within selected folder

Folders

Information about
selected photo
Photo Tray

Function buttons

Figure 13.1 The Picasa photo Library.

When you select a photo, it's surrounded by a blue border and displayed as a thumbnail in the ***Photo Tray*** at the bottom left of the screen. You can select more than one picture at a time; the thumbnails are then resized to all fit within the Photo Tray.

Picasa displays a toolbar of key operations at the top of the window, along with a selection of function buttons at the bottom of the window. These function buttons are described in Table 13.1.

Photo Tray That area of the Picasa Library screen that temporarily stores selected photographs.

Table 13.1—Picasa's Function Buttons	
Button	**Description**
Hold selected items	Holds selected pictures in the Photo Tray
Clear items from the selection	Clears all pictures from the Photo Tray
Add selected items to an album	Adds the selected picture to the screensaver, your Starred Photos album, or a new album
Add/Remove Star	"Stars" selected photos for future use or removes previously applied stars
Rotate counter-clockwise	Rotates the picture 90 degrees to the left
Rotate clockwise	Rotates the picture 90 degrees to the right
Upload	Uploads selected photos to Picasa Web Albums
Email	Emails pictures to selected recipients, using either your default email program or Gmail
Print	Prints the selected pictures

(Continued)

Table 13.1—(Continued)

Button	Description
Export	Saves a copy of any photo you've edited
Shop	Orders prints of selected photos from an online photo-printing service
Blog This!	Sends the selected photo to your Blogger blog (as a new photo posting)
Collage	Creates a collage of the selected photos
Movie	Creates a Movie presentation with selected photos
Geotag	Places pictures at selected locations in Google Earth
Show/Hide People Panel	Shows or hides a panel that lists people displayed in selected photo(s)
Show/Hide Places Panel	Shows or hides a panel that displays a map of where selected photos were taken
Show/Hide Tags Panel	Shows or hides a panel that displays keywords related to selected photo(s)
Show/Hide Properties Panel	Shows or hides a panel that displays information about selected photo(s)

Just above these function buttons, at the bottom right of the main display, is a Zoom slider control. You use this slider to adjust the size of the photos that appear in the main display.

How does Picasa organize photographs?

Album A virtual folder used to organize similar photographs in Picasa.

By default, Picasa organizes photographs in the same folders in which they were originally stored on your computer. You can, however, create virtual photo *albums* that combine photos stored in multiple locations; these albums enable you to organize your photos by date, location, subject, or other criteria. Note that these albums merely point to individual photos; if you delete or move a photo from a given album, the photo remains in its original location on your computer.

Hands-On Exercises

1 | Organizing Your Photographs

Steps: 1. Filter Photos; **2.** Sort Photos; **3.** Create a New Photo Album; **4.** Move Photos.

Use Figures 13.2 through 13.6 as a guide to the exercise.

Filter Photos

Refer to Figure 13.2 as you complete Step 1.

Filter A means to display a subset of all available photographs in Picasa.

Picasa offers several *filters* that help you determine which photos are displayed in the Library window. These filter buttons are displayed at the top of the Library workspace.

a. To display only those photos you've "starred" as important, click the **Show starred photos only** button.

b. To display only those photos you've uploaded to Picasa Web Albums, click the **Show Uploads to Web Albums only** button.

c. To display only photos of people, click the **Show only photos with faces** button.

d. To display only movie files indexed by Picasa, click the **Show movies only** button.

e. To display only those photos that have been *geotagged* with a specific location, click the **Show only photos with geotag** button.

f. To display only newer photos, drag the **Filter by date range** slider to the right.

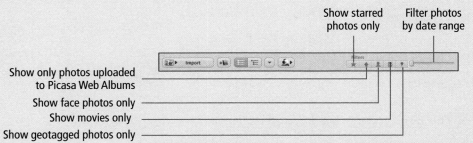

Show starred photos only   Filter photos by date range

Show only photos uploaded to Picasa Web Albums
Show face photos only
Show movies only
Show geotagged photos only

Figure 13.2 Hands-On Exercise 1, Step 1.

Step 2   Sort Photos

Refer to Figure 13.3 as you complete Step 2.

By default, Picasa displays your photos in order of date taken. You can, however, change the sort order for your photos.

a. Click the folder you wish to view.

b. To sort photos by filename, pull down the **Folder** menu and select **Sort By** and then **Name.**

c. To sort photos by file date, pull down the **Folder** menu and select **Sort By** and then **Date.**

d. To sort photos by file size, pull down the **Folder** menu and select **Sort By** and then **Size.**

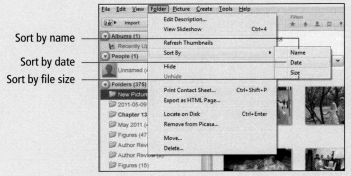

Sort by name
Sort by date
Sort by file size

Figure 13.3 Hands-On Exercise 1, Step 2.

Step 3   Create a New Photo Album

Refer to Figures 13.4 and 13.5 as you complete Step 3.

a. Click the **File** menu and select **New Album.**

Click to create new
photo album

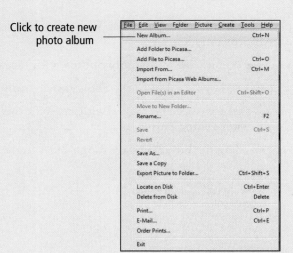

Figure 13.4 Hands-On Exercise 1, Step 3a.

This displays the *Album Properties* dialog box.

b. Enter a name for the new album into the *Name* field.

c. Accept the current date for the new album, or enter a different date into the *Date* field.

d. If this album is to hold photos for a slideshow or movie presentation, check the **Music** box, click the **Browse** button, and select an audio file for background music.

e. To identify the folder by specific geographical location, enter a location name into the *Place taken* field.

f. Enter an optional description of the album's contents into the *Description* field.

g. Click the **OK** button.

The new album appears in the *Albums* panel on the left side of the page. You can now move photos into this new album.

Enter album name
Accept or change date
Check if adding music
for slideshow or movie
Enter geographic location
of album photos
Enter description

Click to create album

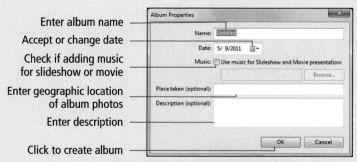

Figure 13.5 Hands-On Exercise 1, Steps 3b through 3g.

Step 4 Move Photos

Refer to Figure 13.6 as you complete Step 4.

a. Click and hold the thumbnail for the photo you wish to move.

b. Drag the thumbnail to the desired folder in the *Folders* pane.

c. Drop the photo into the folder and then release the mouse button.

Drop thumbnail into desired folder

Click and drag thumbnail

Figure 13.6 Hands-On Exercise 1, Step 4.

Objective 2

Edit Your Photographs

Does Picasa enable you to edit your digital photos?

Picasa is more than a photo organizer; it's also a full-featured photo-editing program. When you want to edit a picture, you start by double-clicking it in the photo Library. This opens Picasa's photo editor, which contains a variety of controls for editing and fixing digital photographs.

What editing functions are available?

Picasa offers a variety of common photo-editing operations, including cropping, red eye removal, auto contrast, and auto color. The most common fixes are found on the *Basic Fixes* tab in the editing window, as detailed in Table 13.2.

Table 13.2—Picasa's Basic Fixes	
Fix	**Description**
Crop	Trims unwanted areas from a picture
Straighten	Tilts a picture to a horizontal axis
Redeye	Removes the red eye effect from portraits
I'm Feeling Lucky	Applies any and all fixes that Picasa deems are necessary; does not always offer the best results
Auto Contrast	Automatically adjusts a picture's brightness and contrast levels
Auto Color	Automatically adjusts a picture's color and tint levels
Retouch	Enables you to remove blemishes in a photo by painting over them with the cursor (brush)
Text	Superimposes text over the picture
Edit in Picnik	Exports the picture to the Picnik online photo-editing service for corrections
Fill Light	Adjusts the brightness level of the picture

In addition, Picasa offers a number of special photographic effects found on the *Effects* tab in the editing window. These special effects are described in Table 13.3.

Table 13.3—Picasa's Special Effects	
Special Effect	**Description**
Sharpen	Sharpens the photo's edges
Sepia	Converts the photo to sepia tone, like old-time photos
B&W	Removes all color from the photo
Warmify	Boosts the warm tones in the photo (good for skin tones)
Film Grain	Adds a film-like grain to the photo
Tint	Lets you adjust the photo's tint
Saturation	Lets you adjust the photo's color saturation
Soft Focus	Adds a soft-focus effect to the photo's edges while keeping the center of the photo in sharp focus
Glow	Adds a gauzy glow to the photo
Filtered B&W	Creates the effect of a black-and-white photo taken with a color filter
Focal B&W	Similar to the soft-focus effect, removes color from the photo's edges while keeping the center of the photo in full color
Graduated Tint	Applies a graduated filter to the photo (useful for shooting skies and landscapes)

Hands-On Exercises

2 | Editing Your Photographs

Steps: 1. Adjust Contrast and Brightness; **2.** Adjust Color; **3.** Remove Red Eye; **4.** Crop a Picture; **5.** Save an Edited File.

Use Figures 13.7 through 13.19 as a guide to the exercise.

Step 1 Adjust Contrast and Brightness

Refer to Figures 13.7 and 13.8 as you complete Step 1.

If you shoot a lot of photos indoors, chances are you'll run across a few shots that are underlit—that is, the photos appear too dark. Conversely, shooting outdoors in bright sunlight can result in some photos being too light, or washed out. Fortunately, Picasa can fix both these problems.

a. From the Picasa Library, double-click the photo you wish to edit.

Picasa changes to display the editing window. The editing pane, on the left, offers three tabs of different types of editing operations. The photo being edited appears on the right; it changes to reflect the edits you apply.

b. Select the **Basic Fixes** tab in the editing pane.

c. Click the **Auto Contrast** button.

This simple automated operation will fix many brightness-related problems. If not, you can proceed to more involved editing.

d. Move the **Fill Light** slider to the right to lighten the picture; move the slider to the left to darken the picture.

 Undo Editing

You can undo any editing change you make by clicking the **Undo <operation>** button in the editing pane. Reapply the change by clicking the **Redo <operation>** button.

If this doesn't fix the problem, you can further fine-tune the photograph.

Click to access basic fixes

Click to automatically adjust contrast

Slide to adjust brightness level

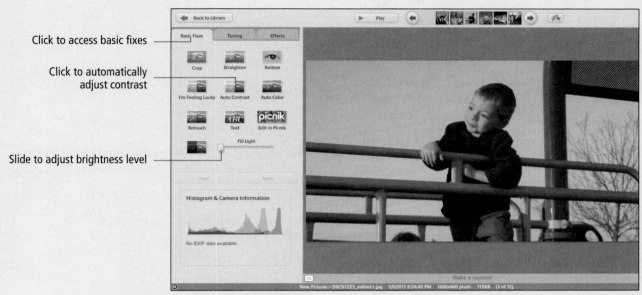

Figure 13.7 Hands-On Exercise 2, Steps 1b through 1d.

e. Select the **Tuning tab** in the editing pane.

f. Adjust the **Fill Light, Highlights,** and **Shadows** sliders until you've achieved the desired brightness and contrast levels.

Click to access more advanced editing controls

Slide to adjust fill lighting

Slide to adjust highlights

Slide to adjust shadows

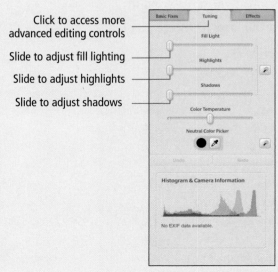

Figure 13.8 Hands-On Exercise 2, Steps 1e and 1f.

Step 2 Adjust Color

Refer to Figures 13.9 through 13.13 as you complete Step 2.

Another problem with taking photographs indoors is that you don't always get the proper colors. Shooting under fluorescent lights can turn everything a little green, and shooting under too low a light can give everything a warmish orange cast.

a. In the editing pane, select the **Basic Fixes** tab.

b. Click the **Auto Color** button.

If this doesn't fix the problem, you can further fine-tune the photograph.

Click to access basic fixes ——

Click to automatically adjust color and tint ——

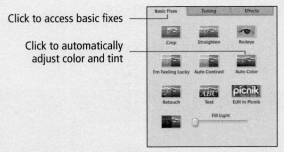

Figure 13.9 Hands-On Exercise 2, Steps 2a and 2b.

c. Select the **Tuning** tab in the editing pane.

d. Move the **Color Temperature** slider to the right to create a "warmer" picture (more red) or to the left to create a "cooler" picture (more blue).

Click to fine-tune the photograph ——

Move slider to adjust color temperature ——

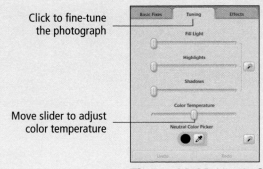

Figure 13.10 Hands-On Exercise 2, Steps 2c and 2d.

More sophisticated color adjustments are available on the *Effects* tab.

e. Select the **Effects** tab in the editing pane.

Tint A color variation, such as red or blue.

f. To adjust the photo's *tint*, click **Tint**.

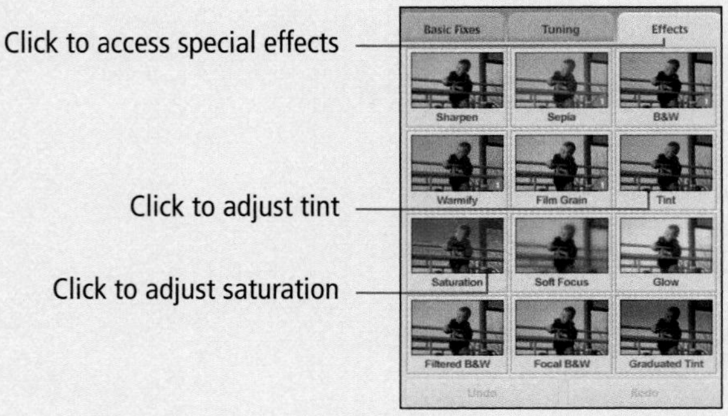

Click to access special effects ——

Click to adjust tint ——

Click to adjust saturation ——

Figure 13.11 Hands-On Exercise 2, Steps 2e, 2f, and 2h.

This displays the *Tint* control.

g. Click within the **Pick Color** box and then move the cursor around the resulting color box until you find the proper tint; click **Apply** when done.

Click to pick new tint level

Click to apply changes

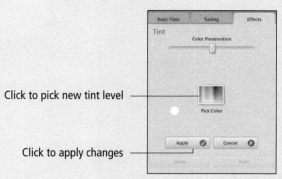

Figure 13.12 Hands-On Exercise 2, Step 2g.

Saturation The amount of color—too much or too little.

h. To adjust the photo's color *saturation*, return to the **Effects** tab and click **Saturation**.

This displays the *Saturation* control.

i. Adjust the **Amount** slider to the left to remove color from the picture or to the right to increase the amount of color; click **Apply** when done.

Move to adjust saturation level

Click to apply changes

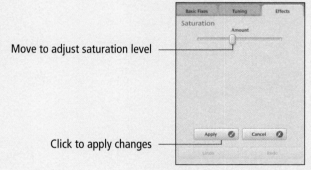

Figure 13.13 Hands-On Exercise 2, Step 2i.

Step ③ Remove Red Eye

Refer to Figures 13.14 and 13.15 as you complete Step 3.

Red eye An undesired photographic effect, most often caused by camera flash, which results in red irises in photographed subjects.

When you shoot indoors with a flash, you sometimes get what is called the *red eye* effect. Fortunately, Picasa makes it easy to remove most instances of red eye.

a. In the editing pane, select the **Basic Fixes** tab.

b. Click **Redeye**.

Click to access basic fixes

Click to automatically
remove red eye

Red eye

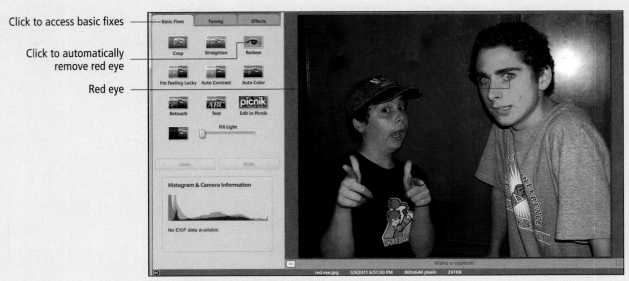

Figure 13.14 Hands-On Exercise 2, Steps 3a and 3b.

Most of the time, Picasa will automatically detect and fix instances of red eye within the selected photo. Picasa then displays the *Redeye Repair* panel.

c. To accept and save the results, click **Apply**.

Click to accept changes

Figure 13.15 Hands-On Exercise 2, Step 3c.

Step 4 Crop a Picture

Refer to Figures 13.16 and 13.17 as you complete Step 4.

Sometimes, for whatever reason, you don't properly compose a picture. Maybe your subject isn't centered; maybe your subject appears too small or far away. Whatever the case, Picasa enables you to *crop* the photo to put the subject front and center in the picture.

Crop An operation that cuts out or trims unwanted portions of an image.

a. In the editing pane, select the **Basic Fixes** tab.

b. Click **Crop**.

Click to access basic fixes —

Click to crop the photo —

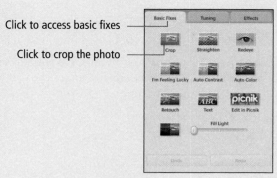

Figure 13.16 Hands-On Exercise 2, Steps 4a and 4b.

The *Crop Photo* control now appears.

c. Click the crop size arrow and select the size you want the resulting picture to be; this fixes the dimensions of the crop area.

d. Click one of the three preselected crop areas, as represented by the thumbnails under the crop size list.

e. Move the crop area on the preview picture until it is centered on what you want to retain in the photo.

f. Drag any corner or edge of the crop area on the preview picture to resize the crop area, while retaining the selected dimensions.

g. Click the **Apply** button to confirm the crop.

> **Tip** **Manual Cropping**
>
> To apply a free-form crop to a photograph, select **Manual** from the pull-down list in the *Crop Photo* pane. Click at the top left of the photo, where you want the crop to start, and then continue holding down the mouse button as you drag the cursor diagonally (down and to the right) until you have selected the area you want to remain in the final picture. Release the mouse button to set the crop area and then click **Apply**.

Select crop dimensions —

Click pre-selected crop area —
Move crop area as necessary —

Click to crop —

Click and drag edge to resize crop area —

Figure 13.17 Hands-On Exercise 2, Steps 4c through 4g.

Step 5 Save an Edited File

Refer to Figures 13.18 and 13.19 as you complete Step 5.

After you're done editing and adding special effects to your photos, it's time to save your changes. Since Picasa retains the original version of your file under the original filename, you need to save the edited file under a new name.

a. From the *Picasa Library* screen, select the photo to save.

b. Click the **File** menu and select **Save As**.

Select photo to save

Click to save file

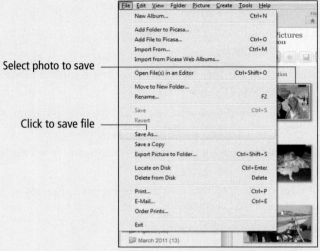

Figure 13.18 Hands-On Exercise 2, Steps 5a and 5b.

This displays the *Save As* dialog box.

c. Navigate to and select the folder where you want to store the edited file.

d. Click the **Save** button.

Select file location

Click to save file

Figure 13.19 Hands-On Exercise 2, Steps 5c and 5d.

Objective 3

Print and Share Your Photographs

How can you use Picasa to share your photos?

Picasa offers many ways to share your digital photos with others. You can make and share photo prints, email the photos, or burn them onto a picture CD. (You can also share your photos online with Picasa Web Albums, which we'll discuss in Objective 4.)

Can Picasa send photos to an online photo-printing service?

Online photo-printing service A service that creates hardcopy prints, on special photo paper, of digital photos you upload.

If you don't have a photo printer, or you prefer more professional prints, Picasa lets you send your photos to an *online photo-printing service*, such as Snapfish or Shutterfly. Most of these services will send your prints to you via postal mail; some services with local locations let you pick up your prints, instead. You can upload photos directly from Picasa to a participating photo-printing service; you typically pay a few cents per print.

Hands-On Exercises

3 | Printing and Sharing Your Photographs

Steps: 1. Print a Photo on Your Personal Printer; **2.** Print Photos to an Online Printing Service; **3.** Email Photos.

Use Figures 13.20 through 13.26 as a guide to the exercise.

Step 1 Print a Photo on Your Personal Printer

Refer to Figures 13.20 and 13.21 as you complete Step 1.

a. From Picasa's photo Library, select the photo you want to print.

b. Click the **Print** button.

Selected photo ——

Click to print ——

Figure 13.20 Hands-On Exercise 3, Steps 1a and 1b.

The Picasa window changes to display *Print Layout* controls and a *Preview* pane.

c. In the *Print Layout* section, select the print size or layout you want.

You can select from nine wallet-sized prints, four 3.5 × 5 prints, two 4 × 6 prints, two 5 × 7 prints, one 8 × 10 print, or a full-page print.

d. To print a larger picture on a smaller page, click the **Shrink to Fit** button. If you'd rather crop a larger picture to fit, click the **Crop to Fit** button instead.

e. If the correct printer isn't selected, click the **Printer** button and select a different printer.

f. If you need to further configure your printer for printing, click the **Printer Setup** button and proceed from there.

g. In the *Copies per Photo* section, click the + and − buttons to select how many copies you want to print.

h. Click the **Print** button.

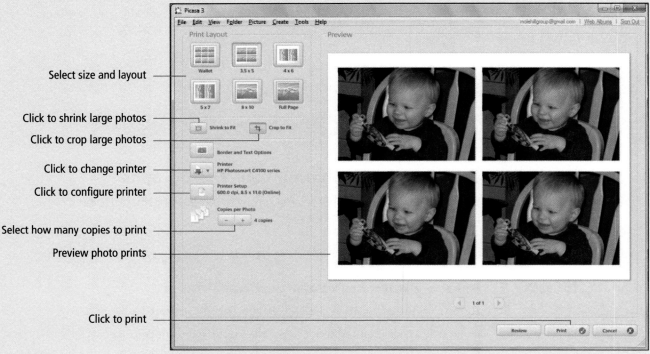

Select size and layout

Click to shrink large photos
Click to crop large photos

Click to change printer
Click to configure printer

Select how many copies to print
Preview photo prints

Click to print

Figure 13.21 Hands-On Exercise 3, Steps 1c through 1h.

 Print Photos to an Online Printing Service

Refer to Figures 13.22 and 13.23 as you complete Step 2.

a. From Picasa's photo Library, select the photos you want to print.

Hold down the **Ctrl** key to select multiple photos.

b. Click the **Shop** button.

Selected photos

Click to print online

Figure 13.22 Hands-On Exercise 3, Steps 2a and 2b.

Picasa opens a new *Shop* window that displays participating online printing services.

c. Select your country from the *Location* list.

d. Click the printing service you wish to use.

Each online photo-printing service has its own distinct operations from this point. Follow the onscreen instructions to complete and pay for your order.

Select country

Select photo-printing service

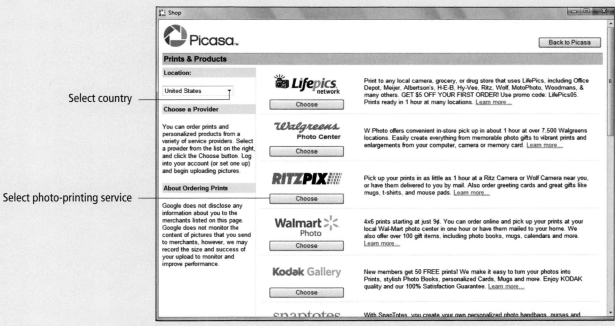

Figure 13.23 Hands-On Exercise 3, Steps 2c and 2d.

Step ③ Email Photos

Refer to Figures 13.24 through 13.26 as you complete Step 3.

a. From Picasa's photo Library, select the photo you want to email.

b. Click the **Email** button.

Click to email ——

Figure 13.24 Hands-On Exercise 3, Steps 3a and 3b.

Picasa displays the *Select Email* dialog box.

c. Select which email service you want to use to send your photo—Gmail or your default email program.

Click to send via your default email program —

Click to send via Gmail —

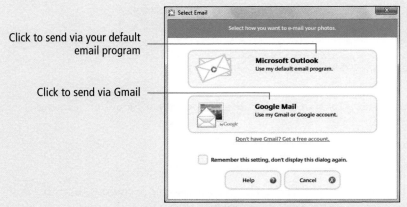

Figure 13.25 Hands-On Exercise 3, Step 3c.

If you select Gmail, you see the *Gmail* dialog box. (If you select your default email program, you see that application's send email screen.)

d. Enter the email address of the recipient into the *To:* box.

e. Enter a subject for the message into the *Subject:* box.

f. Enter an accompanying message into the large text box.

g. Click the **Send** button to send the email message.

Enter recipient's email address —

Enter message subject —

Attached photo —

Enter message text —

Click to send email —

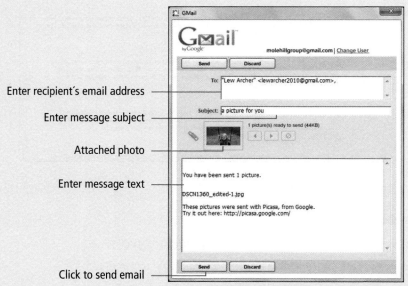

Figure 13.26 Hands-On Exercise 3, Steps 3d through 3g.

Objective 4

Share Your Photographs with Picasa Web Albums

Can you share photos online?

Aside from sharing digital photos via email, you can also share photos via online photo-sharing sites. These sites let you upload photos into digital albums and then have your friends and family view those online photo albums.

What is Picasa Web Albums?

Picasa Web Albums Google's web-based photo-sharing site.

Picasa Web Albums, also known as Google Photos, is Google's online photo-sharing site (**picasaweb.google.com**). As the name implies, Picasa Web Albums is tightly integrated with the Picasa application, although it can also be accessed by anyone with an Internet connection. Photos uploaded to Picasa Web Albums are stored in virtual photo albums; you can create separate photo albums for different types of photos.

How much does it cost to use Picasa Web Albums?

Picasa Web Albums is free to use. You can upload and store a set number of photos for free; others can view your photos, also for free. All you need is a Google account.

Does Picasa Web Albums have a storage limit?

Picasa Web Albums lets you store photos and videos up to 50 megapixels in size, or up to 20MB in file size. You can create a maximum of 10,000 web albums, each containing up to 1,000 photos. Google offers 1GB in free storage; if you exceed this space, you can purchase additional storage for $0.25 per GB per year.

Hands-On Exercises

4 | Sharing Your Photographs with Picasa Web Albums

Steps: 1. Upload Your Photos from Picasa; **2.** Upload Your Photos from Your Web Browser; **3.** View Photos Online; **4.** Share Your Photos Online.

Use Figures 13.27 through 13.35 as a guide to the exercise.

Step 1 Upload Your Photos from Picasa

Refer to Figures 13.27 and 13.28 as you complete Step 1.

a. From Picasa's photo Library, select the photos you want to upload.

b. Click the **Upload** button.

Click to upload ——

Figure 13.27 Hands-On Exercise 4, Step 1b.

If this is your first time to use Picasa Web Albums, you're prompted to sign in or create a new account. You can use your normal Google account or create a separate account just for Picasa Web Albums.

On subsequent uses, Picasa displays the *Upload to Picasa Web Albums* dialog box.

c. To upload to a new photo album, click the **New** button and then enter a name into the *Album Title* box and an optional description into the *Description* box.

d. To upload to an existing photo album, select that album from the *Upload to this album* pull-down list.

e. Click the **Size to upload** arrow and select the desired size for the uploaded photos.

You can select from *Original size* (best for archival purposes), *Recommended: 1600 pixels* (good for photo prints), *Medium: 1024 pixels* (good for viewing online), or *Small: 640 pixels* (good for displaying on web pages).

f. By default, others can view your uploaded photos only if they have the link to the photos. To make the album totally public, so anyone can view your photos, click the **Visibility for this album** arrow and select **Public on the web**. To make the photos visible only to you, select **Private** instead.

g. To share your photos with specific people, click the + button and select from an existing group of contacts, or create a new contact group.

h. Click the **Upload** button to upload the photos.

Select album to host photos →

Select upload size →
Select visibility →
Click to share with specific people →
Click to complete upload →

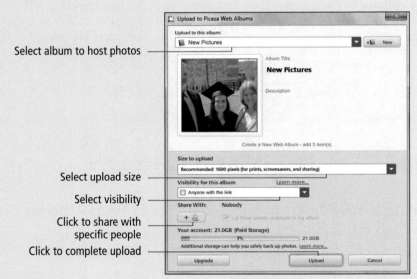

Figure 13.28 Hands-On Exercise 4, Steps 1c through 1h.

Step Upload Your Photos from Your Web Browser

Refer to Figures 13.29 through 13.32 as you complete Step 2.

You don't have to use the Picasa application to upload your photos to Picasa Web Albums. You can upload photos from any web browser.

a. Go to the Picasa Web Albums website (**picasaweb.google.com**).

b. Click the **Upload** button.

Click to upload photos

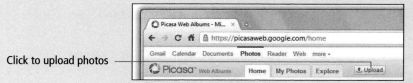

Figure 13.29 Hands-On Exercise 4, Steps 2a and 2b.

This displays the *Upload Photos: Create or Select Album* dialog box.

c. To create a new photo album for your uploaded photos, enter the title for the new album into the *Title* box and then pull down the *Visibility* list and determine who can view the photos in this album—*Public on the web, Limited, anyone with the link,* or *Only you*. Click **Continue** when ready.

d. If you prefer to upload a photo into an existing photo album, click the **choose an existing album** link and then select an album from the resulting list and click the **Select Album** button.

Click to upload to existing photo album

Enter album title
Select who can view album
Click to continue

Figure 13.30 Hands-On Exercise 4, Steps 2c and 2d.

This displays an *Upload Photos and Videos* page.

e. Click the **Select photos from your computer** button.

Click to choose photos to upload

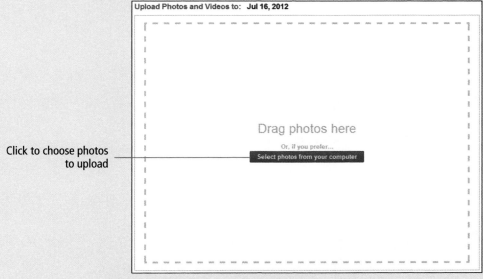

Figure 13.31 Hands-On Exercise 4, Step 2e.

f. When the *Open* dialog box appears, navigate to and select the photos to upload and then click **Open**.

The photos you selected are now displayed on the *Upload Photos and Videos to:* page.

g. Click **OK**.

Google now displays the contents of the album to which you uploaded new photos.

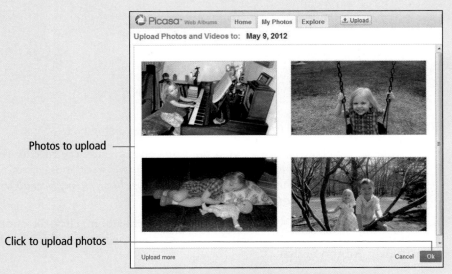

Photos to upload

Click to upload photos

Figure 13.32 Hands-On Exercise 4, Step 2g.

Step ③ View Photos Online

Refer to Figure 13.33 as you complete Step 3.

a. Go to the Picasa Web Albums homepage, located at **picasaweb.google.com**.

b. Click the **Home** tab to display your recent albums and activity, as well as featured photos selected by Picasa staff.

c. Click the **Explore** tab to view featured photos.

d. Click the **My Photos** tab to view all photo albums you've uploaded; click a photo album to view all photos in that album.

Click to go to Picasa Web Albums homepage

Click to view your photos

Click to view Picasa-selected photos

Click to view photos in this album

Figure 13.33 Hands-On Exercise 4, Step 3.

Step ④ Share Your Photos Online

Refer to Figures 13.34 and 13.35 as you complete Step 4.

Picasa Web Albums is designed for sharing—that is, for sharing your photos online with friends and family. To that end, Picasa lets you share individual photos or complete photo albums with other users, via email.

a. From the Picasa Web Albums homepage, click the **My Photos** tab.

b. Click the photo album that contains the photos you want to share.

c. If you want to share a specific photo, click that photo.

If you don't select a photo, you'll share all the photos in the currently selected album.

d. Click the **Share** icon at the top of the page.

Click to display your photos —

Click to share the selection —

Click to select a photo —

Figure 13.34 Hands-On Exercise 4, Steps 4a through 4d.

This displays either the *Share Album* or the *Share Photo* page, which are functionally identical.

e. Enter the email addresses of those with whom you wish to share into the *To:* box.

Separate multiple addresses with commas.

f. Enter the text of your message.

g. Click the **Share via Email** button.

The selected recipients receive an email message inviting them to view the album or photo, along with a link to the shared item online.

Enter recipients' email addresses —

Enter message —

Click to send link via email —

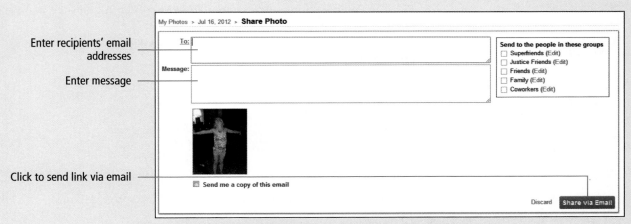

Figure 13.35 Hands-On Exercise 4, Steps 4e through 4g.

Summary

In this chapter, you learned how to manage and organize photos using Google's Picasa software. You also learned how to edit your photos, as well as print and share them with others. In addition, you learned how to use the Picasa Web Albums site to share photos online with others.

Key Terms

Album	312	Photo Tray	311
Crop	320	Picasa	310
Filter	312	Picasa Web Albums	327
Geotag	313	Red eye	319
Library	310	Saturation	319
Online photo-printing service	323	Tint	318

Multiple Choice Questions

1. What is the difference between Picasa and Picasa Web Albums?

    (a) Picasa Web Albums offers additional photo-editing functionality.

    (b) Picasa Web Albums is a web-based version of Picasa.

    (c) Picasa is a photo-editing software program; Picasa Web Albums is a web-based photo-sharing site.

    (d) Picasa is a photo-sharing application; Picasa Web Albums is a web-based photo-editing application.

2. How much does it cost to use Picasa?

    (a) $99.95 one-time purchase

    (b) $9.95 per month usage fee

    (c) $0.99 per picture

    (d) Nothing; it's free.

3. What is the largest sized picture you can upload to Picasa Web Albums?

    (a) 10 megapixels

    (b) 50 megapixels

    (c) 100 megapixels

    (d) Picasa Web Albums has no file size limit.

4. Where on your hard drive does Picasa look for photos to organize?

    (a) only in the Picasa folder

    (b) only in the My Pictures folder

    (c) only in the My Pictures, My Documents, and Desktop folders

    (d) anywhere on your computer's hard disk

    (e) Either (c) or (d)

5. Which of the following is *not* a special effect in Picasa?

(a) Sharpen

(b) Warmify

(c) Coldify

(d) Soft Focus

6. When you want to quickly fix a photo's brightness and contrast in Picasa, click this button:

(a) Auto Contrast

(b) Auto Brightness

(c) Auto Exposure

(d) Auto Levels

7. When you want to quickly fix a photo's color, click this button:

(a) Auto Tint

(b) Auto Saturation

(c) Auto Temperature

(d) Auto Color

8. An online photo-printing service enables you to

(a) print photos on your own computer.

(b) print photos on other printers on your network, wirelessly.

(c) order prints of photos you upload.

(d) Both (a) and (b)

9. Which of the following is *not* a Basic Fix feature in Picasa?

(a) Tint

(b) Straighten

(c) Crop

(d) Fill Light

10. How many photo albums can you create with Picasa Web Albums?

(a) up to 100

(b) up to 1,000

(c) up to 10,000

(d) an unlimited number

Fill in the Blank

Write the correct word or words in the space provided.

1. When you want to trim unnecessary portions of a picture, use the _____ command.

2. In the Picasa Library, selected photos are displayed in the _____.

3. When you _____ a photo, you embed location information into the photograph.

4. In Picasa, a(n) _____ is a virtual folder used to organize photographs of a given type.

5. _____ is an undesired effect that results in red irises in photographed subjects.

Practice Exercises

1. **Import a Photo**

   (a) Open your web browser and type **www.pearsonhighered.com/nextseries** in the browser address bar. Press **Enter**.

   (b) From the list of books provided, locate this textbook and click the **Companion Website** link. This will take you to the companion website for the book.

   (c) Click the **Student Data Files** link.

   (d) Download the photo IntroGoogleApps01.jpg from the site and save it in your *My Documents* folder.

   (e) Open Picasa.

   (f) Within Picasa, navigate to the IntroGoogleApps01.jpg photo.

2. **Crop a Photo**

   (a) Open the previously downloaded IntroGoogleApps01.jpg photo for editing.

   (b) Select the **Basic Fixes** tab.

   (c) Use Picasa's crop tool to crop the photo to a 5×7 landscape photo that trims out the trees on the left side of the photo.

   (d) Save the edited photo as IntroGoogleApps02.jpg.

   (e) Print the photo as four 3.5×5 prints and hand in to your instructor.

3. **Apply Special Effects**

   (a) Open the previously downloaded IntroGoogleApps01.jpg photo for editing.

   (b) Select the **Effects** tab.

   (c) Turn the photo into a black and white photo.

   (d) Apply the Soft Focus effect.

   (e) Save the edited photo as IntroGoogleApps03.jpg.

   (f) Print the photo as two 5×7 prints and hand in to your instructor.

4. **Share a Photo with Picasa Web Albums**

   (a) If you haven't shared photos earlier, open an account with Picasa Web Albums.

   (b) Upload the IntroGoogleApps02.jpg and IntroGoogleApps03.jpg photos to a new album titled **Introduction to Google Personal Apps**.

   (c) Share the contents of this folder with your instructor, via email.

Critical Thinking

1. Many companies, such as Adobe, sell photo-editing programs for $100 or more. Google provides Picasa as a free download. Write a short paper speculating on why Google distributes Picasa for free—what does Google hope to achieve with this strategy?

2. Professional photographers tend to use expensive photo-editing programs, such as Adobe Photoshop CS, which have many more features than are found in Picasa. Write a short paper examining Picasa's feature set, and speculating as to what additional features not found in Picasa professional photographers might desire.

Credits

Google, Blogger, and Picasa screenshots reprinted by permission.

CHAPTER 14

Using YouTube

Objectives

After you read this chapter, you will be able to:

1. Search for and Watch Videos

2. Share Your Favorite Videos

3. Upload Videos

The following Hands-On Exercises will help you accomplish the chapter objectives:

Hands-On Exercises

EXERCISES	SKILLS COVERED
1. Searching for and Watching Videos	**Step 1:** Search for Videos **Step 2:** Browse for Videos **Step 3:** View a Video
2. Sharing Your Favorite Videos	**Step 1:** Share a Video via Email **Step 2:** Post a Video to Facebook **Step 3:** Post a Video to Twitter
3. Uploading Videos	**Step 1:** Upload a Video File **Step 2:** Upload a Webcam Video

Objective 1

Search for and Watch Videos

What is YouTube?

YouTube The video-sharing community owned by Google.

YouTube is, in its own words, "the world's most popular online video community." It is a site that enables users to upload their own digital videos and share those videos with other users. It is also a site where viewers can find millions of short videos for viewing on their computers and other devices.

> **Note** **The YouTube Community**
>
> YouTube claims more than 300 million users worldwide, with more than 120 million videos available for viewing. It would take more than 600 years to view all the videos currently available and there are 200,000 new videos uploaded every day.

What types of videos can be found on YouTube?

YouTube offers an interesting and ever-changing mix of amateur and professionally produced videos. Many videos on YouTube are the Internet equivalent of *America's Funniest Home Videos*, amateur videos of everything from birthday parties to "stupid human tricks." Also popular are video blogs, or *vlogs*, video versions of traditional text-based blogs; these are personal journals, typically captured via webcam and posted to YouTube on a regular basis.

Vlog A video blog, or a personal journal in video form.

YouTube is also host to a variety of educational and informational videos, which makes the site ideal for finding "how to" information on a variety of topics. In addition, many businesses post both informational and promotional videos to the YouTube site.

YouTube also serves as a repository for "historical" items, such as old television commercials, music videos, and clips from classic television shows. It's also host for a large number of music videos from both past and present, as well as a growing number of current television programs, documentaries, and feature films.

Does YouTube offer movies and other commercial programming?

Streaming video A technology that enables the viewing of videos over the Internet in real time, without having to first download a video file.

YouTube now competes with Netflix and other *streaming video* services in offering movies, television shows, and other commercial programming to viewers. Most of this programming is available for a price (e.g., typically $2.99 to $3.99 to watch a movie), although some free content is also offered. This commercial content is available by clicking the **Movies** link at the top of any YouTube page. You'll need a Google Checkout account to pay for any movies you purchase.

Can you watch YouTube videos on any computer?

To watch YouTube videos, you must be connected to the Internet. It helps if you have a broadband Internet connection, as videos do not stream well or quickly on slower dial-up connections.

> **Alert** **Blocking YouTube**
>
> Some companies and organizations block access to YouTube and similar streaming video sites, thinking that watching videos on company time is not a good use of their employees' time.

Resolution A measurement of the picture quality of a video, measured in terms of picture elements (pixels).

High definition Also known as HD, the current high resolution digital picture format.

Widescreen A video aspect ratio where the width greatly exceeds the height; the HD format has a widescreen aspect ratio of 16:9 (16 units wide by 9 units tall).

Aspect ratio A measurement that compares picture width by picture height.

What is the playback quality of YouTube videos?

YouTube lets users upload videos at all different levels of *resolution*. Some videos are relatively low quality (as low as 320×240 pixel resolution); others are available in full 720p or 1080p *high definition*. Most newer videos are in *widescreen* format, although some older videos are in standard 4:3 *aspect ratio*. Higher-quality videos can be watched in their full resolution on your computer screen.

Hands-On Exercises

1 | Searching for and Watching Videos

Steps: 1. Search for Videos; **2.** Browse for Videos; **3.** View a Video.

Use Figures 14.1 through 14.6 as a guide to the exercise.

 Step 1 **Search for Videos**

Refer to Figure 14.1 as you complete Step 1.

You can find videos to watch by either searching or browsing the YouTube site.

a. Go to **www.youtube.com**.

> **Note** **Create an Account**
>
> To best use the YouTube site, in terms of saving favorites and uploading your own videos, you should sign in to YouTube with your Google account or create a new YouTube account. You can do this from the YouTube homepage, by clicking the **Create Account** or **Sign In** links.

b. Enter one or more keywords that describe what you want to view into the search box at the top of any YouTube page.

c. Click the **Search** button.

YouTube displays videos that match your query on the resulting search results page.

Enter keywords

Click to search

Figure 14.1 Hands-On Exercise 1, Step 1.

Step 2 **Browse for Videos**

Refer to Figures 14.2 through 14.4 as you complete Step 2.

You can also browse YouTube videos by category.

a. From the top of any YouTube page, click the **Browse** link.

YouTube displays the *All Categories* page.

b. Click the **Categories** arrow to display a list of all video categories: *Autos & Vehicles, Comedy, Education, Entertainment, Film & Animation, Gaming, Howto & Style, Music, News & Politics, Nonprofits & Activism, People & Blogs, Pets & Animals, Science & Technology, Sports, and Travel & Events.*

Click to browse videos by category
Click to display categories

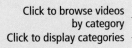

Figure 14.2 Hands-On Exercise 1, Steps 2a and 2b.

c. Click the category in which you're interested.

Click to view videos in this category

Figure 14.3 Hands-On Exercise 1, Step 2c.

YouTube displays the appropriate category page for the specific category you chose. This page contains sections for *Popular Around the Web* and *Most Viewed Today*.

d. Click the **View all** link at the top of the *Most Viewed Today* category.

YouTube displays the first of several pages of matching videos.

Click to view all videos in this category

Figure 14.4 Hands-On Exercise 1, Step 2d.

Step ③ View a Video

Refer to Figures 14.5 and 14.6 as you complete Step 3.

a. Search or browse for a video you want to watch.

b. To view a video, click either the video title or the thumbnail.

Click to view video

Figure 14.5 Hands-On Exercise 1, Steps 3a and 3b.

YouTube displays a separate page for the video you selected. The video is displayed in its own playback window; playback starts automatically.

c. To pause playback, click the **Pause** button, which then changes into a **Play** button. To resume playback, click the **Play** button.

d. To mute the audio, click the **Audio** button. To adjust the volume, place your cursor over the **Audio** button to display the Volume slider; use your mouse to adjust the slider left (softer) or right (louder).

e. To display the video at a higher resolution (if available), place your cursor over the **Resolution** button and click a different resolution.

f. To display the video in a larger playback window across the width of your web browser, click the **Expand** button.

g. To display the video full screen, click the **Full screen** button. To exit full screen mode, press **Esc**.

h. To view more details about the video, click the down arrow next to the description beneath the video.

i. To vote for the video, click either the **Like** (thumb up) button or the **I dislike this** (thumb down) button.

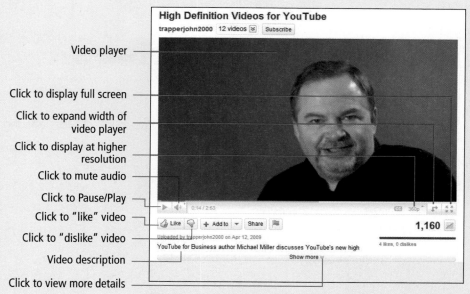

Video player
Click to display full screen
Click to expand width of video player
Click to display at higher resolution
Click to mute audio
Click to Pause/Play
Click to "like" video
Click to "dislike" video
Video description
Click to view more details

Figure 14.6 Hands-On Exercise 1, Steps 3c through 3i.

Objective 2

Share Your Favorite Videos

Is YouTube a social network?

Social network A website where users can form communities with like-minded users and share details of their lives with friends, family, fellow students, and coworkers.

YouTube is a video-sharing community; it's the community aspect that makes YouTube a *social network*. You can comment on other users' videos, share videos with other users or non-YouTube members, subscribe to other users' videos, and post YouTube videos on your blog or Facebook page. The key is to participate; while you can be a passive viewer, social networking comes from fully participating in the YouTube community.

How can you share YouTube videos?

If you have a YouTube account, YouTube offers several ways to share a video you like with your friends. You can share a link to the video via email, post the video to a Blogger-hosted blog, or post the video as a status update or tweet to a variety of social media, including Facebook, Twitter, MySpace, Google Buzz, orkut, hi5, tumblr, Bebo, and StumbleUpon.

What is a viral video?

Viral video A video that attracts large numbers of viewers through Internet sharing.

A *viral video* is one that achieves large viewership through sharing over the Internet. Viewers share videos via links in email messages, embedding videos in blogs and web pages, and "liking" videos on Facebook, Twitter, and other social networks. Viral videos can attract thousands or even millions of viewers, and even migrate to traditional media, such as cable news networks and late-night comedy shows.

Hands-On Exercises

2 | Sharing Your Favorite Videos

Steps: 1. Share a Video via Email; **2.** Post a Video to Facebook; **3.** Post a Video to Twitter.

Use Figures 14.7 through 14.11 as a guide to the exercise.

Step 1 Share a Video via Email

Refer to Figure 14.7 as you complete Step 1.

a. Navigate to the YouTube video you want to share.

b. Click the **Share** button beneath the video player.

   The *Share* panel is displayed beneath the video player.

c. Click the **Email this video** button.

   The *Share* panel is expanded.

d. Enter the recipient's email address into the *To* box.

   Separate multiple addresses with commas.

e. Enter an accompanying message into the *Additional note* box.

f. Click the **Send Email** button.

Click to share —

Click to compose email —

Enter email addresses —

Enter message —

Click to send email —

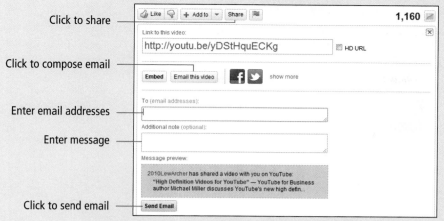

Figure 14.7 Hands-On Exercise 2, Step 1.

Step ② Post a Video to Facebook

Refer to Figures 14.8 and 14.9 as you complete Step 2.

a. Navigate to the YouTube video you want to share.

b. Click the **Share** button beneath the video player.

The *Share* panel is displayed beneath the video player.

c. Click the **Facebook** button.

Click to share —

Click to post to Facebook —

Figure 14.8 Hands-On Exercise 2, Steps 2a through 2c.

The *Facebook* window opens.

d. Enter a short message to accompany the video link.

e. Select a thumbnail image to accompany the post, if multiple thumbnails are available.

f. Click the **Share Link** button.

A status update containing an embedded version of this video is now posted to your Facebook account.

 Note **Signing In**

The first time you try to share a video with your Facebook, Twitter, or other social media account, you will be prompted to sign in to your account. Follow the onscreen instructions to enter your username and password and sign in.

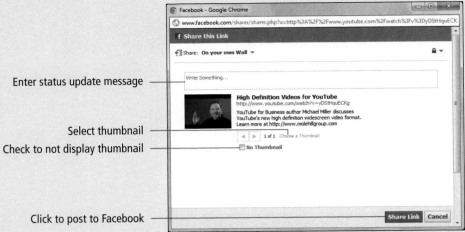

Enter status update message

Select thumbnail

Check to not display thumbnail

Click to post to Facebook

Figure 14.9 Hands-On Exercise 2, Steps 2d through 2f.

Step 3 Post a Video to Twitter

Refer to Figures 14.10 and 14.11 as you complete Step 3.

a. Navigate to the YouTube video you want to share.

b. Click the **Share** button beneath the video player.

The *Share* panel is displayed beneath the video player.

c. Click the **Twitter** button.

Click to share

Click to post to Twitter

Figure 14.10 Hands-On Exercise 2, Steps 3a through 3c.

The *Twitter* window opens.

d. Confirm or edit the text for the tweet.

e. Click the **Tweet** button.

A tweet containing a link to this video is now posted to your Twitter feed.

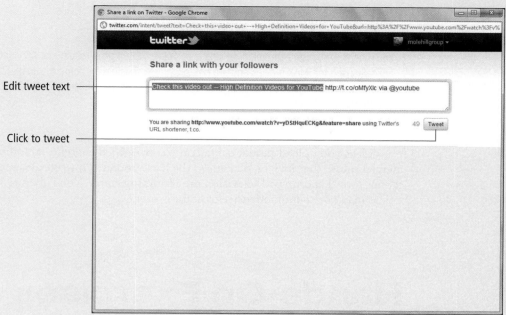

Edit tweet text

Click to tweet

Figure 14.11 Hands-On Exercise 2, Steps 3d and 3e.

Objective 3

Upload Videos

Who can upload videos to YouTube?

Any registered YouTube user can upload videos to the YouTube site. You can sign in to YouTube with your Google account, or create a new account just for YouTube.

How can you upload a video to YouTube?

There are two ways to upload videos to YouTube. You can transfer videos to YouTube "live" from a computer webcam or upload digital videos shot on a video camcorder and edited with a computer video-editing program.

What are the specifications for uploading a video to YouTube?

Before you upload a video to YouTube, you must sign in with your Google Account or register for a free account at **www.youtube.com**. YouTube accepts videos that meet the following specifications:

- Length: No longer than 15 minutes
- File size: No larger than 2GB
- File formats: 3GPP (cell phone video), AVI, FLV, MK4 (h.264), MOV, MP4, MPEG, WebM, WMV
- Resolution: Up to 1080p (1920 × 1080 pixels), in either standard or widescreen aspect ratio

Videos you upload cannot contain any copyrighted content, including any commercial music that may be playing in the background. This rule also means that you cannot record and upload television programming to the YouTube site. In addition, videos may not contain offensive or adult content.

Hands-On Exercises

3 | Uploading Videos

Steps: 1. Upload a Video File; **2.** Upload a Webcam Video.

Use Figures 14.12 through 14.22 as a guide to the exercise.

Step 1 **Upload a Video File**

Refer to Figures 14.12 through 14.15 as you complete Step 1.

a. Click the **Upload** link at the top of any YouTube page.

Click to upload a video

Figure 14.12 Hands-On Exercise 3, Step 1a.

This displays the *Video File Upload* page.

b. Click the **Upload video** button.

Click to upload video

Figure 14.13 Hands-On Exercise 3, Step 1b.

The *Select file(s) to upload* or *Open* window now opens.

c. Navigate to and select the desired video file and then click the **Open** button.

Click to select video —

Click to open video
for uploading —

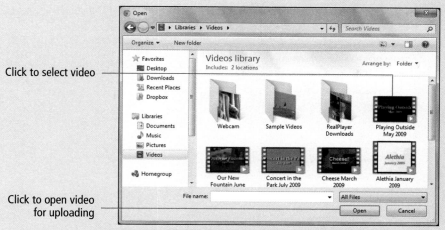

Figure 14.14 Hands-On Exercise 3, Step 1c.

Your file now begins to upload, and YouTube displays the *Video File Upload* page. The progress of your upload is displayed at the top of this page; uploading a video can take several minutes—longer for longer videos, or if you have a slow Internet connection.

d. Click the thumbnail image you'd like displayed for the video.

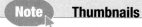 **Thumbnails**

Thumbnails may not be displayed until the video is almost finished uploading.

e. Enter a title for the video into the *Title* box.

f. Enter a short description of the video into the *Description* box.

g. Enter one or more keywords that describe the video into the *Tags* box.

h. Click the *Category* list and select the appropriate category for the video.

i. If you want all YouTube viewers to see your video, select the **Public** option in the *Privacy* setting section. (This is the default.) If you want to share your video only with viewers you invite, select the **Private** option. If you want your video to be accessible only by those who know the specific URL, select the **Unlisted** option.

j. Click the **Save changes** button.

When your video is uploaded, YouTube displays a link to the video. Click this link to view the video.

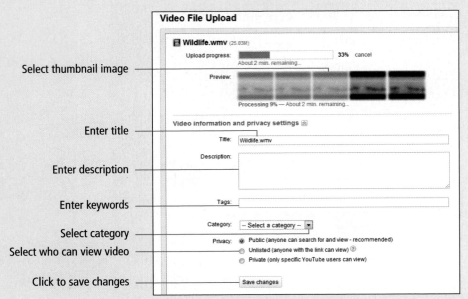

Select thumbnail image

Enter title

Enter description

Enter keywords

Select category

Select who can view video

Click to save changes

Figure 14.15 Hands-On Exercise 3, Steps 1d through 1j.

Step 2 Upload a Webcam Video

Refer to Figures 14.16 through 14.22 as you complete Step 2.

YouTube also enables you to record video from a computer webcam directly to the YouTube site. Before you proceed, make sure your webcam is enabled and functional.

a. Click the **Upload** link at the top of any YouTube page.

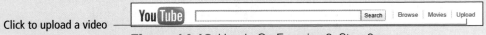

Click to upload a video

Figure 14.16 Hands-On Exercise 3, Step 2a.

This displays the *Video File Upload* page.

b. Click the **Record from webcam** link.

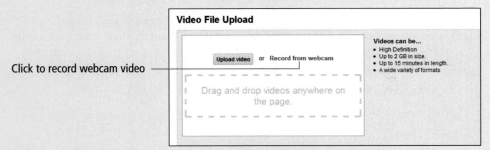

Click to record webcam video

Figure 14.17 Hands-On Exercise 3, Step 2b.

YouTube displays the *Record Video from Webcam* page, along with the *Adobe Flash Player Settings* dialog box.

c. Click the **Allow** option in the *Adobe Flash Player Settings* dialog box and then click the **Close** button.

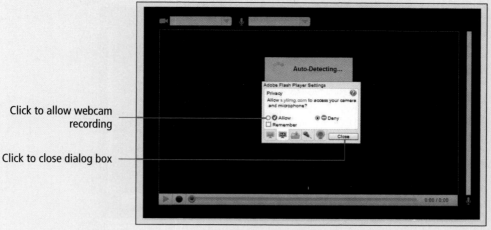

Click to allow webcam recording

Click to close dialog box

Figure 14.18 Hands-On Exercise 3, Step 2c.

The live picture from your webcam is now displayed. Make sure you have the proper webcam and microphone selected from the drop-down lists above the picture.

Tip **Audio Level**

The audio level is displayed in a vertical meter to the right of the picture on the *Record Video from Webcam* page. As you talk, watch the audio level meter rise and fall. Try to keep the audio level in the green range; if the meter goes higher into the red, you're talking too loud and the sound on your recording could be distorted.

d. Click the **Record** button to begin recording.

Click to begin recording

Adjust audio level

Figure 14.19 Hands-On Exercise 3, Step 2d.

The *Record* button changes to a red *Stop* button.

e. Click the **Stop** button when you're done with recording.

Click to stop recording

Figure 14.20 Hands-On Exercise 3, Step 2e.

When you stop recording, YouTube gives you the options to *Preview* your recording, *Re-record* the video, or *Publish* the video.

f. Click **Publish** to publish the video to the YouTube site.

Click to publish video

Figure 14.21 Hands-On Exercise 3, Step 2f.

YouTube now displays the *Video Information* page for this video.

g. Edit the title information in the *Title* box.

h. Enter a short description of this video into the *Description* box.

i. Enter one or more keywords to describe the video into the *Tags* box.

j. Click the **Category** list to select a category for this video.

k. Click the thumbnail image you want to display for this video. (Thumbnails may not appear until after YouTube has finished processing the video.)

l. If you want all YouTube viewers to see your video, select the **Public** option in the *Privacy* setting section. (This is the default.) If you want to share your video only with viewers you invite, select the **Private** option. If you want your video to be accessible only by those who know the specific URL, select the **Unlisted** option.

m. Set any other settings as desired in the *Broadcasting and Sharing Options* section of the page.

n. Set the current date and your location in the *Date and Map* section of the page, if desired.

o. Click the **Save Changes** button.

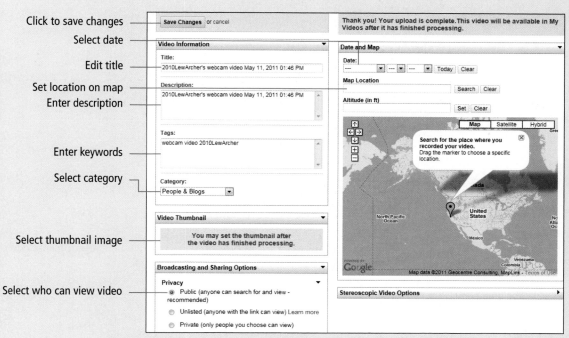

Figure 14.22 Hands-On Exercise 3, Steps 2g through 2o.

Summary

In this chapter, you learned how to find and view videos on the YouTube site. You also learned how to upload both webcam videos and traditional video files.

Key Terms

Aspect ratio 337
High definition...................................337
Resolution..337
Social network....................................339
Streaming video 336

Viral video 340
Vlog...336
Widescreen...337
YouTube...336

Multiple Choice Questions

1. What is the maximum practical resolution you can use when you upload a video to YouTube?

    (a) 320 × 240 pixels

    (b) 640 × 480 pixels

    (c) 1280 × 720 pixels

    (d) 1920 × 1080 pixels

2. YouTube lets you share videos with the following social media:

    (a) Facebook

    (b) Twitter

    (c) MySpace

    (d) All of the above

3. What do you need to watch a video on YouTube?

    (a) Internet connection

    (b) paid subscription

    (c) 3D glasses

    (d) Both (a) and (b)

4. YouTube's widescreen aspect ratio is

    (a) 4:3.

    (b) 16:9.

    (c) 10:1.

    (d) 1.66:1.

5. Which of the following is *not* a YouTube video category?

    (a) Sports

    (b) Howto & Style

    (c) Advertisements

    (d) People & Blogs

6. When you want to "like" a video, click this button:
   - (a) Vote
   - (b) Like (thumb up)
   - (c) Star
   - (d) Favorite

7. How long a video can you upload to YouTube?
   - (a) up to 5 minutes
   - (b) up to 15 minutes
   - (c) up to 30 minutes
   - (d) up to 60 minutes

8. If you want to share a video only with invited viewers, select this privacy option:
   - (a) Public
   - (b) Invitation-only
   - (c) Private
   - (d) Unlisted

9. How can you upload a video to YouTube?
   - (a) from a video file
   - (b) from a webcam
   - (c) from a video hosted on another website
   - (d) Both (a) and (b)

10. What types of videos can you *not* upload to YouTube?
   - (a) home movies
   - (b) copyrighted content
   - (c) video blogs
   - (d) how-to tutorials

Fill in the Blank

Write the correct word or words in the space provided.

1. YouTube is a _____-sharing community.
2. A video blog is called a(n) _____.
3. YouTube uses _____ _____ technology to offer movies and television shows to viewers.
4. Both 720p and 1080p are _____ _____ video formats.
5. A(n) _____ video is one that is shared among large numbers of viewers over the Internet.

Practice Exercises

1. **Find and Share a YouTube Video**

   YouTube makes it easy to find and share your favorite videos. Any public video on the YouTube site can be shared via email or social media.

   (a) Search the YouTube site for a video that demonstrates how to make an omelet.

   (b) Share this video via email with your instructor.

2. **Upload and Share a Video (optional)**

   (a) Upload a video of your own to the YouTube site. (You can either upload an existing video file or create a new webcam video.)

   (b) Share this video via email with your instructor.

Critical Thinking

1. YouTube lets you upload both videos taken with a camcorder and videos created with a webcam. Write a short paper discussing why you might prefer to create one type of video over the other, and for which purposes.

2. YouTube was created as a community for individuals to share videos for free, but is now being expanded to include paid viewing of movies, television shows, and the like. Write a short paper discussing why YouTube might be expanding into paid viewing, what competition it will encounter, and why you personally might or might not watch paid videos on the YouTube site.

Credits

YouTube screenshots reprinted by permission.

Glossary

@replies In Google Buzz, a way to direct a buzz to a particular contact, by putting an @ sign in front of a contact's name.

Album A virtual folder used to organize similar photographs in Picasa.

Anchor text The text that links to another web page.

Archive A means of storing older or inactive email messages.

Article A message posted on a Usenet newsgroup.

Aspect ratio A measurement that compares picture width by picture height.

Attachment A file that is attached to a normal text email message.

Autofill A feature in Google Chrome that lets you save frequently entered form data for future entry.

Automatic word stemming A feature that enables Google to automatically search for all possible word variations.

Bcc Blind carbon copy; sends a message to additional recipients without displaying their addresses.

Blog A diary-like website that features commentary about a given topic.

Blog address For Blogger blogs, the part of the blog's URL that appears before the blogspot.com domain.

Blogger Google's blog-hosting service, also known as Google Blogs.

Blog-hosting service A website that offers easy-to-use tools to build, host, and maintain a blog—typically for free.

Blogosphere All the blogs on the Internet.

Bookmark A means of storing links to favorite web pages for quick recall.

Boolean operators Words that are used to refine a search and that come from Boolean logic and mathematics, such as AND, OR, and NOT. Google supports only the Boolean OR operator.

Cache A temporary storage area on your hard disk where recently visited web pages are stored.

Cached page A page that is stored on Google's document servers, and that may be slightly older than the current version of the page, or outdated.

Cc Carbon copy; sends a message to additional recipients.

Citation A short note recognizing a source of information or of a quoted passage.

Comment moderation A means of blocking unwanted blog comments by requiring the owner's approval of all comments before they are displayed.

Comment spam Unsolicited commercial messages (spam) placed in the comments section of a blog post.

Computer virus A malicious computer program capable of reproducing itself and causing harm to files or programs on a computer system.

Constant A number representing a fixed value in a specified mathematical context.

Contact A person to whom you send email messages.

Contact group A group of contacts, typically used to send email mailing lists.

Conversation A grouping of related email messages.

Cookie A small text file, stored on your computer, used to track your web browsing behavior.

Crawler A software program, also known as a spider, that automatically and regularly visits websites to read and index them for search engine use.

Crop An operation that cuts out or trims unwanted portions of an image.

Dashboard In Blogger, the page that enables you to manage all your blogs and blog-related activities.

Database An organized collection of related information.

Discussion In Google Groups, a collection of messages on a specific topic.

Domain A specific type of site on the web, indicated by the domain name after the final "dot" separator. For example, the .edu domain is used to indicate education sites.

Earth view A Google Maps view that displays a 3D version of a satellite photo.

eBook Short for electronic book, a digital version of a traditional printed book.

eBook reader A handheld device designed specifically for reading electronic books.

Email Electronic mail, a way of delivering messages over the Internet.

EPUB A popular eBook format, the official standard of the International Digital Publishing Forum and compatible with most eBook readers and applications.

Event An item scheduled with Google Calendar.

Executable program file A computer file that contains a software program.

File extension A three- or four-character suffix that usually indicates the program in which a file was created.

File type A particular way of encoding data in a computer file. Most programs store their data in their own file types; file types are indicated by specific file extensions.

Filter A means of applying one or more actions to incoming messages that meet specific criteria in Gmail; a means to display a subset of all available photographs in Picasa.

Gadget A content module on an iGoogle page; in Blogger, a small application module that displays in your blog's sidebar.

Geotag A means of embedding location information about where a photo was taken into the photo file.

Gmail Google's web-based email service.

Google The Internet's most popular search engine.

Google account An individual user account for all Google services.

Google Blog Search A service that searches blogs and blog posts.

Google Books Google's searchable online repository of book content.

Google Books Library Project Google's program that encourages partner libraries to scan books in their collections for submission to the Google Books database.

Google Books Partner Program Google's program that enables book publishers to submit books to the Google Books database.

Google Buzz A social networking tool that integrates data from a variety of social networks, including Twitter, Blogger, and FriendFeed. Google Buzz was launched in 2010, and integrates with Gmail, Google's web-based email service.

Google Calendar Google's web-based calendar application.

Google Chrome Google's web browser.

Google Directory Google's hand-assembled web directory.

Google Earth A software program that generates high-resolution, 3D flybys of any location on the planet.

Google Fast Flip A visual display of the day's top stories that users can "flip" through.

Google Groups A collection of web-based special interest discussion groups, both based on Google and hosted on Usenet.

Google Image Search A subset of Google's basic web search that lets you search for photos, drawings, logos, and other graphics files on the web.

Google Instant Technology on the Google site that displays search results as a query is entered.

Google Maps Google's online mapping service.

Google News Google's news aggregation service.

Google Places A program, supplemental to Google Maps, that gathers information about local businesses.

Google Product Search Google's shopping search engine, for comparing prices from multiple retailers.

Google Reader A Google site that aggregates news feeds from blogs, news sites, and Twitter feeds.

Google Realtime Search A service that searches social media and news sites in near real time.

Google Scholar A database of scholarly journals and articles.

Google Translate Google's automatic translation service.

GoogleBot Google's web crawler software.

High definition Also known as HD, the current high resolution digital picture format.

iGoogle A customizable homepage from Google.

Inbox The main storage area for new incoming email messages.

Incognito mode A form of anonymous browsing offered in Google Chrome.

ISBN Short for International Standard Book Number, a unique numeric identification code for commercially published books.

ISSN Short for International Standard Serial Number, a unique numeric identification code for periodical publications.

Keyword A term used in a search query.

Label A keyword or tag that describes an email message in Gmail; a keyword that helps describe or categorize a specific blog post in a Blogger blog.

Layer In Google Earth, a set of data overlaid on the basic map.

Library The main view in Picasa that displays photos stored on your computer.

Malware Any type of malicious software, including computer viruses and spyware.

Mashup A custom map that includes personal data overlaid on a Google map.

My Places A subset of Google Maps that lets you create, save, and share custom maps.

News alert An email notification of new stories about a given news topic.

News Archive Search Google's database of older news articles—up to 200 years old.

News feed Also known as a site feed, an automatically updated stream of contents for a blog or news site.

Newsgroup A topic-specific discussion group on Usenet.

Newsreader A software program or website that aggregates news feeds.

Omnibox The combination address box and search box at the top of the Chrome web browser window.

OneBox Specialized search results.

Online photo-printing service A service that creates hardcopy prints, on special photo paper, of digital photos you upload.

Organic Nonpaid search results; results generated directly from a Google search.

Overlay A layer of data displayed on top of a Google map.

PageRank Google's algorithm for ranking web pages in its search results.

Phishing A type of web-based scam that typically involves an official-looking (but fake) website designed to solicit your personal information.

Photo Tray That area of the Picasa Library screen that temporarily stores selected photographs.

Photoblog A blog consisting primarily or solely of photographs.

Picasa Google's photo-editing application.

Picasa Web Albums Google's web-based photo-sharing site, also known as Google Photos.

Pinpoint A specific location or business marked on a Google map.

Place page A page of information about a given business, as compiled by Google.

Placemark A marker on a map that pinpoints a specific location.

Places of interest Specific locations overlaid on a Google Earth map.

POP email A type of email service where messages are stored on an email server and delivered directly to users' computers via email client software. (POP stands for Post Office Protocol, the protocol used to retrieve email messages from the server.)

Post A message posted to a blog; another word for a message or article in a group.

Price-comparison site A website that compares prices on given merchandise from multiple retailers.

Priority Inbox A special Gmail inbox that organizes messages in order of importance.

Public domain Any intellectual property whose rights are not held or controlled by any entity; the rights are held by the public at large.

Query A search for information.

Quick Add An "intelligent" feature that lets you quickly add an event to a Google calendar.

Red eye An undesired photographic effect, most often caused by camera flash, which results in red irises in photographed subjects.

Resolution A measurement of the picture quality of a video, measured in terms of picture elements (pixels).

Restricted group A Google group that requires members to join before viewing or posting messages.

RSS Short for Really Simple Syndication, a popular format for news feeds.

SafeSearch Google's content filter for search results.

Saturation The amount of color—too much or too little.

Search engine A website that enables users to search the web for specific information.

Search index A database that stores information about web pages, in order to provide fast and accurate searching.

Search operator A symbol or word that causes a search engine to do something special with the word directly following the symbol.

Search tools A means of filtering Google search results.

Seller rating In Google Product Search, a rating of a given seller, on a scale of one to five stars, as determined by that seller's customers.

Shortcut A small file, often appearing as a desktop icon, that points to and opens an associated application or document.

Signature Personalized text that appears at the bottom of an email message.

Site feed An automatically updated stream of contents for a blog or news site that readers can subscribe to.

Snippet A short excerpt from a book or an email message.

Social network A website or service, such as Facebook or MySpace, where users can form communities with like-minded people and share details of their lives with friends, family, fellow students, and coworkers.

Spam Unsolicited commercial email.

Star A means of flagging important email messages.

Statistical machine translation Also known as SMT, an approach to language translation based on statistical models derived from the analysis of previous documents.

Stop word A small, common word, such as "and," "the," "where," "how," and "what," that Google ignores when performing a query.

Streaming video A technology that enables the viewing of videos over the Internet in real time, without having to first download a video file.

Street View A Google Maps view that displays street-level photos of a given location.

Tab In Google Chrome, a means of displaying multiple web pages within a single browser window.

Task list A to-do list of upcoming tasks managed in Google Calendar.

Template Designer Blogger's web-based application for formatting the look and feel of a blog.

Thread On Usenet, a collection of posts on a specific topic.

Tint A color variation, such as red or blue.

Universal Search The display of different types of search results on a single results page.

URL Uniform resource locator, the address of a specific web page.

Usage rights The permissions that specify in what context web page content can be reused.

Usenet A subset of the Internet comprised of tens of thousands of online discussion groups.

Vacation mode When enabled, puts a Gmail account on hold while the user is on vacation.

Viral video A video that attracts large numbers of viewers through Internet sharing.

Vlog A video blog, or a personal journal in video form.

Web browser An application designed to view HTML-based pages on the web.

Web server A specialized computer, connected to the Internet, that hosts web content.

Widescreen A video aspect ratio where the width greatly exceeds the height; the HD format has a widescreen aspect ratio of 16:9 (16 units wide by 9 units tall).

Wildcard A character that enables you to search for all words that include the first part of a keyword. Google does not support wildcard searches.

YouTube The video-sharing community owned by Google.

Index

& (ampersands), 132
- (minus sign) operators, 21, 25–26, 28
+ (plus sign) operators, 21, 24–25
~ (tilde) operators, 21–22, 26–27

A

Abbreviations (Google Maps), 132
ABC News, 57
Accounts. *See also* Google accounts
  creating Blogger, 279–280
  creating Gmail, 166–169
  creating YouTube, 337
Accounts tab (Gmail), 197
Adding
  books to libraries, 105–106
  gadgets
    in Blogger, 291–292, 296–299
    to iGoogle pages, 73, 74–75
  labels to posts, 282, 290–291
  links to posts, 285–286
  new tabs to iGoogle pages, 77–78
  photos to posts, 283, 286–288
  placemarks to maps, 145, 147–149
  RSS feeds to iGoogle pages, 75
  videos to posts, 288–290
Addition function, 83
Add/Remove Star button (Picasa), 311
Address book (Gmail), 190–195
Address formats (Google Maps), 132
Add selected items to an album button (Picasa), 311
Adobe Acrobat (.pdf) files, 22, 102
Adobe PostScript (.ps) files, 22
AdSense gadget, 292
Advanced searches. *See* Google search
Advertisements (Google Product Search), 63
Aerial photography, 130
AIM (AOL Instant Messenger), ⓒⓦ A2
Albums, defined, 312
Aligning text (Blogger), 284
allinanchor: operators, 32–33
allintext: operators, 31–32
allintitle: operators, 29–30
allinurl: operators, 30–31
Ampersands (&), 132
Anchor text, 32–33
AND Boolean operators, 21
AND/OR queries, 21, 23–24, 54
AOL Instant Messenger (AIM), ⓒⓦ A2
Apple iBooks, 102
Applications, Google. *See specific applications*
Archiving messages (Gmail), 171, 176–177
Articles, 112, 125
Aspect ratio, 337
Atom feeds, 123

Attachments
  in Gmail, 179, 185–187
  to messages (Google Buzz), 268
Audio level (YouTube), 347
Austrian National Library (Austria), 95
Authors, searching for, 54
Auto Color option (Picasa), 315, 318
Auto Contrast option (Picasa), 315
Autodesk (.dwf) files, 22
AutoFill feature (Google Chrome), 256
Automatic word stemming, 22

B

Background colors, 216, 295
Bargains, searching for, 62–66
Barnes & Noble NOOK, 102
Basics tab (Google Chrome), 240
Bavarian State Library (Germany), 95
BBC, 57
Bcc (blind carbon copy) field, 184
Bebo, 340
Bicycling directions, 150
Bicycling overlays, 131
BizRate, 62
Blind carbon copies (Gmail), 184
Blocking
  comments (Blogger), 300
  messages (Google Talk), ⓒⓦ A13–A14
  YouTube access, 336
Blog address, defined, 281
Blog Archive gadget, 292
Blogger. *See also* Blogs
  blog posts
    adding labels to, 290–291
    adding links to, 285–286
    adding photos to, 286–288
    adding video to, 288–290
    Blogger Dashboard, 281, 283–291
    categories of, 282
    contents of, 283
    creating new, 283–284
    formatting, 284–285
    frequency of, 282
    length of, 282
  costs of, 279
  creating an account, 279–280
  creating blogs, 281–282
  customizing blogs
    adding gadgets, 291–292, 296–299
    changing page elements, 295–296
    choosing a template, 293–295
    rearranging page elements, 299–300
    Template Designer, 291
  defined, 279
  managing blog comments, 300–305

posting YouTube videos on, 339–340
  signing up for, 279–280
  viewing blogs from, 282
  web address, 2, 279
Blogger Dashboard
  blog posts
    adding labels to, 282, 290–291
    adding links to, 285–286
    adding photos to, 283, 286–288
    adding video to, 288–290
    creating, 283–284
    formatting, 284–285
  creating blogs from, 281
  defined, 283
  viewing blogs from, 282
Blogger templates, 281
Blog-hosting services, 279
Blog List gadget, 292
Blogosphere, 278
Blogs. *See also* Blogger
  creating, 279
  defined, 123, 278
  layout, 278
  reasons to blog, 278
  searching for, 124–125
Blog This! button (Picasa), 312
Bloomberg, 57
Bolding text (Blogger), 284
Bookmarks
  defined, 248
  in Google Chrome, 248–254
  organizing, 249–251
  synchronizing between computers, 248, 252–254
  to Web pages, 249
Bookreport.com, 100
Books. *See* Google Books
Boolean operators, 21
Borders and Labels layer (Google Earth), 157
Brightness, photo, 316–317
British Library Direct, 56
Browsing
  books/magazines, 97
  groups, 113
  history (Google Chrome), 254–256
  news articles, 58–59
  for videos, 337–338
Bulleted lists (Blogger), 285
Businesses, searching for, 141–144
Buttons. *See specific buttons*
Buzz overlays, 131
Buzz tab (Gmail), 197
B&W special effect (Picasa), 316

C

Cached pages, 15
Caches, 256
Calculations, 83–84, 87

Calculator functions, 83
Calendars. *See* Google Calendar
Carbon copies (Gmail), 184
Case sensitivity (Google search), 14
CBS News, 57
Cc (carbon copy) field, 184
Changing
  fonts (Blogger), 284, 296
  page elements (Blogger), 295–296
  themes
    Gmail, 198–199
    iGoogle, 78
Chats (Google Talk)
  starting a session, (CW) A5–A6,
    (CW) A11–A12
  video, (CW) A11, (CW) A12
  voice-based, (CW) A8–A10
Chat tab (Gmail), 197
Choose function, 83
CIC (Committee on Institutional
  Cooperation), 95
Citations, 52, 55–56
Clear items from the selection button
  (Picasa), 311
CNN, 57
Collage button (Picasa), 312
Colors
  in blogs, 284, 295–296
  in calendars, 216
  in photos, 315, 318–319
Color Temperature slider (Picasa), 318
Columbia University, 95
Comment moderation, 300, 303–305
Comments
  in Blogger
    blocking, 300
    disabling, 302–303
    limiting, 300, 301–302
    managing, 300–305
    moderating, 300, 303–305
    spam, 300–301
  in Google Buzz, 270–271
Commercial programming
  (YouTube), 336
Committee on Institutional
  Cooperation (CIC), 95
Computer viruses, 187–190
Constants, 84, 87–88
Contact groups (Gmail), 190, 193,
  194–195
Contact information (Google
  accounts), 8–9
Contacts (Google Talk), (CW) A2,
  (CW) A13–A14
Contacts lists (Gmail), 190–195
Contrast, photo, 315, 316–317
Conversations (Gmail), 179, 180–181
Conversions, 84, 88
Cookies, defined, 241
Copyrighted images, 44
Cornell University Library, 95
Cosecant function, 84
Cosine function, 84
Costs

of Blogger, 279
of Gmail, 166
of Google accounts, 2
of Google Books, 94–95
of Google Earth, 154
of Picasa Web Albums, 327
of YouTube commercial programming, 336
Cotangent function, 84
Courts, searching specific, 55
Crawler, defined, 13
Create Event button, 219–221
Creating
  Blogger accounts, 279–280
  blog posts (Blogger)
    adding labels to, 290–291
    adding links to, 285–286
    adding photos to, 286–288
    adding video to, 288–290
    Blogger Dashboard, 283–291
    categories of, 282
    contents of, 283
    creating, 283–284
    formatting, 284–285
    frequency of, 282
    length of, 282
  blogs, 279, 281–282
  calendars, 208–210
  custom maps, 145–150
  events, 219–221
  Gmail accounts, 166–169
  Google accounts, 2–6
  new groups, 119–122
  new messages (Gmail), 183–184
  new message threads in groups,
    118–119
  new photo albums, 313–314
  YouTube accounts, 337
Crop operation (Picasa), 315,
  320–321
Customizing
  blogs (Blogger)
    adding gadgets, 291–292,
      296–299
    changing page elements, 295–296
    choosing a template, 281,
      293–295
    rearranging page elements,
      299–300
    Template Designer, 291
  individual gadgets (iGoogle), 76
  maps, 145–150

D

Dashboard (Blogger). *See* Blogger
  Dashboard
Database, defined, 12
Dates
  searching
    articles by, 54
    for web pages by, 38–39
  search results by, 19
define: operators, 83, 86
Definitions, word, 82–83, 85–86

Deja.com, 112
DejaNews, 112
Deleting
  browsing history, 255–256
  gadgets, 76
  Gmail messages, 171, 178, 189–190
Detachable tabs, 246
Dictionary pages, displaying, 85–86
Digital Globe Coverage layer (Google
  Earth), 157
Digital photographs. *See* Photographs;
  Picasa
Directions
  bicycling, 150
  driving
    Google Earth, 159–161
    Google Maps, 150–153
  multiple-stop, 152
  public transit, 150
  reversing, 152
  walking, 150
Directories, 121
Disabling blog comments, 302–303
Discussions, defined, 115
Displaying
  dictionary pages, 85–86
  Gmail messages, 170
  layers (Google Earth), 157–158
  single definitions, 85
Division function, 83
Documents, translating, 81–82
Document servers, 12
Domains, 23, 28–29, 95
Downloading
  books online, 102–103
  Google Chrome, 241
  Google Earth, 154
  Google Talk, (CW) A3–A4
  Picasa, 310
Driving directions
  Google Earth, 159–161
  Google Earth *vs.* Google Maps, 159
  Google Maps, 150–153
Dual mode (Google Chrome), 241

E

Earth view (Google Maps), 130, 131,
  138–139
eBook readers, 102
eBooks, 56, 94. *See also* Google
  Books
Editing photos (Picasa), 315–322
Edit in Picnik option (Picasa), 315
Email button (Picasa), 311
Email(ing). *See also* Gmail
  adding additional addresses, 7
  defined, 166
  from Google Groups, 116–117
  news alerts, 60–61
  photos (Picasa), 323, 325–326
  YouTube videos, 340–341
Enabling comment moderation
  (Blogger), 303–304
EPUB format, 102

ESPN, 57
Event maps, 220
Events, calendar
    adding
        with Create Event button, 218,
            219–221
        directly, 218–219
        from Gmail, 218, 221–222
        overview, 217–218
        using Quick Add, 217, 221
    defined, 217
    inviting others to existing, 222–224
    notification of, 227
Exact phrases, searching for, 37
Excluded titles (Google Books), 96
Excluding
    files types from search, 28
    words from search results, 21, 25–26
Executable (.exe.) program files
    (Gmail), 179
Exponent function, 83
Export button (Picasa), 312

F

Facebook, 272, 339, 340, 341–342
Factorial function, 83
Feed gadget, 292
Feeds
    atom, 123
    news, 123, 124–125
    Twitter, 124–125
Fees. *See* costs
File extensions, defined, 22
Files
    attaching to Gmail, 179, 185–187
    sending (Google Talk), 🔵 A2,
        🔵 A6–A7
File types, 22, 28, 179
Fill Light option (Picasa), 315
Film Grain special effect (Picasa), 316
Filtered B&W special effect
    (Picasa), 316
Filtering
    on Advanced Search page, 34–35
    defined, 312
    messages (Gmail), 171, 177–178
    offensive pages, 35
    photos, 312–313
    search results, 17
Filters tab (Gmail), 197
Finding. *See* Searching
Flagging messages (Gmail), 171,
    174–175
Flickr, 272
Focal B&W special effect (Picasa), 316
Follow back button (Google Buzz), 269
Follow by Email gadget, 292
Followers gadget, 292
Following (Google Buzz), 268–270
Fonts, changing (Blogger), 284, 296
Forbes, 57
Formats
    address (Google Maps), 132
    eBooks, 102

PDF file, 22, 102
    video (Blogger), 289
Formatting posts (Blogger), 284–285
45° overlays, 131
Forwarding messages (Gmail),
    182–183
4K videos, 344
Fox News, 57
Froogle, 62
Functions. *See specific functions*

G

Gadgets. *See also specific gadgets*
    in Blogger, 291–292, 296–299
    defined, 73, 291
    in iGoogle, 73, 74–77
Gallery layer (Google Earth), 157
General tab (Gmail), 196
Generating
    Google Earth driving directions,
        159–161
    Google Maps, 132–133
    Google Maps directions, 150–153
GeoEye Featured Imagery layer
    (Google Earth), 157
Geographic Features layer (Google
    Earth), 157
Geotag button (Picasa), 312, 313
Ghent University Library
    (Belgium), 95
Global Awareness layer (Google
    Earth), 157
Glow special effect (Picasa), 316
Gmail. *See also* Email
    Accounts tab, 197
    adding calendar events from, 218,
        221–222
    attaching files, 179, 185–187
    Buzz tab, 197
    Cc/Bcc fields, 184
    Chat tab, 197
    contact groups, 190, 193, 194–195
    contacts list, 190–195
    conversations, 179, 180–181
    cost of, 166
    creating accounts, 166–169
    customizing, 196–202
    defined, 166
    Filters tab, 197
    Forwarding and POP/IMAP tab, 197
    General tab, 196
    Google Buzz and, 272–273
    Google Talk in, 🔵 A11–A12
    inbox, priority, 169, 200–202
    Labels tab, 196
    messages
        archiving, 171, 176–177
        creating new, 183–184
        deleting, 171, 178, 189–190
        displaying, 170
        filtering, 171, 177–178
        flagging, 171, 174–175
        forwarding, 182–183
        labeling, 169, 175–176

    organizing, 169
    reading, 180
    replying to, 181–182
    searching, 172–173
    starred, 170, 174
    unarchiving, 177
    viewing with common labels,
        175–176
    Offline tab, 197
    passwords, 167
    POP email *vs.,* 166
    priority inbox, 169, 200–202
    Priority Inbox tab, 197
    secondary email addresses, 167
    signatures, 179, 184–185
    signing in, 169
    snippets, 170
    spam, 187–190
    spell-checking, 184
    themes, 198–199
    Themes tab, 197
    usernames, 167
    vacation mode, 198, 199
    viewing trash, 178
    views, 170
    viruses, 187–190
    web address, 2
    Web Clips tab, 197
Goodreads, 100
Google. *See* Google search
Google, Inc., 12
Google accounts
    contact information, 8–9
    costs, 2
    creating, 2–6
    defined, 2
    email addresses, adding additional, 7
    linking web pages to, 8–9
    managing settings, 6–8
    passwords, 4–5, 7
    personal information, 8–9
    sharing calendars, 226
    signing in to, 5–6
    user profiles, 8–9
    viewing data stored with, 7
Google Applications. *See specific
    applications*
Google Blog Search, 2
Google Books
    book search, 97–99
    browsing books/magazines, 97
    cost of, 94–95
    defined, 2, 94
    downloading books, 102–103
    eBook formats supported, 102
    Google Books Library Project, 94,
        95–96
    Google Books Partner Program, 94
    library management, 105–106
    overview, 94
    purchasing books, 102, 104
    reviewing books, 100–102
    search results, 96
    viewing book content, 99–100

Google Books (*Continued*)
viewing options, 96
web address, 96
Google Books Library Project, 94, 95–96
Google Books Partner Program, 94
GoogleBot, 13
Google Buzz
adding photographs to posts, 271
attachments to messages, 268
comments on posts, 270–271
connecting websites to, 266–268
following, 268–270
overview, 272
Picasa Web Albums and, 272
posting, 268, 270–273
posting YouTube video on, 340
putting in an inbox, 266
showing in Gmail, 265
social networks and, 268–273
Twitter *vs.,* 272
Google Calendar
adding events
with Create Event button,
219–221
directly, 218–219
from Gmail, 218, 221–222
overview, 217–218
using Quick Add, 217, 221
calendar colors, 216
creating calendars, 208–210
defined, 2
event maps, 220
holiday calendars, 210–211
inviting others to existing event,
222–224
multiple calendars, 208, 209–210,
215–216
notification of events, 227
permission settings, 210
printing calendars, 216–217
sharing calendars, 222–224
specialty calendars, 208
sports calendars, 210–211
task lists, 227–232
to-do lists, 227–232
viewing calendars, 211–217
views, 212–215
Google Checkout, 2
Google Chrome
Basics tab, 240
bookmarks, 248–254
browsing history, 254–256
changing search providers, 243
defined, 238
downloading, 241
Dual mode, 241
history, 254–256
homepages, 245–247
Under the Hood tab, 240
incognito mode, 241, 244–245
installing, 241
Internet Explorer *vs.,* 238–239
launching, 242
malware, 240–241
navigating to web pages, 242–243

overview, 238
Personal Stuff tab, 240
phishing, 240–241
printing web pages, 244
searching the web, 243
setting configurations, 239–240
shortcuts, 258
speed of, 239
system requirements, 241
tabs, 245–247
using with Google Apps, 257–259
versions of, 241
web address, 2
Google Code, 2
Google Desktop, 2
Google Directory, 2
Google Docs, 2, 3
Google Earth
costs of, 154
defined, 3, 154
downloading/installing, 154
generating driving directions,
159–161
Google Earth Enterprise, 154
Google Earth Pro, 154
Google Maps driving directions
vs., 159
(.kml, .kmz) files, 22
layers, 156–158
navigating with the mouse, 155–156
onscreen navigation controls, 154–155
overview, 154
plug-in, 138
printing directions, 161
searching for places, 156
system requirements, 154
versions of, 154
Google Earth Enterprise, 154
Google Earth Pro, 154
Google Earth view, 138–139
Google Fast Flip, 59
Google Finance, 3
Google Groups
browsing, 113
creating
new groups, 119–122
new message threads, 118–119
defined, 3, 112
directory, 121
email from, 116–117
identifying, 114
inviting members to, 121–122
joining groups, 115–117
managing, 122
moderation of, 112
page layout, 115
reading posts, 117–118
replying to posts, 117–118
searching
for groups, 113–114
for posts across groups, 114–115
unsubscribing from, 117
Usenet, 112, 119
Google Health, 3
Google Images, 3

Google Image Search, 41
Google Instant, 17, 18
Google Knol, 3
Google Labs, 3
Google Local, 130
Google Maps
abbreviations, 132
adding placemarks to, 145,
147–149
address formats, 132
creating custom maps, 145–150
defined, 130
displaying
Google Earth view, 138–139
overlay data, 139–140
satellite images, 137–138
street view photos, 130, 135–136
driving directions, 150, 151
Earth view, 130, 131, 138–139
generating, 132–133
generating directions, 150–153
Google Earth driving directions
vs., 159
Google Local *vs.,* 130
map views available, 130–131
navigating, 133–134
overlays, 131
overview, 130
printing directions, 152–153
printing maps, 140–141
saving to My Places, 146
searching for nearby businesses,
141–144
sharing custom, 149–150
Street View, 130, 135–136
Traffic View, 134–135
viewing custom maps, 147
web address, 3
Google Mobile, 3
Google News, 3, 57–62
Google Patent Search, 3
Google Photos. *See* Picasa Web
Albums
Google Places, 142
Google products, 2–3
Google Product Search, 3, 62–66
Google Reader, 3, 123–125, 272
Google Realtime Search, 3
Google Scholar, 3, 52–57
Google search. *See also* Restricting
searches; Results, search;
Searching
advanced, 34–41
AND/OR queries, 21, 23–24, 54
conducting, 14
entering a query, 18
excluding words from results, 21,
25–26
extending search results, 18–19
filtering results, 17
Google Blog Search, 2
GoogleBot, 13
Google Directory, 2
Google Image Search, 41
Google Instant, 17

Google News, 3, 57–62
Google Product Search, 3, 62–66
Google Realtime Search, 3
Google Scholar, 3, 52–57
from iGoogle, 73
index building, 12–13
links/link text, 13
News Archive Search, 57, 61–62
OR searches, 36
overview, 12
page organization, 14
queries with wildcards, 22
with quotation marks, 27
ranking results, 13
refining
queries, 21–34
search results, 19–20
results page layout, 14–17
SafeSearch filtering, 40
search tools, 19–20
stop words, 21, 24–25
Universal Search, 17
using wildcards, 22
Google Search button, 14
Google services/applications, 2–3
Google Sites, 3
Google Talk
blocking messages, **CW** A13–A14
chat sessions, **CW** A5–A6
defined, **CW** A2
downloading, **CW** A3–A4
in Gmail, **CW** A11–A12
history, **CW** A3
launching, **CW** A4–A5
managing contacts, **CW** A13–A14
navigating clients, **CW** A2–A3
online status, **CW** A7–A8
sending files, **CW** A2, **CW** A6–A7
signing in, **CW** A4–A5
signing out, **CW** A8
voice-based chats, **CW** A8–A10
web address, 3
Google Toolbar, 3
Google Translate, 3, 78–82
Google Trends, 3
Google Videos, 3
Google Voice, 3
Google Web Search, 3
Graduated Tint special effect
(Picasa), 316
Groups. *See* Google Groups
Groups, contact (Gmail), 190, 193,
194–195

H

Harvard University, 95
hi5, 340
High definition video, 337
History
Google Chrome, 254–256
Google Talk, **CW** A3
Hold selected items button
(Picasa), 311
Holiday calendars, 210–211

Homepages
Google Chrome, 245–247
iGoogle, 72–78
HTML/JavaScript gadget, 292
Hyperbolic cosine function, 84
Hyperbolic functions, 84
Hyperbolic sine function, 84
Hyperbolic tangent function, 84

I

ICQ, **CW** A2
iGoogle
adding gadgets to, 73, 74–75
adding new tabs to, 77–78
adding RSS feeds to, 75
changing visual themes, 78
customizing individual gadgets, 76
Google accounts, 2
as homepage, 72
overview, 72
rearranging gadgets, 77
removing gadgets, 76
searching Google from, 73
viewing content on, 73
web address, 3, 72–78
Images, 41–46. *See also* Photographs;
Picasa
Imax movies, 344
I'm Feeling Lucky
Google search, 14
Picasa, 315
Importing
bookmarks (Google Chrome), 248,
251–252
settings (Google Chrome), 251–252
inanchor: operators, 32–33
Inbox, 169, 266. *See also* Gmail
Incognito mode (Google Chrome),
241, 244–245
Indenting blocks of text (Blogger), 285
Index, search, 12–13
Index servers, 12
Inserting
photos in posts (Blogger), 286–288
videos in posts (Blogger), 288–290
Installing
Google Chrome, 241
Google Earth, 154
Google Talk, **CW** A3–A4
Picasa, 310
Instant messaging, **CW** A2. *See also*
Google Talk
International Herald Tribune, 57
International Standard Book Number
(ISBN), 98–99
International Standard Serial Number
(ISSN), 98–99
Internet connections (YouTube), 336
Internet Explorer, Google Chrome *vs.,*
238–239
intext: operators, 31–32
intitle: operators, 29–30
inurl: operators, 30–31
Inverse cosecant function, 84

Inverse cosine function, 84
Inverse cotangent function, 84
Inverse secant function, 84
Inverse sine function, 84
Inverse tangent function, 84
Inverse trigonometric function, 84
Invitations
to events, 222–224
members to groups, 121–122
ISBN (International Standard Book
Number), 98–99
ISSN (International Standard Serial
Number), 98–99
Italicizing text (Blogger), 284

J

Joining groups, 115–117
Junk mail, 187–190

K

Keio University Library
(Japan), 95
Keywords, defined, 14, 172

L

Labeling
messages (Gmail), 169, 175–176
posts (Blogger), 282, 290–291
Labels gadget, 292
Labels overlays, 131
Labels tab (Gmail), 196
Languages
searching for pages with specific,
37–38
translating, 79–82
Layers (Google Earth), 156–158
Layouts
blog, 278
Blogger, 296
Google Groups page, 115
Google search results page, 14–17
Legal databases, searching (Google
Scholar), 55
Libraries
Google Books, 105–106
Google Scholar, 56
online, 94
Picasa, 310
Library view (Picasa), 310–311
Limitations, storage (Picasa Web
Albums), 327
Limiting blog comments, 300,
301–302
Linking
web pages to Google accounts, 8–9
websites to Google Buzz, 266–268
Link List gadget, 292
Links
adding to Blogger posts, 285–286
opening as new tabs, 246
to posts on Google Buzz, 271
Links/link text (Google search), 13
Linux operating system, 12

List gadget, 292
Lists
   bulleted, 285
   contact, 190–195
   numbered, 285
   task, 227–232
   to-do, 227–232
Logarithm base e function, 84
Logarithm base 2 function, 84
Logarithm base 10 function, 84
Logarithmic functions, 84
Logo gadget, 292
Los Angeles Times, 57
Lotus 1-2-3 files, 22
Lyon Municipal Library (France), 95

M

MacWrite (.mw) files, 22
Magazines. *See* Google Books
Malware, 240–241
Managing
   comments (Blogger), 300–305
   contacts
     in Gmail, 190–195
     in Google Talk, (CW) A13–A14
   Google account settings, 6–8
   groups, 122
   homepages (Google Chrome),
     245–247
   tabs (Google Chrome), 245–247
Manual cropping (Picasa), 321
Mapping events, 220
Maps. *See* Google Maps
Map views (Google Maps), 130–131
Mashups, map, 145
Matching, automatic (Gmail), 172
Mathematical functions, 83
Measurement, converting units of, 88
Members, inviting to groups, 121–122
Messages
   Gmail
     archiving, 171, 176–177
     creating new, 183–184
     deleting, 171, 178, 189–190
     displaying, 170
     filtering, 171, 177–178
     flagging, 171, 174–175
     forwarding, 182–183
     labeling, 169, 175–176
     organizing, 169
     reading, 180
     replying to, 181–182
     searching, 172–173
     starred, 170, 174
     unarchiving, 177
     viewing with common labels,
       175–176
   Google Buzz, attachments to, 268
   Google Talk
     blocking, (CW) A13–A14
     voicemail, (CW) A8, (CW) A9–A10
Messages threads, creating new,
   118–119
Microsoft Excel (.xls, .xlsx) files, 22

Microsoft PowerPoint (.ppf, .ppfx)
   files, 22
Microsoft Word (.doc, .docx) files, 22
Microsoft Works (.wdb, .wks, .wps)
   files, 22
Microsoft Write (.wri) files, 22
Minus sign (-) operators, 21,
   25–26, 28
Moderation, comment (Blogger), 300,
   303–305
Moderation (Google Groups), 112
Modulo function, 83
Movie button (Picasa), 312
Movies, 336, 344. *See also* YouTube
Moving
   elements on pages (Blogger),
     299–300
   gadgets (iGoogle), 77
   photos (Picasa), 314–315
MSNBC, 57
Multiple-stop directions, 152
Multiplication function, 83
My Places, 145, 146
MySpace, 340

N

National Library of Catalonia, 95
Navigating
   clients (Google Talk), (CW) A2–A3
   Google Maps, 133–134
   with the mouse (Google Earth),
     155–156
   with onscreen controls (Google Earth),
     154–155
   to web pages, 242–243
Netflix, 336
News alerts, email, 60–61
News Archive Search, 57, 61–62
News articles, 57–60, 61–62
News feeds, 123, 124–125
Newsgroups, defined, 112
Newsreaders, defined, 123
Newsreel gadget, 292
New York Public Library, 95
New York Times, 57
NexTag, 62
NOT Boolean operators, 21
Notifications, 227
Numbered lists (Blogger), 285
Numeric ranges, searching within,
   39–40

O

Ocean layer (Google Earth), 157
Offensive pages, filtering, 35
Offline tab (Gmail), 197
Omnibox, 238
OneBox results, 16
Online libraries, 94
Online photo-printing services, 323,
   324–325
Online Status (Google Talk),
   (CW) A7–A8
Opening links as new tabs, 246

Operators
   AND, 21
   allinanchor:, 32–33
   allintext:, 31–32
   allintitle:, 29–30
   allinurl:, 30–31
   Boolean, 21
   define:, 83, 86
   intext:, 31–32
   intitle:, 29–30
   inurl:, 30–31
   minus sign (-), 21, 25–26, 28
   NOT, 21
   OR, 21
   plus sign (+), 21, 24–25
   related:, 33–34
   search, 21–22
   what is:, 83, 86
Organic, defined, 15
Organizing
   bookmarks, 249–251
   messages (Gmail), 169
   photos (Picasa), 312–315
Orkut, 3, 340
OR searches, 36
Overlays
   Google Earth, 139–140
   Google Maps, 131
Overstock.com, 100
Oxford English Dictionary, 12
Oxford University, Bodleian Library
   (UK), 95

P

Page elements (Blogger), 295–296,
   299–300
Page Header gadget, 292
Page organization (Google search), 14
PageRank, 13
Pages
   cached, 15
   dictionary, 85–86
   offensive, 35
   searching, 29–34
Pages gadget, 292
Panoramio, 3
Park/Recreation Areas layer (Google
   Earth), 157
Passwords
   Gmail, 167
   Google accounts, 4–5, 7
Patents, searching for, 53
PDF file formats, 22, 102
Percent function, 83
Performing calculations, 83–84, 87
Permission settings, 210
Personal information (Google
   accounts), 8–9
Personal Stuff tab (Google
   Chrome), 240
Phishing, 240–241
Phone calls (Google Talk), (CW) A8
Photo albums (Picasa), 313–314
Photoblogs, 283

Photographs. *See also* Picasa
adding to Blogger posts, 283, 286–288
adding to Google Buzz posts, 271
aerial, 130
profile, 8
Photos layer (Google Earth), 157
Photos overlays, 131
Photo Tray (Picasa), 311
Phrases, 27, 37, 86
Picasa. *See also* **Picasa Web Albums**
creating new photo albums, 313–314
defined, 3, 310
downloading, 310
editing photos, 315–322
filtering photos, 312–313
function buttons, 311–312
installing, 310
moving photos, 314–315
organizing photos, 312–315
overview, 310–312
printing photos, 323–325
saving edited files, 322
sharing photos, 323, 325–326
sorting photos, 313
system requirements, 310
uploading photos to Picasa Web Albums, 327–328
Picasa Web Albums
attaching hyperlinks to Google Buzz, 268
costs of, 327
Google Buzz and, 272
sharing photos with, 327–331
uploading photos to Blogger, 283, 286, 288
web address, 3
Picnik, 3
Picture gadget, 292
Pinpoints, 142–143
Place Categories layer (Google Earth), 157
Placemarks, 145, 147–149
Place page, 142, 143–144
Places layer (Google Earth), 157
Places of interest (POIs), 157, 158
Playback controls (Google Earth), 160
Playback quality (YouTube), 337
Plug-ins (Google Earth), 138
Plus sign (+) operators, 21, 24–25
POIs (Places of Interest), 157, 158
Poll gadget, 292
POP (Post Office Protocol) email, 166
Popular Posts gadget, 292
Posting
YouTube video
to Blogger, 339–340
to FaceBook, 341–342
on Google Buzz, 340
to Twitter, 342–343
Posts
adding
labels to (Blogger), 290–291
links to (Blogger), 285–286

photos to (Blogger), 286–288
video to (Blogger), 288–290
comments on (Google Buzz), 270–271
creating new (Blogger), 283–284
defined, 114, 278
to Google Buzz, 268, 270–273
reading
from Google Groups, 117–118
from Google Reader, 125
replying to (Google Groups), 117–118
searching across groups (Google Groups), 114–115
Price-comparison sites, 62
PriceGrabber.com, 64
Princeton University, 95
Print button (Picasa), 311
Printing
calendars, 216–217
directions
Google Earth, 161
Google Maps, 152–153
maps, 140–141
photos, 323–325
web pages, 244
Priority inbox, 169, 200–202
Priority Inbox tab (Gmail), 197
Privacy (Google Buzz), 268, 272–273
Products, searching for, 65
Profile gadget, 292
Profile photos, 8
Profiles (Google Buzz), 269
Publications, searching for, 54
Public calendars, 224–227
Public domain, defined, 95
Public transit directions, 150
Purchasing, online, 65, 102, 103–104

Q

Queries. *See also* **Google search; Searching**
AND/OR, 21, 23–24, 54
defined, 14
search, 18
suggested, 18
wild cards in, 22
Quick Add link (Google Calendar), 217, 221
Quotation marks, searching with, 27
Quoting original posts, 118

R

Ranking Google search results, 13
Ratings, seller, 64, 65–66
Reading
articles, 125
book reviews, 101
messages (Gmail), 180
posts
Google Groups, 117–118
Google Reader, 125
tweets, 125
Real-time Simple Syndication (RSS), 75, 123

Rearranging
elements (Blogger), 299–300
gadgets (iGoogle), 77
photos (Picasa), 314–315
Red eye fix (Picasa), 315, 319–320
Redo button (Picasa), 317
related: operators, 33–34
Related search results, 16–17
Removing
formatting (Blogger), 285
redeye in photos (Picasa), 315, 319–320
@replies function, 266
Replying
to messages (Gmail), 181–182
to posts (Google Groups), 117–118
ResellerRatings.com, 64
Resolution, video, 337
Restricted groups, defined, 115
Restricting searches
to page's
anchor text, 32–33
body text, 31–32
title, 29–30
URL, 30–31
to specific domains/websites, 28–29
to specific file types, 28
Results, search
by date range, 19
excluding words from, 25–26
extending, 18–19
filtering, 17
fine-tuning, 17
Google Books, 96
Google page layout, 14–17
Google Product Search, 63–63
Google Scholar, 55–57
image, 42–43
ranking Google, 13
refining with search tools, 19–20
related, 16–17
types of, 19
Universal Search, 17
Retouch option (Picasa), 315
Reuters, 57
Reverse stemming, 22
Reversing directions, 152
Reviews, 64, 100–102
Rich Text Format (.rtf) files, 22
Roads layer (Google Earth), 157
Root function, 83
Rotate clockwise button (Picasa), 311
Rotate counter-clockwise button (Picasa), 311
Routes, modifying (Google Map), 150
RSS (Real-time Simple Syndication) feeds, 75, 123

S

SafeSearch filtering, 35, 40
Satellite view (Google Maps), 130, 136–138
Saturation special effect (Picasa), 316, 319

Saving
  edited photo files (Picasa), 322
  maps to My Places, 146
School libraries, searching, 56
Search Box gadget, 292
Search engine, defined, 12
Search index, 12–13
Searching. *See also* Google search;
  Restricting searches; Results, search
  articles by dates, 54
  for authors, 54
  for bargains, 62–66
  for blogs, 124–125
  for books, 97–99
  for eBooks, 56
  for exact phrases, 27, 37
  for files on the web, 22
  for groups, 113–114
  from iGoogle, 73
  for images, 41–46
  legal databases, 55
  for messages, 172–173
  for nearby businesses, 141–144
  news feeds, 124–125
  within a numeric range, 39–40
  pages, 29–34
  for pages in specific languages, 37–38
  for patents, 53
  for places, 156
  for posts across all groups, 114–115
  for products, 65
  for publications, 54
  for recent web pages, 38–39
  school libraries, 56
  smart, 132
  specific courts, 55
  specific domains, 23, 28–29
  for specific file types, 28
  for specific subject areas, 55
  specific websites, 23, 28–29
  for synonyms, 21–22, 26–27
  Twitter feeds, 124–125
  for videos, 337
  web pages by dates, 38–39
  the web using Google Chrome, 243
Search operators, 21–22, 34
Search providers, 243
Search tools, defined, 15
Secant function, 84
Seller ratings/reviews, 64, 65–66
Sepia special effect (Picasa), 316
Servers, web, 12
Sharing
  calendars, 222–227
  custom maps (Google Maps), 149–150
  libraries, 105
  photos
    Picasa, 323, 325–326
    Picasa Web Albums, 327–331
  videos (YouTube), 339–343
Sharpen special effect (Picasa), 316
Shockwave Flash (.swf) files, 22
Shop button (Picasa), 312
Shopping.com, 62, 64
Shortcuts (Google Chrome), 258

Show/Hide People Panel button
  (Picasa), 312
Show/Hide Places Panel button
  (Picasa), 312
Show/Hide Properties Panel button
  (Picasa), 312
Show/Hide Tags Panel button
  (Picasa), 312
Signatures (Gmail), 179, 184–185
Signing in
  to Gmail account, 169
  to Google account, 5–6
  to Google Talk, (cw) A4–A5
Signing up for Blogger, 279–280
Sine function, 84
Size, image, 44
SketchUp, 3
Slideshow gadget, 292
Smart searching, 132
SMT (Statistical machine
  translation), 79
Snippets, defined, 96, 170
Social media, 272
Social networks
  defined, 272, 339
  Google Buzz and, 268–273
Soft Focus special effect
  (Picasa), 316
Software. *See also specific software*
  crawler, 13
  spider, 13
Sony eBook readers, 102
Sorting photos (Picasa), 313
Spam, 187–190, 300–301
Special effects (Picasa), 316
Specifications, uploading video to
  YouTube, 343–344
Spelling, checking, 184
Spider software, 13
Sports calendars, 210–211
Spot Image layer (Google Earth), 157
Square root function, 83
Stanford University, 95
Starred messages, 170, 174
Statistical machine translation
  (SMT), 79
Stemming, 22
Stemming, automatic word, 22
Stop words, 21, 24–25
Storage limitations (Picasa Web
  Albums), 327
Straighten fix (Picasa), 315
Streaming videos, 336
Street View (Google Maps), 130,
  135–136
Strikethrough text (Blogger), 284
StumbleUpon, 340
Subject areas, searching specific, 55
Subscription Links gadget, 292
Subscriptions, news feeds, 123–125
Subtraction function, 83
Synchronizing bookmarks/settings
  between computers, 248, 252–254
Synonyms, searching for, 21–22,
  26–27

System requirements
  Google Chrome, 241
  Google Earth, 154
  Picasa, 310

T
Tabbed browsing, 245–246
Tabs
  adding to iGoogle, 77–78
  managing Google Chrome, 245–247
Tangent function, 84
Task lists (Google Calendar), 227–232
Template Designer, 291
Templates (Blogger), 281, 293–295
Terrain overlays, 131
Text
  anchor, 32–33
  formatting, 284–285
  translating selected, 79–80
Text analysis (Google search), 13
Text (.ans, .txt) files, 22
Text fix (Picasa), 315
Text gadget, 292
Themes
  Gmail, 198–199
  iGoogle, 78
Themes tab (Gmail), 197
Third-party gadgets, 291, 298
Threads, defined, 115
3D Buildings layer (Google Earth), 157
Thumbnails, 15–16, 345
Tilde () operators, 26–27
Timelines, news article, 61–62
Tint special effect (Picasa), 316,
  318–319
To-do lists (Google Calendar),
  227–232
"to google," 12
Touring your route (Google
  Earth), 160
Traffic layer (Google Earth), 157
Traffic overlays, 131
Traffic view (Google Maps), 130,
  134–135
Transit overlays, 131
Translation. *See* Google Translate
Transportation layer (Google
  Earth), 157
Trash mailbox (Gmail), 178
Trigonometric functions, 84
tumblr, 340
Tweets, 125
Twitter, 123, 124–125, 272, 340,
  342–343

U
UCE (Unsolicited commercial email),
  187–190
Unarchiving messages (Gmail), 177
Underlining text (Blogger), 284
Under the Hood tab (Google Chrome),
  240
Undo button (Picasa), 317
Universal Search, 17

University Complutense of Madrid (Spain), 95
University Library of Lausanne (Switzerland), 95
University of California, 95
University of Michigan, 95
University of Texas at Austin, 95
University of Virginia, 95
University of Wisconsin-Madison and Wisconsin Historical Society Library, 95
Unsolicited commercial email (UCE), 187–190
Unsubscribing from groups, 117
Upload button (Picasa), 311
Uploading
    images to Blogger, 283, 286–288
    photos to Blogger, 283, 286, 288
    photos to Picasa Web Albums
        from Picasa, 327–328
        from web browsers, 328–330
    videos
        to Blogger posts, 288–290
        to YouTube, 343–349
URLs. *see also* Web addresses
    defined, 23, 242
    navigating to web pages (Google Chrome), 242–243
    public calendars, 226
U.S. Government layer (Google Earth), 157
Usage rights, defined, 35
USA Today, 57
Usenet, 112, 119
Usernames (Gmail), 167
User profiles (Google accounts), 8–9

V

Vacation mode (Gmail), 198–199, 199
Video Bar gadget, 292
Video chats, ⓒⓌ A11, ⓒⓌ A12
Videos. *See also* YouTube
    adding to Blogger posts, 288–290
    adding to blogs, 283
    4K, 344
    high definition, 337
    resolution, 337
    viral, 340
    widescreen, 337
Videos overlay, 131

Viewing
    blogs, 282
    book content, 99–100
    books in libraries, 106
    browsing history, 254–255
    business information, 143–144
    calendars, 211–217
    custom maps, 147
    Gmail messages with common labels, 175–176
    Gmail trash, 178
    Google account data, 7
    online photos, 330
    posts (Google Buzz), 270–271
    videos (YouTube), 338–339
Viewing options (Google Books), 96
Views
    Gmail, 170
    Google Calendar, 212–215
Viral video, 340
Viruses, computer, 187–190
Visiting groups, 115–117
Vlogs, 336
Voice-based chats (Google Talk), ⓒⓌ A8–A10
Voicemail messages (Google Talk), ⓒⓌ A8, ⓒⓌ A9–A10
Voice-Over Internet Protocol (VOIP), ⓒⓌ A8

W

Walking directions, 150
Wall Street Journal, 57
Warmify special effect (Picasa), 316
Washington Times, 57
Weather layer (Google Earth), 157
Web, searching the (Google Chrome), 243
Web addresses. *see also* URLs
    for excluding titles (Google Books), 96
    Google homepage, 14
    Google services/applications, 2–3
    WordNet, 83
Web browsers
    defined, 238
    history (Google Chrome), 254–256
    uploading photos to Picasa Web Albums, 328–330
Webcams overlays, 131
Webcam Video, uploading (YouTube), 346–349

Web Clips tab (Gmail), 197
Web pages
    bookmarking, 249
    navigating to, 242–243
    printing, 244
    searching for recent, 38–39
    translating, 79, 80–81
Webpage thumbnails, 15–16
Web server, defined, 12
Websites
    book review, 100
    connecting to Google Buzz, 266–268
    searching specific, 23, 28–29
what is: operators, 83, 86
Where2 Technologies, 130
Widescreen video, 337
Width, adjusting (Blogger), 295–296
Wikipedia layer (Google Earth), 157
Wikipedia overlays, 131
Wildcards, 22
Windows Live Messenger, ⓒⓌ A2
Word definitions, 82–83, 85–86
WordNet, 83
Word stemming, automatic, 22
Writing book reviews, 101–102

Y

YouTube
    accounts, 2, 337
    blocking access to, 336
    browsing for videos, 337–338
    commercial programming, 336
    creating accounts, 2, 337
    defined, 336
    inserting videos in Blogger, 289
    internet connections, 336
    movies, 336
    playback quality, 337
    posting video
        on Blogger, 339–340
        on Google Buzz, 340
    searching for videos on, 337
    sharing videos, 339–343
    uploading videos to, 343–349
    video types, 336
    viewing videos, 338–339
    web address, 3

Z

Zoom detail (Google Maps), 134